THE SATANISM SCARE

SOCIAL INSTITUTIONS AND SOCIAL CHANGE

An Aldine de Gruyter Series of Texts and Monographs

EDITED BY

Michael Useem • James D. Wright

THE SATANISM SCARE

James T. Richardson
Joel Best
David G. Bromley
(*Editors*)

ALDINE DE GRUYTER
New York

ABOUT THE EDITORS

James T. Richardson is Professor of Sociology and Judicial Studies at the University of Nevada, Reno, where he directs the Master of Judicial Studies Degree Program. He does research in sociology of religion (on new religions or "cults") and social psychology of law. He has co-authored several books, along with many articles in professional journals. His Ph.D. is in Sociology from Washington State University (1968), and his J.D. Degree is from Old College, Nevada School of Law (1986).

Joel Best is Professor and Chair of Sociology at Southern Illinois University at Carbondale. His principal research interests are deviance and social problems. He is the editor of *Images of Issues* (1989) and author of *Threatened Children* (1990).

David G. Bromley is Professor of Sociology in the Department of Sociology and Anthropology and Senior Project Director in the Survey Research Laboratory at Virginia Commonwealth University.

Copyright © 1991 Walter de Gruyter, Inc., New York

ALDINE DE GRUYTER
A division of Walter de Gruyter, Inc.
200 Saw Mill River Road
Hawthorne, New York 10532

The paper used in this publication meets the minimum requirements of American National Standard for Information Sciences—Permanence of Paper for Printed Materials, ANSI Z39.48-1984. ∞

Library of Congress Cataloging-in-Publication Data
The Satanism scare / edited by James T. Richardson, Joel Best, and
    David G. Bromley.
        p.   cm — (Social institutions and social change)
    Includes index.
        ISBN 0-202-30378-0 (alk. paper). — ISBN 0-202-30379-9 (pbk. :
    alk. paper)
        1. Satanism—United States—History—20th century.   2. Satanism—
United States—Public opinion.   3. Public opinion—United States.
4. United States—Religion—1960-   5. United States—Social
conditions—1980-   I. Richardson, James T., 1941-   . II. Best,
Joel. III. Bromley, David G. IV. Series.
BL2525.S27   1991
133.4'22'0973—dc20   90-25504
                                                            CIP

Manufactured in the United States of America
10 9 8 7 6 5 4 3 2

CONTENTS

INTRODUCTION ——————————————— 1

Satanism as a Social Problem $\underline{\hspace{3cm}}$ 1

James T. Richardson, Joel Best and David Bromley

Why a collection of scholarly articles about contemporary satanism? Many academics would consider the topic unworthy of serious consideration; they equate antisatanism with flying saucer cults, parapsychology enthusiasts, and other causes at or beyond the lunatic fringe. We disagree.

Contemporary antisatanism warrants serious examination, if only because this movement's influence now extends into important segments of American society. Long a staple topic for religious broadcasters and "trash TV" talk shows, satanism has crept into network news programs and prime-time programming, with news stories, documentaries, and made-for-TV movies about satanic cults. Growing numbers of police officers, child protection workers, and other public officials attend workshops supported by tax dollars to receive formal training in combating the satanist menace. Authority figures ranging from New York's Cardinal O'Connor to federal "drug czar" William J. Bennett warn against the threat of satanism. The general public has responded to these messages: when a Texas poll recently asked "How serious a problem do you think satanism is to our society, if at all?" 63 percent of Texans responded "very serious," and another 23 percent said "somewhat serious."

Satanism—a subject of denunciations by media and public figures, and an issue of some concern to a large segment of the general public—has attracted surprisingly little serious attention from social scientists. We believe it is time to address this neglect.

CONSTRUCTING THE SATANIST PROBLEM

This volume's contributors have backgrounds in several of the social sciences, in particular sociology, anthropology, folklore, and history. Each chapter uses its own set of concepts and offers its own stance on satanism as a contemporary social problem. There is, however, a general approach that provides a foundation for the book as a whole. Our perspective toward satanism is *constructionist*.

Constructionism contrasts with more traditional orientations toward the study of social problems. Traditionally, researchers took for granted the objective reality of their subject matter—say, crime. That is, they made an assumption that the real world contained crimes and criminals, objective phenomena that could be studied. These researchers measured crime rates, searched for the causes of crimes, examined the characteristics of criminals, and so on, never questioning why something was designated a crime or someone was called a criminal. This approach is sometimes called *objectivist*, because it takes for granted the objective reality of the phenomena under study.

Constructionists criticize objectivism on the ground that our world is socially constructed. There is no natural phenomenon "crime"; all crimes are identified through social processes. Legislative bodies write criminal codes that define some acts as crimes, and those laws are enforced (that is, interpreted) by police officers, prosecutors, and other agents of the criminal justice system who must ask themselves whether the events they encounter fit the legal definition of crime, and if so, what to do about it. All "crimes" and "criminals" are identified through these social processes, and all other social problems are constructed in similar fashion. These processes of social construction are the focus of constructionists' attention, as they try to understand the social construction of reality, including social problems.

Most warnings about satanism make objectivist assertions—that satanic cults conduct human sacrifices; that listeners are influenced by satanic messages backmasked onto heavy metal records, that much child sexual abuse is motivated by satanism, and so on. Social scientists guided by objectivist assumptions might try to study coven members and the effects of listening to backmasked lyrics, or accept at face value sometimes bizarre statements made by allegedly abused children.

In contrast, essays in this volume view the social problem of satanism as a *social construction*. In this view, warnings about covens, backmasking and ritual abuse should be seen as *claims,* and, for constructionists, the *process of making claims is the essence of social problems.*[1] Once the researcher's focus shifts to the process of claimsmaking, an entirely new set of research questions emerges, focused on production and validation of claims.

Perhaps the most basic questions for constructionists are: Who is making claims? Why are they making them? What do they say? and How do others respond? Claims about satanism may come from various sources such as preachers and parents, journalists and ex-cult members, therapists and political leaders. Each of these claimsmakers has a distinctive approach to the topic; presumably preachers see satanism in essentially religious terms, while journalists apply the canons of their profession when reporting on alleged satanists and their activities. Claimsmaking therapists may be justifying a new therapeutic practice or diagnosis, and politicians may be seeking political advantage. Obviously, claimsmakers have different audiences (e.g., the preacher's congregation, the journalist's readers or viewers, the therapist's potential clients) and different objectives (e.g., preachers want to win souls, journalists seek to inform, therapists want clients).

Constructionist analysts look carefully for the claimsmakers' interests—what do they stand to gain by making claims and having those claims taken seriously? This is one of the most important questions to ask when examining the process of constructing a social problem. Finding out what advantages accrue to claimsmakers when claims are made and accepted often reveals motivations hidden from casual observers.

Claimsmaking is a form of persuasion; claimsmakers call attention to a social phenomenon and, in the process, attempt to shape perceptions of that phenomenon. Thus, we need to be concerned, not only with people making claims, but with the rhetoric of those claims. If satanism is a social problem, exactly what sort of social problem is it? It makes a big difference whether satanists are characterized as alienated loners, members of small, basically harmless cults, or as participants in a vast, powerful, criminal conspiracy.

Whether the audience takes claims seriously depends, in part, on the claims' content. Are they plausible? Do they mesh well with cultural beliefs and values? Whether people accept and act on claims is the ultimate test of claimsmakers' impact.

Claimsmakers must compete in a social-problems marketplace (Hilgartner and Bosk 1988; Best 1990). At any given moment, many causes demand our attention and concern. Some claimsmakers fail to influence others; their claims do not shape policy or even public opinion. Other claims are more successful: people believe them and social policies change.

Currently, claims about the menace of satanism enjoy some success—even if most academics do not yet take the topic seriously. Many ordinary people, as well as opinion leaders in society, appear to take these claims seriously, which suggests that scholars should do so as well. We need to know why the antisatanists' campaign is working, and what the future holds for this movement.

THE ROOTS OF CONTEMPORARY ANTISATANISM

Antisatanism's appeal has several sources, each of which has contributed to the construction of satanism as a contemporary social problem. During the 1980s, elements of apparently unrelated social movements converged in the cause of antisatanism. Each movement brought its own set of concepts and concerns. Five precursor movements—fundamentalist Christianity, the anticult movement, the development of "satanic churches," the new wave of child saving, and the survivor/recovery movement—made particularly important contributions to social construction of the satanist menace.

Fundamentalist Christianity

During the 1970s, fundamentalism became a powerful political and economic force in American society (Bromley and Shupe 1984; Jorstad 1990). There has been a strong fundamentalist undercurrent since the early part of this century, but it was relatively invisible to many Americans, and was ignored or ridiculed for decades by intellectuals. This view of fundamentalism changed dramatically in the 1970s, as fundamentalists were invited into the political arena by conservative political leaders with common interests (Jorstad 1990:58).

The "new" fundamentalism was led symbolically and (to a degree) literally by the Reverend Jerry Falwell, who established the Moral Majority in 1979. Fundamentalism had been quietly gaining strength in numbers and economic power, and fundamentalist leaders and conservative political organizers decided to make its new–found strength felt. Fundamentalists became involved in politics, registering tens of thousands of new voters, and endorsing candidates. They burst on the national scene, and became involved in political races at all levels, even presidential politics. The New Right also became involved in other social issues, such as sex education and prayer in the schools, abortion, and the Equal Rights Amendment.

Fundamentalists of Protestant, Catholic and Mormon persuasion have found that they share common interests, and can work together to achieve joint political goals (Chandler 1984; Richardson 1984). The alliance of various threads of the new fundamentalist movement help create an infrastructure (Hadden 1984; Jorstad 1990; Latus 1984). Thus, it became easier for the religious right to take a united stand on new concerns—rock music, or censoring books in schools, or satanism—simply because they had worked together on other matters. Fundamentalists could receive new "marching orders" quickly through this network.

This fundamentalist infrastructure, with its organizations, publications, and television and radio broadcasts, has responded vigorously to the perceived threat of satanism. Fundamentalists take an objectivist view, treating the growth of satanism very matter of factly; after all, holy scripture predicts the spread of satanism and the growth of Satan's power. The issue is not whether Satan exists and is gaining power, but what this means and what people should be doing about it. The message is clear and simple: all real Christians should be warning others about the satanic threat.

Belief in Satan is an essential element of Christian fundamentalist cultural heritage, part of the cultural baggage fundamentalists carry. This belief has spread as fundamentalism has grown. National survey data show a significant increase in belief in the Devil from 1964 to 1973 (Nunn 1975). Nunn adds (1975:87):

> The evidence also showed Devil-believers to be not the unchurched but God-fearing Christians who actively participate in their Protestant and Catholic Churches, especially in the Bible-belts of America. . . . Consistently, . . . the more active the participation in religious services, the greater the likelihood people were certain the Devil was around.

The fundamentalist infrastructure regularly promotes warnings about the satanic menace. Shelves in religious bookstores are filled with titles on satanism, and major televangelists warn of Satan's growing threat. People, including many only peripherally involved in fundamentalism, apparently accept the antisatanist message. Acceptance is more likely when the message comes from sources that conceal its fundamentalist origins. For instance, when the press, law enforcement, and psychiatrists appear to take satanism seriously, others are encouraged to do so. If the secular press and the usually antireligious therapeutic community seem to accept the objective reality of satanism, then the satanism scare gains considerable momentum.

The Anticult Movement

The Anticult Movement (ACM) emerged in the late 1960s and early 1970s (Shupe and Bromley 1980), focused on getting young people out of new religious groups (popularly called cults) that had proliferated in the late 1960s. Once America found out that the new religions were serious, "high demand" groups, which sought to change youths' lives in ways strange and unacceptable to their parents, society counterattacked.

The ACM emerged as a coalition of distraught parents, religious leaders, former members, and others, including a few professional therapists and academics. ACM groups exchanged information, lobbied politicians, and presented their views to the press, which was always on the look-out for a good "human interest" story. Cult stories qualified because they could be "framed" as child-stealing stories that characterized gurus as "Pied Pipers" who could turn political recruits into mental captives.

Accusations of brainwashing by cults became a "social weapon" (Robbins, Anthony and McCarthy 1978), justifying attacks—even extralegal ones—against new religions, while excusing parents and recruits from responsibility. After all, how could children stand up against the cult's psycho-technology, even if properly raised and educated? To counteract the cult's powerful tactics, the ACM turned to forcible "deprogramming" (Bromley and Richardson 1983). Thousands of members were kidnapped by agents of their parents, incarcerated, and put through rigorous resocialization until they either recanted their beliefs or escaped. The label "deprogramming" served to make the point that the recruit had first been "programmed" by the cult.

The ACM's account of cult brainwashing was readily accepted by the media, which in turn passed the tale on to the general public. Many, if not most, people believe that cults brainwash their members, and that cults are evil groups which should be controlled. Cults are the most despised groups in America, according to a recent Gallup Poll (Richardson 1990). The ACM message has been received, and accepted.

The ACM used the Jonestown tragedy to promote its view of exotic religions, even though the People's Temple was vastly different from the groups on which the ACM had focused attention (Richardson 1980). In 1988, a major ACM drive promoted the tenth anniversary of the Jonestown tragedy with widely dispersed press packets stressing that cults brainwash members, and keep them through mind control practices. The ACM's claims were accepted without question, and the nation was reminded again of the social problem of cults.

In recent years the ACM has exploited the growing attention paid to satanism. ACM literature regularly reports on "satanic cult" activities, presenting them as another example of evil cults at work. ACM conferences have sessions dealing with satanism, and ACM press releases comment on events such as the killings at Matamoros. Satanic cults are accused of brainwashing victims, and using mind control to get their followers to commit unspeakable acts. Thus, satanism has been incorporated within the broader anticult framework promoted by the ACM for over two decades. This tactic has benefited ACM interests, and contributed to the rising satanism scare.

Growth in Satanic Churches

There is a temptation to dismiss antisatanists' claims as illusory; as sociologist Marcello Truzzi says, "Satanists are better scapegoats than Jews, because they don't exist (in Lyons, 1988:179). Although the vast conspiracy denounced by the antisatanist crusade may be exaggerated, satanists do exist; there are members of organized satanist churches in our society. These satanist groups are important to the antisatanist movement: they furnish a "kernel of truth" that antisatanists can expose. Groups such as Anton LaVey's Church of Satan "prove" that the satanic threat exists. The Church of Satan is not large; estimates range from 2000 to 5000 active members (Melton 1986:77; Lyons 1988:115). Still, the publicity showered on LaVey since he founded his San Francisco church in 1966 has made him and his group a part of American popular culture. Nearly everyone knows about LaVey's church, even though it is quite small.

What the Church lacks in size it has made up for in attention paid to it and its activities. Anton LaVey, a colorful character with a flare for the dramatic, gained considerable publicity by performing satanic weddings of famous people, satanic baptisms of children, and satanic last rights for a sailor member who died—all deliberately staged as media events. LaVey sought celebrities as members, and for a time claimed such stars as Sammy Davis, Jr. and Jayne Mansfield as active participants, gaining national attention as a result (Lyons 1988). He also served as a consultant to the film *Rosemary's Baby*, even playing a part in the film.

There is considerable debate about what the Church of Satan stands for, and what its members believe. Some analysts treat the Church as a spoof, deliberately designed to upset Christians. Others take it more seriously, and look to LaVey's writings, such as his *The Satanic Bible* (LaVey 1969), to understand his philosophy.

> The church actively rejects spirituality and mysticism of any sort; it espouses an elitist, materialist, and basically atheistic philosophy. Satan constitutes a worship of one's own ego. . . . In its major features, the Church of Satan takes a position of Extreme Machiavellianism and cynical-realism toward the nature of man. . . . Its major feature . . . is its emphasis upon the importance of myth and magic and upon their impact in a world of people who can still be manipulated through such beliefs and emotions. This Satanist, then is the *ultimate pragmatist.* (Truzzi 1974:220)

Moody (1974) discusses the Church of Satan's redefinition of Christianity's seven deadly sins—greed, pride, envy, anger, gluttony, lust, and sloth—as virtues within satanic theology. Melton (1988:145) describes satanic churches' relationship to Christianity:

> Satanism is logically subsequent to Christianity and draws on it in representing an overthrow of the Christian deity in favor of his adversary. It stands in polemical relation to Christianity and . . . uses Christian elements, which are changed and given new meaning.

Although LaVey's Church of Satan is the most visible satanic church, others exist. The Temple of Set, a small off-shoot group organized by Michael Aquino, a former disciple of LaVey, has attracted attention (Melton 1989:805; Lyons 1988:125). The small size of these organized satanic groups is less important than the cultural meaning attached to them. As a radical rejection of Christian culture, they are symbolically significant. Their very presence has contributed to the concern about satanism in America.

The New Child Savers

Campaigns to protect children from victimization provided a fourth influence on contemporary antisatanism. Beginning with identification of the "battered-child syndrome" in 1962, late twentieth-century America experienced a series of campaigns to protect child victims (Best 1990). Originally typified in terms of physical brutality against small children, child abuse was redefined to include neglect, emotional abuse, and sexual abuse by both family members (incest) and outsiders (molestation). By the late 1970s, concern with sexual abuse, in turn, extended to sexual exploitation via child pornography and adolescent prostitution. The early 1980s saw the rise of a movement to locate missing children, with claims that strangers abducted 50,000 children per year. Also, a campaign began against objectionable content in "porn rock" music and videos, on the grounds that these messages harmed their young audience.

By 1985, members of these new child-saving movements began talking about another form of child victimization—"ritual abuse." Claims of ritual abuse combined diverse concerns about child victims; such as "ordinary" physical and psychological abuse, orgies of sexual abuse, links to child pornographers, and human sacrifice of missing children in satanic rituals.

It was difficult to criticize these child-saving movements, which depicted children as vulnerable innocents exploited by deviant adults. The alleged crimes were almost too awful to imagine; motives such as sadism, profit, and depravity seemed inadequate to account for these terrible acts. Claims that satanic cults were at work helped make the inconceivable somehow more plausible.

Further, because concern for child victims led to laws requiring that suspected abuse be reported, child saving produced a large child-protection apparatus—a network of protective services workers, police officers, and other specialists with a mandate to do something to help child victims. These workers had a vested interest in expanding their organizational turf by discovering and assuming responsibility for new forms of child victimization. The child-saving industry gained considerable momentum from this self-interest, which made many in the child-saving industry receptive to antisatanist ideas.

The Survivor/Recovery Movement

Child-protection agents were not the only professionals to extend their influence. Twentieth-century America was marked by the growing influence of medical authorities; a wide range of social problems were medicalized (Conrad and Schneider 1980). At the same time that physicians expanded their influence, self-help groups of ex-deviants, such as Alcoholics Anonymous, adopted the medical model for their own use, defining their deviance as medical problems.

During the 1980s, some medical authorities began talking about post-traumatic stress disorder, a label used to explain maladaptive behavior in terms of traumatic experiences in the individual's past. The term first achieved popular attention as an explanation for troubled behavior by Vietnam veterans, but other movements soon began identifying other sorts of "survivors." Feminists, in particular, began speaking of "rape survivors" and "incest survivors," but the term also was applied to former members of new religions (sometimes called cults) by some in the ACM. Following the publication of *Michelle Remembers* (Smith and Pazder 1980), which allegedly detailed one psychiatrist's efforts to help a woman reconstruct her childhood experience as a victim of ritual abuse within a satanic cult, "occult survivors" began to surface.

The notion that the trauma of sexual abuse could be repressed deeply enough so that the victim might have no recollection of the experience underpinned therapists' efforts to reconstruct patient's past histories. Adult and child victims were thought to need help recognizing and understanding their traumatic experiences; patients' denials of having been exploited were dismissed as a typical symptom of the underlying disorder. Thus, suspicions of ritual abuse led to therapists helping dozens—in some cases hundreds—of children to acknowledge and understand alleged exploitation which they initially denied having experienced. This application of a medical model to behavior that may well have been illusory was a crucial element in the rise of antisatanism. When a growing number of individuals believe that they experienced satanic rituals as children, their beliefs become, in effect, "eyewitness testimony." Refuting such testimony becomes a formidable task for those questioning the satanic conspiracy's existence. Indeed, those who question such claims run the risk of being accused of revictimizing the person making the statements.

DISSEMINATING ANTISATANIST CLAIMS

The several movements which voiced claims of antisatanism found their task made easier by developments in the news media and in methods for training social-service professionals.

The News Media

Sensational claims about deviants are a standard topic for news coverage, and it is no surprise that the press covered the antisatanists' warnings. True, the "prestige press" (e.g., the networks' evening news broadcasts, the major newsweeklies, and the *New York Times* and *Washington Post*) paid relatively little attention to satanism. But satanism became a popular topic for those sectors of the press that run less "hard news" and more feature stories and sensationalism, sectors made increasingly visible by developments during the 1980s.

Consider the case of television. The growth of cable and satellite broadcasting meant more channels available for viewing. Under this increased competition, each channel could anticipate a smaller audience, and programmers sought ways to cut production costs. Because talk shows are reasonably popular and relatively inexpensive to produce, they proliferated. But a talk show broadcast every weekday, such as *Donahue,* requires up to 250 topics per year. By the late 1980s, there were enough syndicated talk shows with large appetites for fresh topics to ensure that almost any movement's claims could receive a hearing on national television. In addition, the growth of televangelism, the emergence of religious cable broadcasting, and the adaptation of the talk-show format by religious broadcasters provided a media forum in which antisatanists were especially welcome.

As an entertaining topic, satanism also found a place in the networks' prime-time programming. In 1988, NBC broadcast a two-hour Geraldo Rivera documentary on satanism that received record ratings. Satanist ritual abuse figured in CBS's 1989 "Do You Know the Muffin Man?" and other made-for-TV movies. Kenneth Wooden, an investigator for ABC's *20/20* who had been active in the anticult and missing-children movements, became visible in the antisatanist crusade. Thus, while the prestige press virtually ignored satanism, the topic received plenty of coverage in the media, contributing to the perception that satanism must be increasing.

Training Social Service Professionals

The growing numbers of child-protection workers joined the ranks of social workers, police officers, and other social-service professionals. Increasingly, as part of our "credentialing society's" demand for formal training, people in these positions must demonstrate that they are keeping abreast of their fields by attending special workshops and training sessions. Individuals can usually choose their training sessions, and sessions about satanism and occult crime—exotic, sensational topics—have drawn large audiences.

These workshops are important for two reasons. First, they provide an effective way of disseminating information about satanism. Because those giving workshops emphasize that they are experts with first-hand knowledge, many people treat this information as accurate and authoritative. Second, it is important to note that police and protective-services workers who attend these seminars have real powers: they can make arrests and remove children from homes. If these agents begin believing in the satanic threat, we can expect those beliefs will shape their official actions. When public officials take actions in their official capacities, it lends an air of credibility to antisatanists' claims, giving greater impetus to the satanism scare.

THE PLAN OF THE BOOK

Because antisatanism had roots in several social movements, including fundamentalism, the anticult movement, child-saving, and the survivor/recovery movement, once reports of satanic activities began to circulate, they seemed to receive confirmation from several quarters. What they rarely received was any sort of critical examination. That is the purpose of this book. We have organized the essays in this volume under seven general headings, starting with this introductory overview of satanism's emergence as a significant social problem.

The chapters in the second section attempt to locate the contemporary concern over satanism in its broader anthropological, sociological, and historical context. Phillips Stevens, an anthropologist, offers an examination of "demonology," by which he means an "ideology of evil, an elaborate body of belief about an evil force that is inexorably undermining society's most cherished values and institutions." Stevens views satanism as a modern form of demonology, one which shares themes with demonologies in other times and places.

Stevens' essay is followed by a brief history of the concept of Satan by historian Jeffrey Russell, whose several books on this topic have become standard references. Russell argues that monotheistic religions require a concept of an evil power doing battle with an all-powerful god, in order to relieve that preeminent entity of responsibility for evil and suffering. He describes development of this antigod concept in Western culture.

David Bromley's sociological look at satanism as a new "cult scare" notes similarities between the ACM that developed two decades ago and the more recent Antisatanism Movement. Bromley locates antisatanism within a broader frame of countersubversion ideologies, then discusses specific allegations surrounding satanism.

Part III explores the theme of satanic threats to children. Journalist Debbie Nathan presents a history of the notion of "ritual abuse." She discusses the famous McMartin case in detail, and examines the recent political history of child abuse. Joel Best's paper demonstrates the importance to the antisatanist movement of the "threatened children" motif, focusing on two variants, abuse and corruption. He argues that evidence for both phenomena is weak, and asks why these claims are taken seriously.

Daniel Martin and Gary Alan Fine's chapter examines the role of fantasy games played by adolescents in promoting satanism. They address three prevalent claims about "Dungeons & Dragons": that the game is directly linked to satanism; that mind control is used on participants; and that violence results from participation. They close with a discussion of fantasy games as a means of "reenchantment" of the world.

Part IV deals with a critical problem facing those who question the antisatanists' claims—the reports of so-called "occult survivors." Adults who claim, usually under hypnosis, that they were abused by satanic cults as children serve an important legitimating role in the antisatanism movement. The essay by Philip Jenkins and Daniel Maier-Katlin sets survivor stories in a historical context that reveals their similarities to earlier anti-Catholic accounts. Jenkins and Maier-Katkin examine some of the best-known survivor tales in depth, and find them implausible.

The next paper, by anthropologist Sherrill Mulhern, asks how mental health professionals could come to accept survivor tales. Her methodological critique of what therapists do in working with occult survivors is a milestone study. The discussion of "highly hypnotizable," "multiple personality disorder" persons whose "memories" are developed in lengthy interactions with therapists using questionable methods raises serious questions about the efficacy of survivor accounts.

Part V presents three studies of how law enforcement and the legal system handle antisatanists' claims. Robert Hicks' chapter outlines the "police model" of satanic crime that has evolved in recent cult crime seminars. Hicks offers a thorough critique of the model, explains how and why law enforcement agencies get involved in antisatanism, and discusses the consequences of this involvement.

The chapter by Ben Crouch and Kelly Damphousse presents original data from a survey of "cult cops"—police personnel who specialize in and accept the reality of antisatanism. Their analysis of demographic and personal features of cult cops is revealing, as well as disquieting.

The section closes with a paper by James Richardson, examining how satanism has come to play a role in four types of legal actions—"satanic murder" cases, child "ritual abuse" cases, "cult brainwashing" cases, and "heavy metal" cases. The latter discussion focuses on the widely publicized "Judas Priest" trial, a case on which Richardson consulted with the defense team.

Part VI contains four empirical studies of the ways news spreads. Jeffrey Victor's paper explores satanic "rumor panics" in which satanism becomes a focus of local concern. He argues that such panics tend to develop in rural

America, and he offers a natural history of why and how such panics occur. Folklorist Thomas Green compares folk and media treatments of the Matamoros tragedy, probably the most heavily-publicized crime recently attributed to satanists. Green notes that the interpretations given the Matamoros murders were colored by racism, as well as regional considerations.

Robert Balch and Margaret Gilliam present a case study of the development and spread of a satanic rumor following two murders in Montana. This study is valuable for its detailed portrait of a panic's development, as well as its demise, once the crimes were eventually solved.

Laurel Rowe and Gray Cavender's comparison of media treatments of witches and satanists closes the section. They find important differences in how the media treat the two phenomena, with witches and witchcraft being handled much more positively. Rowe and Cavender offer interesting speculation on why this occurs, focusing on the tendency to view witchcraft in terms of feminism, while satanists are usually viewed as criminals.

The two papers in Part VII discuss "real satanists," the activities of people who think they are doing some form of satanism. Folklorist Bill Ellis' paper develops the concept of "ostension," which means, literally, "acting out." He is interested particularly in teenagers who act out local supernatural legends, including many tied to satanism. Ellis suggests that "legend trips" often give rise to rumors of satanic activity.

The book closes with William Bainbridge's account of the fate of a satanic group—The Process—which he first studied some years ago. The Process started in England as a spin-off of Scientology, migrated to various places around the world, divided into factions, and still exists in small, mutated forms. Bainbridge describes the Processeans' creativity as they developed an eclectic, evolving theology which gave a prominent place for Satan.

This collection offers, then, a wide range of scholarly and professional opinion on the growing interest in satanism. We hope that other scholars will, after examining the substance of this collection, take the topic of satanism more seriously. We would welcome assistance in developing more information which might help an informed citizenry understand the growing satanism scare.

NOTE

1. For detailed discussions of constructionism, see Best (1989), Schneider (1985), and Spector and Kitsuse (1977). Within the constructionist camp, there is debate over the theoretical assumptions that should guide social-problems research, appropriate topics for study, and other issues. Although we would locate the essays in this volume within the constructionist tradition, we should note that some constructionists would review our work as unacceptably tainted by objectivist assumptions.

REFERENCES

Best, Joel (ed.). 1989. *Images of Issues*. New York: Aldine de Gruyter.

———. 1990. *Threatened Children*. Chicago: University of Chicago Press.

Bromley, David, and Richardson, James T. (eds.). 1983. *The Brainwashing/ Deprogramming Controversy*. New York: Edwin Mellen.

Bromley, David, and Shupe, Anson, Jr., (eds). 1984 *New Christian Politics*. Macon, GA: Mercer University Press.

Conrad, Peter, and Joseph W. Schneider. 1980. *Deviance and Medicalization*. St. Louis: Mosby.

Chandler, Ralph C. 1984. "The Wicked Shall Not Bear Rule: The Fundamentalist Heritage of the New Christian Right." In Bromley, D. and A. Shupe, *op. cit.*

Hadden, Jeffrey. 1984. "Televangelism and the Future of American Politics." In Bromley, D. and A. Shupe, Jr., *op. cit.*

Hilgartner, Stephen and Bosk, Charles. 1988. "The Rise and Fall of Social Problems." *American Journal of Sociology* 94:53–78.

Jorstad, Erling, 1990. *Holding Fast/Pressing On: Religion in America in the 1980s*. New York: Preager.

Latus, Margaret Ann. 1984. "Mobilizing Christians for Political Action: Campaigning with God on your Side." In D. Bromley and A. Shupe, *op. cit.*

LaVey, Anton. 1969. *The Satanic Bible. New York: Avon.*

Lyons, Arthur. 1988. *Satan Wants You*. New York: Mysterious Books.

Melton, Gordon. 1986. "Satanism and The Church of Satan.: In *Encyclopedic Handbook of Cults in America*, edited by G. Melton, New York: Garland Publishing.

Moody, Edward. 1974. "Urban Witches." In *On the Margin of the Visible: Sociology, the Esoteric, and the Occult*, edited by E. Tinyakian, New York: John Wiley & Sons.

Nunn, Clyde. 1975. "The Rising Credibility of the Devil in America." In *Heterodoxy: Mystical Experience, Religious Dissent and the Occult*, edited by R. Wood, River Forest, IL: Listening Press.

Richardson, James T. 1980. "People's Temple and Jonestown: A Corrective Comparison and Critique." *Journal for the Scientific Study of Religion* 19(3):239–255.

———. 1984. "The 'Old Right' in Action: Mormon and Catholic Involvement in an Equal Rights Amendment Referendum." In Bromley, D. and A. Shupe, *op. cit.*

———. 1990. "Definitions of Cult: From Sociological-Technical to Popular Negative." Paper presented at annual meeting of the American Psychological Association, Boston.

Robbins, Thomas, Anthony, Dick and McCarthy, James. 1983. "Legitimating Repression." In D. Bromley and J. Richardson, *op. cit.*

Shupe, Anson, Jr., and Bromley, David. 1980. *The New Vigilantes*. Beverly Hills, CA: Sage.

Schneider, Joseph W. 1985. "Social Problems Theory." *Annual Review of Sociology* 11: 209–29.

Smith, Michelle, and Pazder, Lawrence. 1980. *Michelle Remembers*. New York: Congdon & Lattes.
Spector, Malcolm, and Kitsuse, John. 1977. *Constructing Social Problems*. Menlo Park, CA: Cummings.
Truzzi, Marcello. 1974. "Witchcraft and Satanism." In *On the Margin of the Visible*, edited by E. Tiryakian. New York: Wiley and Sons.

ANTHROPOLOGICAL AND HISTORICAL PERSPECTIVES ON SATANISM

II

The Demonology of Satanism: An Anthropological View

2

Phillips Stevens, Jr.

Throughout the decade of the 1980s vast numbers of people, apparently many millions, throughout North America and western Europe have become alarmed about allegations of satanic cult activity. There are varying details, but mainly the fears have focused on a mysterious Satan-worshipping cult whose members subject human victims, preferably children, to obscene torments, then slash them to death, dismember them, and drink their blood and eat their flesh and vital organs. This central theme is couched in two main variants. One is rather vague, saying that somewhere just outside the community there is a satanic cult whose members are planning to kidnap a child for use in a sacrificial ritual. The other variant is detailed: the cult has an organized ritual whose main elements are travesties of Christian liturgy; prominent authority figures in the community are members; it actively seeks new members, preying especially on insecure, alienated, lonely young people who are attracted to it by prospects of identity, self-esteem, and a sense of belonging; and the local cult is interlinked with others across the nation and around the world in a coordinated conspiracy. Bound by their pact with Satan, and invigorated by the blood of their victims, the satanists are bent on an international mission of subversion.

The allegations and their variants constitute a Christian form of a body of beliefs of a universally standard type, which we may call a demonology. The term most commonly refers to an institutionalized set of beliefs in evil spirits, or demons; I will use it here to mean an ideology of evil, an elaborate body of belief about an evil force that is inexorably undermining society's most cherished values and institutions. Historical and anthropological studies have shown that such beliefs invariably develop in times of intense, prolonged social anxiety, times when a significant proportion of people who share cultural values have come to feel that they are being let down or ignored by the social or governmental institutions that they have always supported and in which they have placed their trust. Something is very seriously wrong in society, and they are feeling increasingly helpless. The demonology provides an explanation for this state of affairs.

It may allege that the evil is embodied in and perpetrated by a specific group of people, a minority that becomes the scapegoat for the people's pent-up frustrations. Or the evil force may be a set of ideas, a pervasive ideology that spreads as if driven by a will of its own or by a supernatural will, and that may seduce and subvert any individuals or groups within society.

The demonology usually labels its referents as horribly, unspeakably evil. When it refers to a specific group of people it often dehumanizes them, describing their bestial habits, or declaring their association with certain animals; or by reference to a new interpretation of some old myth, it may declare that these people were execrated by the gods or culture founders themselves, for some horrendous act or accident of birth. When it refers to supernatural or other-worldly evil it may acknowledge that the human agents have been seduced by the evil and are not entirely to blame, but it explicitly states that their rights as human beings, even their lives, must be forfeit to the necessity of expunging the evil from society.

In either case, the demonology both sanctions and gives impetus to the persecutory social-cleansing movement or witch hunt. A demonology can be an awful, powerful thing, snowballing and engulfing people far beyond its cultural source. It generates rage, which wedges its way into culturally prescribed norms of reasonable behavior, obscures whatever was considered due process, and motivates people into mob-type actions. When the rage dissipates and reason returns—suddenly, as often happens, it is followed by general shock and remorse, and almost always by a change in the social order. Demonologies and the social movements they generate can change the course of history.

DEMONOLOGIES AND SOCIETY

Social scientists agree that witch-hunting movements develop during, and are themselves indicative of, intolerable social stress. The formulation of general theories with predictive capability is, however, probably impossible because of uncountable sociocultural variables—but also, as all agree, because of problems in the definition and measurement of "stress." The processes of such movements, however, and their impacts on society, are strikingly similar to those in revitalization movements (Wallace 1956) and can be analyzed using similar processual models (e.g., Schoeneman 1975).

In historical perspective, it is evident that witch hunts and revitalization movements in small-scale societies are both products of and agents of social change, responding to stress and instituting a new order. It has been suggested, too, that they are a form of periodic social regulator. The most dramatic of revitalization movements, such as Melanesian cargo cults, the Ghost Dance religions of the Plains in the late nineteenth century, and African witch-purging movements, are most neatly described as reactions to stressful colonial experiences. But there must exist some critical factors in societies that enact revitalization that enable such movements to develop; stress of similar intensity is surely experienced in the great majority of oppressed groups who do not instigate such movements. Indeed, some research has shown that earlier forms of some revitalization movements occurred at periodic intervals before foreign contact. Seligmann (1910), Williams (1923), and Lanternari (1963) have shown this for prototypes of cargo cults, through analysis of oral traditions. Bohannan (1958) has shown that witch hunts occurred well before the European presence among the Tiv of central Nigeria. And witch hunts have occurred fairly regularly throughout Western history. Dorothy Rabinowitz (1990:63) suggests that "an orgy of self-cleansing" occurs in American society "every fifty years or so."

Historians and social scientists have written much on the sociology of such movements. And psychological interpretations have been brought to bear: what is really going on in a witch hunt? What deep psychic needs are being satisfied in actions motivated by bigotry, by prejudice against people of different race, religion, culture, or life-style, by what are today called "hate crimes?" Evolutionary anthropology has suggested that cultural intolerance may have evolved as an adaptive defense/survival mechanism. The "we–they" attitudes evident among so many neighboring societies, expressed in translations of societies' names for themselves as "people" or "human-beings," and their names for others as something else, are cultural manifestations of such adaptively advantageous attitudes. Displacement of frustration in the form of aggression against those others is a natural result. It has been suggested that scapegoating behavior is a human universal; with the discovery of similar behavior among primates (DeVore and Washburn 1960), primatological bases for this type of behavior were suggested.

Ernest Becker (1975) argued that all ideas of evil are reactions by people against the awareness of their own mortality; in difficult times people become acutely aware of their own fragility and the nearness of their own deaths, and scapegoating is a "heroic" effort at combatting that eventuality. The Devil, said Becker, is the ultimate symbol of the finality of people's mortal condition, and to do battle with him or his earthly agents is people's ultimate act of valiant heroism (Becker 1975:122–123). Some researchers have recently tested and reaffirmed Becker's propositions (Greenberg et al. 1990).

But few scholars have focused on the demonology that drives the witch hunt. Norman Cohn's *Warrant for Genocide* (1981) is one notable exception. The book's subtitle is nearly sufficient to explain its contents: "The Myth of the Jewish World-Conspiracy and the *Protocols of the Elders of Zion*." Cohn carefully documents the development of this terrible hoax: its origin, first publication in 1905 and rapid dissemination, tacit acceptance by the media (including the London *Times*), social conditions that enhanced its credibility, and its influence on the antisemitic demonology of the Nazis.[1] This case is important to our discussion because it shows parallels to the development of the satanic demonology, especially to the efforts of some satan hunters to stress a "world conspiracy" idea. And Cohn's study is instructive to any who would more clearly understand the strong psychopathology that can overcome people during times of stress and uncertainty.

Demonologies catch on at the local level because they touch certain basic fears in people, because they express terrifying prospects that are immediately threatening to individuals. In the following sections I will show how some of the basic premises of anthropology, and some of its insights gained from studies in non-Western situations, can help us understand the specific, horrible contents of the satanic demonology, why such incredible allegations are believed, and how they can trigger near-hysterical reactions in people.

BLOOD, CANNIBALISM, AND CHILD MURDER

Certain elements in the satanic demonology, specifically blood, cannibalism, and child murder, are ancient, have widespread cultural parallels, and are indicative of deep subcultural human drives. Each of these topics has received lengthy anthropological and psychological treatment. Each is at once symbolic, metaphorical, and real. Each can express deep cultural values, evoking awe and fascination—or absolute horror and revulsion. All three are found together in countless demonologies created by people about others; in these contexts they are intertwined, and so our discussion of each must make reference to the others.

Blood and Sacrifice

The ritual of sacrifice, or offering, is universally central to religious liturgy, no matter the material offered. It is best explained as the symbolic return of life to its ultimate source, to replenish that source and keep the cycle going. The most effective sacrifice is that of a living being, and the blood of the victim is always allowed to flow freely during the rite. The ultimate sacrifice, in probably all the world's cosmologies, is human. The purest human is a child: innocent, untainted by adult emotion, physiologically unsexed, and ritually "clean," unpolluted by the sexual power of the other gender (see Douglas 1966).

These sentiments, we must note, exist in peoples' abstract realm of the *ideal*, a level of cultural "reality" that often does not correspond with what actually goes on. Human sacrifice among such celebrated theocracies as the

Aztecs is frequently cited as evidence of its place in primitive and tradition-bound cultures. But we should be aware that throughout history and around the world, *human sacrifice is actually very rare*. When it does occur, the Aztecs notwithstanding, it is almost always at times of severe social crisis. In fact, most striking ethnologically are cultural explanations for the *absence* of human sacrifice. Myths may explain that the gods honored the intentions of culture founders to offer one of their own, but said don't, your people are too precious, give us this or that animal instead. This theme appears in the Biblical account of Abraham and Issac (a basis for the "scapegoat" idea) in *Genesis* 22, and there are parallels in mythologies around the world. Among the Bachama in northeastern Nigeria, I recorded a myth with precisely the same theme.

In all cultures, blood is life, really and symbolically. Life—all life—is infused with supernatural power, and all living things contain a "life force" or "soul." Blood (or the corresponding fluid in invertebrates and plants) is a favored sacrificial material; wine, beer brewed from the staple crop, or distilled liquids carry their respective life force in concentrated form and are ritual counterparts to blood. Blood, containing the life force, is powerful. Menstrual blood, through its own extraordinary generative power, is "polluting," taboo, ritually unclean, "dangerous" (see Douglas 1966); the clash of its power with other powers in nature might bring down horrible consequences on people. The color of blood is magically powerful, too, because of its symbolic connection; and things colored red are used in magical rites the world over; in sorcery, in generative magic, and in talismanic or protective magic. Red is vital, energetic, turbulent; it is also powerfully negative: anger, rage, violence. Red is fire, in many cultures the ultimate destroyer, an effective weapon against spirits and witches; in some African cosmologies the god of Death burns with live fire. Satan is often depicted in red (and black, sometimes evil by association with night).

Cannibalism

The idea of the human consumption of human flesh is also deeply embedded in the subcultural psyche, surely universally. It is the stuff of nightmares, a subject of revulsion and horror. As I. M. Lewis demonstrates in his very insightful book, *Religion in Context* (1986), cannibalism is inextricably associated with witchcraft beliefs. For the first few months of my fieldwork among Bachama in 1969, while I was still groping with the language, my English-speaking informants frequently referred to "the cannibals" in discussions of cosmology. I had learned that cannibalism in Africa was extremely rare, limited to a very restricted ritual context, and none at all had been documented in this area; this was a disturbing puzzle. I realized later that the people were using the most appropriate English word for witches.

Anthropologists use the term "witchcraft" to refer to beliefs in a mystical or "psychic" power in certain people that can work evil directly, without magic or spiritual assistance. In this sense it is distinct from sorcery, which is evil magic, involving the learned use of objects and words to affect things in nature symbolically, through principles of similarity. This distinction in beliefs is made by peoples everywhere: the English referents follow the terminology used by the pioneers in witchcraft studies, Fortune (1932) and Evans-Pritchard (1937). Universally, witches are believed to be able to change their shapes, work through animal or spirit familiars, and fly at great speeds directly to their targets. Witches in late medieval Europe received their powers from Satan; otherwise, their attributes are identical to witches elsewhere.

A universal attribute of the witch is its lust for human flesh and blood, which it consumes, symbolically, by "eating" the life-force of its victim, causing debilitating illness and death. Beliefs in werewolves, or *loup garou* in France and areas of French influence, vampires (from Slavic *vampir*, a blood-sucking ghost); the Italian *strega*, the *nagual* of Central America, and the blood-sucking spirits that abound in Caribbean cultures are variants of this aspect of witch beliefs.

The witches of the Middle Ages demanded child sacrifices, which they consumed in their orgiastic *sabbats*. The term for the nocturnal gatherings of medieval witches (another aspect of witch behavior, believed universally) in wild places, or in cemeteries where they would exhume corpses, was taken from the Hebrew word for the Jews' holy day. Jews, as we know so well, have been the victims of the most vicious witch hunts in the history of civilization. They were charged by Greeks with kidnaping, murdering, and cannibalizing babies before the Christian era, and by Christians periodically thereafter (see Ellis 1983). The association of Jews with Satan by late medieval Christians, charges of spreading plague during the horrible scourge of the Black Death, and the kidnaping and butchering of Christian children were documented in detail by Joshua Trachtenberg (1943; see also Hsia 1988) just before the world was to learn of the enormity of the Nazi Holocaust, the next great Jewish witch hunt.

First-century Christians were themselves charged, both by Romans and by other sects of Christians, with ritual murder and cannibalism of children (Wilken 1984; Fox 1989). And nearly identical allegations have been made around the world—in Islamized areas, and by tribal peoples against each other, against colonial governments, even against anthropologists! They have been explained in terms of power and powerlessness, and sexuality. In most traditional areas that have experienced colonialism, European power has been regarded not only in political and military terms, but also as magical and mystical power. This explained their good health (sick Europeans were cared for in isolation, or sent home), eternal youth (infants and elderly were seldom seen by natives), and the fact that they had more than they needed but were seldom seen to work. Bachama people, as some told me, were certain I had special power, which was why I was never bothered by evil spirits or witches. And in colonial Africa from time to time, when some inexplicable disruption occurred in the social order, rumors spread about cannibalism of African children by the Europeans. Fraenkel (1959) describes reactions to the distribution of cans of meat marked "For African Consumption," in Northern Rhodesia; the people were sure it was human flesh that would weaken them and force them to agree to an unpopular political proposition. When a colonial administrator, to allay such fears, publicly opened and ate from a can, it simply confirmed native suspicions about European cannibalism and power. Epstein (1979) offers a psycho-analytic interpretation of this and similar incidents.

The introduction of Western medicine to Third World areas has often contributed to fears of cannibalism. Western-trained family-planners have been suspect, and Friedland (1960) links African failures of Red Cross blood drives to these beliefs—and Lewis (1986:66) notes how suspicions were bolstered by Europeans' fondness for tinned tomato juice. Hypodermic injections and surgery are powerful and magical, but are also sometimes seen as Europeans' refinements on the methods of witches. During the political crisis in Northern Rhodesia, Epstein noted

> a resurgence of the belief in *banyama,* or vampire-men. Once again *banyama* were stalking the land, seizing their victims at night, *injecting* them so they became docile, then taking them off to some remote place, there to suck their blood and feast on their flesh. . . . Unlike the vampire of European legend, *banyama* were not men who returned to walk the land, they were living persons. Anyone could be a *banyama,* a European or an African, one's next-door neighbor, or someone hitherto held in high public regard or esteem. Many ugly incidents were reported, and for a time as night fell many terrified Africans took to their houses and barred the doors. The *banyama* outbreak expressed perfectly the breakdown of trust in social relations. (1979:6)

I italicized *injecting;* without this feature Epstein's description expresses perfectly the general social response to a witch scare. The location might be a late medieval European community . . . or Jamestown, New York, in the spring of 1988 (Victor 1989). Southern American blacks from slavery times until early in this century held a parallel belief in the "night doctors," evil people who had sold their souls to the medical establishment and stalked the night looking for victims to kill and sell (Fry 1975:170ff.).

Dr. Christian Bernard's heart transplant surgery in south Africa, which in some cases utilized African hearts to give new life to whites, confirmed such suspicions throughout the African continent. And Campion-Vincent (1990) describes a modern Latin American demonology about Americans operating an international trade in baby parts. The rumors developed in areas of high infant mortality and feelings of oppression by the United States, and were seized on by political opportunists both there and in Europe.

Elsewhere, Margaret Mead reported allegations of cannibalism between tribes in the Sepik River area of New Guinea (1950). My colleague Don Pollock told me how the Sharanaua of eastern Peru suspected the Culina of western Brazil of cannibalism (among other charges typically made between unrelated societies who share the same ecology: they are dirty and never wash, they eat snakes and rodents, which is why their minds are dulled, etc.) and how, when he inquired of the Culina what they thought about it, they suspected him. For some days in 1981 he feared not only for his field-work, but for his life. William Arens reported similar, though less threaten-ing, experiences in Tanzania (Kolata 1987). Folklorist Lydia Fish suggested that Vietnamese fears of American cannibalism were aroused by President Lyndon Johnson's determination to "win their hearts and minds," and confirmed by the response of ground troops: "Get 'em by the balls, and their hearts and minds will follow."

Lewis (1986) relates suspicions of cannibalism, not only to witchcraft, but also to expressions of power and powerlessness, and to sexual aggression. This latter interpretation had earlier been offered by Sagan (1974), who noted psychoanalytic similarities between eating and sexuality, and be-tween cannibalism and incest. Robert Knox Dentan informs me that in much of Southeast Asia, and throughout Malaysia, cannibalism and incest are referred to by the same term. Cannibalism is also related to sodomy in some of these areas. Arens' ground-breaking study of "the man-eating myth" surveys reports of cannibalism through history and around the world, and concludes: "The cannibalistic epithet at one time or another has been applied by someone to every human group" (1974:13).

Live sacrifice is often followed by a communal meal in which the commu-nicants prepare, cook, and share the sacrificial animal. The cannibalistic meal in the satanic demonology is a travesty of the Eucharist, as we shall see in the section on the "Satanic Mass." The widespread idea among Third World peoples that Europeans are cannibals may have been planted in some areas by early missionaries who stressed Christ's prescription for this holiest of sacraments, in such New Testament passages as John 6:53–58.

Cannibalism as a repugnant idea is clearly a cognitive universal with deep psychological significance. But does it really happen? Arens (1979) said no; unconfirmed allegations have been taken as fact. Others (Brown and Tuzin 1983; Sanday 1986) countered with some evidence, mostly of a ritual sort associated with the flow of life or continuity of the social order, e.g., eating a bit of the corpse of one's kin to identify with and appease ancestors, or the custom in some monarchies of the new king eating a bit of his predecessor's brain and heart to gain wisdom and courage. But all subsequent researchers have agreed that, as an actual practice, cannibalism is extremely rare; and it does not really matter, anyway. It is the symbolism of the idea that is important; as Marshall Sahlins (1983:88) put it: "Cannibalism is always symbolic, even when it is real."

Children

All the above discussion finds a locus in children, surely the most significant of the three central elements in the satanic demonology. The principal actors in demonologies frequently focus their evil ambitions on children. Children are kidnapped, abused, subjected to obscene torments, sold into slavery or to pornography rings or to childless or lecherous adults (or monsters); or killed, butchered, and dismembered, their blood and parts saved for ritual consumption or sold to the oppressed poor. Similar charges are found in pre-Christian and Christian demonologies, into the modern era. Robert Tallant (1983:15) reports persistent fears among white residents of New Orleans in the mid-nineteenth century, that "every small child that vanished had become a Voodoo sacrifice." Modern Satan hunters emphasize the enormity of the problem with figures of 50,000 to 60,000 ritual murders of children per year; late medieval allegations against Jews were similar. Satan demands human lives, according to the lore. Late medieval art showed him devouring live victims, and witches presenting the horned god with children they had stolen, or conceived through an *incubus*.

The role of children in society may seem clear and straightforward. They are valuable beyond economic measure; indeed, they are "priceless," as satanic claims-makers often assert (Best 1987). They are real and tangible, physically here; the other elements in demonologies are removed, outside. But I think the depth of the cultural significance of children, which prompts such quick response from alarmed parents, has not been fully appreciated by social scientists. Let us consider, again, family-planning efforts among impoverished Third World peoples. Even when improved health care has decreased infant mortality, and economic hardship makes supporting large families increasingly difficult, and even when family-planning agencies have established trust and rapport with the people, fertility rates often remain high. Something else is going on.

Children represent the fulfillment of adult potential. Parenthood is a supremely important stage in the life cycle. Childlessness is a grievous condition, perhaps a mark of supernatural displeasure, and may affect the quality of one's afterlife. It is more than failure to produce heirs, or to expand one's kin group, or to provide for security in one's old age; it means failure to achieve a fundamental expectation of adult life, a basic measure of self-worth. And what the family planners may fail to recognize is that when modernization and the money economy erode the social structure, labor and land and livestock are sold for necessary cash, and other measures of adult success such as hunting and warfare are banned by law, then the ability to produce children may be *all* a person has left.

Culturally, of course, children are blessed, pure and innocent, dependent and vulnerable, and trustworthy. Children are open to spiritual insight. Some Melanesian cargo cults were based on the visions of children (Belshaw 1951); visions that sanctioned great Christian pilgrimage sites were experienced by children; the claims of two young girls gave the impetus to the religion of Spiritualism. Children were the first to be afflicted by, and to accuse, witches in Salem. The ordeal of Raymond Buckey and his mother and grandmother in the McMartin Preschool case, referred to as a "witch hunt" by some journalists (Charlier and Downing 1988), depended on the testimony of children. Buttons proclaiming "Believe the Children" were worn by outraged adults in Newark, New Jersey, at the 1987 child sexual abuse trial of Margaret Kelly Michaels, who was sentenced to 45 years in prison (Rabinowitz 1990).

A function of demonologies is that they can distract people from immediate yet daunting social problems. Social conditions in late medieval Europe were horrendous, but officials spent considerable time and money ferreting out witches. In late 1944 when German front lines were collapsing, Nazi leaders *diverted* supply trucks and trains to intensify the extermination of Jews. Elsewhere (Stevens 1990b) I have suggested that this sort of thing may be going on in the satanism scare, and the efforts to search out "ritual abusers" today: we are distracted from addressing serious problems affecting our children.

Worries about the welfare of children have been central to our social concerns for three decades. In the 1960s it was "flower children" and Vietnam war protests that led to campus protests and a generation of disenchanted kids in the 1970s who were vulnerable to alternative religious philosophies and "cults." In the 1980s concerns focused on missing or kidnapped or run-away (or "thrown-away") children (Best 1987; Finkelhor et al. 1990). These fears were exacerbated by public statistics about alcohol and other drug use, pregnancy, pornography, violence, suicide, and declining academic performance among children. And consider the *general* social problems and concerns throughout this period: terrorism, drugs, sexual promiscuity, homosexuality, AIDS, secular humanism, economic deterioration, poverty and homelessness, political corruption and ineptitude, social unrest, racism, increased lawlessness, earthquakes, environmental disasters, radically changed weather patterns, constant warnings from all sorts of "experts." This has been the breeding ground for the demonology of satanism, and it is revealing to note that it has coalesced around concerns for children.

Children are the ultimate measure of adult success. The value of children derives directly from deep cultural sentiments, themselves having deep roots in the evolutionary biology of our species. This is one of the fundamental premises of sociobiology (Wilson 1975); indeed, the quickness with which parents respond to danger that threatens their children is evident throughout the animal kingdom. Cultural is the human elaboration on animalian neuro-biological structures, and allows a unique and powerful response to emotion. The victimization of children, especially when blood sacrifice and cannibalism are involved and all is sanctioned by supernatural evil, comprises the worst imaginable cultural nightmare.

THE SATANIC MASS

The specific form and content of a demonology are the products of local cultural tradition, and the social researcher should investigate such tradition and its history. The central theme in today's satanic demonology derives from the so-called "Satanic Mass," or "Black Mass," known in various forms throughout Christendom. Variations on this story include saying the Mass backward over the naked body of a young girl (a virgin, parodying the Immaculate Conception) followed by copulating with her on the altar; desecration of the sacraments, fouling the chalice with human and animal excretory fluids, and sacrificing children for a cannibalistic Eucharist. These blasphemous acts may be performed in black-draped rooms lit with black candles, by persons in black robes and hoods. The ceremony may feature the appearance of Satan himself, or one of his demons.

Those unaware of the history of this tradition have wondered at the appearance of this motif, apparently spontaneously, in distinctly separate geographic regions. So many different communities of people could not be making up such similar stories, say the satan hunters; these things must really be happening.

In fact, today's demonology is a legend (see Stevens 1990a) containing some elements that have appeared periodically in Western history for over 2000 years; others have been introduced fairly recently. And through popular literature, movies, and rock music lyrics and album covers, it has become firmly embedded in our popular culture.

Jeffrey Russell (1980:128–131) has traced the origin of the Black Mass motif to the reign of Louis XIV (b. 1638, d. 1715) in France. Historians of the period have focused on the grandeur of Louis' monarchy; because of his enlightened accomplishments he was called the "Sun King." But there was a dark underside to his reign. In 1679 Louis established a secret commission to investigate allegations of poisonings and political and sexual improprieties against certain influential people, including clergy. The windows of the room in which this investigative body sat were draped in black, the room was lit with candles, and the judiciaries wore black robes. The court was referred to as *Chambre ardente*.

The peasantry of France had endured severe economic hardships and disruptive civil unrest in the period prior to Louis' reign. His focus on lavish building projects (exemplified by the palace at Versailles), keeping his disgruntled nobility occupied with elaborate courtly ceremonies, and a series of costly wars against the Habsburgs did little to ease the widespread sense of alienation among the common people. The earliest forms of the Satanic Mass idea developed among them out of their speculation over the mysterious *Chambre ardente* affair.

These were the waning years of the Great Witch Hunt. With the Industrial Revolution, Church and society backed away from a central concern with Satan (although the Roman ritual of exorcism remained on the books). But in the late nineteenth century (the period of the development of the *Protocols*, we might note), in the shadows of the "Gilded Age," a number of new "occult" groups emerged, including the Order of the Temple of the Orient (O.T.O.) and the Hermetic Order of the Golden Dawn. These organizations attracted several intellectuals and writers of the period; their most notorious member was Aleister Crowley. They were influenced by the notion, elaborated a bit later by Margaret Murray (1921), that there really was a "witch cult" of enlightened pagans, almost exclusively liberated women who worshiped a horned goatish figure, which had operated continuously in western Europe since Druidic times. It was by serious misinterpretation of the harmless aims of such seekers of spiritual insight that the excesses of the Inquisitions were perpetrated. Crowley and his fellows disclaimed any reality in Satan, but they resurrected and reworked much medieval magic and demon lore, and concocted new rituals. Prominent among their emblems was the "Baphomet," the bizarre androgynous, winged, goat-headed figure created earlier by French occultist Eliphas Lévi.

Although Murray's arguments have been thoroughly discredited (see Cohn 1975), they were widely influential, and formed the guiding philosophy of some modern "neopagan" groups, several of which chose to call themselves witches. The late medieval image of Satan as a winged, goat-headed figure persisted in popular lore, and an unintentional result of the "esoteric magic" of the Crowleyites was that the Satanic Mass became firmly rooted in modern popular culture. One influential book on this motif was written by Henry Rhodes, a British criminologist, and published in 1954 by Rider & Co., the earlier occultists' publisher (Rhodes 1954). It is based on rumor, allegation, and popular folklore; in it, "satanic" refers to anything eccentric or outside the mainstream, and anything non-Christian. The books of Church of Satan founder Anton LaVey (1969, 1972) were apparently strongly influenced by this "occult tradition." (LaVey also popularized the "satanic pentagram," the five-pointed star with one point downward and the head of a goat superimposed. The origin of this emblem is not clear, but it was not used by the Crowleyites, nor was it medieval.) Lévi's major work, originally intended for exclusive distribution, was republished in the United States in 1970 (Lévi 1970); and the Baphomet is regarded in some communities today as the most ominous of all satanic emblems and graffiti. Michelle Smith's and Lawrence Pazder's influential book, *Michelle Remembers* (1980), which brings child molestation and Satan himself into the Black Mass theme, appeared 10 years later. And Crowley and the O.T.O. are invoked by occult dabblers today; some of their motifs and slogans have been picked up by heavy metal musicians.

The Black Mass theme, central to the satanic demonology today, has a continuous 300-year history. Its modern version owes its form to a few creative imaginations of our century. As social scientists, our major task is to discover how and why it has moved from the fringes of society into the mainstream.

SOME FURTHER CONSIDERATIONS

The prophet and the doomsayer are always with us; at what point do their messages become widely acceptable? In small-scale homogeneous societies we can find answers in traditional cosmologies and in people's perceptions of their position in society. Demonologies are constructed around elements that are culturally true. Witch hunts are mass expressions of the reality of witches; the idea that supernatural evil is spreading among the populace is credible because the problems traditionally thought to be caused by witches have been increasing. Satan was thought to be real, and central, in late medieval Europe, and horrendous social conditions were clear evidence of his increasing activity.

But the question of credibility presents an unprecedented challenge in the case of today's satanic demonology. Satan has not been on such a rampage since the New England witch hunts of the seventeenth century (Demos 1982), which culminated in the Salem terror of 1692–1693, nearly 300 years ago. And the fears have snowballed over nearly an entire decade, even though there is no hard evidence that any of the horrible things described in the demonology have actually happened.

The social sciences, collectively, have the expertise to discover what is going on. I have indicated some research directions throughout this chapter, and will refer to some of them, and suggest some others by way of conclusion.

We should ask who accepts the demonology, what socioeconomic conditions prevail in their areas, and what are their culturally shaped perceptions of those conditions. How long have such conditions obtained, and what factors shaped their development; how have people been reacting to them, and what were the outcomes of such reactions? Can we devise research strategies that can demonstrate direct causal links between social conditions and perceptions, and the satanism fears? In framing our research we should take into consideration models from history, anthropology, and the other social sciences (Stevens 1988).

Jeffrey Victor's (1989) discussion of the evolution of a satanic rumor panic in a small western New York community is a good model. His research shows that rumor panics, in which whole communities have been disrupted, are largely a *rural* phenomenon. This is significant, and his discussion addresses some of the above questions for rural communities. A recent study (Helge 1990) suggests that certain socioeconomic stresses on rural people, especially school children, may be more severe than those in urban areas.

Demonological fears, especially those associated with blood, cannibalism, and child molestation, have been referred to as "the stuff of nightmares." Nightmares, too, are reactions to severe stress and anxiety; they, and "night terrors" with varying cultural contents, are universal human phenomena. Understanding the cultural, psychological, and physiological bases for nightmares will yield insight into such collective phenomena as demonologies. Monica Wilson (1950) suggested this 40 years ago. Hufford (1982) and Hartmann (1984) have offered guidelines such research might follow.

The religious content of revitalization and witch-hunting movements are often framed in millennial expectations, usually the hastening of a utopia or paradise by human action. It seems that the satanic demonology took root and is most widespread among fundamentalist Christians; is this so? We are rapidly approaching the end of the second thousand years of Christian history, and many people perceive the world to be in dire shape. The first millennium, as prophesied in *Revelation,* failed, but people in subsequent centuries found reasons for its postponement (Stevens 1989). There are striking similarities between social conditions today and those that correlated with the great witch hunts of the late Middle Ages when many people fully expected the trumpets of the Apocalypse to sound; but today, dire events and predictions, and chronological time, are correlating perfectly. Are some Christians gearing up for the *real* Apocalypse?

There is one further important question. As pointed out earlier in this chapter, in our eagerness to explain why social movements occur, we tend to forget about the greater number of situations of similar stressful conditions in which such movements have not developed. As well as asking why, it may be profitable to ask, *why not?* The answer, again, should be sought in specific cultural patterns. Hill (1944), for example, showed that the Navaho did not accept the great Ghost Dance of 1890, even though all their neighbors embraced it with intense fervor, because for the Navaho the idea that ancestral ghosts would return was an absolutely terrifying prospect.

Persons of any ethnic background may have reason to fear the operation of alleged satanic cults, but the demonology of satanism is a Christian phenomenon. Since slavery days American blacks have devoutly embraced Christianity; yet the demonology seems not to find widespread acceptance among urban or rural blacks. Why not? No human group has experienced such oppression, and there is certainly a strong history of fears of nocturnal evil, as Fry (1975) has shown.

At least part of the answer may lie in the image of Satan in black culture. The old mainstream American churches, to which the fundamentalist traditions are heir, derived directly from European Christianity, which has kept alive the terrible image of Satan that drove the Inquisition and the New England witch hunts. But in black Christianity, Satan is quite a different character. Since the first baptisms on sixteenth-century slave ships, and manifested later most strongly in the syncretistic traditions of Brazilian *candomblés,* Cuban and Puerto Rican *Santería,* and Haitian *Vodun,* black Christianity has maintained strong African elements.[2] African (and most of the world's) religions have no counterpart to Satan or to Hell. The first missionaries saw Satan in the "devilish" behavior of trickster deities, and his demons in the wide range of ghosts and spirits like the *jombees, zombies,* or *duppies* of various Afro-Caribbean cultures. New World blacks retained elements of the old trickster character in their idea of Satan. He is clever, even dangerous, but he has human foibles, and he can be outwitted. He is more a principle of unpredictability than of evil. Jay Dobbin's description of beliefs in Montserrat are generalizable:

> on several occasions I heard "Feed dee debil, but wif' a long spoon," . . . the devil, in the saying quoted above and in others, does not appear as the horrendously terrifying figure of, for example, the Christian *Epistle of Peter,* where he "prowls around like a roaring lion, seeking anyone to devour" (1 Peter 4:8). The devil in Montserratian sayings has more the trickster character and is comparable with the folklore character, Bo-Ananci [the spider trickster in Akan folklore of Ghana]. The devil is here not like Satan in *The Book of Job,* who watches the affairs of man from above and at a distance. The devil here is more like the close at-hand jombees and Bo-Ananci. This Montserratian devil is close enough to feed. He is not the Christian source of evil, for he lives within the intimacy of the Montserratian countryside. (Dobbin 1986:30–31)

The satanic demonology, a product of northern Christianity, could find no basis for credibility in this character.

Analyses of witch hunts and demonologies from hindsight can establish correlations, but hypotheses about direct causes are untestable. Today, social science has an unprecedented opportunity[3]—a demonology is flourishing, and variants of it have inspired some local witch hunts, among our contemporaries. Things may get worse. Through careful study of the satanism scare we can make significant contributions to understanding human behavior, *and* we might help to alleviate fears.

NOTES

1. The Nazi demonology about the Jews drew from some medieval ideas, but emphasized their financial dealings, treachery, and world conspiracy plans. It touched on their personal habits and appearance, and as the Final Solution got under way it dehumanized them, referring to them as unnatural, vermin, or as "Night and Fog," from Hitler's *Nacht und Nebel* decree issued on December 12, 1941.
  At this point we should address a premise frequently used by satan hunters today: that Hitler was "into satanism." It is true that the framers of Third Reich philosophy were interested in pre-Christian and other "pagan" sources of justification for their new "German Faith" and the Aryan "Master Race" idea (cf. Sklar 1977), but there is no evidence at all of the invocation of Satan, anywhere. Indeed, they conscientiously sought to declare *all* tenets of Christianity null and void—but here, of course, is all the evidence fundamentalist Christians need, and this fact is probably the basis for allegations of satanism in the Third Reich.
  2. Many would be surprised to hear these belief systems spoken of as expressions of "black Christianity." In fact, they are blends of Christian and African religious beliefs. They are *not* systems of sorcery or "witchcraft," and Satan is not in their pantheons. They are full-fledged religions, their adherents united *against* evil. They are older than the United States, having flourished continuously since at least the early seventeenth century, but they have always been misunderstood by mainstream Christian institutions. And this misunderstanding has generated much inaccurate, sensationalistic material about them, and some satan hunters have recently pointed at them, causing no little concern to their thousands of North American adherents. See my earlier discussion: Stevens (1989); and for a general overview: Simpson (1978); for *Santería:* González-Wippler (1982) and Murphy (1988); for *Vodun:* Métraux (1959) and Thompson (1983).
  3. In my research for this paper I have become aware, again, of the dangers of fragmentation within the social sciences. Sociologists, psychologists, folklorists, and anthropologists have all been asking similar questions, although from different perspectives; they are coming up with similar answers, though with different kinds of evidence, and they seldom cite each other. This breakdown in communication among our disciplines wastes time and effort. This book is a unique collaboration. Let up hope it will be exemplary.

REFERENCES

Arens, William. 1979. *The Man-Eating Myth: Anthropology & Anthropophagy.* New
    York: Oxford University Press.
Becker, Ernest. 1975. *Escape from Evil.* New York: Free Press.
Belshaw, Cyril. 1951. "Recent History of Mekeo Society." *Oceania* 22:1.

Best, Joel. 1987. "Rhetoric in Claims-Making: Constructing the Missing Children Problem." *Social Problems* 34:101–102.

Bohannan, P.J. 1958. "Extra-Processual Events in Tiv Political Institutions." *American Anthropologist* 60:1–12.

Brown, Paula, and Tuzin, Donald. eds. 1983. *The Ethnography of Cannibalism.* Washington: Society for Psychological Anthropology.

Campion-Vincent, Veronique. 1990. "The Baby-Parts Story: A New Latin American Legend." *Western Folklore* 49(1):9–25.

Charlier, Tom, and Downing, Shirley. 1968. "Justice Abused: A 1980s Witch-Hunt." Memphis, TN, *Commercial Appeal,* January 17–22.

Cohn, Norman. 1975. *Europe's Inner Demons: An Enquiry Inspired by the Great Witch-Hunt.* New York: Basic Books.

————. 1981. *Warrant for Genocide,* 3rd ed. Brown Judaic Studies, 23. Chico, CA: Scholars Press (1st ed. 1967).

Demos, John Putnam. 1982. *Entertaining Satan: Witchcraft and the Culture of Early New England.* New York: Oxford University Press.

De Vore, Irven, and Washburn, S.L. 1960. *Baboon Behavior.* 16-mm film. Berkeley, CA: University Extension, University of California.

Dobbin, Jay D. 1986. *The Jombee Dance of Montserrat.* Columbus, OH: Ohio State University Press.

Douglas, Mary. 1966. *Purity and Danger: An Analysis of the Concepts of Pollution and Taboo.* London: Routledge & Kegan Paul.

Ellis, Bill. 1983. "*De Legendis Urbis:* Modern Legends in Ancient Rome." *Journal of American Folklore* 96:380, 200–208.

Epstein, A.L. 1979. "Unconscious Factors in the Response to Social Crisis: A Case Study from Central Africa." Pp. 3–39 in *The Psychoanalytic Study of Society,* Vol. 8, edited by W. Muensterberger and L. Byrce Boyer. New Haven: Yale University Press.

Evans-Pritchard, E.E. 1937. *Witchcraft, Oracles and Magic among the Azande.* Oxford: Clarendon Press.

Finkelhor, David, Hotaling, Gerald, and Sedlak, Andrea. 1990. *Missing, Abducted, Runaway, and Thrownaway Children in America.* First Report, May. Washington, DC: Office of Juvenile Justice and Delinquency Prevention.

Fortune, Reo. 1932. *Sorcerers of Dobu.* New York: E.P. Dutton.

Fox, Robin Lane. 1989. *Pagans and Christians.* New York: Knopf.

Fraenkel, P.J. 1959. *Wayaleshi.* London: Weidenfeld and Nicolson.

Friedland, W.H. 1960. "Some Urban Myths in East Africa." Pp. 83–97 in *Myth in Modern Africa,* edited by A. Dubb. Lusaka: Rhodes Livingstone Institute.

Fry, Gladys Marie. 1975. *Night Riders in Black Folk History.* Knoxville: University of Tennessee Press.

González-Wippler, Migene. 1982. *The Santería Experience.* Englewood Cliffs, NJ: Prentice-Hall.

Greenberg, Jeff, Pyszczynski, Tom, Solomon, Sheldon, Rosenblatt, Abram, Veeder, Mitchell, Kirkland, Shari, and Lyon, Deborah. 1990. "Evidence for Terror Management Theory II: The Effects of Mortality Salience on Reactions to Those Who Threaten or Bolster the Cultural Worldview." *Journal of Personality and Social Psychology* 58:308–318.

Hartmann, Ernest. 1984. *The Nightmare: The Psychology and Biology of Terrifying Dreams.* New York: Basic Books.

Helge, Doris. 1990. "National Study Regarding Rural, Suburban and Urban At-Risk Students." Bellingham, WA: National Rural Development Institute.

Hill, W.W. 1944. "The Navaho Indians and the Ghost Dance of 1890." *American Anthropologist* 46:523–527.

Hsia, R. Po-chia. 1988. *The Myth of Ritual Murder: Jews and Magic in Reformation Germany.* New Haven: Yale University Press.

Hufford, David J. 1982. *The Terror That Comes in the Night: An Experience-Centered Study of Supernatural Assault Traditions.* Philadelphia: University of Pennsylvania Press.

Kolata, Gina. 1987. "Cannibalism: Fact Or Fiction?" *Smithsonian Magazine* 17:150–172.

Lanternari, Vittorio. 1963. *The Religions of the Oppressed: A Study of Modern Messianic Cults.* New York: Mentor Books.

LaVey, Anton Szandor. 1969. *The Satanic Bible.* New York: Avon Books
————. 1972. *The Satanic Rituals.* New York: Avon Books.

Lévi, Eliphas (Alphonse Louis Constant). 1970. *Transcendental Magic.* A.E. Waite, trans. York Beach, ME: Samuel Weiser (orig. London: Rider, 1898).

Lewis, I.M. 1986. *Religion in Context: Cults and Charisma.* Cambridge: Cambridge University Press.

Mead, Margaret. 1950. *Sex and Temperament in Three Primitive Societies.* New York: Mentor Books.

Metraux, Alfred. 1959. *Voodoo in Haiti.* New York: Oxford University Press.

Murphy, Joseph M. 1988. *Santeria: An African Religion in America.* Boston: Beacon Press.

Murray, Margaret Alice. 1921. *The Witch-Cult in Western Europe.* London: Oxford University Press.

Rabinowitz, Dorothy. 1990. "From the Mouths of Babes to a Jail Cell. Child Abuse and the Abuse of Justice: A Case Study." *Harper's Magazine.* May, 52–63.

Rhodes, Henry T. F. 1954. *The Satanic Mass.* London: Rider.

Russell, Jeffrey Burton. 1980. *A History of Witchcraft: Sorcerers, Heretics and Pagans.* New York: Thames & Hudson.

Sagan, Eli. 1974. *Cannibalism: Human Aggression and Cultural Form.* New York: Harper & Row.

Sahlins, Marshall. 1983. "Raw Women, Cooked Men, and Other 'Great Things' of the Fiji Islands." Pp. 72–93. In *The Ethnography of Cannibalism,* edited by Paula Brown and Donald Tuzin. Washington: Society for Psychological Anthropology.

Sanday, Peggy Reeves. 1986. *Divine Hunger: Cannibalism as a Cultural System.* Cambridge: Cambridge University Press.

Schoeneman, Thomas J. 1975. "The Witch Hunt as a Social Change Phenomenon." *Ethos* 3(4):529–554.

Seligmann, C.G. 1910. *The Melanesians of British New Guinea.* Cambridge: Cambridge University Press.

Simpson, George Eaton. 1978. *Black Religions in the New World.* New York: Columbia University Press.

Sklar, Dusty. 1977. *Gods and Beasts: The Nazis and the Occult.* New York: Thomas Y. Crowell.

Smith, Michelle, and Pazder, Lawrence. 1980. *Michelle Remembers.* New York: Congden & Lattes.

Stevens, Phillips, Jr. 1988. "The Appeal of the Occult: Some Thoughts on History, Religion and Science." *The Skeptical Inquirer* 12:376–385.

———. 1989. "Satanism: Where Are the Folklorists?" *New York Folklore* 15 (1–2):1–22.

———. 1990a. " 'New' Legends: Some Perspectives from Anthropology." *Western Folklore* 49(1):121–133.

———. 1990b. "The Dangerous Folklore of Satanism." *Free Inquiry* 10(3):28–34.

Tallant, Robert. 1983. *Voodoo in New Orleans.* Gretna, LA: Pelican (orig. New York: Macmillan, 1946).

Thompson, Robert Farris. 1983. *Flash of the Spirit: African and Afro-American Art and Philosophy.* New York: Random House.

Trachtenberg, Joshua. 1943. *The Devil and the Jews.* New Haven: Yale University Press.

Victor, Jeffrey S. 1989. "A Rumor-Panic about a Dangerous Satanic Cult in Western New York." *New York Folklore* 15 (1–2):22–49.

Wallace, A.F.C. 1956. "Revitalization Movements." *American Anthropologist* 58:264–281.

Wilken, Robert L. 1984. *The Christians as the Romans Saw Them.* New Haven: Yale University Press.

Williams, F.E. 1923. *The Vailala Madness and the Destruction of Native Ceremonies in the Gulf Division.* Port Moresby, New Guinea: Papuan Anthropology Reports.

Wilson, E.O. 1975. *Sociobiology: The New Synthesis.* Cambridge, MA: The Belknap Press.

Wilson, Monica Hunter. 1950. "Witch Beliefs and Social Structure." *American Journal of Sociology* 56:307–313.

The Historical Satan 3

Jeffrey Burton Russell

Most societies have a variety of demons, spirits, or gods, which are morally ambivalent: that is to say, the gods can be kind or unkind to humanity. One might argue that this amoral or dimoral polytheism fits the human experience of the cosmos well: we see things happening mysteriously, without reason, for good or ill, and call it fate, chance, or an "act of God."

Few religions have one figure specifically symbolizing evil, although Buddha's tempter Mara comes close. No religion has a single entity personifying evil except those of the Jewish–Christian–Muslim (and "Zoroastrian") tradition, which have Satan or the Devil.[1]

The problem of evil confronts every worldview, but none so poignantly as great monotheistic religions. Theologically the problem is simply stated. God is all-powerful and all-good. But an all-powerful, all-good God would not allow evil in the cosmos he creates. Therefore evil cannot exist. But we observe that evil exists. We are therefore forced to reject the existence of God (at least as great monotheistic religions define it) or qualify our definition. If we choose the latter, we can save God's pure goodness by limiting his omnipotence, or else save his omnipotence by qualifying his goodness. This is a sharp theological choice; few theologians choose to face it that explicitly.

To avoid this choice, a variety of strategies have been employed over the millennia. One solution, however unsatisfactory philosophically, is to resort to the notion of a spiritual power antagonistic to God, such as Satan.

The Old Testament has relatively few references to Satan as a personality. Most Hebrew thought before the second century B.C.E. accepted destruction and suffering as originating in God's inscrutable will. But some Old Testament passages lent themselves to an interpretation that mysterious spiritual powers, subordinate to a God, often did destructive things. In some passages—most dramatically in the Book of Job—this power is portrayed as having an independent, malevolent existence.

The idea of the Devil, very fuzzy in the Old Testament, becomes clear and sharp in the era from the second century B.C.E. to the second century C.E. One reason is the influence of Iranian dualism. The ancient Iranian religion of Mazdaism (sometimes called Zoroastrianism) had its origins in the teachings of Zarathushtra, a prophet whose dates are unknown. It is a dualist religion, explaining evil by positing a continual cosmic warfare between the God of Light and the God of Darkness. Mazdaism had some influence in Babylonia, where Hebrews in Exile were liberated by Iranian Shah Cyrus. A tendency toward dualism seems also to have grown indigenously among Jews, as they developed a darker view of the world during the times they were invaded, enslaved, and persecuted by a variety of conquerors—Egyptians, Assyrians, Babylonians, Persians, Greeks, and finally Romans.

The Jews reacted to this suffering partly by blaming it on their own sins (a stance of the great prophets), but partly by blaming exterior forces. The Devil or his deputies were the powerful spirits backing evil Gentiles against the Chosen People. Some Jewish sects, such as the Essenes, conceived (like the Mazdaists) of a vast cosmic warfare between the Lord of Light and the Prince of Darkness, a warfare in which each nation and each person was called to stand on one side or the other. For Jewish apocalyptics, the cosmic struggle was coming to its end; there would be one last, vast war between sons of darkness and sons of light, and then the good God would triumph eternally.

In the context of this heavily dualistic Jewish thought, Christianity came into being. Ideas similar to those of apocalyptic writers appear in the Christian Gospels, notably the Gospel of John, with its imagery of light against darkness, in miracle stories of Jesus' ability to cast out and defeat demons and their leader the Devil, and in the Book of Revelation (The Apocalypse).

However, after the destruction of Jerusalem by Romans in 70 C.E., and the diaspora of the Jews, Pharisees were left as the surviving leading Jewish group. Their tradition downplayed Satan's power so much that he seldom appears in works of the rabbis, although he does retain a presence in Jewish folklore.

Although Judaism downplayed Satan's power, Messianic trends that faded in Judaism after 70 C.E. remained strong in Christianity. For Christianity, Jesus was the Messiah. In Christian thought, God is good. Opposed by the Devil, he sends Jesus his Messiah to destroy the Devil's power. Unlike many Jewish sects, such as the Zealots, Christians believed that the Messiah was not a military victor over Satan and gentile nations, but rather the Suffering Servant, who took upon himself all sins of the people and, in dying for them, broke Satan's power. Virtually all early Christian writers granted Satan great power throughout the cosmos and also in the life of each human. Christ and Satan vie for each soul, and each person must choose between them.

Like Judaism, Christianity is a monotheistic religion. But by using the Devil to explain the existence of evil, some early Christian groups, such as Gnostic sects of the first two centuries C.E., pulled strongly in the direction of dualism. For them, Satan was an anti-God of enormous power. This power was to be fought, exorcised, and struggled against. But because it was so vast, Satan's power could also be manipulated, harnessed to one's own will, even, in extreme cases, worshipped. There was no organized Satanism in early Christianity, but some Gnostic sects seem to have verged on it by practicing orgiastic rites.

Many of the Gnostics melded Iranian dualism with Greek dualism, which identified spirit with good and matter with evil. By naming the Devil as creator and lord of matter, Gnostics opened the door for extremists to worship this material lord to obtain material goods. Thus Gnosticism bred both extreme asceticism and, occasionally, gross orgiasticism.

The vast majority of the educated Christian elite rejected such ideas, branding Gnostics as heretics. They saw that such extreme dualism was inconsistent with monotheism, and insisted that one Lord God had created all the cosmos, both spiritual and material. They counted the Devil's power as impotent before Christ. Still, they did not and could not dismiss it, for the dilemma posed to monotheism by evil is even worse for Christianity than for Judaism and Islam. In Christianity, the messiah has already come to save the world and destroy Satan's power over us. We should therefore observe the end of evil. If the Evil Lord held his grip on humanity before Christ's Incarnation and Passion, and Christ shattered that grip, evil should be no more. But evil continues. This dilemma could be resolved only by positing a Second Coming. Christ's First Coming, with his ministry, death, and resurrection, broke Satan's power in eternity, but the kingdom of God will not fully be realized until Christ returns. However, the longer his return delayed, the more continuing power of Satan in the world posed a serious theological problem.

To understand Christian ideas of Satanism we must first look at theories held by the elite, and then turn to the meager evidence that illustrates more popular beliefs.

The three most influential sources of Christian thought on the Devil were the Greek Alexandrian Egyptian, Origen; the "desert fathers"—hermits and monks who withdrew into the margins of vast deserts of Egypt and Syria; and Saint Augustine of Hippo, who set the theological tone for the Latin, Western church.

Through Origen and his older compatriot Clement of Alexandria, Christianity was influenced by a strong stream of Greek dualism. Greek dualism expressed itself classically in Plato's theories, and then with Neoplatonists who were Origen's near contemporaries. Unlike Iranian dualism, which posited a struggle between a spirit of light and a spirit of darkness, Greek dualism posited a struggle between spirit (which was good) and matter (which was evil). Early Christians Montanus and Tertullian envisioned matter as the Devil's tool to pry humanity away from the spirit, which comes from God. Such Christian writers viewed evil as a descent from spirituality into matter and the flesh.

Origen argued that God was the highest order of being, and that God created pure spirits and pure intelligences. For early Christian Platonists, goodness, spirit, intelligence, and pure being were equated. But one salient characteristic of intelligence is its ability to make free choices, including moral ones. Of the intelligences created, many chose to remain with God, but many others chose to pursue their own wills. The more drastically an intelligence chose to bend away from God, the farther into matter it fell. Some fell so low as to become humans and dwell on the earth's surface; others fell further, and became demons, imbedded in the grossest matter— hell, the center of the earth—where they are imprisoned, obeying their leader, the anti-God Satan.

Even as Origen was writing, a movement began in Egypt and spread to Syria that had important effects on Christianity and on beliefs about Satan, in particular. In the third century a rich young man, Anthony, decided to heed the Gospel injunctions to abandon all material concerns and follow Christ. He left his business, family connections, and even a young dependent sister (not without making provisions for her), moved from the city, and took up residence on the fringe of the Egyptian desert, thus becoming the first hermit. For a variety of complex reasons, this behavior caught on in solitary places of Egypt, Syria, Asia Minor, and elsewhere. Often the hermits remained alone; more often they attracted followers, who grouped together in monasteries.

One prominent characteristic of these holy men and women was their struggle against the Devil. From ancient Egyptian times, the red, dry, barren desert had been a symbol of evil, the haunt of demons. When Christ went out into the wilderness, he was tempted there by Satan. As Christianity gradually permeated cities, Satan's forces were believed to withdraw into remote places to escape the power of the cross; monks went forth in pursuit of them. For this reason, lurid stories arose of the Devil or his demons attacking these voluntary martyrs. The act of withdrawing into the desert was a deliberate act of defiance against Satan, and Satan seldom failed to take up the challenge.

The influence of such stories of struggle was twofold. They became a model for the lives of future saints. Jesus, after all, had struggled with the demonic. Stories of struggle also entered Christian (and later Muslim) folklore, so that the Devil was increasingly believed to be active everywhere. Whenever a temptation occurs to your senses or mind, and you assent to it for a moment, the Devil rushes in with his hordes to establish his kingdom in the citadel of your heart. You are powerless to dislodge him, but can save yourself by calling on Christ's help, for the power of Christ will always be stronger than Satan.

By the fifth century a standard "theology of Satan" had been established, though no church council or decree ever defined belief in Satan's existence as essential to Christian faith. Saint Augustine was in general the most influential of the western church fathers; his ideas set the tone of Christian belief even through the Reformation. Augustine's view was that God created the world to pour forth goodness beyond his own essence. But moral goodness requires a choice. If creatures were only robots programmed to act a certain way, they would be incapable of moral goodness. Hence God created intelligent creatures with real free choice between good and evil. The intelligent creatures known to Augustine were humans and angels. Many angels remained loyal in God's love; many others chose evil: that is, to love themselves more than God, and to do their own will rather than God's. These angels, fallen from grace, became demons, and their leader was the Devil or Satan. God next creates humanity also with completely free will. Adam and Eve, as representative of the human race, are created pure, with an endless life of joy before them. But they must have choice, so God forbids them to pluck the fruit of one tree. Satan tempts them to pick the forbidden fruit, they yield, and are banished from paradise. After this fall from grace, God could, in strict justice, abandon all of us to eternal separation from him. But because God's love is greater than his justice, he plans to redeem us from our own folly. First he gradually prepares his chosen Israel for the coming of the Messiah, Christ, who takes on himself all the sins of the world and liberates humans from the Devil's power. Next, between the initial coming of the messiah and his second coming, the Devil is allowed power to tempt, and humans are still free to love Christ or reject him.

This theory entailed many sophisticated questions. For instance, was Christ's salvation a true redemption—a ransom paid to induce Satan to relinquish the hold over us that original sin had given him? More troublesome were questions of predestination and free will. Such questions left room for a theology (and a folklore) giving Satan continued power in the world.

Early medieval literature, especially in Anglo-Saxon England, framed mighty epics of warfare between Christ and Satan, heaven and hell. Profound shocks to medieval society by repeated invasions and migrations, which upset civil, economic, ecclesiastical, and educational order, encouraged belief in supernatural powers of evil. German and Norse mythology added their demonic figures to legends of Mediterranean peoples. At the same time, domination of education by monasteries meant that monastic houses spread the desert fathers' tales of struggling against the Devil and fit new stories into the same pattern.

Neither scholastic theology of the twelfth through fifteenth centuries nor Protestant theological leaders of the sixteenth century such as Luther and Calvin advanced the theology of the Devil substantially beyond the basic picture painted by Saint Augustine. However, from the fourteenth through sixteenth centuries there developed a large body of visionary, spiritual, "mystical" writing. The Devil played a major part in this writing, partly because it drew again on lurid stories of the desert fathers, partly because political, epidemical, demographic, and economic problems of the period made the powers of evil seem closer to hand, and partly because the deeply religious felt that in approaching God through contemplation they were attracting the particular ire of the Devil.

Luther, far from changing Catholic theology of the Devil, incorporated it into his teachings. In fact, of all leading Christian theologians Luther pays most attention to Satan. Satan is everywhere, physically tormenting him, distracting him with temptations, stirring up enemies against him. As Luther's teachings were circulated in popularized form by Lutheran preachers to sixteenth-century audiences of literate and semiliterate people, belief in the Devil's power grew, rather than declined.

The most significant late Middle Ages development affecting modern ideas of Satanism was the alleged rise of diabolical witchcraft. Before roughly 1250, practicing magic had generally been considered a sin, but not particularly linked with the Devil. With the rise of Aristotelianism, attempts were made to distinguish the natural from the supernatural world, and magic was placed on the supernatural side. If magic was being worked, it could be only through the help of demons. Hence sorcerers were implicitly, even if not explicitly, calling on Satan's help. This constituted a turning away from God, to love and worship of Satan.

The theory of diabolical witchcraft existed from the thirteenth century, but only became a significant social problem in the fifteenth and sixteenth centuries. Religious and intellectual fermént enhanced insecurities: the immediateness of Satan's power, as expressed by mystics, Luther, and other writers, created a fear of Satanic witchcraft frequently called the witch craze. The witch craze began in the late fifteenth century, but after the Middle Ages it reached a fever peak, during the Reformation and religious wars of the sixteenth and seventeenth centuries. After 1700, it declined rapidly.

The witch craze was based on belief of a widespread conspiracy of witches (male and female) actively worshipping the Devil by calling up his presence, kidnapping babies, sacrificing them to him or eating or making ointments out of their flesh, and having sexual intercourse with Satan. Witches allegedly flew through the air and had other magical powers given them by demons, allowing them to work harm against their neighbors. Occasionally some anomic or psychotic people attempted to summon and worship Satan, but there was no basis for belief in a widespread conspiracy. The craze began and centered in France and Germany, but spread to Italy, Scandinavia, the British Isles, and eventually America.

Whatever the macrosocial causes for the craze, its rapid spread can be set down to a few definable causes. First, the background of Aristotelian scholastic theology declared any act of magic to be demonic. Second, there existed a long tradition in literature and folklore of persons calling up Satan (the sixteenth century Faust story was such a tale). Third, and most important were formal inquiries by local civil and ecclesiastical leaders into witchcraft. After several decades of investigating witch charges, inquisitors drew up manuals stating what questions should be put to the accused and in what order. Torture or threat of torture was commonplace. Terrified, the accused would confess, and, since one of the standard questions concerned who else was involved, they inculpated other innocent victims. If, again, it is assumed that some few antisocial people did practice witchcraft, their number was certainly tiny in comparison with the millions accused during the two worst centuries of the craze. At least a hundred thousand people were put to death.

The craze waned in the later seventeenth century and was extinct in most regions by the early eighteenth. One reason was growth of Cartesian and other rationalism that had no place in its worldview for such beliefs. More important, inquisitions produced so many accusations under torture that mayors, merchants, knights, judges, clergymen, and noblemen were sometimes implicated. Power elites, seeing themselves threatened, withdrew their support and brought the inquisitions to an end.

Satan's greatest moment in art came just as the craze was beginning to fade—in John Milton's epic poem *Paradise Lost* (seventeenth century). The reader is invited to admire Satan's pomp and glory and then, gradually, to perceive his treachery and his final humiliation. The literary Satan was a powerful figure in both sixteenth and seventeenth centuries, but the skepticism of eighteenth-century Enlightenment dismissed belief in the Devil as nonsense. By the early nineteenth century this intellectual skepticism came to permeate all educated classes, and Satan's powers were seen as absurd.

The Devil had a curious rebirth in the nineteenth century. Conservative Christians of all denominations continued to believe in him, but he was also revived by Romantic writers, sometimes as a figure of horror, but more often of sympathy, or even a hero. Romantics who supported popular revolutions from 1789 onward made Satan a symbol of liberty. If revolutions were against kings and priests, Romantics admired Satan as the enemy of the greatest king and Priest of all, Christ himself. Permutations were nearly infinite. In one great poem, Victor Hugo portrays Satan as a lonely hero, cast out from the world, full of love and longing, thrust out beyond the planets and stars into the empty coldness of space. At last he can see only three stars; he strains his wings and courage to reach a refuge, but one by one the stars die out and he is left in utter darkness. For some Romantics, Satan was a redeemer who bought human liberty at the cost of his own ruin.

Toward the nineteenth century's end, a number of literary and artistic figures such as J. K. Huysmans entertained belief in Satan as a kind of snub to society. It was a period when the occult was popular in many forms, and Satanism was clearly the way to flout and shock societal values most luridly. Huysmans' novel La-bas described the persona's visit to an orgiastic Black Mass (the Black Mass had been invented in the eighteenth century at the court of Louis XV). It was a best seller, and numerous writers turned to the Satanic, treating their subject as horror fiction, satire, whimsy, or, in some cases, allegedly "true" stories. It is likely that in the time's decadent atmosphere a few did engage in Satanic rites, but, there was no craze. The rational, materialistic worldview that had supplanted a theological worldview would not support taking such ideas seriously.

Interest in Satanism and the occult gradually declined in the early twentieth century and was virtually defunct by the end of World War II, possibly because there were so many more tangible evils. Conservative Christians continue to affirm the Devil's existence, and some psychologists and historians still find the idea of an evil that transcends individual human sins plausible. Liberal Christians and almost all Jews join in the general mindset that the Devil is a quaint anomaly, a silly superstition. It is curious, then, that beginning in the 1950s, Satan and the terror of satanism made something of a reappearance. Reasons for this are for other chapters of this book to address.

NOTE

1. A number of good sources exist for detailed information on the historical satan or devil, terms which will be used interchangeably herein. See Forsyth (1987), Kelly (1974), and Russell (1977,1981,1984,1986, and 1988) for more information.

REFERENCES

Forsyth, Neil. 1987. *The Old Enemy: Satan and the Combat Myth.* Princeton: Princeton University Press.

Kelly, Henry Ansgar. 1974. *The Devil, Demonology, and Witchcraft,* 2nd ed. New York: Doubleday.

Russell, Jeffrey B. 1977. *The Devil: Perceptions of Evil from Antiquity to Primitive Christianity.* Ithaca: Cornell University Press.

———. 1981. *Satan: The Early Christian Tradition.* Ithaca: Cornell University Press.

———. 1984. *Lucifer: The Devil in the Middle Ages.* Ithaca: Cornell University Press.

———. 1986. *Mephistopheles: The Devil in the Modern World.* Ithaca: Cornell University Press.

———. 1988. *The Prince of Darkness: Radical Evil and the Power of Good in History.* Ithaca: Cornell University Press.

Satanism: The New Cult Scare 4

David G. Bromley

The satanism scare has been to the 1980s and early 1990s what the religious cult scare was to the 1970s (Bromley and Shupe 1981). In the 1970s, a diverse cohort of alternative religious movements that represented a continuation of the 1960s counterculture attracted young adults. These new religious movements were opposed by the Anticult Movement (ACM), a coalition of family-based groups supported by a small subgroup of religious leaders (primarily from conservative wings of their respective traditions), mental health professionals and social scientists, and local law enforcement officers and political officials (Shupe and Bromley 1980). During the 1980s, even more diverse groups and activities came to be viewed as manifestations of satanism. As in the case of the religious cult scare, an Antisatanism Movement (ASM) formed to meet the threat posed by satanic cults. The coalition comprising the ASM resembled the ACM; it was led by family-based groups and conservative religious interests with strong support from some mental health professionals and local law enforcement officers. The trajectories of the two scares crossed in the early 1980s; about the time the religious cult scare began to recede, public concern about satanic cults began to escalate.

What is referred to as satanism in the mass media and by the ASM involves a number of distinct elements: local incidents (e.g., church and grave desecrations, animal mutilations, and community or regional rumors of impending abductions and ritual sacrifice of children); claims that heavy metal rock music (or fantasy games) containing occult themes or satanic messages caused homicides and suicides; confessions by convicted murderers attributing their crimes to involvement in satanism; and accounts by "ritual abuse survivors" who claimed to have participated in satanic rituals involving human sacrifice and even cannibalism. The ASM links these phenomena through an assertion that a nationally organized, underground, hierarchically structured cult is the ultimate source of these forms of deviance. This allegation is explosive, both because the underground cult network purportedly has sponsored and organized other forms of satanic activity, and because of the diabolical, antisocial nature of cultic rituals.

49

Subversion fears have recurred through American history; countersubversion ideologies have targeted witches, Indians, Catholics, Mormons, the mafia, communists, and religious cultists (Bromley 1987). In each case, fears emerged during a period of significant social conflict. This chapter argues that the current satanism scare is similarly rooted in an institutional crisis. Structural incompatibility between family and economy confronts individuals with contradictory behavioral imperatives. The tensions individuals experience as a product of this institutional crisis are explained in terms of satanists by the ASM, which depicts satanists, not as ordinary deviants, but as subversives who embody ultimate evil. The ASM's countersubversion ideology delineates the origin, nature, operation, and impact of the satanic cult network. As the ideology has gained credence, anxiety has intensified; mounting tension has launched a countersubversion campaign relatively unaffected by lack of evidence of subversives' existence. This chapter begins by defining the basic characteristics of countersubversion ideology, then applies those characteristics to the satanic cult case. A second section documents the scare's considerable social impact, despite the absence of validating evidence. The final section analyzes how incompatibility between family and economy makes the countersubversion ideology culturally plausible.

COUNTERSUBVERSION IDEOLOGY

Swidler (1986:279) defines ideology as "a highly articulated, self-conscious belief and ritual system, aspiring to offer a unified answer to problems of social action." All ideologies manifest general similarities; they identify and describe troubling conditions in the contemporary social environment, placing these problems in a temporal context such that they can be viewed as products of historical forces that have logical consequences not previously recognized.

A central element of ideology, identifying and defining a social problem, involves claimsmaking. The source of the problem is directly or indirectly attributed to people designated as morally inferior by virtue of their inability or unwillingness to avoid or remedy the problematic condition. The construction of moral imbalance through some combination of elevation and degradation of respective moral statuses justifies social control measures based on these moral claims (Katz 1975; Garfinkel 1956). The more central the conduct deemed unacceptable, the stronger the impetus to exert social control and the greater likelihood of *extreme* moral degradation of the target individual's or group's status. The social construction of extreme degradation moves the target individual or group to a symbolically distant, alien position, which in turn mandates repression. Ideologies also elevate concern about problems they identify through assertions that the targeted problem is novel or neglected, large and growing, and dangerous if immediate remedial action is not undertaken.

Countersubversion movement ideologies are distinctive in the extreme degree of moral imbalance constructed, and hence the degree of social control that is warranted. They depict subversives as embodying ultimate evil. This construction involves three symbolic dimensions: physical/objective, moral/normative, and cathectic/subjective (Geertz 1966; Habermas 1984). On the physical/objective dimension, subversives are cast as aliens, residents of a separate domain, proximate to and interconnected with the endangered social domain, such that subversives periodically can penetrate the endangered society's terrain. The conspiracy's history transcends not merely biographies of the living, but the history of the society or civilization itself.

On the moral/normative dimension, subversives are attributed a qualitatively different, inferior moral essence. They are quintessentially evil. This evil is symbolized through representations of subversive beliefs and practices as inversions of the sacred in the endangered society's moral order and/or by attributing the subversives' evil acts to their essentially evil character and purpose.

On the cathectic/subjective dimension, subversives are attributed the capability of reconfiguring and redirecting the basis for adaptation, loyalty, and mutual expectations in the social order to evil purpose. Subversives are corrupting. This capacity for undermining individuals is depicted as *irresistible* (all individuals are vulnerable and any contact or involvement is subverting), *irreversible* (once individuals become ensnared they are unable to break subversive control and extricate themselves, even if involvement results in self-destruction), and *inexorable* (vulnerability to subversive control is progressive and capacity for resistance continuously declines). The danger posed by subversive power is increased by its captivating quality: individuals find themselves alternatively paralyzed, fascinated, or even attracted to it.

Countersubversion ideologies assert a maximum degree of threat. Subversives are depicted as having infiltrated once secure terrain. Initially undetected, they have become a large, rapidly growing, highly organized and entrenched presence, possessing the capacity for corrupting or destroying ordinary, unsuspecting individuals. They are ruthless and unscrupulous in their tactics; some major institution or even the entire social order is depicted as in imminent danger of falling prey to domination.

SATANIC COUNTERSUBVERSION IDEOLOGY

Like other countersubversion ideologies, antisatanist ideology can be viewed as a narrative that describes in detail the shape of subversion: (1) its origins, (2) the size of the subversive network, (3) its organizational structure and growth, (4) the pattern of nefarious activities, (5) the motives for those activities, (6) the mechanism through which innocent individuals are ensnared, (7) how subversives manage to elude or neutralize social control agents, and (8) the catastrophic consequences of permitting subversive activities to continue unopposed.

Origins and Locations

According to the ASM, contemporary satanism is the latest episode in a long, recurrent pattern of intrusion by evil forces that have taken diverse forms in different historical eras (Hill and Goodwin 1989). Although the timing and form of this latest episode could not be predicted, it was inevitable. Some antisatanists, such as cult specialist Kurt Jackson, assert that such episodes occur on a 28-year cycle, with 1982 being a peak year in the cycle (*Geraldo*, "Satanic Cults and Children," Nov. 19, 1987).

Because satanic cults operate underground, their destructive activities do not become apparent until considerable damage already has been done. The increasing number of abuse victims being recorded is taken as proof of an established, active satanic network. Descriptions emphasize satanism's underground, secret, hidden nature, its appearance in contested terrain such as cemeteries, isolated wooded sites, and underworld criminal rings, and the chameleon-like disguises that allow satanists to "pass" and infiltrate legitimate and presumably secure locations like childcare facilities.

> I found a hidden society, much larger and more disquieting than the world of Satanism alone, a place few people know exists . . . It is the underworld of "occult crime" . . . The crimes are frightening: a homicide where the decapitated victim is surrounded by colored beads, seven coins and chicken feathers; ritual sacrifices at wooded sites where black-robed cultists mutilate animals on altars; other homicides where the corpses are found drained of blood with symbols such as a pentagram or inverted cross carved into their chests; drug and pornography rings with nationwide connections to occult groups; carefully executed grave robbing; Satanic rituals and human sacrifices involving children—fantastic stories told by hundreds of children in scores of preschools throughout the United States, all of them relating similar horrors. (Kahaner, 1988:vii)

Dimensions of the Problem

Estimates by the ASM of the number of satanists vary considerably because the core organization and its members have been elusive, but even the most conservative assessments would evoke public alarm. Since satanists exist largely undetected in underground organizations, their numbers often are inferred from the number of victims. For example, the number of children reportedly victimized in community daycare abuse cases would suggest a menace of staggering proportions, if generalized to the nation as a whole. One McMartin Preschool parent asserted that 1200 children had been molested in the city of Manhattan Beach alone:

> that's a third of the school system in the city of Manhattan Beach that's been molested. We have eight preschools closed here. This is the child molestation capital of the world. (*Geraldo*, "Devil Worship: Exposing Satan's Underground," October 25, 1988)

The extraordinary accusations of ritual abuse and sacrifice have evoked considerable skepticism. However, ideology proponents contend that the sudden surge of ritual abuse reports is evidence of the seriousness of this recently discovered problem, not a reason for mistrusting the reports:

> Skeptics of the devil-cult scenario should acknowledge the sheer number of child-victim allegations (over 800 in Los Angeles County alone) and the fact that from the beginning of the investigations the children have been talking to therapists about sexual games with adults wearing robes and talking in funny languages. (*Penthouse*, "The Devil Made Me Do It," January, 1986, p. 48)

Victims requesting therapists' services are another source of estimates. A therapist working with ritual abuse victims has counted 250 therapists currently working on satanic ritual abuse cases (*Insight Magazine*, "Battling Satanism a Haunting task," 11 January 1988, p. 49). These therapists claim to be overwhelmed with clients. Other projections have been derived from national data on missing children. Some ideology proponents insist that most of these children are satanic ritual victims, which has yielded widely publicized estimates of 50,000–60,000 ritual sacrifice victims annually. Over time, the dimensions of this problem could only expand as abuse victims become adult abusers. All of these inferences lead to dire predictions about the scope and impact of satanic cult activity. In congressional testimony on ritual child abuse, Kee MacFarlane, who interviewed children at the McMartin Preschool, said:

> I believe we're dealing with an organized operation of child predators designed to prevent detection. The preschool, in such a case, serves as a ruse for a larger, unthinkable network of crimes against children. If such an operation involves child pornography or selling of children, as is frequently alleged, it may have greater financial, legal and community resources at its disposal than those attempting to expose it. (*New York Times*, 18 September 1984)

Satanist Organization

According to the countersubversion ideology, satanists are members of a complex network with different levels of involvement, age-graded participation, and a division of labor. Workshops for police and social workers frequently identify four levels of satanic activity (Hicks 1990:283). At the lower level are *dabblers,* young people who experiment with satanic materials such as heavy metal rock music and fantasy games like "Dungeons & Dragons." The second level is *self-styled satanists,* criminals who create or borrow satanic themes as a rationale for their antisocial acts. Some of these individuals also have been linked to underground cult activity. For example, Terry (1987) argues that the Son of Sam killer did not act alone, but was a member of a satanic cult. And the Manson Family's Susan Atkins was once a member of the Temple of Set. A third level involves *organized satanists,* members of public, satanic churches such as the Church of Satan and Temple of Set. These public groups may be connected to other types of satanic activity. Thus, ideology proponents note that Michael Aquino, high priest of the Temple of Set, was once charged with ritual child abuse. At the highest level are the *traditional satanists,* individuals organized into a secret cult network engaged in child abuse and sacrifice. Satanists' careers frequently begin at lower levels and progress to involvement at higher levels.

Another organizational dimension is age, at least for ritual abuse victims. According to the ASM, initial victimization usually occurs when children are between 4 and 6 years old. They then return to their biological parents with the memories of abuse buried deep in their unconscious, as a result of the terror and brainwashing that they experienced during their indoctrination. In early adolescence, females are impregnated by cult members and used to breed babies for future ritual sacrifices. Older teens are once again separated from the cult and become walking "time bombs" in conventional society. In their late twenties, these individuals are reintroduced to cult activity, this time as abusers and molesters of others. Finally, in their mid-50s, individuals join the cult in an "upper echelon status" (Massachusetts State Police, *Roll Call Newsletter,* January, 1989, p. 4). Individuals also perform different roles within the cult, primarily related to child abuse and sacrifice, such as "spotters," "transporters," physicians who perform abortions to obtain "near term babies," and morticians who provide cremation services (see Best, Chapter 6, this volume). This complex organization serves to recruit additional cult members and infiltrate and exploit legitimate social institutions.

Satanic Rituals

Surprisingly little detail about satanic rituals is available; no outsiders have reported witnessing one, and ritual abuse survivors have been able to reconstruct only fragmentary accounts. For example, two therapists report the following account of a woman in her mid-twenties:

Candles in a circle-someone cutting the bottoms with a huge butcher knife. I'm on a table. My arms are up. I think I'm tied down. It smells. It's dark. The walls move. He's there in front of me. Got something shiny on. It smells. He's doing something. Can't see. Can't move. See his face, its ugly. Satan. Shiny cape or something. Puts my legs up. Putting something in me. Cold. Don't know what it is. He's talking slow like a record in slow speed. Don't know what he's saying. I sink to the floor. I'm under the floor. Can't see me. I sing to myself. . . . He's got a candle. I can't see what else he's got. It's going in me, it hurts. I feel sick, don't move . . . Now he's on me. He twisted me around, stay still. It hurts and he's breathing. The table's hard. Twisted me again on my back. My legs are up and it hurts and I feel sick and I can't breathe and I can't move. I want to get down. There's candles. He's still on me, in me. I go away with the flickering candles. I don't know where I am. In a room with candles and a table. (Hill and Goodwin 1989:42)

According to sympathetic therapists, some survivors were abused at such a young age as to prevent meaningful recollection, and adults who have attempted to reconstruct childhood abuse confront recall problems created by the effects of satanists' brainwashing and terror tactics. Survivors report a variety of macabre events that were components of satanic rituals in which they were involved, including being fondled, raped, and sodomized, used as subjects in pornographic photography sessions and sexual games, being urinated on and smeared with fecal matter, and being placed into caskets and lowered into graves. In a number of cases, these events allegedly took place in preschools or at other, sometimes distant locations to which children were taken in their teacher's custody.

Still, ideology proponents describe rituals involving child abuse, animal and human sacrifice, and procurement of new cult members. One ritual abuse survivor described a satanic ritual involving abduction, illicit drug use, and animal and human sacrifice in which the main focus was rape of an abducted female victim (Menendez 1986:6–7). In another, the central activity was human sacrifice:

The sacrifice is performed with a circle on the surface of the sacrificial area. The circle serves as a containment field for the energy released from the victim. It is believed that there is a great amount of energy unleashed when the victim is killed and those who conduct the sacrifice must guard against being overwhelmed by the force. The slaughter is preceded by silent concentration, incantations, and burning of incense. A gradual build-up of exitement [sic] culminates in a frenzy at the time of death and the discharge of blood from the victim. An even greater frenzy is reached if there is a simultaneous release of sexual energy through orgasm. (Massachusetts State Police, Roll Call Newsletter, January, 1989, p. 3)

Other rituals supposedly use abuse and brainwashing to disrupt victim's bonds to families and build ties with satanist groups that can be exploited later in their lives.

Procuring Victims

Contentions that satanists sexually abuse and murder tens of thousands of children per year raise questions about how the cult obtains and exercises absolute control over these children. Satanists allegedly abduct missing and "throwaway" children, purchase children on the black market, and operate childcare centers, orphanages, and foster homes in order to exploit children placed in their care (see *Style Weekly*, "Satan's Victim: One Woman's Ordeal," 19 January, 1988). Preschool children are controlled by being terrorized, implicated in criminal acts, and threatened with loss of parental love. For example, relatively young children are used as subjects for "kiddie porn," then threatened that the films will be released if they reveal the activities; adolescents have been lured into drug and sex parties and then similarly blackmailed. Therapist Catherine Gould contends the pornography serves both economic and intimidation objectives (*Geraldo*, "Satanic Cults and Children," November 19, 1987). In addition, adolescent females who have fallen into satanists' hands supposedly become "breeders." Kept as virtual slaves, they are terrorized, brainwashed, and repeatedly impregnated, with their babies taken at birth for use in ritual sacrifices.

Sources of Motivation

The basic motivation attributed to satanists is a quest for power. While they seek political power, satanists' most important objective is personal power. Satanists are thought to believe that life energy stored in the blood and body is released at the moment of death. In this instant, the energy can be appropriated by those participating in or witnessing a sacrifice. During child sacrifice, then, satanists literally absorb the life energy of their young victims (Kahaner 1988:140–141). The cannibalism of vital organs such as the heart appears to serve much the same function.

Avoidance of Detection

The frequency and enormity of the offenses attributed to satanists raise questions about how such activities go undetected. Several explanations have been advanced. First, children have indeed divulged the satanists' activities to adults, but the stories have been so fantastic that they were dismissed as child fantasy. Second, children have been intimidated and terrorized so that they cannot reveal their victimization. Children have been terrorized through threats against themselves or those they love. They have been forced to witness mutilation or murder of animals or even humans as a warning against exposing the satanists. In some cases, they are taken to satanist therapists who further undermine the children's belief that confiding in adults will have any effect. This apparently explains why older victims recall childhood abuse only after prolonged therapy has helped them break through both defenses they have built up and blocks implanted during brainwashing.

Third, some high ranking police officials are thought by the ASM to be satanists who use their positions to deflect investigations or warn perpetrators. Satanists also take advantage of constitutionally protected religious liberties to thwart police inquiries. Even if law enforcement officials could gain access to satanic cults, undercover agents infiltrating these groups would be forced to witness and engage in satanic rituals: "There's a real problem in terms of investigating these things. You can't get into it without being part of it. And you can't be part of it without doing things that are unspeakable" (*Chicago Tribune*, "Satanism Haunts Tales of Child Sex Abuse," 29 July 1985).

Finally, mental health professionals who assist ritual abuse victims and, in the process, accumulate evidence about satanists' identities and operations are warned about the consequences of revealing what they discover. Therapists report satanists' efforts to reprogram their clients, break-ins to mental health facilities and therapists' automobiles, surveillance of clients and therapists, tapped phones, and even physical threats. One therapist working with ritually abused children stated:

> It's something I don't want to be identified as knowing that much about. I think anybody who woks in this area ought to carry a badge and wear a gun. And not have a family. (*Chicago Tribune*, "Satanism Haunts Tales of Child Sex Abuse," 29 July 1985)

A therapist in the Seattle area reported receiving a warning through his client in which the "client who was believed to be 'cult-involved' brought a human penis to the therapist, saying it had been mailed to the client" (*Seattle Times*, "Searching for Evidence," 20 February 1989, pp. A12–A13).

Satanists as Subversives

The countersubversion ideology depicts satanists as subversives par excellence. They are an alien force occupying such contested terrain (i.e., outside the perimeter of full social control) as basements, abandoned buildings, cemeteries, wooded areas, underground bunkers and tunnels, or secret locations to which victims are transported for rituals. The current outbreak of satanic activity is the latest in a long series of intrusions, during which satanists have penetrated otherwise safe terrain and operated outside societal surveillance. These incursions are all the more dangerous because satanists are able alternatively to remain hidden, "pass" as normal, or operate through individuals who have been compromised.

Morally, satanists embody quintessential evil. Satanists are not simply child molesters or pedophiles. Such child abusers are defined as sick and usually social isolates. Satanists, by contrast, organize specifically to engage in abusive, destructive practices and even sacralize them through ritual. The existence of rituals is critical to the countersubversion ideology. Rituals demonstrate a high degree of organization, patterned and repetitive activity, and endowment of antisocial, diabolical activity with an aura of the sacred. Individuals are labeled molesters because they engage in abusive acts; but satanists engage in abusive acts because they are satanists.

That satanism is essentially evil is conveyed symbolically in the inversions that fill descriptions of satanic rituals. Rather than preserving and protecting burial sites, satanists desecrate and loot them. Rather than expelling urine, satanists drink urine. Rather than giving blood to others to strengthen or save lives, satanists drink others' blood to enhance their own strength at the expense of others' lives. Even more graphically, descriptions of ritualistic cannibalism assume the form of an inverted eucharist, as consumption of human organs is transformed into enhanced personal power. Rather than marriage being a voluntary bond consummated through sexual union, satanic rituals parody and mock this ritual with abducted victims being first drugged and then incapacitated during a marriage ceremony consummated through rape. Rather than murder committed as a product of inflamed passion, satanists commit murder as a means of igniting their passions. Rather than nourishing, nurturing, and fostering the unique selfhood of children, satanists consume, exploit, terrorize, brainwash, and destroy children. Indeed, they seek to absorb the unique life energy of sacrificial victims to enhance their own life energy, thereby making evil collectively strongly and good collectively weaker. Satanists also deliberately promote such deviant activities as violence and murder, child abuse, sexual abuse, drug use, pornography, and teen suicide.

Seeking to ensnare innocent individuals, satanists employ lures such as drugs, sex, rock music, and fantasy games, or they rely on brainwashing and terror tactics. Although all individuals are susceptible to the coercive techniques, satanists have begun their subversion campaign with the most accessible, vulnerable members of the population. Once enmeshed in a satanic network, individuals find escape virtually impossible, as they face physical captivity, continued brainwashing, threats against their lives or lives of loved ones, and complicity in heinous crimes. The relatively few survivors who provide evidence of the satanic cults' activity are eloquent testimony to its ruthlessness and effectiveness. Individuals caught up in satanic networks become agents themselves, infiltrating childcare facilities or recruiting future victims, sometimes even members of their own families. Lower levels of involvement, such as dabbling with rock music or fantasy games, inevitably lead to more serious involvement from which escape becomes ever less likely.

IMPACT OF THE COUNTERSUBVERSION IDEOLOGY

Linking satanists to diverse forms of deviance kept satanism in the forefront of public attention through the 1980s and created an amplification process in which allegations of satanic activity fed on one another. Allegations do not necessarily translate into credibility, but the satanism scare sometimes approached panic levels. The impact of the countersubversion ideology is demonstrated by the response of the general public, media, law enforcement agencies, mental health professionals, and government officials.

Responses to the Scare

Public Reaction. There is considerable public concern about satanism. Local rumor panics across the nation have deluged officials with reported sightings of black-robed, hooded figures in wooded areas; discoveries of ritual sites, artifacts, and sacrificial remains in out of the way locations; and rumors of impending child abductions and sacrifices. These various reports and rumors sometimes achieve surprising credibility, and defensive measures are common. For example, following the discovery of the Matamoros murders, cross-border traffic dropped 80 percent in the El Paso area *(El Paso Times,* "Kidnap Scare Sweeps Matamoros," 20 April 1989). Rumors of satanist plots to abduct children have led many parents to temporarily withdraw their children from school. Further, the failure of official investigations to substantiate rumors has met considerable public skepticism. In Jordan, Minnesota, even after charges of ritual abuse and murder were dropped against two dozen adults, 80 percent of community residents continued to believe the children's stories, which were the primary evidence in the case *(Penthouse,* "The Devil Made Me Do It," January, 1986).

Governmental, Criminal Justice, and Mental Health Responses. Law enforcement officials have dragged rivers and excavated fields in search of ritual murder victims, launched investigations of daycare centers, and reviewed unsolved crime files for previously overlooked evidence of a satanic connection. Between 1983 and 1988, ritual child abuse investigations were initiated in more than 100 communities across the country (Charlier and

Downing 1988). Social workers, child welfare workers, and therapists have begun searching for and reporting evidence of ritual satanic abuse. Police and therapists have established networks to exchange information through newsletters, professional conferences, and training workshops. Special investigatory techniques for searching crime sites and interviewing potential victims are being developed, and treatment programs have been instituted. Legislators have begun proposing bills to facilitate prosecution of ritual crimes. Senator Jesse Helms proposed a bill revoking tax exemptions for any religion that "has as a purpose, or that has any interest in, the practice of Satanism or 'witchcraft' Provided . . . 'Satanism' is defined as the worship of Satan or the powers of evil and 'witchcraft' is defined as the use of powers derived from evil spirits, the use of sorcery, or the use of supernatural powers with malicious intent" (Congressional Record—Senate, September 26, 1985, S12171). Legislation recently has been introduced or passed in Idaho, Illinois, Louisiana, Pennsylvania, and Washington, and legislative task forces have been established in California and Virginia (State of California, 1989–1990; State of Idaho, 1990; New Orleans Times-Picayune, "Bill Would Outlaw Blasphemy," 2 May 1989; The New Federalist, "Pennsylvania Legislature to Get Anti-Satanism Bill," 3 March 1989; Seattle Times, "Tough Penalties Being Proposed for Satanic Rituals," 28 February 1989). For example, Illinois revised the criminal code to include a definition of ritual mutilation: "A person commits the offense of ritual mutilation when he mutilates, dismembers or tortures another person as part of a ceremony, rite, initiation, observance, performance or practice, and the victim did not consent or under such circumstances the defendant knew or should have known that the victim was unable to render effective consent." Investigations and prosecutions of child abuse cases involving allegations of satanic or ritual abuse have consumed enormous public resources, and penalties have sometimes been draconian. For example, seven Bakersfield, California defendants received a total of 2619 years in prison (an appeals court reversed the convictions). The now legendary McMartin Preschool case, which produced no convictions, was one of the longest, costliest trials in American history.

   The Mass Media.   Local panics, criminal investigations, conferences and workshops on satanism, and testimonials from ritual abuse survivors all have received extensive media coverage. With some significant exceptions (e.g., Charlier and Downing 1988) media coverage has been uncritical and sensationalized. Journalists often reported fantastic, implausible claims that would provoke immediate skepticism under most other circumstances. Even where satanic cult allegations ultimately are dropped, initial reports featuring satanism in cases such as Matamoros and McMartin received much greater fanfare than subsequent disclaimers. Further, in the intense competition for audiences, national talk shows such as Geraldo, Oprah, and Sally Jesse Raphael have featured numerous unsubstantiated or fabricated allegations. Media coverage has amplified reports of satanic activity and social control responses, fostering further concern.

Unsubstantiated Claims

The countersubversion campaign's influence is remarkable, given the lack of hard evidence to support its claims. It is precisely this combination of heightened anxiety, expanded control activity, and lack of corroborating evidence that characterizes a scare. In this instance, virtually all of the evidence offered in support of the countersubversion ideology is seriously flawed; it is convincing only if one begins by assuming that a subversive group exists.

Local Outbreaks. Church and grave desecrations and animal mutilations have a long history in America but only recently have been regarded as evidence of satanic cult activity, as the work of satanic "dabblers," or even a harbinger of abductions and sacrifices. However, there is no evidence of an increase in the number of these events, particularly when inevitable reporting increases are taken into account. Virtually all investigations have led to the conclusion that unexplained animal deaths are the product of roadkills, trapping, disease, or poisoning. The "surgically precise" wounds observed on "mutilated" animal carcasses are almost exclusively the work of predators and scavengers (e.g., Cade 1977).

A Perfect Conspiracy. The diabolical cleverness attributed to satanists runs afoul of other contentions by ideology proponents. On the one hand, satanists allegedly have a tightly organized, powerful, infallible network that leaves no evidence of its large-scale abduction, breeding, and human sacrifice activity. On the other hand, these groups supposedly leave behind an easily discovered trail of clues such as animal carcasses and open graves that invite official investigation. Although satanists are very powerful, they allow ritual abuse survivors to recount their stories publicly, and use easily discovered intimidation techniques such as tapping phones, breaking and entering, mailing warning messages, and planting explosive devices. Finally, satanists maintain perfect discipline and secrecy despite the fact that their network consists of teenage dabblers, sociopathic criminals, public satanists, and prominent, powerful individuals who secretly occupy positions of cult leadership. Not a single defector has managed to leave with any type of organizational records. This absence of defectors who could furnish hard evidence is striking since radical groups historically have been particularly prone to schism, defection, and internecine conflicts.

A large, diverse, powerful, active satanic network would have to be very complex indeed. However, there is no substantial evidence of a common belief system, a set of rituals, or an organizational apparatus. Despite the descriptions of elaborate rituals, no written sources have been discovered that would trace their historical evolution or spell out the substance and process of secret ceremonies. Despite the alleged existence of an elaborate organizational network, no organizational apparatus—correspondence, membership lists, phone logs, travel records, bank accounts, buildings or meeting places, ritual implements, crematoriums, pornographic filming equipment or films produced—have ever been discovered.

Misleading Statistics.   Assertions that there are tens of thousands of ritual sacrifice victims each year simply are not credible. In particular, the notion of a decades-old satanic cult network in widespread child sacrifice strains credulity. Many of the individuals claiming to be ritual abuse survivors are in their forties. If they were abused as young children, then satanic cults were active during the 1950s. Moreover, since this abuse involved adults who must have joined the cult through some prior recruiting process, the cult network must have existed well before the 1950s. Assuming a network of roughly constant size and activity, satanic cult victims would number in the millions. Even if satanists sacrificed only 10,000 children per year, the period covered by current survivors' claims would have produced 400,000 victims, a total rivaling of 517,347 war–related deaths from World War II, Korea, and Vietnam combined. Yet, not a single casualty of the satanic cult network has been discovered.[1] The FBI's Kenneth Lanning concludes:

> a satanic murder can be defined as one committed by two or more individuals who rationally plan the crime and whose primary motivation is to fulfill a prescribed satanic ritual calling for the murder. By this definition, the author has been unable to identify even one documented murder in the United States. Although such murders may have and can occur, they appear to be few in number. In addition, the commission of such killing would probably be the beginning of the end for such a group. It is highly unlikely that they could continue to kill several people, every year, year after year, and not be discovered. (1989:82)

The claim that satanists obtain victims by abducting children is equally unconvincing. The best estimate places the number of children abducted by strangers annually between 200 and 300 (Finkelhor et al. 1990). Even if all of the stranger abductions were by satanists, they would not begin to meet the demand for sacrifice victims. Estimates of ritual abuse of children in daycare facilities appear similarly inflated.

Ritual Abuse and Survivor Accounts.   Since the early 1980s, claims of satanic sexual abuse of children have mounted (e.g., Kelly 1988). Some adults, primarily women, report having been victimized as children; in other cases, children of various ages claim recent victimization. In most instances, there is no conclusive physical evidence. Although some early cases relied on medical data thought to constitute strong evidence of abuse, recent research indicates that naturally occurring anatomical variations make it difficult to identify cases of sexual abuse (Coleman 1989; Nathan 1989). As a result, most cases hinge on the testimony of "ritual abuse survivors."

There are a number of serious problems with survivors' accounts. First, satanic material has been introduced by therapists, rather than raised by clients. In one series of ritual abuse allegations in Utah, each case surfaced shortly after the same therapist arrived in the community (Shupe 1987). Leading questioning by therapists created sufficient doubt in the minds of the McMartin juries to produce acquittals.

Second, therapists make little effort to corroborate survivors' accounts. Therapists view verification as a secondary concern, both because they lack the capacity to conduct independent investigations and because their primary concern is with treating their clients. When efforts at corroboration have been made, they have been consistently unsuccessful. The most dramatic recent example involved self-identified abuse survivor Lauren Stratford (1988), author of the autobiographical *Satan's Underground*. When journalists began checking her story, they discovered, for example: Stratford's friends, neighbors, and relatives did not confirm her claimed pregnancies; several individuals asserted that they observed her engage in self-mutilation which she later asserted was the work of satanists; and Stratford had accused a wide range of individuals of sexual abuse over a 30-year period prior to her 1985 satanic abuse claims (Passantino et al. 1989). In 1990, Harvest House Publishers withdrew her book from the market (American Library Association 1990).

A lack of evidence characterizes other cases as well. In the McMartin and Jordan, Minnesota cases, pornographic filming of children was alleged, but no films were uncovered. Some claims appear to have been intentionally fraudulent. Missouri law enforcement officials investigated two incidents of satanic sacrifices reported in a Geraldo series on satanism and concluded that both were fabricated (*Religious Freedom Alert*, "Missouri Police Waste Time, Money On False Rumor of Satanic Activity," May, 1989). In still other instances, investigations of leads provided by abuse survivors have yielded no hard evidence. In Toledo, Ohio in 1985 and El Paso, Texas in 1986, police excavated locations where survivors claimed sacrifice victims were buried, but they found no bodies (Lyons 1988:143–145).

An Irrefutable Argument.   The argument for an organized network of satanists is virtually irrefutable. Ritual abuse survivors' reports contain many fantastic elements. Rather than regard the implausible features of these accounts as grounds for skepticism, however, proponents of the satanic conspiracy theory insist that it is precisely these elements that mean the stories must be true. No one, they insist, would or could make up such bizarre, macabre stories. Sometimes proponents retreat to the position that satanists commit bizarre activities precisely so that victims will not be believed when they recount their experiences. This latter tack illustrates the problem of infinite regress.[2] When confronted with the difficulty of concealing so many homicides, proponents explain that satanists dispose of bodies in ways that make them difficult or impossible to find, such as in double-decker graves. Challenges to this argument lead to assertions that bodies are burned. The observation that bodies cannot be burned in ordinary fires leads to the assertion that they are cremated. The problems of gaining access to crematoriums lead to contentions that satanists use special portable crematoriums. Further protestation may yield the argument that child-witnesses may be mistaken about some deaths because satanists sometimes use life-like dolls rather than live humans to terrorize children into silence. The continual retreat from the lack of confirming evidence shifts the burden of proof from those seeking to demonstrate a satanist network to those questioning such assertions.

THE DEMONIZATION OF DAYCARE

A number of observers have dismissed the extreme claims in the counter-subversion ideology as "absurd" (Forsyth and Oliver 1990:287) or a "straw-man view" (Langone 1990:56), which divert attention from more substantial public issues. From one perspective, dismissal makes sense since the allegations are both extreme and unsubstantiated. However, extraordinary claims make satanism intriguing sociologically. An extreme form of deviance has been constructed, with little evidence of its existence. Despite a lack of confirmation, the claims have achieved considerable credibility and, faced with disconfirming evidence, proponents have banded together even more tightly to reaffirm the ideology. One important sociological issue, therefore is identifying the structural conditions that make satanic subversion claims culturally plausible.

Both the religious cult scare of the 1970s and the satanic cult scare of the 1980s occurred in the context of heightened tensions between covenantally structured forms of organization (familial, religious) and contractually structured forms (economic, state-administrative/bureaucratic) (Bromley and Busching 1988). The covenantally organized family and contractually organized economy are interdependent. The family is the locus for socialization through which basic individual character is shaped, and has served as the basis for forging and preserving a societal moral consensus. The economy, in turn, constitutes the legitimate opportunity system though which adults generate economic resources to support independent nuclear families. The two spheres coexist in varying states of tension with one another as a result of qualitative difference in their premises and structures for social action and individual character.

> The objective of interaction in contractual social relations, where pledges are to specific activity (e.g., purchase, employment), is mutual agreement on terms of exchange (e.g., price, wage). In covenantal social relations, where pledges are to one another's well being (personal happiness, spiritual enlightenment), the objective is mutual commitment to one another (e.g., mutual caring, nurturance, love). The process through which individuals express their intentions in contractual social relations is negotiation (e.g., bargaining, bidding) while the corresponding process in covenantal social relations is bonding (uniting, fostering community, worship). (Bromley and Busching 1988:18)

Contractualism and covenantalism also value and foster different individual attributes. For example, contractual individuals ideally are relationally reliable, astute, and fair while covenantal individuals are loyal, sensitive, and caring.

Changing Family Forms and Childcare

There has been a notable expansion of contractualism through the conversion of traditional family functions into contractually provided products and services. These products and services have empowered families by giving family members greater opportunity to generate financial resources through labor force participation, but greater career involvement has also increased dependence on externally supplied products and services. The result has been a self-reinforcing process of expansion of the contractual sphere and contraction of the covenantal sphere.

During the affluent 1950s and 1960s, middle-class families mediated conflicting family-economy demands through a division of labor in which males assumed primary responsibility for contractual sphere activities and females for the covenantal sphere. Alternatively, economic responsibility was shared in a two-person career in which "women channeled their talents and energies into an auxiliary role relative to their husbands' careers, rather than pursuing their own mobility" (Hunt and Hunt 1986:276). This contractual–covenantal role partitioning matched traditional bases of individual identity, with male career pursuits symbolized as "breadwinning" on behalf of the family and women's domestic activities symbolized as "home-making." Family values were celebrated and female domesticity idealized.

Over the last two decades, this once culturally celebrated family form has progressively given way to families organized around dual careers, which are more compatible with expanding contractualism in at least three ways. First, a high level of individual consumption has become increasingly critical as a means of fueling economic expansion; for individuals, personal freedom has come to be defined in terms of maximizing life-style choice through consumption patterns. Given the wage stagnation and growing income inequality that began in the 1970s, dual incomes increasingly became a sine qua non for the middle classes in living out the American dream. Second, declining family size, serial marriage, and reduced social viability and cultural legitimacy accorded to domesticity have increased the attractiveness and impetus for female careers. Third, the dual career family offers an avenue for self-fulfillment through both individual career development and mutual commitments to one another's self-actualization as a basis for marriage. Children constitute another important, but now culturally optional, vehicle for achieving mutual personal fulfillment through "parenting."

This recent change in family form is reflected in the increasing proportion of women in the labor force and an even more rapid increase in women with children in the labor force. According to the U.S. Bureau of Labor Statistics, the percentage of women in the labor force increased from 39 percent in 1970 to 49 percent in 1978 and to 56 percent by 1988. Between 1978 and 1988, the percentage of working women with children increased from 53 to 65 percent and the proportion of working women with children under 6 years of age from 44 to 56 percent. There has been a nearly fivefold increase in working women with young children since 1950, when only 12 percent of these women worked. This shift of women from home to workplace has created the growing demand for childcare. Indeed, half of the young children in the United States currently are cared for by persons other than their parents. Although some parents rely on family networks for such services, contractual daycare services have proliferated.

Parents express serious qualms about entrusting their young children to strangers, however. Public opinion surveys indicate that a solid majority of men and women in the age groups most likely to need daycare services regard them as a change for the worse from their parent's generation, and an even larger majority of women state that they would prefer to stay at home with young children if it were economically feasible. Further, a third of the women interviewed in one survey asserted they would be afraid to leave their children in a daycare facility (*Christian Science Monitor,* "The Politics of Child-Care Polls," 8 August, 1988). Such fears are hardly unjustified; parents often find these services expensive, difficult to obtain, and of poor quality, conditions that have been recounted as horror stories in the popular media (Wallis 1987; Orth 1975).

Loss of Family Control

As an attempt to "have it all" in cultural terms, the dual career family creates a demanding, complex life-style:

> The dual-career family means the addition of a high-demand work role to the couple's commitments and creates the problem of career coordination between spouses. No matter how housekeeping and childcare are apportioned, the dual-career family is over extended and faces great logistic difficulties. (Hunt and Hunt 1986:279)

One major problem is attempting to orchestrate the constellation of external groups that now provide products and services to the family. Kenneth Keniston (1971:18) sensed this trend emerging in the early 1970s:

> the parent today is usually a coordinator without voice or authority, a maestro trying to conduct an orchestra of players who have never met and who play from a multitude of different scores, each in notations the conductor cannot read. If parents are frustrated, it is no wonder: for although they have the responsibility for their children's lives, they hardly ever have the voice, the authority, or the power to make others listen to them.

Quite simply, parents have been losing control over the socialization process to various external service providers that operate relatively independently of individual families. Visible evidence of family resistance to this trend is found in the plethora of family-based, grassroots movements seeking to reassert control by nominating as social problems such family-related issues as drug use, missing and abducted children, heavy metal rock music, fantasy games, religious cults, sexuality and violence in the media, pornography, drunk driving, incorrigibility, suicide, and abortion.[3] In most instances, however, parents cannot reassert familial control by increasing their own involvement in child-rearing; success in the competitive contractual sphere requires a committed pursuit of self-interest. Even temporary "stop-outs" associated with child-rearing can exact significant career penalties. The tension experienced by parents, then, is twofold. On the one hand, parents have a commitment to and a responsibility for socializing their children, but face increased vulnerability as the contractual sphere intrudes into the covenantal. On the other hand, parents have a commitment to and a responsibility for career achievement but face increased vulnerability as the covenantal sphere impinges on the contractual. Ultimately, the contradiction is that time and energy invested in either sphere have negative implications for functioning in the other. If contractual childcare seems the only means for meeting both family and career responsibilities, it is not surprising that apprehension and suspicion about these childcare arrangements run high.

Creating Satanists

Socially constructed reality, the human defense against chaos, becomes ever more precarious when culturally legitimated social patterns lead individuals away from stability toward the boundary between order and chaos. When the source of tension is integral to the very social order, humans are likely to reason metaphorically by "effecting instantaneous fusion of two separated realms of experience into one illuminating, iconic, encapsulating image" (Beit-Hallahmi 1989:75–76). In this sense, satanism claims may be metaphorically true even if empirically false. Rather than being confronted by troublemakers for whom an appropriate label must be found, there is a source of trouble inherent in the pattern of social relations to which no existing type of troublemaker corresponds. One way of preserving (or restoring) order in this circumstance is to identify symbolically the source of tension. The social construction of satanism reasserts control by naming the problem, giving it human shape, and locating its source outside the matrix of social relations to which the social actors are committed. The problems confronting families thereby become the product, not of inappropriate parental conduct but rather of irresponsible or malevolent others. The appropriate response is intensified alertness, surveillance, and social control.

The satanic subversion narrative gives human shape to the sense of danger and vulnerability, in this case the tension between family and economy, that individuals experience. Allegations of satanic cults infiltrating childcare facilities coincided closely with a sharp increase in the number of women with young children in the labor force who faced a pressing need for reliable daycare. The individuals making the initial allegations of satanic subversion were family members who entrusted their children to daycare facilities about which they had significant reservations and apprehensions. The accused childcare workers occupied a pivotal point of tension between covenantal and contractual spheres and thereby embodied both sets of expectations—as managers (who manipulate "human resources" to maximize organizational profit), on the one hand, and as surrogate parents (who nurture and protect children in their care), on the other hand. They were accused of satanic activity rather than child molestation because the tension emanated from structural tension and not ordinary, individualistically based deviance. The victims were children entrusted to strangers during their critical formative years. Accusations most frequently involved sexual abuse, widely thought to have reached almost epidemic proportions in American society and to produce devastating, long-term psychological consequences. Indeed, given the significance of sexual development for maturation and of sexuality for interpersonal bonding and family formation, in a larger sense the narrative warns that the capacity of covenantal family to recreate itself is at risk. The heroic figures in the narrative were therapists (and their allies) who, despite risk of personal harm and rejection by fellow professionals, committed themselves to healing and vindicating their clients. The irony, of course, is that the logical solution to preventing repetition of such disasters would be the further extension of state-sponsored and contractually organized control over childcare. However, in the near term, at least, the narrative might be functional for families. Once the premise is accepted that children lack the motivation and capacity to concoct subversion narratives, families possess a powerful weapon. Any alleged improprieties in daycare centers would unleash severe sanctions. This threat alone should increase the responsiveness of daycare providers to give parents and children a sense of control.

CONCLUSIONS

This chapter outlines the key elements of one major strand of the satanic cult narrative, that involving ritual abuse and sacrifice of children in daycare facilities. I have argued that the satanic cult narrative is best interpreted as countersubversion ideology. The narrative postulates the existence of an underground, national network of satanists with an elaborate organizational apparatus and rituals that have as their primary objective the exploitation and ritual sacrifice of innocent children. This narrative has had considerable social impact despite the fact that virtually no validating physical evidence has been produced. Its cultural plausibility derives from contractual–covenantal tensions that have recently been exacerbated by expansion of the contractual sphere and increased vulnerability of the family. Satanism constitutes a metaphorical construction of a widely experienced sense of vulnerability and danger by American families. Indeed, in late twentieth-century America a convincing portrait of ultimate evil might well be a group of individuals who for their own power, pleasure, and profit exploit the vulnerability of American families and the trust reposed in them as surrogate parents by so abusing and terrorizing the children in their care as to create profound psychic wounds that permanently impair their capacity for full expression of selfhood.[4]

In closing, two important caveats need to be added to this argument. First, this analysis is incomplete. The impact of the satanism scare cannot be explained simply in terms of the cultural plausibility of the countersubversion ideology. The countersubversion campaign's impact is a product of mobilizing key resources that lend physical form to the ideology's claims: networks of professionals pursuing satanists, cultural performances by ritual abuse survivors, new laws and investigatory techniques, and claims linking a variety of events and marginal groups to satanism (Bromley 1987). Other chapters in this volume address some of these issues. Second, asserting that the countersubversion narrative is metaphorically but not empirically true does not mean that allegations in any specific case are unfounded. Indeed, the likelihood of events matching the countersubversion narrative in certain respects may well have increased, thanks to both the publicity given to the narrative and to the coincidental existence of isolated deviant groups.

ACKNOWLEDGMENTS

This chapter is a revision and extension of a paper. "Subversion Mythology and the Social Construction of Social Problems," presented at the annual meeting of the Society for the Scientific Study of Religion, Lexington, KY, November, 1987. I would like to thank J. Gordon Melton, Director of the Institute for the Study of American Religion, and also Robert Hicks for providing me with some of the data on which this paper is based. Grant support from the Society for the Scientific Study of Religion, the American Sociological Association/National Science Foundation, and the Virginia Commonwealth University College of Humanities and Sciences Research Support Fund is gratefully acknowledged. Bruce Busching contributed helpful theoretical insights throughout the development of this chapter, and Diana Gay Cutchin was central to the coordination of the project in her capacity as a research assistant.

NOTES

1.   The scope of the subversion claims now has become international as satanic activity has been reported in Canada, England, and the Netherlands [*The Independent On Sunday* (London), 12 August, 1990].
2.   Robert Dahl (1961) noted this phenomenon among proponents of power elite explanations. Where involvement of a conspiratorial group could not be confirmed, another more secret group operating behind the visible group was postulated.
3.   Elements of subversion ideology can be found in the way some of these threatening conditions are constructed. For example, the power attributed to subliminal messages (backmasking) in rock music, drug "pushers," and religious cult "brainwashing" all raise the specter of loss of personal autonomy and voluntarism.
4.   In discussing the historical development of sexual crime, Foucault et al. (1988:276–278) note that the "sexuality of the child is a territory with its own geography that the adult must not enter" but rather must act as a "guarantor of that specificity of child sexuality in order to protect it." The apprehension about the fear and trauma that can accompany adult–child sexual contact has led to the construc-

tion of a "particular category of the pervert, in the strict sense, of monsters whose aim in life is to practice sex with children." They conclude that "What we are doing is constructing an entirely new type of criminal, a criminal so inconceivably horrible that his crime goes beyond any explanation, any victim."

REFERENCES

American Library Association. 1990. "Satanism Book Withdrawn." *Newsletter on Intellectual Freedom* 39:81.

Beit-Hallahmi, Benjamin. 1989. *Prolegomena to the Psychological Study of Religion.* Lewisburg: Bucknell University Press.

Bromley, David. 1987. "Subversion Mythology and the Social Construction of Social Problems." Paper presented at the annual meeting of the Society for the Scientific Study of Religion, Lexington, KY.

Bromley, David, and Busching, Bruce. 1988. "Understanding the Structure of Contractual and Covenantal Social Relations: Implications for the Sociology of Religion." *Sociological Analysis* 49:15–32.

Bromley, David, and Shupe, Anson. 1981. *Strange Gods: The Great American Cult Scare.* Boston: Beacon Press.

Cade, Leland. 1977. "Cattle Mutilations—Are They for Real?" *Montana Farmer-Stockman,* March 3.

California, State of. 1989–1990. *Occult Crime: A Law Enforcement Primer.* Office of Criminal Justice Planning.

Charlier, Tom, and Downing, Shirley. 1988. "Justice Abused: A 1980s Witch-Hunt." (series). *Memphis Commercial Appeal* (January).

Coleman, Lee. 1989. "Medical Examination for Sexual Abuse: Have We Been Misled?" *The Champion* 13:5–12.

Dahl, Robert. 1961. *Who Governs: Democracy and Power in an American City.* New Haven: Yale University Press.

Finkelhor, David, Hotaling, Gerald, and Sedlak, Andrea. 1990. *Missing, Abducted, Runaway, and Thrownaway Children in America.* Washington: Office of Juvenile Justice and Delinquency Prevention.

Forsyth, Craig, and Oliver, Marion. 1990. "The Theoretical Framing of a Social Problem: Some Conceptual Notes on Satanic Cults." *Deviant Behavior* 11:281–292.

Foucault, Michel, Hocquenghem, Guy, and Danet, Jean. 1988. "Sexual Morality and the Law." Pp. 271–285 in *Michel Foucault: Politics, Philosophy, Culture,* edited by Lawrence Kritzman. New York: Routledge.

Garfinkel, Harold. 1956. "Conditions of Successful Degradation Ceremonies." *American Journal of Sociology* 61:420–424.

Geertz, Clifford. 1966. "Religion as a Cultural System." Pp. 1–46 in *Anthropological Approaches to the Study of Religion,* edited by Michael Banton. London: Tavistock.

Habermas, Jurgen. 1984. *Theory of Communicative Action.* Vol. 1. Boston: Beacon Press.

Hicks, Robert. 1990. "Police Pursuit of Satanic Crime." *Skeptical Inquirer* 14:276–286.

Hill, Sally, and Goodman, Jean. 1989. "Satanism: Similarities Between Patient Accounts and Pre-Inquisition Historical Sources." *Dissociation* 2:39–44.

Hunt, Janet, and Hunt, Larry. 1986. "The Dualities of Careers and Families: New Integrations or New Polarizations?" Pp. 275–289 in *Family in Transition,* edited by Arlene Skolnick and Jerome Skolnick. Boston: Little Brown.

Idaho, State of. 1990. "An Act Relating to Ritualized Abuse of a Child." House of Representatives, House Bill No. 817.

Kahaner, Larry. 1988. *Cults That Kill: Probing the Underworld of Occult Crime.* York: Warner Books.

Katz, Jack. 1975. "Essences as Moral Identities: Verifiability and Responsibility in Imputations of Deviance and Charisma." *American Journal of Sociology* 80:1369–1390.

Kelly, Susan. 1988. "Ritualistic Abuse of Children: Dynamics and Impact." *Cultic Studies Journal* 5:228–236.

Kenniston, Kenneth. 1971. *Youth and Dissent: The Rise of a New Opposition.* New York: Harcourt, Brace, Jovanovich.

Langone, Michael. 1990. *Satanism and Occult Related Violence: What You Should Know.* Weston, MA: American Family Foundation.

Lanning, Kenneth. 1989. "Satanic, Occult, Ritualistic Crime: A Law Enforcement Perspective." *The Police Chief* 56:62–83.

Lyons, Arthur. 1988. *Satan Wants You.* New York: Mysterious Press.

Menendez, Florangel. 1986. "Violent Ritualistic Victimization: An Attack on the Mind, Body, and Spirit." *NCASA News* Summer:7–7.

Nathan, Debbie. 1989. "Child Abuse Evidence Debated: New Data May Aid in Sex-Crime Cases." *Ms. Magazine* March:81.

Orth, Maureen. 1976. "The American Child-Care Disgrace." Pp. 279–287 in *Confronting the Issues: Sex Roles, Marriage and the Family,* edited by Kenneth Kammeyer. Boston: Allyn and Bacon.

Passantino, Gretchen, Passantino, Bob, and Trott, Jon. 1989. "Satan's Sideshow." *Cornerstone Magazine* 18 (December):24–28.

Shupe, Anson. 1987. "The Lehi Sexual Child Abuse Scare." Paper presented at the annual meeting of the Society for the Scientific Study of Religion, Lexington, KY.

Shupe, Anson, and Bromley, David. 1980. *The New Vigilantes: Deprogrammers, Anticultists and the New Religions.* Beverly Hills, CA: Sage Publications.

Stratford, Lauren. 1988. *Satan's Underground: The Extraordinary Story of One Woman's Escape.* Eugene, OR: Harvest House.

Swidler, Ann. 1986. "Culture in Action: Symbols and Strategies." *American Sociological Review* 51:273–286.

Terry, Maury. 1987. *The Ultimate Evil: An Investigation into America's Most Dangerous Satanic Cult.* Garden City: Doubleday.

Wallis, Claudia. 1987. "The Child-Care Dilemma." *Time* (June 22):54–60.

THE SATANIC THREAT TO CHILDREN _____ III

Satanism and Child Molestation: Constructing the Ritual Abuse Scare 5

Debbie Nathan

RITUAL CHILD ABUSE: A PUTATIVE DESCRIPTION

In early 1984 the media began publicizing a child sex abuse scandal of unprecedented proportions at McMartin Preschool in suburban Los Angeles. Investigating authorities alleged that seven teachers (six of them women) and possibly many other adults in the community had molested hundreds of children over two decades. To accept the possibility of such prolonged abuse by so many perpetrators against so many victims, one would have to assume a far-reaching conspiracy. Indeed, later that year, Kee MacFarlane, a social worker who interviewed McMartin students for the District Attorney's office, told Congress she believed "we're dealing with an organized operation of child predators. . . . The preschool, in such a case, serves as a ruse for a larger, unthinkable network of crimes against children" (*New York Times* September 18, 1984).

McMartin involved even more remarkable allegations. Students talked of experiencing bizarre abuse such as sadistic animal killings, sex acts performed during clandestine rites in churches, and exposure to corpses in graveyards (Charlier and Downing 1988; Nathan 1990). During 1984 and 1985, these reports were widely discussed at child protection conferences nationwide (Charlier and Downing 1988) and were detailed—virtually always unskeptically—by journalists (Fisher 1989; Shaw 1990).

Some McMartin parents with professional connections to the media claimed the case was an instance of "satanic" abuse (Charlier and Downing 1988). As McMartin made headlines, similar reports surfaced across the country involving children and adults in neighborhoods, small towns, preschools, and daycare centers. These cases were so strikingly similar that by 1985 child abuse experts had coined the term "ritual abuse" to denote sex offenses occurring "in a context linked to some symbols or group that have a religious, magical, or supernatural connotation, and where the invocation of these symbols or activities, repeated over time, is used to frighten and intimidate the children" (Finkelhor and Williams 1988:59). Lanning

(1989a,b) characterized ritual abuse as including some of the following: multiple offenders and child victims (usually ranging from 2 to 6 years of age), use of fear as a controlling tactic, and bizarre or ritualistic activity such as chanting, cannibalism, drinking "magical" liquids, or animal sacrifice.

Claims by children that they were ritually abused first surfaced in the United States in about 1983. By mid-1984, the number of such reports had skyrocketed, and by the end of 1987, child protection agencies and police across the country had validated about 100 cases (Charlier and Downing 1988). District attorneys declined to prosecute many of these, citing lack of sufficient admissible evidence. By the mid-1980s, though, many states had reformed criminal evidence statutes to make it easier to try child sex abuse cases (Whitcomb 1985; Whitcomb et al. 1985). Arbitrary minimum ages for competency were eliminated and hearsay admissibility was expanded. Adult witnesses were allowed to take the stand to describe children's behavioral changes—such as bedwetting and phobias—that supposedly indicated prior sexual abuse. At the end of the decade, 37 states allowed videotaped testimony of children and 24 authorized the use of closed-circuit television (Supreme Court of the U.S. 1990). By 1989, some 50 people had gone to trial on charges stemming from ritual abuse cases. Of these, approximately half were acquitted, while half were convicted and typically given prison sentences (Charlier and Downing 1988; Nathan 1990).[1] Since 1986, the number of ritual abuse cases proceeding to indictment stage has tapered off, but new ones continue to surface (Nathan 1990) in the United States and other countries. Defendants were still being prosecuted even after McMartin ended in 1990 with acquittals and hung verdicts.

INCONSISTENCIES REGARDING THE CLAIMS

Despite continuing concern about ritual abuse, investigations have uniformly failed to turn up the adult witnesses or physical evidence[2] that would be associated logically with ongoing group rites, extreme violence, and pornography production alleged in these cases. Furthermore, several children have recanted their charges during investigations, on the witness stand, and after trials. (Humphrey 1985; Rigert et al. 1985; Snedeker 1988). Child protection workers were grappling with these discrepancies as early as 1986. Many grew skeptical, noted the growing problem of false sex abuse allegations in divorce custody disputes, and began speculating that ritual abuse cases might be similarly based on fictitious charges. In trying to explain why children would talk about events that seemingly never happened, researchers began examining investigators' contacts with children. Records have demonstrated many questionable practices; e.g., cross-germination of allegations from one witness to another, leading use of props (e.g., "anatomically correct" dolls), repetition of leading and suggestive questions (especially whenever a child denied abuse had occurred), use of pressure questions and statements, and offering positive reinforcement to elicit affirmations of abuse and negative reinforcement to discourage denials (Benedek et al. 1987; Jones and McQuiston 1988; Raskin and Yuille 1989; Yates and Musty 1988).

Also, researchers and parents of children involved in the cases—even those convinced of the defendants' guilt—have noted that during ritual abuse investigations alleged victims and their families develop extraordinarily close relationships with prosecutors, police, prosecution-oriented therapists, and child protection workers. Furthermore, through professional contacts, conferences, and national parents' groups such as Believe the Children, adults and children in individual cases often become closely connected to their counterparts scattered throughout the country. Such networks, coupled with widespread media claims about ritual abuse, could well have encouraged rapid spread of allegations that, though false, remained remarkably consistent over great geographic distances (Charlier and Downing 1988; Crowley 1990; Manshel 1990; Nathan 1987, 1988b, 1990).

Other child protection professionals, however, insist that ritual abuse is widespread, pointing to consistency of children's stories as strong proof, and believe that lack of evidence demonstrates satanists' superior organizing abilities and their entrenchment in government, law enforcement, and medical professions (Nathan 1987). Others are more cautious. They doubt bizarre elements of the stories, but speculate that adults may have nevertheless perpetrated real abuse. One theory has it that victims may overlay childish fantasies onto their memories of the trauma (Charlier and Downing 1988; Lanning 1989b). Another is that isolated individuals or small groups of molesters/pornographers are using ritual trappings while they molest children, either as an expression of psychopathology, or as a cynical way to manipulate or confuse a child, and thus confound police investigation (Finkelhor and Williams 1988; Lanning 1989a,b).

The belief that ritual abuse is perpetrated primarily by a satanic conspiracy seems particularly attractive to fundamentalist Christians, including law enforcement authorities professing such religious beliefs. The alternative, more secular, explanation has been adopted by professionals skeptical of conspiracy theories or religious claims about the existence of the Devil or an "Ultimate Evil." This latter belief is no more scientific than the former; it actually reinforces the religious current of thought and provides potent justification for further construction of the ritual myth. But a myth such as ritual child abuse cannot be fully described without commenting on cultural conditions that spawn it. One must examine how social anxieties have been articulated within the child protection movement—and how this effort has been shaped by feminism, religious fundamentalism, and popular American folklore since the 1970s.

IDEOLOGICAL AND INSTITUTIONAL FOUNDATIONS

Historically, when Western societies suffer economic difficulties and rapid change, moral panics develop about their children being in imminent danger.[3] Currently, the United States and other industrialized countries seem to be experiencing cultural unease about structural shifts in the family and concomitant changes in sex roles and sexual behavior—particularly of women and teenagers (D'Emilio and Freedman 1988:328–360). During the 1970s and 1980s, for instance, the divorce rate rose dramatically, as did the proportion of never-married women (many of whom opted for single motherhood), working wives, feminine poverty, and declining living standards for children. At the same time, women and adolescents, especially girls, have become increasingly overt in their sexual behavior. Meanwhile, many see sex—especially extramarital, nonmonogamous, or gay sex—as threatening. AIDS has become one symbol of fears about family issues. Another is the idea of endangered children—especially, children threatened sexually by "strangers." This notion cropped up earlier in U.S. history, but has achieved special currency recently. Child protection is now an entrenched cultural value—one that generally tries to safeguard child welfare by focusing more on the idea of deviancy than on what are perhaps normative, structural problems in families.

Child Protection: Family Versus Stranger Danger

In 1962, when C. Henry Kempe and his colleagues published "The Battered Child Syndrome," press and public rediscovered child protection, from turn-of-the-century Progressivism's agenda. By 1967 every state had passed child abuse reporting laws; government-sponsored research on the subject burgeoned. Abuse was generally viewed as an outgrowth of individual deviance, but studies soon made it clear that child neglect was connected to structural social problems such as poverty, joblessness, and inadequate housing.

These findings were anathema to conservative politicians, who feared government impingement on family privacy and self-sufficiency. Thus, in 1971, President Nixon refused to sign the Comprehensive Child Development Act (which proposed broad expansion of public-funded daycare), warning that federal sponsorship of child development outside the home "would commit the vast moral authority of the National Government to the side of communal approaches to child rearing over [and] against the family-centered approach." Liberals became increasingly wary of opposition other human service legislation would face unless they disassociated their rhetoric from class and racial issues. So, when Senator Walter Mondale, chairman of the Senate Subcommittee on Children and Youth, took up a national child protection act, he downplayed child neglect and focused on the far less controversial problem of abuse. The resulting 1974 Child Abuse Protection and Treatment Act (CAPTA) emphasized physical assaults. Not surprisingly, when dealing with sex abuse, the Act played up offenses committed by adults *outside* the family. CAPTA established the National Center for Child Abuse and Neglect (NCCAN) and authorized disbursing $85 million over the next 4 years. To receive funding, states had to adopt procedures to prevent, identify, and treat child abuse (Nelson 1984). Consequently, though researchers knew that the problem lay by and large within the family, by the mid-1970s, the federal government was financing a focus on "stranger danger" to children.

Child Sexual Exploitation and Missing Children

Beginning in the late 1970s, a few self-appointed spokespeople began promoting claims that American children were gravely endangered by prostitution and child pornography industries (Stanley 1989). For instance, author Robin Lloyd (1976) described an international male prostitution ring involving hundreds of thousands of minors. Law enforcement officials repeated this figure to the press and at Congressional hearings; later, Judianne Denson-Gerber, director of several drug rehabilitation centers, doubled it to include girls, then arbitrarily doubled it again (Stanley 1989:312 n. 94,95). Denson-Gerber toured the country claiming links between child prostitution and pornography, and by mid-1977, NBC news reported "it's been estimated that as many as two million American youngsters [some four percent of all minors over five years old] are involved in the fast-growing, multi-million dollar child pornography business" (Best 1989:21).[4]

During the late 1970s, media began playing up the issue of missing children. At first the emphasis was on parents' illegally snatching their children after losing custody during divorces (Eliasoph 1986). Then claims began circulating about a supposedly urgent problem of stranger-abducted children. Politicians and journalists estimated as many as 400,000 kidnappings annually (Best 1989:23–24).[5] Not surprisingly, much rhetoric around this issue linked the "missing children" problem to sexual abuse. Stranger abduction was "a crime of predatory cruelty usually committed by pedophiles, pornographers, black-market baby peddlers, or childless psychotics bidding desperately for parenthood . . . the pedophile [is] perhaps the largest category" (Gelman 1984:78,85).

Women Versus the Devil: Belief Versus Doubt

About the same time, a spate of rumors, or "urban legends" with satanist themes began spreading throughout the country. Concurrently, a small number of people, mostly women, became the focus of media reports with lurid claims about having escaped from satanic cults that tortured them as children. Though no credible evidence has since surfaced to substantiate these stories, many child protection workers believed them unstintingly. These claims resonate with concern many contemporary feminists have about violence against women, and about authorities' traditional disbelief when women reported sexual assaults.

By the mid-1970s, this concern was being aired publicly; the main focus was adult rape, both inside and outside the family. Indeed, American feminist theoreticians, psychologists, and sociologists redefined rape as a form of violence rather than—as had traditionally been articulated—a mere sexual misunderstanding (Herman 1981; Rush 1980). A conservative or "cultural" feminist theoretical current also developed (Echols 1989:243–295), which described men as inherently sexually predatory and genitally fixated, as opposed to women, who were considered naturally gentle and physically diffuse in their sexuality. This idea has buttressed the notion, most radically articulated by feminists such as Dworkin (1988), that heterosexual contact of any type is at best inherently exploitative to women, and in any case invariably violent. These concepts dovetail with patriarchal celebrations of the eternal "differences" between sexes and with a morally conservative assumption that, by nature, women need "protection" from male passions.

While studying rape, feminists encountered the problem of child sexual abuse. At first they focused on incest perpetrated against girls, demonstrating that it was much more common than previously acknowledged (Rush 1980; Herman 1981; Russell 1983). Researchers pointed out that despite incest's prevalence, girls who reported it seldom were believed. They also described victims' tendency to deny the abuse or recant charges, out of fear that disclosure would cause family discord or dissolution (Summit 1983). Denial or recantation, then, might be evidence of incest. This reasoning led many child protection workers to ask leading questions of *all* alleged sex abuse victims, and in general, "do whatever it takes to get children to talk" (MacFarlane 1985:152).

Many feminists also leveled strong criticisms against Freud and Freudians for ascribing women's reports of childhood sex abuse to mere fantasy (Masson 1984; Rush 1980). But, by applying notions about women's passive sexuality and need for protection to children, feminists have contributed to exaggerated claims of child endangerment by assigning the label "child sexual abuse" to a broad range of conduct: everything from forced sodomy to an unsolicited hug from an age-peer boyfriend (Nathan 1990; Okami 1990). Equating all intergenerational sex with exploitation and violence has deflected attention from earlier findings about incest and power imbalances in families. It has also put a large group of secular, feminist-minded professionals in ideologically and politically friendly relationships with moral conservatives, including people who expound satanic conspiracy theories to explain women and children's "memories" of ritual abuse.

The Mouths of Babes

During the 1970s, women diagnosed as suffering from Multiple Personality Disorder, while undergoing hypnotherapy, told therapists they "remembered" having been sexually assaulted by groups of adults performing sadomasochistic acts. Satanism first appeared in these stories in the bestselling book *Michelle Remembers* (Pazder and Smith 1980). By 1982 or 1983, the FBI began receiving similar reports from women around the country; soon thereafter, similar stories surfaced among children.

In October, 1983, for instance, a California girl accused her stepfather of participating in a satanic cult that had forced her to kill an infant, eat feces, and engage in ritualistic sex. During the same month, children in foster care in Omaha claimed that children had been drugged, abused, and sacrificed during satanic rituals in Arizona. The victims were said to have been kidnapped from shopping malls—an echo, perhaps, of an "urban legend" widespread during this period (Brunvand 1984:79–85). Investigation of the Nebraska/Arizona case produced no evidence to substantiate the bizarre allegations. These cases are significant in that they surfaced *before* the national media began covering the McMartin or Jordan, Minnesota ritual child sex abuse cases (Charlier and Downing 1988:A-10). This suggests that adult women's stories, which *were* being highly publicized at the time, may have been the cultural source of the first children's claims of ritual abuse.

McMartin was not widely publicized until February, 1984, but the case surfaced in August, 1983, after the mother of a 2-year-old boy made a series of bizarre allegations to Los Angeles officials. She alleged, for instance, that her son was abused not only by his teachers, but also by strangers following her on the highway and by male models she saw pictured in an advertisement. She claimed that the perpetrators had worn masks and capes, taped the boy's mouth, hands, and eyes, stuck an air tube in his rectum, made him ride naked on a horse, jabbed scissors and staples into him, stuck his finger into a goat's anus, and made him drink the blood of a murdered baby. The mother was later hospitalized and diagnosed as a paranoid schizophrenic (Nathan 1990), which suggests similarities between the etiology of her allegations and those of women claiming to be adult survivors of satanic abuse.[6]

Regardless of whether a connection can be made between allegations of child sexual abuse and claims by alleged adult survivors of satanic abuse, it is clear that adults in this case quickly adopted satanic conspiracy theories. McMartin parent Bob Currie takes credit for explaining the children's allegations by introducing the theory that devil-worshipping practitioners were infiltrating preschools (Charlier and Downing 1988). During the 2 years after the case surfaced, the parents met with Michelle Smith and Lawrence Pazder (co-authors of *Michelle Remembers*). They also conferred with self-styled ritual abuse survivor Lauren Willson (whose claims were recently exposed as a hoax) (Passantino et al. 1989), and with Joan Christianson (who makes claims similar to Willson's) (Nathan 1988c).

According to Charlier and Downing, McMartin and the other 35 cases they studied were replete with similar opportunities for contamination with adults' stories. In some, investigators admitted speaking or meeting with satanic conspiracy theorists, or using written information they supplied. In 1985, for instance, conspiracy theorist Ken Wooden mailed 3500 district attorneys a questionnaire to ask children in ritual abuse cases. Prosecutors and police also used *Michelle Remembers* as an investigative guide (Charlier and Downing 1988; Ross and Sharpe 1986).

The Government and the Sex Ring

When prosecutors went to the press and juries with cases that included allegations of satanism, the conspiracy theory often evoked skepticism. Also, its Christian fundamentalist tinge was offensive to secular-minded child protection workers who nevertheless were inclined, primarily because of feminist concerns, to accept children's allegations literally. Indeed, among such people, the label "satanic abuse" was quickly replaced by "ritual abuse," a term with fewer religious connotations.

Federal investigators also were skeptical of religious conspiracy theories, but the government's proactive, ongoing involvement with the child endangerment scare provided other avenues for developing and justifying cases. Indeed, during the 1980s, the idea that children were at great risk for abuse by strangers continued to captivate politicians, particularly when the issue was narrowed to sexual abuse. From 1983 to 1986, Congress held 13 hearings on the subjects of child pornography and sex between adults and minors; 194 bills were introduced (Stanley 1989:309n., 314n., 316n., 349n.). Also in 1983, Congress asked the FBI to focus on solving cases involving missing, murdered, and sexually exploited children. In May, 1983, the FBI invited law enforcement officers from around the country to a national seminar to discuss the subject; participants agreed on the need to share more information among investigators (Charlier and Downing 1988).

During the same period, a new federal law enforcement apparatus was created to coordinate child pornography and sex abuse investigations among FBI, U.S. Postal Service, Customs and police officials, as well as researchers and social workers. In 1984 Congress passed the Sexual Exploitation Act, which revised child pornography statutes by removing previous requirements that depictions be obscene or produced for commercial use, making it a crime to receive or import child pornography, and upping the age limit defining who was a "child" from below 16 to 18 years of age (Stanley 1989:302, 319). Also in 1984 the *FBI Law Enforcement Bulletin* devoted an issue to pedophilia and "sex rings," said to be composed primarily of male pedophiles who abuse children (usually older boys), and who often form networks with fellow pedophiles via computer, phone, and the mail (Burgess 1984; Burgess and Grant 1988). The bulletin was distributed to 25,000 FBI agents and other law enforcement agencies, and was the first to ever go into a second printing (Charlier and Downing 1988).

Thus, by the time McMartin and other similar cases surfaced, many investigators assumed that accused perpetrators must be members of groups organized, not into religious cults, but rather as "sex rings" formed to bring male pedophiles together to abuse children and/or produce child pornography. During 1985, the apex year for reports of ritual child abuse, this dominant secular theory was used to explain and develop what previously had often been called "ritual" abuse cases. At hearings for the Attorney General's Commission of Pornography (the Meese Commission) in 1985, the label "ritual" abuse was used interchangeably with "multivictim, multioffender" abuse, a term more compatible with the sex ring concept. At the hearings, parents who believed their children had been brutally molested in daycare gave testimony (U.S. Dept Justice 1986:773), but there was little official mention of satanic sex abuse conspiracies—even by participants such as Roland Summit, a leading proponent of the theory (Nathan 1987; Summit 1988).

The Meese Commission reported with concern testimony about

> alleged multi-victim, multi-perpetrator child sexual molestation rings throughout the country. Few . . . have resulted in successful prosecutions. Multitudes of children have related experiences of being photographed by the alleged molesters. . . . Even in the face of clear medical evidence of sexual molestation, the young ages of the children and the procedures in the criminal courts have combined to undermine and destroy effective prosecution. (U.S. Dept. of Justice 1986:688–689)

The Meese Commission recommended creating a national task force to investigate possible links between "multivictim, multiperpetrator child sex rings" and pornography, links between such sex rings nationwide, and whether they were connected with pornography distribution or organized crime. The report reiterated Summit's call for research into effects of sexual abuse of children, and noted the $450,000 federal grant received in 1985 by UCLA researchers sympathetic to the McMartin prosecution to study "the McMartin Pre-School child victims" (Dept. of Justice 1986; *Los Angeles Times* 1985). The Meese report also recommended that investigators in child sex abuse cases always ask alleged victims if he or she had been photographed or filmed (1986:449, 451–52).

MORE DOUBTS, MORE THEORIES

Shortly after release of the Meese Commission report, the Los Angeles District Attorney dropped all charges against five of seven McMartin defendants, stating that evidence against them was "incredibly weak" (Charlier and Downing 1988). The Jordan, Minnesota case had largely fallen apart by then, too, and the Minnesota Attorney General had issued a report severely criticizing the investigators' methods (Humphrey 1985; Rigert 1985). By 1987, media were taking a more critical attitude toward ritual abuse cases (Ross and Sharpe 1986; Mann and Stevens 1987). Press skepticism reflected doubts that child protection professionals were raising about some of their own methods and concepts—for example, about the theory, widely expounded during the early 1980s (Sgroi et al. 1982), that it is rare for children to make false sex abuse charges (Green 1986; Jenkins and Katkin 1988; Jones and McGraw 1987; King and Yuille 1987; Moss 1987, 1988; Raskin and Yuille 1989; Renshaw 1985). Still, new ritual cases continued to crop up, and many cases that had surfaced earlier were still being investigated or prosecuted.

Prosecutors had already learned that juries and media might scoff at cases in which "satanic" or ritual allegations were publicized (Hollingsworth 1986). Even the sex ring approach could prove problematic, because behavior commonly observed in such groups has little to do with that described in ritual cases. Sex rings are said to be almost always composed exclusively of male pedophiles, whereas most groups of adults accused in ritual cases have contained both men and women, including elderly women. And even when only men were named as ritual abuse perpetrators, there was seldom any evidence uncovered to suggest they were pedophiles (Burgess 1984; Burgess and Grant 1988; Lanning 1987:7–25, 1989b:11–15). Lanning (1987:10) has stated that "it is rare to find a case . . . in which a female offender fits the dynamics of the [pedophile]." Thus, it would be unlikely to find women in sex rings, unless they participated not to fulfill sexual desires, but to make pornography for profit, because they were dominated by the males in the group, or were reenacting abuse they suffered as children.[7] Again, however, no child pornography has ever turned up in a ritual sex abuse case, despite extensive investigations and reward offers (Charlier and Downing 1988). Although recent research done on self-admitted female incest molesters suggests that some helped domineering spouses or male lovers abuse children (Mathews et al. 1989; McCarty 1986; Travin et al. 1990), in many groups of adults accused in ritual cases, there is no suggestion that men were dominating women. In some, there were no males at all. Finally, although harder to demonstrate, it seems apparent that in general, these defendants lack a history of childhood physical or sexual victimization.

The Search for a Profile

However, an alternative, more convincing secular explanation for ritual abuse began evolving as investigators and prosecutors characterized ritual abuse defendants of both sexes with simplified behavioral "profiles" derived from traditional, male perpetrator cases. The primary source of the profile concept has been the FBI, via Kenneth Lanning, the Bureau's Behavioral Science Unit specialist in child sex abuse. Lanning has long been vocally skeptical of the satanic megacult conspiracy theory as an explanation for ritual abuse cases: he has suggested that witness contamination, leading interviewing, and children's exposure to mythical and sadomasochistic motifs in the media may explain the allegations. On the other hand, Lanning seems compelled to justify these cases, at least those that have resulted in convictions. Thus, he has discarded the term "ritual" abuse and renamed them "multidimensional sex rings" (Lanning 1989b). This semantic turn further distances "ritual" abuse from its religious context and tends to validate the phenomenon on its face, by linking it to "sex rings," whose reality is seldom disputed.

Even earlier, Lanning—who was studying sex abuse before the ritual cases surfaced—took data from conventional cases and elaborated a "Behavioral Typology" of male child molesters. The typology began appearing in print in the mid-1980s (Lanning 1985), and was widely read after it appeared in the Meese Commission report. It deals with male child molesters, as individuals, prior to any involvement in groups, and purports to describe, among other things, behaviors that motivate or correlate with child sex abuse. Thus, according to Lanning, "situational" molesters (i.e., those who are not pedophiles) are: regresses (with "poor coping skills"), morally indiscriminate ("users of people"), sexually indiscriminate (bored and looking for "sexual experimentation"), or inadequate (social misfit, "unusual") (Lanning 1987:6,8). These categories could encompass almost anyone's behavior, of course. Lanning has broadened them by suggesting that in "ritual" abuse cases, an "inadequate" personality type might not even have a sexual motive for brutalizing children:

> What you are dealing with is individuals who have emotional, psychological
> problems, hostilities, pent up emotions, and they are simply taking them out
> on available targets . . . who in this case are children. But the individual who
> is working at, this time, ABC nursery school, today, molesting children . . .
> could be . . . working at the XYZ nursing home and be doing the same thing to
> 85-year-old senile people laying [sic] in bed. (Transcript of Proceedings, U.S.
> Dept. of Justice, the Attorney General's Commission on Pornography, Public
> Hearing, Miami, Florida, November 20–22, 1985, in Stanley [1989:301])

This and other statements by Lanning (1987) imply that the typology can be
used to describe defendants in ritual cases. Lanning has been reluctant to
use his typology on female offenders, but many officials involved in ritual
abuse prosecutions have applied it to both sexes, indiscriminately mixing it
with unsubstantiated assertions about women defendants derived from recent research on female sex offenders.

A federally funded study by Finkelhor and Williams (1988) on sexual
abuse in daycare centers is particularly significant in this regard because it
clearly illustrates how staunch believers in ritual abuse use pseudoscientific
profiles and concepts from female offender research to rationalize otherwise
inexplicable behavior. The study, *Nursery Crimes: Sexual Abuse in Daycare*, accepts the validity of ritual abuse accusations. After a brief caveat, it
proceeds to include data from any daycare sex abuse report validated by
one protective agency, even if the police later closed the investigation due
to lack of evidence, and even though only a third of the cases were
prosecuted (with many ending in hung juries or acquittals). Although most
cases in the sample involved "traditional" relatively nonviolent (e.g., pe-
dophilic) abuse by lone males, those that alleged ritual abuse supplied most
of the data base for the "victims" component of the study, as well as many
adults for the "perpetrator" section.

In attempting to characterize ritual defendants psychologically, Finkelhor
and Williams had virtually no contact with defendants, their friends, relatives, or attorneys. Instead, they relied almost exclusively on anecdotal
interviews with police, prosecutors, and social workers involved in prosecutions. The study conflated the data on "conventional" and ritual male
defendants, but all the women were involved in ritual cases, so data on
them are instructive. The researchers point out that objective studies of these
women reveal very low incidences of drug abuse and alcoholism. To
explain why they would commit continuing crimes such as urinating and
defecating on children, raping and stabbing them with sharp implements,
threatening them with death, killing animals, etc., Finkelhor and Williams
imply Lanning's "inadequate" personality type by suggesting that such
women are suffering from "isolation and stress" (p. 46) or seeking "power
and control" (p. 47). For instance, in discussing motivations of convicted
teacher Kelly Michaels (Nathan 1988b; Rabinowitz 1990), who was living

with a lesbian when arrested, researchers write that she was "a very quiet young woman" (an echo of the "inadequate" personality?), and "isolated from heterosexual relationships" ("sexually indiscriminate," "inadequate," or both?).[8] On the other hand, Michelle Noble (pseudonymed "Eagle's Nest"), who has since been acquitted at retrial (Nathan 1987, 1988a), is fitted into a "profile" derived from female offender research. She is described as having suffered from "isolation," as a "battered wife who had been abused as a child," and as possibly vulnerable "to a more aggressive, sexually abusive friend" (referring to a *woman* co-worker). None of these claims is substantiated by the facts of the case or by Noble's history. They are merely rumor and innuendo, which are nevertheless significant in rationalizing belief in widespread ritual child abuse.

Some law enforcement officials have begun to attribute ritual abuse cases to hysteria. Montgomery County, Maryland police detective Richard Cage (1990), for example, has detailed a daycare ritual abuse case that surfaced recently after a 3-year-old complained of a nonexistent "bruise" on his buttocks and blamed a person he called David. After repeated questioning by his anxious parents, the child said "David" was a "midget doctor." Cage describes how leading interrogations and cross-germination spread allegations from parent to parent and child to child, and how therapists and investigators unwittingly encouraged the process. Children were soon accusing their women teachers of sadomasochistic acts, "satanic" rites, and animal killing. Police eventually determined that all such stories were confabulations: the first child's original statement referred to the fact that his best friend, a 4-year-old named David, had hit him in the buttocks while playing at the daycare. Rossen (1989) and District Attorney Rubenstein (1990) describe similar cases.

But although skepticism grows in some quarters, blind faith abounds in others. More and more papers given at professional conferences and articles in academic journals report ritual abuse research using highly controversial data that the authors nevertheless accept at face value (Cozolino 1989; Faller 1988, 1990; Finkelhor and Williams 1988; Hunt and Baird 1990; Kelly 1988, 1989, 1990; McCord et al. 1990; Ramsey-Klawsnik 1990; Waterman et al. 1990).[9] The federal government continues to support production of materials promoting investigative techniques that critics say buttress false allegations. At federally sponsored conferences, such as the annual (San Diego) Children's Hospital "Health Science Response to Child Maltreatment" program, speakers promote a belief in existence of widespread "ritual" abuse and satanic conspiracies (Summit 1990; Summit and Lanning 1990). State and municipal governments play a part, too. The Los Angeles County Commission for Women, for instance, has a task force on ritual abuse, and distributes an uncritical description of the phenomenon to the public (Los Angeles County Commission for Women 1989). Several states have considered or passed laws specifically outlawing "ritual" abuse, thus further legitimizing the concept (Nathan 1989b). The mass media, meanwhile, continue to play up the scare—popular true-crime books assume that convicted defendants are guilty (Crowley 1990; Hollingsworth 1986; Manshel 1990), and "made-for-TV" movies, docudramas, and tabloid talk shows describe mass daycare abusers, satanist preschool molesters, and devil-worshipping kiddie porn producers (Nathan 1990). Not surprisingly, then, ritual abuse cases continue to surface. In the United States, many now originate in divorce custody disputes (Hoffman 1990), while others continue to emanate from preschool and daycare settings.

CONCLUSION

Several years and scores of cases since allegations of ritual child sexual abuse first surfaced throughout the United States, authorities still have no more evidence of such crimes than they did when McMartin parents and children began talking. But even though many child protection professionals have suggested that the investigative process itself is what causes this phenomenon, researchers have failed to do a thoroughgoing review of that process. Many have instead countered skepticism with new theories that attempt to secularize and "deconspire" ritual abuse by suggesting novel, scientifically untested ideas about individual psychopathology, or by conflating the putative behavior of ritual abusers with that of pedophiles in sex rings. This seemingly unceasing activity, the support it has garnered from the government, and the acceptance it has won from the media and public suggest that the ritual abuse scare is a deeply rooted expression of anxieties this culture harbors about unresolved family and sexual issues. Without thoughtful, public discussion of such problems, the moral panic about diabolic, conspiratorial child molesters will no doubt continue to victimize adult defendants—and children—at least for the foreseeable future.

ACKNOWLEDGMENTS

The author would like to thank Robert Hicks and Ellen Willis for generously sharing ideas and materials that have helped develop this paper.

NOTES

1. Since the mid-1980s, numerous articles and books have appeared containing detailed narratives of particular ritual abuse cases. Works that primarily argue for the defendants' guilt include those by Hollingsworth (1986), Crowley (1990), Manshel

(1990); and Raschke (1990). Those suggesting that the accused were not guilty include Eberle and Eberle (1986), Fisher (1988), Mann and Stevens (1987), Nathan (1987, 1988b), Rabinowitz (1990), and Snedeker (1988).

2.   The "Country Walk" (Dade County, Florida) case described by Hollingsworth (1986) is a possible exception. In Country Walk, which surfaced in the spring/summer of 1984, a 36-year-old man with a criminal record for murder and for molesting a 9-year-old girl was accused, along with his 17-year-old wife, of sexually assaulting toddlers and preschoolers who attended their in-home babysitting service. Much has been made of the fact that the couple's 7-year-old son tested positive for gonorrhea of the throat, and that the wife pleaded guilty and testified against her husband (who was convicted). Though Country Walk became something of a model for investigators and prosecutors in later cases, it was fraught with the same problems that have plagued other investigations. Many interviews with the children were leading and suggestive, and children's statements from one interview to another were highly contradictory. In addition, after her arrest, the woman defendant insisted for months that she and her husband were innocent. Only after spending a long period in jailhouse isolation and being actively plea-bargained, did she plead guilty; but she continued to claim she was innocent and was pleading guilty only "to get all of this over" (Hollingsworth, 1986:424). Subsequent research has discredited many medical findings in child sexual abuse cases (see Coleman 1989; Krugman 1989; McCann et al. 1989; Nathan 1989a; Paradise 1989), including previously used tests for gonorrhea now shown to produce frequent false-positive results. This is not to say that no plausible evidence of child sexual abuse existed in the Country Walk case; indeed, it appears that the husband perpetrated sadomasochistic assaults against the wife (who was legally a minor) and possibly against the younger children, including abuse involving the use of urine and excrement. However, it is not at all clear that the children's "ritual" stories—about pornography making, masks, animal killing, satanic prayers, etc.—were factual.

3.   The term "moral panic" refers to a situation "in which a minor social problem expresses and preempts a deeper related one" (see Cohen 1972).

4.   Subsequent government investigations have debunked the claims, finding instead that, until its prohibition in the United States, only 5000 to 7000 children worldwide were involved in child pornography production. Further, the preprohibition industry had estimated revenues of only about $5 million, and since 1978, the U.S. commercial market for child pornography has been virtually wiped out (Stanley 1989:307–317). These facts have failed to dampen the child pornography myth in popular culture or the government.

5.   These figures have been discredited. In 1985, for instance, the FBI investigated only 67 such cases (Eliasoph 1986) and a Justice Department-funded study released in 1990 estimated that strangers abduct, at most, 300 children per year for more than a few hours (Finkelhor et al. 1990).

6.   Since McMartin surfaced, other sex abuse cases have been dismissed after investigators and courts found that the adult reporting the abuse (usually the child's mother or other female caretaker) was mentally ill and delusionary about sex abuse (Jones and McGraw 1987; Ross and Sharpe 1986).

7.   Traditionally, child sexual abuse by women has been considered extremely rare (Finkelhor and Russell 1984) and it was assumed that female offenders were psychotic or mentally retarded. In recent years anecdotal accounts (Hollingsworth 1986) and research with self-admitted teen-age and adult women perpetrators, primarily in incest cases, has shown that such offenders, while seldom mentally retarded or psychotic, typically were sexually abused themselves as children, suffered substance abuse problems at the time of the offense, or offended at the behest

of a dominating male (McCarty 1986; Mathews et al. 1989; Travin et al. 1990). In such cases, abuse was generally perpetrated against the women's own children or against pubescent boys; it consisted of fondling and/or oral-genital contact with younger children or having intercourse with older boys, and it did not resemble the sadomasochistic and terroristic acts alleged in the ritual abuse cases.

8. Finkelhor and Williams (1988) assigned pseudonyms to the cases they describe in *Nursery Crimes*, which makes it hard to compare the authors' accounts with others. *Nursery Crimes* refers to Kelly Michaels' case in New Jersey as "Welcome Child" (p. 48).

9. The UCLA study, for example, has provided all or a significant part of the data for Finkelhor and Williams (1988); McCord et al. (1990); and Waterman et al. (1990). Yet, of the dozens of children (and their parents) in the UCLA study, very few ever testified in any legal proceeding involving McMartin or any other ritual abuse case. The studies consistently fail to point this out or to give serious consideration to the possibility that these children were *not* ritually abused.

REFERENCES

Benedek, E. P., and Schetky, D. H. 1987. "Problems in Validating Allegations of Sexual Abuse. Part I: Factors Affecting Perception and Recall of Events." *Journal of the American Academy of Child and Adolescent Psychiatry* 26:912–915.

Best, Joel. 1989. "Dark Figures and Child Victims: Statistical Claims About Missing Children." Pp. 21–37 in *Images of Issues: Typifying Contemporary Social Problems,* edited by Joel Best. New York: Aldine de Gruyter.

Brunvand, Jan Harold. 1984. *The Choking Doberman and Other "New" Urban Legends.* New York: W. W. Norton.

Burgess, Ann W. 1984. *Child Pornography and Sex Rings.* Lexington, MA: Lexington Books.

Burgess, Ann W., and Grant, Christine A. 1988. *Children Traumatized in Sex Rings.* Washington, D.C.: National Center for Missing and Exploited Children.

Cage, Richard. 1990. "Problems in Multiple Victim Cases." (Audio recording of presentation before the Health Science Response to Child Maltreatment Conference, Children's Hospital, San Diego, January 17–20, 1990. Available as Tape No. 200-19 from Convention Recorders, 5401 Linda Vista Road, San Diego, CA 92110.)

Charlier, T., and Downing, S. 1988. "Justice Abused: A 1980s Witch-hunt." *The Commercial Appeal,* Memphis, Tennessee, January.

Cohen, Stanley. 1972. *Folk Devils and Moral Panics.* London: Granada.

Coleman, Lee. 1989. "Medical Examination for Sexual Abuse: Have We Been Misled?" *The Champion* 13:5–12.

Cozolino, Louis, J. 1989. "The Ritual Abuse of Children: Implications for Clinical Practice and Research." *Journal of Sex Research* 26:132–133.

Crowley, Patricia. 1990. *Not My Child: A Mother Confronts Her Child's Sexual Abuse.* New York: Doubleday.

D'Emilio, John, and Freedman, Estelle. 1988. *Intimate Matters: A History of Sexuality in America.* New York: Harper & Row.

Dworkin, Andrea. 1988. *Intercourse*. New York: Free Press.

Eberle, P., and Eberle, S. 1986. *The Politics of Child Abuse*. Secaucus, NJ: Lyle Stuart.

Echols, Alice. 1989. *Daring to be Bad: Radical Feminism in America, 1967–1975*. Minneapolis: University of Minnesota Press.

Eliasoph, Nina. 1986. "Drive-In Morality, Child Abuse, and the Media." *Socialist Review* 90:7–31.

Faller, Kathleen, C. 1988. "The Spectrum of Sexual Abuse in Daycare: An Exploratory Study." *Journal of Family Violence* 3:283–298.

———. 1990. *Understanding Child Sexual Maltreatment*. Newbury Park, CA: Sage Publications.

Finkelhor, D., Hotaling, G., and Sedlak, A. 1990. *Missing, Abducted, Runaway, and Thrownaway Children in America: Executive Summary*. Washington, D.C., U.S. Department of Justice, Office of Justice Programs (May).

Finkelhor, D., and Russell, D. 1984. "Women as Perpetrators: Review of the Evidence." In *Child Sexual Abuse: New Theory and Research*, edited by D. Finkelhor. New York: Free Press.

Finkelhor, D., and Williams, L. M. 1988. *Nursery Crimes: Sexual Abuse in Day Care*. Newbury Park, CA: Sage.

Fischer, Mary A. 1988. "Flip-Flop: Why, Four Years later, the Press is Taking a Strikingly Different Approach to the McMartin Preschool Scandal." *Los Angeles Magazine* 33 (December):85–94.

———. 1989. "A Case of Dominos?" *Los Angeles Magazine* 34 (October):126–135.

Gelman, David. 1984. "Stolen Children." *Newsweek* 103 (March 19):78–86.

Green, Arthur H. 1986. "True and False Allegations of Sexual Abuse in Child Custody Disputes." *Journal of the American Academy of Child Psychiatry* 25:449–56.

Herman, Judith Lewis. 1981. *Father-Daughter Incest*. Cambridge, MA: Harvard University Press.

Hoffman, Jan. 1990. "The Devil and Faye Yager." *Village Voice*, June 12:39.

Hollingsworth, Jan, 1986. *Unspeakable Acts*. New York: Congdon and Weed.

Humphrey, Hubert H., III. 1985. *Report on Scott County Investigations*. State of Minnesota Attorney General's Office.

Hunt, P. and Baird, M. 1990. "Children of Sex Rings." *Child Welfare* 69:195–207.

Jenkins, Philip, and Katkin, Daniel. 1988. "Protecting Victims of Child Sexual Abuse: A Case for Caution." *The Prison Journal* 68(2):25–35.

Jones, D. P. H., and McGraw, J. M. 1987. "Reliable and Fictitious Accounts of Sexual Abuse to Children." *Journal of Interpersonal Violence* 2:27–45.

Jones, D. P. H., and McQuiston, M. G. 1988. *Interviewing the Sexually Abused Child*. London: Royal College of Psychiatry.

Kelly, Susan. 1988. "Ritualistic Abuse of Children: Dynamics and Impact." *Cultic Studies Journal* 5:228–236.

———. 1989. "Stress Responses of Children to Sexual Abuse and Ritualistic Abuse in Day-Care Centers." *Journal of Interpersonal Violence* 4:501–12.

———. 1990. "Parental Stress Response to Sexual Abuse and Ritualistic Abuse of Children in Day-Care Centers." *Nursing Research* 39(1):25–29.

King, M. A., and Yuille, J. C. 1987. "Suggestibility and the Child Witness." Pp. 24–

35 in *Children's Eyewitness Memory,* edited by S. J. Ceci, M. P. Toglia, and D. F. Ross. New York: Springer-Verlag.

Krugman, R. D. 1989. "The More We Learn the Less We Know With 'Reasonable Medical Certainty'?" *Child Abuse and Neglect* 13:165–166.

Lanning, Kenneth V. 1985. "The Investigation and Prosecution of Pedophiles: An Interview with Supervisory Special Agent Kenneth V. Lanning," *Law Enforcement Coordinating Committee (LECC) Network News:* U.S. Department of Justice, Executive Office for U.S. Attorneys (Fall).

———. 1987. *Child Molesters: a Behavioral Analysis* (2nd ed.). Washington, D.C.: National Center for Missing and Exploited Children.

———. 1989a. "Satanic, Occult, Ritualistic Crime: A Law Enforcement Perspective." *Police Chief* 56(10):62–83.

———. 1989b. *Child Sex Rings: A Behavioral Analysis for Criminal Justice Professionals Handling Cases of Child Sexual Exploitation.* Washington, D.C.: National Center for Missing and Exploited Children.

Lloyd, Robin, 1976. *For Money or Love: Boy Prostitution in America.* New York: Vanguard Press.

Los Angeles County Commission for Women. 1989. "Ritual Abuse: Definitions, Glossary, the Use of Mind Control." Report of the Ritual Abuse Task Force. Los Angeles County Commission for Women, 500 W. Temple St., Los Angeles, Calif.

Los Angeles Times. 1985. "UCLA to Study Development of Victims of Alleged Abuse." October 20:II-1,9.

MacFarlane, Kee. 1985. "Diagnostic Evaluation and the Use of Videotape in Child Sexual Abuse Cases." *University of Miami Law Review* 40:135–65.

Mann, Abby, and Stevens, Glenn. 1987. "The McMartin Tapes." *California Magazine* 12 (February):57–65, 90–92, 104–105.

Manshel, Lisa. 1990. *Nap Time.* New York: Morrow.

Masson, J. M., 1984. *The Assault on Truth: Freud's Suppression of the Seduction Theory.* New York: Farrar, Straus & Giroux.

Mathews, Ruth, Matthews, June Kinder, and Speltz, Kathleen. 1989. *Female Sexual Offenders: An Exploratory Study.* Orwell, VT: The Safer Society Press.

McCann, John, Voris, Joan, Simon, Mary, and Wells, Robert. 1989. "Perianal Findings in Prepubertal Children Selected for Non-abuse: A Descriptive Study." *Child Abuse and Neglect* 13:179–193.

McCarty, L. 1986. "Mother-Child Incest: Characteristics of the Offender." *Child Welfare* 65:447–58.

McCord, Jane, Kelly, Robert, Waterman, Jill, and Oliveri, Mary Kay. 1990. "Therapist Ratings of Parental Reactions to Child Sexual Abuse: A Comparison of Mothers and Fathers," in *The Center for Child Protection (Welcomes You to the) Health Science Response to Child Maltreatment 1990,* (Program Guide). San Diego, CA: Children's Hospital and Health Center.

Moss, Debra Cassens. 1987. "Are the Children Lying?" *American Bar Association Journal* May 1:59–62.

———. 1988. " 'Real' Dolls Too Suggestive." *American Bar Association Journal* December 1:24–5.

Nathan, Debbie. 1987. "The Making of a Modern Witch Trial." *The Village Voice,* September 29:19–32.
_____. 1988a. "Day-Care Witch Trials: One Acquittal, One Conviction, and a Lot of Bad Testimony." *The Village Voice,* April 26:17.
_____. 1988b. "Victimizer or Victim?" *The Village Voice,* August 2:31–39.
_____. 1988c. "Stories Could Lead to Witch Hunt." *El Paso Times,* September 21:B6.
_____. 1989a. "False Evidence: How Bad Science Fueled the Hysteria Over Child Abuse." *Los Angeles Weekly,* April 7–13:15–19.
_____. 1989b. "The Devil and Mr. Mattox." *Texas Observer,* June 2:10–13.
_____. 1990. "The Ritual Sex Abuse Hoax." *The Village Voice,* June 12:36–44.
Nelson, Barbara J. 1984. *Making an Issue of Child Abuse.* Chicago: University of Chicago Press.
Okami, Paul. 1990. "Sociopolitical Biases in the Contemporary Scientific Literature on Adult Human Sexual Behavior with Children and Adolescents." Pp. 91–121 in *Pedophilia: Bio-Social Dimensions,* edited by J. Feierman. New York: Springer-Verlag.
Paradise, Jan. 1989. "Predictive Accuracy and the Diagnosis of Sexual Abuse: A Big Issue about a Little Tissue." *Child Abuse and Neglect* 13:169–76.
Passantino, Gretchen, Passantino, Bob, and Trott, Jon. 1989. "Satan's Sideshow." *Cornerstone Magazine* 18(90):24–28.
Pazder, L., and Smith, M. 1980. *Michelle Remembers.* New York: Congdon and Lattes.
Rabinowitz, Dorothy. 1990. "From the Mouths of Babes to a Jail Cell: Child Abuse and the Abuse of Justice: A Case Study." *Harpers* 280 (May):52–63.
Ramsey-Klawsnik, Holly. 1990. "Sexual Abuse by Female Perpetrators: Impact on Children," in *The Center for Child Protection (Welcomes You to the) Health Science Response to Child Maltreatment 1990,* (Program Guide). San Diego, CA. Children's Hospital and Health Center.
Raschke, Carl. A. 1990. *Painted Black.* San Francisco: Harper & Row.
Raskin, David, and Yuille, John. 1989. "Problems in Evaluating Interviews of Children in Sexual Abuse Cases." Pp. 184–207 in *Perspectives on Children's Testimony,* edited by S. J. Ceci, D. F. Ross, and M. P. Toglia. New York: Springer-Verlag.
Renshaw, Domeena. 1985. "When Sex Abuse is Falsely Charged." *Medical Aspects of Human Sexuality* 19(7):116–122.
Rigert, J., Peterson, D., and Marcotty, J. 1985. The Scott County Case/How it Grew; Why it Died." *Minneapolis Star and Tribune,* May 26.
Ross, A. S., and Sharpe, Ivan. 1986. "Ritualistic Child Abuse? A Presumption of Guilt." *San Francisco Examiner,* September 28, 29.
Rossen, B. 1989. "Mass Hysteria in Oude Pekela." *Issues in Child Abuse Accusations* 1:49–51.
Rubenstein, Alan M. 1990. *Report: Investigation into Breezy Point Day School.* Office of the District Attorney, Bucks County Courthouse, Doylestown, PA: 18901.
Rush, Florence. 1980. *The Best Kept Secret: Sexual Abuse of Children.* New York: McGraw-Hill.

Russell, Diana. 1983. "The Incidence and Prevalence of Intrafamilial and Extra-
familial Sexual Abuse of Female Children." *Child Abuse & Neglect* 7:133–146.
Sgroi, Suzanne, Porter, Frances Sarnacki, and Blick, Linda Canfield. 1982. "Valida-
tion of Child Sexual Abuse." Pp. 39–79 in *Handbook of Clinical Intervention in
Child Sexual Abuse*, edited by S. M. Sgroi. Lexington, MA: Lexington Books.
Shaw, David, 1990. "McMartin Verdict: Not Guilty: Where Was Skepticism in
Media?" (Jan. 19, 1A); "Reporter's Early Exclusives Triggered a Media Frenzy
(Jan. 20, 1A); "Media Skepticism Grew on McMartin Case," (Jan. 21, 1A);
"Times McMartin Coverage was Biased, Critics Charge" (Jan. 22 1A). *Los
Angeles Times,* January 19–22 (series).
Snedeker, Michael. 1988. "Servants of Satan: The Rise and Fall of the Devil in Kern
County, California" (two-part series). *California Prisoner,* April, June.
Stanley, Lawrence A. 1989. "The Child Porn Myth." *Cardozo Arts and Entertain-
ment Law Journal* 7:295–358.
Summit, Roland. 1983. "The Child Sexual Abuse Accommodation Syndrome."
Child Abuse and Neglect 7:177–193.
———. 1988. (Audio tape recording) Tape No. 4D-436-88; Fifth International
Conference on Multiple Personality/Dissociative States (Rush-Presbyterian-St.
Luke's Medical Center, Department of Psychiatry), Chicago, Illinois, October.
———. 1990. "Cults and Rituals: Relationships to Child Abuse." (audio recording
of presentation before the Health Science Response to Child Maltreatment
Conference, Children's Hospital, San Diego, January 17–20, 1990. Available
as Tape No. 200-22 from Convention Recorders, 5401 Linda Vista Road, San
Diego, CA 92110.)
Summit, Roland, and Lanning, Kenneth. 1990. "Cults and Rituals: Relationships to
Child Abuse." in *The Center for Child Protection (Welcomes You to the) Health
Science Response to Child Maltreatment 1990,* (Program Guide). San Diego,
CA: Children's Hospital and Health Center.
Supreme Court of the United States. 1990. No. 89-478. Maryland, Petitioner v.
Sandra Ann Craig. On Writ of Certiorari to the Court of Appeals of Maryland:
June 27. Opinion: p. 14n.; p. 15n.
Travin, Sheldon, Cullen, Ken, and Protter, Barry. 1990. "Female Sex Offenders:
Severe Victims and Victimizers." *Journal of Forensic Sciences* 35:140–50.
U.S. Department of Justice. 1986. *Attorney General's Commission on Pornography:
Final Report.*
Waterman, Jill, Kelly, Robert, Oliveri, Mary Kay, and McCord, Jane. 1990. "Speci-
ficity of Effects on Children of Ritualized and Non-Ritualized Sexual Abuse." In
*The Center for Child Protection (Welcomes You to the) Health Science Re-
sponse to Child Maltreatment 1990,* (Program Guide). San Diego, CA: Chil-
dren's Hospital and Health Center.
Whitcomb, Debra. 1985. "Prosecution of Child Sexual Abuse: Innovations in Prac-
tice." National Institute of Justice *Research in Brief,* Washington, D.C.
Whitcomb, Debra, Shapiro, Elizabeth R., and Stellwager, Lindsey D. 1985. *When
the Victim is a Child: Issues for Judges and Prosecutors.* Washington, D.C.:
National Institute of Justice.
Yates, A., and Musty, T. 1988. "Preschool Children's Erroneous Allegations of
Sexual Molestation." *American Journal of Psychiatry* 145:989–992.

Endangered Children in Antisatanist Rhetoric _____ 6

Joel Best

"Child molestation and murder are the two areas where even the most accepting individual becomes wary of people declaring themselves Satanists." Schwarz and Empey (1988:180)

Claims that satanists prey on children are central to contemporary antisatanist rhetoric. Critics charge satanists with kidnapping, molesting, and murdering children, and implicate satanism in child pornography, teenage suicide, and drug abuse. The child threatened by satanists is a powerful image, capable of arousing widespread concern. Antisatanists rely on such images of threatened children, both because general concern for children's well-being makes this imagery effective in mobilizing support for the antisatanist cause, and because defining the satanic threat as criminal helps obscure the religious basis of antisatanism.

The contemporary concern over satanism is notable because it extends to people outside religious groups that have been traditional audiences for such beliefs. The antisatanist movement's success in attracting a broad audience has come through redefining the issue in nonreligious terms. The movement's public claims focus on satanists as criminal, rather than spiritual or religious threats. This is a secular age, when a large proportion of the population doubts that demons and witches exist. However, the American public clearly believes in criminals, and satanism, when presented as a criminal problem, can become a frightening specter.

It is no accident, then, that antisatanists concentrate on linking satanism to serial murders, teen suicides, child abductions, sexual abuse, and child pornography. These seem to be real-world threats, the subjects of news reports, televised docudramas, and 60 Minutes segments. We know that there are serial murderers, that some teens kill themselves, and so on. If satanism is somehow linked to these crimes, then this justifies concern about satanism.

In particular, the antisatanist movement emphasizes satanists' crimes against children. This theme links antisatanists with other contemporary, broad-based, highly visible child-saving movements. During the 1970s and, particularly, the 1980s, threats to children—social problems defined in terms of deviant adults menacing child victims—attracted widespread notice (Best 1990). Reformers drew attention to child abuse, missing children, child molestation, incest, child pornography, and Halloween sadism. The press covered these topics and, in turn, public opinion polls revealed considerable concern for child victims. Because children can be seen as embodying the future, the image of the threatened child is particularly powerful in an era when many people lack confidence in their own futures. The antisatanists' frequent use of child victim imagery links their cause with general contemporary concern for endangered children. Presenting satanism as one more threat to children makes claims about children endangered by satanists seem more plausible.

Two sorts of threats to children—abuse and corruption—figure prominently in antisatanist rhetoric. These threats involve different sorts of harms; warnings about each reveal different sets of concerns about children's safety and play a different role in the movement's rhetoric. After examining each threat, I will consider the meaning of threatened children for antisatanists.

ABUSE

Abuse involves direct physical or sexual exploitation of children by satanists. The child may—but need not—be an unwilling victim. Because children are defined as naive and easily manipulated, their consent is deemed irrelevant; thus, some of what is described as abuse may involve children as willing participants. But such children are not held responsible for their actions; all blame is directed toward their exploiters.

The most dramatic tales of satanic abuse involve allegations of human sacrifice and ritual abuse by satanic cults. Antisatanists describe this as a major problem: "Dr. Al Carlise of the Utah State Prison System has estimated that between forty and sixty thousand human beings are killed through ritual homicides in the United States each year" (Johnston 1989:4). There are various explanations why these crimes go undetected: "the offenders moved the bodies after the [child-witnesses] left, the bodies were burned in portable high-temperature ovens, the bodies were put in double-decker graves under legitimately buried bodies, a mortician member of the cult disposed of the bodies in a crematorium, the offenders ate the bodies, the offenders used corpses and aborted fetuses, or the power of Satan caused the bodies to disappear" (Lanning 1989:20). Although some accounts suggest that adult cult members—"high priests" and "coven women who have been specially trained and educated"—are the ones sacrificed (Holmes 1989:93), warnings about the ritual sacrifice of innocent and unwilling victims—particularly children—are more common.

Ritual sacrifice of children is reported to take several forms. There are "altar babies"—secretly conceived, carried, and born to "breeders" for the sole purpose of sacrifice. "If the mother has not delivered the child in time for the ritual, it is taken by Cesarean section" (Michaelsen 1989:191). These are perfect crimes; because there is no record of these children's existence, it is impossible to prove that sacrifices have occurred. A satanic cult that cannot breed or enlist enough sacrificial victims can turn to kidnapping. Finding enough victims may require a division of labor: "Transporters are the people who take babies and ship them out-of-state. Spotters have the task of looking for recruits or objects" (Lundberg-Love 1989:9). Other cases involve "near-term babies murdered by their own mothers in the abortionists' clinics and then quietly taken by the Satanist nurse or doctor for his or her own use" (Michaelsen 1989:252).

Thanks to the well-publicized efforts of the missing-children movement of the early 1980s, there is a widespread perception that large numbers of children permanently disappear. These children, antisatanists suggest, may well be victims of cult sacrifices: "Officer Mitch White of the Beaumont, California Police Department estimates that *95 percent of all missing children are victims of occult-related abductions*" (Larson 1989:125—emphasis in original). The number of these abductions is controversial; the missing-children movement attracted considerable publicity by claiming that strangers abducted 50,000 children per year, but, by 1985, there were well-publicized charges that the movement had exaggerated the magnitude of the stranger-abduction problem (Best 1990). This criticism proved well founded; when the federal government released its long-awaited report on the incidence of missing children, it estimated that only 200–300 children per year were victims of "stereotypical kidnappings" by strangers (Finkelhor et al. 1990).

Yet the antisatanists' case does not depend on the number of stranger abductions. There are other sorts of missing children who can serve as sacrificial victims:

> how many runaway kids are never heard from again? What about the throw-aways that no one bothers to report missing at all? Some of the kids are taken from transient families who can no longer afford to support their little ones and believe they are giving them away to "good homes," or from unwed mothers who innocently give their little ones over to "agencies" and "reputable" doctors or lawyers who promise to find them "a loving family." (Michaelsen 1989:251)

At another point, Michaelsen suggests that some children are stolen from "illegal aliens, since they are not always likely to report the kidnapping because of fear of the authorities" (1989:191). And there are still other sources:

> Computerized sex bulletin boards list children for sale. . . . In countries where
> poverty is rampant, the selling of children can be a means of financial survival.
> Some families have adopted foreign children specifically for sexual abuse.
> Such commerce in children has made it easy for Satanists to obtain them for
> rituals. (Schwarz and Empey 1988:186)

Still, even with all the available children, human sacrifice is not an everyday
event. According to antisatanists, between major rituals featuring human
sacrifice, cult members must content themselves with ritual abuse—sexual
molestation and orgies involving children. Although some parents introduce
their children to cult practices, other victims are abused in preschools and
daycare centers. The McMartin Preschool is only the best-known of dozens
of widely dispersed cases in which childcare workers have been charged
with ritual abuse (Charlier and Downing 1988; Nathan 1990).

Accounts of ritual abuse often include a supplementary claim that satanists film or photograph the sexual exploitation of the children and distribute
these works of child pornography. Assertions of pornographic exploitation
do not seem central to the antisatanists' depiction of satanism, but they do
link the antisatanist cause to yet another secular child-saving movement.
Warnings about missing children, sexual abuse, and child pornography did
not originate with antisatanists, and the audience for those claims extended
far beyond fundamentalist believers. By the mid-1980s, there were several
popular urban legends featuring threatened children (e.g., a boy castrated in
the shopping-mall restroom; a baby kidnapped in the department store; a
girl nearly abducted by white-slavers from a shopping-mall restroom; and
LSD-laced "lick-on tattoos" being distributed to preschoolers). The fact that
these tales had wide circulation suggests that people were worried about
children. Similarly, public opinion polls revealed general, widespread concern over such threats to children. Many people believed, for instance, that
large numbers of children disappear each year. The antisatanist movement
tapped into concern about missing children, offering an explanation for this
phenomenon and other threats to children.

Evidence of Cult-Based Abuse

The notion that satanic cults constitute a major threat to children in
contemporary America is literally a conspiracy theory. Like communists,
papists, and other conspiratorial villains targeted by social movements
during earlier periods in American history, satanists are described as widespread, powerful, insidious, secretive, and virtually impossible to detect.
These qualities necessarily limit what can be known about satanists' crimes.

Law-enforcement investigations of cult satanism have failed to find proof
of ritualized cult sacrifices:

> Not only are no bodies found, but also, more important, there is no physical evidence that a murder took place. Many of those not in law-enforcement do not understand that, while it is possible to get rid of a body, it is much more difficult to get rid of the physical evidence that a murder took place, especially a human sacrifice involving sex, blood, and mutilation. (Lanning 1989:20)

Antisatanists offer various explanations for the failure of these investigations: child witnesses are young and have been traumatized, satanic conspirators have cleverly concealed their crimes, and so on. Given the lack of physical evidence, antisatanists turn to other sorts of proof. Horrifying examples— atrocity tales—of satanic crimes provide their key evidence for the satanic conspiracy's existence. The most powerful testimony comes from adult "occult survivors" who offer first-person reports of childhood exploitation or adult participation in cult activities. Books such as *Michelle Remembers* (Smith and Padzer 1980), *Suffer the Child* (Spencer 1989), and *Satan's Underground* (Stratford 1988) are regularly cited as proof of satanic crimes, as are accounts of particular crimes said to have been motivated by satanism, e.g., Sean Summers' murder of his parents, and the killings in Matamoros. In addition, antisatanists point to the statements elicited from children by social workers and therapists investigating allegations of ritual abuse in preschools.

Beyond these examples, antisatanist rhetoric often turns to authorities for evidence to support its claims. Thus, in passages quoted above, a prison official and a police officer serve as sources for statistical estimates of human sacrifices. Other experts offer a variety of arcane information about satanic practices, terminology, and symbolism. Presumably, an investigator trained to interpret these symbols can detect signs of satanic involvement in crimes. However, the range of alleged satanic symbols is very broad, encompassing several basic geometric shapes—including circles, crescents, triangles, and five-pointed stars—and such "significant colors" as red, orange, yellow, green, blue, purple, black, and white (cf. Holmes 1989; Johnston 1989).

These interpretive schemes obviously make it easy to find evidence of satanism, but such evidence falls well short of overwhelming proof and is unlikely to convince skeptics. Antisatanists must point to the power of the satanic conspiracy in explaining why they cannot document the satanists' crimes in more detail. For instance, examples of satanic crimes tend to implicate disaffected adolescents (e.g., Sean Summers), while antisatanists often insist that satanism attracts powerful, high-status adults: "Cult Satanists are extremely secretive and difficult to spot. They frequently prove to be those considered the pillars of society: doctors, lawyers, district attorneys, judges, schoolteachers, worship leaders, even ministers" (Michaelsen 1989:258–259). And if some charges against satanists seem implausible, this itself can serve as evidence of a sort: "Satanic cults deliberately fabricate preposterous forms of child victimization, knowing that the more unthinkable their atrocity, the less likely the victim will be believed" (Larson 1989:126).

Thus, antisatanist rhetoric about abuse juxtaposes child victims—vulnerable, innocent, "little ones"—against their exploiters—powerful adults who belong to an even more powerful conspiracy. Perfect villains abuse perfect victims:

> Do things like these really happen? Is it possible that there are really human beings who are capable of such deliberate and calculated assault against the bodies, minds, and spirits of innocent little children? Why would they do such things? The answer is really quite simple: they do it because they worship Satan. They do it because they are evil. . . . It is precisely because children are so pure and precious in the sight of God that they offer them in sacrifice to Satan. (Michaelsen 1989:250)

Linking satanism to terrible crimes serves to make antisatanists' charges seem plausible and, perhaps equally important, secular. The publicity garnered by campaigns against child abuse, sexual abuse, child pornography, missing children, and other threats to children—campaigns that tended to typify those problems in terms of atrocity tales—has accustomed the public to claims that large number of children suffer horrifying mistreatment at the hands of adults. By highlighting stories of kidnapping, human sacrifice, ritual abuse, child pornography, and other satanic abuse, antisatanists portray satanism as part—perhaps a major part—of the crime wave against children. Although they may make reference to children's spirits and children's special status in the eyes of God, claims about satanic abuse usually downplay religion. However, the religious roots of antisatanism become clearer in warnings about popular culture's corrupting influences.

CORRUPTION

American culture idealizes children as innocent and pure. These are precarious virtues, which constantly must be defended from corruption, as the title of Tipper Gore's (1987) book, *Raising PG Kids in an X-Rated Society*, suggests. Child pornography and other forms of abuse are inherently corrupting, but not all corruption involves criminal exploitation. In particular, antisatanists often single out popular culture as a legal, yet corrupting influence on children.

Fears about popular culture's power to corrupt have a long history (Gilbert 1986). Society's innocents—children and, in an earlier era, women—are thought to lose their moral bearings through exposure to the wrong images. Nineteenth-century antiprostitution crusaders argued that reading "yellow-backed novels" could turn a good girl bad. The twentieth century has been marked by campaigns to protect children from the damaging influences of movies, television, rock music, comic books, and most other forms of popular culture. Antisatanism is only the most recent campaign to exploit fears of the media's powers.

Discussions of satanism in the mass media usually begin with heavy metal music. This is an obvious target, since several well-known bands use satanic imagery in their lyrics, album covers, stage sets, and costumes. This can be seen as simply the most recent escalation of the rebellious posture that has always been rock's stock in trade. Each generation needs new symbols of revolt; after all, the blue jeans, leather jackets, and duck-tail haircuts that frightened adults in the 1950s are unlikely to phase parents of today's teenagers. However, heavy metal, with its unfamiliar sounds, bizarre costumes, and offensive lyrics, is well calculated to disturb even the formerly hip.

For antisatanists, heavy metal is threatening, not merely because it is grotesque, but because it sometimes endorses, even celebrates satanism. It is possible to quote satanic sentiments from song lyrics and interviews with musicians, and one can point to instances of corrupted youth—metal fans who have gone on to dabble in satanism. The most frightening examples involve heavy metal listeners who have killed others—or themselves. Popular culture's ability to inspire adolescent suicide is featured in antisatanists' attacks on another favorite target—"Dungeons & Dragons" and other fantasy role-playing games. Here atrocity tales and statistics (e.g., the frequently-cited claim that D & D has been implicated in several hundred teen suicides) are essential, since the crusaders must counter the obvious defense that "it's only a game" with proof of fantasy role-playing's corrupting power.

Although claims linking heavy metal music and "Dungeons & Dragons" to specific cases of adolescents who have turned to violence or suicide are the most visible elements in the antisatanists' campaign against corruption, less-publicized charges reveal more about the movement. Consider, for example, the ouija board, a familiar toy that antisatanists redefine as a powerful satanist tool:

> I have spoken with those who have had close personal associations with Satanism who tell me that some Satanists do indeed use the Ouija board for the purpose of divination. Several police officers have confirmed this fact to me. At least one self-styled Satanist youth gang in Southern California used the Ouija board to select the name of the gang's next victim. (Michaelsen 1989:67)

But the danger is not simply that satanists might use ouija boards:

> the simple fact is that *Ouija is NOT a neutral device. Nor is it a toy. It is a dangerous spiritualistic tool designed to contact spirit beings and develop psychic abilities.* (Michaelsen 1989:64—emphasis in original)

Without exception, those who have asked the board to disclose its source of information have received the response: "demons, devils, Satan, Beelzebub, Lucifer," or a satanic equivalent. Either unconscious assumptions were made by the players, triggering muscular responses to the question, or the reply was truthful. If the latter, the Ouija board is a spiritually dangerous tool of evil invasion. (Larson 1989:57)

Charges of this sort reveal the religious assumptions underpinning the antisatanist movement. Thus, Michaelsen (1989:65) warns that ouija board use can lead to "possession by demonic spirits," and Larson (1989:57) notes that God warned the Israelites against divination. Similarly, religious concerns become explicit in some discussions of heavy metal and fantasy role-playing games: "when an artist sings or speaks of hedonism, licentiousness, or any deviant, felonious deed, he honors the devil. . . . The cassette or CD player in too many teens' rooms is an altar to evil, dispensing the devil's devices" (Larson 1989:81). And Maddux (1986:53) explains: "the D & D advocate . . . should realize that these types of games are based on real principles of witchcraft and magic, and that those who practice witchcraft suffer the danger of being under God's retribution."

The antisatanist movement's most public charges focus on satanism's ties to criminal behavior—kidnappings, murders, and the like. Consider a claim that some youths exposed to, say, satanic heavy metal are influenced to adopt deviant values and turn to deviant behavior. One can accept such a claim without making assumptions about Satan's existence or role on earth. But warnings that ouija boards invite demonic possession or that divination, witchcraft, and magic are forbidden by biblical injunction are a very different matter; accepting such claims requires initial acceptance of a particular cosmology, a set of religious beliefs.

To fundamentalist Christians, much contemporary popular culture seems corrupting, not merely because it is worldly, but because it invokes, even celebrates, non-Christian elements of the occult. For instance, *Masters of the Universe*, the early 1980s sword and sorcery television cartoon series, generated sales of a billion dollars in toys and other licensed products. Fundamentalists warned that many characters in the series had magical powers, that programs contained frequent references to the occult. Moreover,

The name, *Masters of the Universe*, implies that these characters are superior to humans and that they are on the same plane as God . . . children today lift up *He-Man* as the children of Israel lifted up and worshipped pagan gods. (Phillips 1986:91)

Although these critics did not charge that *Masters of the Universe* offered a direct means of invoking spirits, they did argue that the toys and programs might perform the initial role in spiritual corruption of the young: "The seeds of *subtle deception* were planted in the shows and books, but the child's own imagination waters the seed until it grows into a fascination with the occult" (Phillips 1986:94—emphasis in original).

Once we accept these critics' definition of occult, it is impossible to argue that occult imagery played no role in *Masters of the Universe,* given the show's frequent references to demons, sorceresses, and good and evil magic. And *Masters of the Universe* was not unique; the 1980s saw a proliferation of toy lines linked to cartoon series—what were, in effect, half-hour commercials for the toys. The series aimed at boys frequently featured magical spells (a device that let producers inject plenty of action into the plots without crossing the line into the physical violence deplored by liberal critics).

But the fundamentalist critique does not stop with these series. The gentler, pastel fantasies aimed at young girls also come under attack. This includes *Smurfs* ("constantly using occult symbols" [Phillips 1986:77]), *Gummie Bears* ("filled with magic and the occult" [p. 78]), *Care Bears* ("play an almost Godlike, or at least an angelic, role when helping out children in trouble and in establishing their own religious order and rituals" [p. 82]), and *Rainbow Brite* ("any toy or cartoon that employs symbolisms from the *New Age Movement* [rainbows] is also in contradiction to Scripture" [p. 83—emphasis in original]).

The overt message in attacks on heavy metal music and fantasy role-playing games is that some popular culture can corrupt some youths, causing criminal violence. But the mechanism of corruption is rarely made clear when antisatanists present these claims in the secular media. However, indictments against heavy metal, fantasy role-playing games, and a wide range of other forms of corrupting popular culture are available in books from religious presses. These works make it clear that the central nature of corruption is fostering belief and practices involving non-Christian entities and forces.

Religious concern with popular culture's corrupting influence on children is not new. Rock music has been a more-or-less constant target of the fundamentalist youth ministry for 40 years, as shown in periodic news reports of rock records being burned in church parking lots. But much contemporary rhetoric depicts popular culture's corrupting impact in secular terms, linking popular culture aimed at the young to a large-scale criminal conspiracy of satanists.

THE THREATENED CHILD'S IMPORTANCE

Antisatanism is a religious movement. To a fundamentalist Christian audience, the movement's warnings against all occult involvements may seem familiar, sensible, correct. But we live in a secular age. Large numbers of Americans doubt the Devil's existence; no doubt an even larger proportion would question claims that "demons can and frequently do attach themselves to occult tools and books" (Michaelsen 1989:284). Such warnings are likely to be taken seriously by a small proportion of the population, but ignored or ridiculed by the great majority of people. Fundamentalist reformers too often find themselves "preaching to the choir." They seek ways to spread their message to a broader audience.

One method is to redefine the issue in secular terms. A society that believes it is bedeviled by crime may entertain claims that the Devil lurks behind criminals, or at least that some criminals see themselves as doing the Devil's work. Thus, evangelist Bob Larson (1989:31) cites an estimate that "up to 70 percent of all crimes committed by teens under the age of seventeen are motivated by involvement in the occult." If the crime problem is really an occult problem, then occult problems should concern everyone.

Statistical estimates help give the impression that occult crime is a sizable problem. Geraldo Rivera suggests:

> there are over one million Satanists in this country. The majority of them are linked in a highly organized, very secret network. . . . The odds are that this is happening in your town. (Investigative New Group 1987:2)

Such frightening statistics are commonplace:

> In 1946, there were an estimated 10,000 covens in the United States; 48,000 were reported in 1976. In 1985, that figure was estimated at 135,000. (*College Security Report* 1989:5)

> The International Coalition Against Violent Entertainment estimates that 12 percent of the movies produced in the United States can be classified as satanic horror films. (Lanning 1989:23)

We know that crime is common. If satanism is linked to criminality, and if satanism is widespread, then satanism warrants serious attention.

This is especially true if we typify satanic crimes in terms of violence against children. The practice of accusing one's opponents of murdering or otherwise mistreating children has a long history; the centuries-old myth that Jews practiced ritual murder of children is perhaps the most familiar example (Moore 1987). Although these would be serious charges in any society, the image of the threatened child may be especially powerful in modern America, where children are characterized in the most sentimental terms, as priceless, innocent beings (Wishy 1968; Zelizer 1985). This sort of sentimentality has been central to much of the recent rhetoric about child abuse, missing children, and other threats to children, including, of course, warnings of abuse and corruption by satanists (Best 1990).

The danger posed by redefining a religious problem (satanism) in these secular terms (ritual abuse and the like) is that the imagery of the threatened child is so powerful and compelling. Who can resist taking the children's side, joining the cause of child protection? The parents involved in several ritual abuse cases organized around the slogan "Believe the Children," while an article on the clinical problems posed by ritual abuse concludes:

> The decision concerning one's belief in the existence of this phenomenon has to rest, at this time, on an understanding of and concern for the children whose voice society has yet to acknowledge as reality. Learning how to listen for indications of abuse necessitates an identification with a frightened child, even when that child finds him or herself hidden within an apparently well function-ing adult. (Cozolino 1989:137)

But in most cases, the children's voice is heard through their interpreters— the therapists who interview child victims and adult survivors—who, through those interviews, extract the damning testimony of satanic abuse. That testimony is sometimes bolstered by yet another sentimental claim about childhood—that children will tell only the truth about such experi-ences. Too often, there is no other evidence, unless we count the antisatan-ists' claims about the nature of the satanic conspiracy.

Thus, we return to the key issue. Antisatanists depend on images of children endangered by satanists because those images are so powerful. Our horror at the notion of widespread ritual abuse of innocent children is likely to shortcircuit any critical examination of these terrible claims. But we must remember that history contains plenty of examples of frightening rhetoric sparking what in retrospect seem to have been irrational campaigns of societal reaction. The rhetoric of antisatanism—particularly its emotional appeals about threatened children and its casual standards for proof— deserves our careful attention.

ACKNOWLEDGMENT

Loy Bilderback made helpful comments about an earlier draft.

REFERENCES

Best, Joel. 1990. *Threatened Children: Rhetoric and Concern About Child-Victims.* Chicago: University of Chicago Press.
Charlier, Tom, and Downing, Shirley. 1988. "Justice Abused: A 1980s Witch-Hunt" (series). *Memphis Commercial Appeal* (Jan.).

College Security Report. 1989. "Satanic Groups and Cults on Campus." November:5–11.

Cozolino, Louis J. 1989. "The Ritual Abuse of Children: Implications for Clinical Practice and Research." *Journal of Sex Research* 26:131–38.

Finkelhor, David, Hotaling, Gerald, and Sedlak, Andrea. 1990. *Missing, Abducted, Runaway, and Thrownaway Children in America.* Washington: Office of Juvenile Justice and Delinquency Prevention.

Gilbert, James. 1986. *A Cycle of Outrage: America's Reaction to the Juvenile Delinquent in the 1950s.* New York: Oxford University Press.

Gore, Tipper. 1987. *Raising PG Kids in an X-Rated Society.* Nashville: Abingdon.

Holmes, Ronald M. 1989. *Profiling Violent Crimes: An Investigative Tool.* Newbury Park, CA: Sage.

Investigative New Group. 1987. "Geraldo: Satanic Cults and Children" (transcript), November 19.

Johnston, Jerry. 1989. *The Edge of Evil: The Rise of Satanism in North America.* Dallas: Word.

Lanning, Kenneth V. 1989. *Child Sex Rings: A Behavioral Analysis.* Washington: National Center for Missing and Exploited Children.

Larson, Bob. 1989. *Satanism: The Seduction of America's Youth.* Nashville: Thomas Nelson.

Lundberg-Love, Paula K. 1989. "Update on Cults Part I: Satanic Cults." *Family Violence Bulletin* 5:9–10.

Maddux, Bob. 1986. *Fantasy Explosion.* Ventura, CA: Regal.

Michaelsen, Johanna. 1989. *Like Lambs to the Slaughter.* Eugene, OR: Harvest House.

Moore, R. I. 1987. *The Formation of a Persecuting Society: Power and Deviance in Western Europe, 950–1250.* New York: Basil Blackwell.

Nathan, Debbie. 1990. "The Ritual Sex Abuse Hoax." *Village Voice* (June 12):36–44.

Phillips, Phil. 1986. *Turmoil in the Toybox.* Lancaster, PA: Starburst.

Schwarz, Ted, and Empey, Duane. 1988. *Satanism: Is Your Family Safe?* Grand Rapids, MI: Zondervan.

Smith, Michelle, and Pazder, Lawrence. 1980. *Michelle Remembers.* New York: Congdon and Lattes.

Spencer, Judith. 1989. *Suffer the Child.* New York: Pocket Books.

Stratford, Lauren. 1988. *Satan's Underground.* Eugene, OR: Harvest House.

Wishy, Bernard. 1968. *The Child and the Republic.* Philadelphia: University of Pennsylvania Press.

Zelizer, Viviana A. 1985. *Pricing the Priceless Child.* New York: Basic Books.

Satanic Cults, Satanic Play: Is "Dungeons & Dragons" a Breeding Ground for the Devil?

7

Daniel Martin and Gary Alan Fine

Despite its reputation for airy, insubstantial content, the history of leisure activities demonstrates that play can have a significant public policy impact. As Olmsted (1988) suggests in his study of controversial leisure, diverse leisure activities, including billiards, parachuting, surfing, pinball, theater, amateur archeology, horse racing, butterfly collecting, motorcycling, target shooting, and dancing, have been targeted by their opponents as morally disreputable, and even necessary to ban or limit. Stepping slightly further afield, one finds such widely condemned activities as sexual swinging, recreational drug use, or cock fights. In each case moral entrepreneurs claim that the activities permanently harm the participants, on-lookers, the environment, or the social system itself. Debate over *Dungeons & Dragons* is part of the lengthy history of controversial leisure. Leisure tends to be particularly controversial when the activities are widely engaged in by children or adolescents: legitimate leisure for adults, such as drinking alcoholic beverages, is illegitimate for those "under age."

Our study examines rhetorical claims by those on both sides of the argument that fantasy role-playing games are harmful, and are connected to satanic possession. Claims made by *Dungeons & Dragons* opponents that fantasy game play is an occult activity appear at first glance to be consistent with the imagery developed by gamers themselves: dragons, sorcerers, elves, slayers, and soothsayers are part and parcel of the mystical, enchanted, dangerous voyages that players embark on during the game. Thus, the claims have a surface plausibility. According to these claims-making groups, because such play represents "consorting with the Devil," one should expect insidious and diabolical consequences, corrupting naive players who become involved in the game without knowing its dangerous effects. These claims, which gamers dismiss, are ironic in that critics wish to give the games more importance than do the games' defenders. Players argue that these are only "games" having little effect on players, but critics see them as powerful tools of education and socialization. These positions are typical in cases of controversial leisure: participants are, to some degree, placed on the defensive, saying that these activities are "only" fun; their opponents find significance in the activities. It is ironic that prior to the critics' charge, participants recruit others by arguing that these activities promote skills and training, and are worthy of public notice.

Claims confronting fantasy gamers resemble satanic cult rumors spread by radical-right Christian organizations (Victor 1989a; 1989b). Many groups attacking *Dungeons & Dragons* also are associated with fundamentalist Christian sects in the United States and Canada. Organizations that have explicitly attacked *Dungeons & Dragons* include Media Spotlight, Chick publications, Pro-Family Forum, Christian Life Ministries, and The Daughters of St. Paul; two primary claims-making organizations are NCTV (the National Coalition on Television Violence) and BADD (Bothered About *Dungeons & Dragons*). The last group is self-consciously modeled on MADD (Mothers Against Drunk Driving); like MADD, BADD was founded by a mother who lost her child—in this case to a suicide that she claims was caused by *Dungeons & Dragons*. Although BADD has had nowhere near the impact of MADD, it has become the primary media source for materials that oppose fantasy games. A variety of localized, less visible religious and civic groups, including school boards, parents' groups, and ministerial councils, offer similar claims. Opposing these moral entrepreneurs are coteries of gamers (CAR-PGa [The Committee for the Advancement of Role-Playing Games]) and organized gaming interests (Game Manufacturer's Association, an industry trade organization), which offer counterclaims through various gamers' magazines and publications.

We draw most of our evidence from various claims and counterclaims, and from the second author's 18-month ethnographic and interview study of several fantasy gaming groups, published as *Shared Fantasy: Role-Playing Games as Social Worlds* (Fine 1983). We begin by briefly describing fantasy role-playing games, and then examining three related claims about dangers of *Dungeons & Dragons*, most popular of the fantasy role-playing games: the direct link to satanism, the possibility of mind control, and the danger of excessive violence.

FANTASY ROLE-PLAYING GAMES

A "[fantasy] role-playing game" has been defined as "any game which allows a number of players to assume the roles of imaginary characters and operate with some degree of freedom in an imaginary environment" (Lortz 1979:36). Most such games are based on science fiction settings or, like *Dungeons & Dragons*, on scenarios that derive from medieval European fantasy. The games represent a hybrid of war games and educational simulations. TSR Hobbies, producer of *D & D*, describes its structure in a brochure written for hobby store owners:

> While one of the participants creates the whole world in which the adventures are to take place, the balance of the players—as few as two or as many as a dozen or more—create "characters" who will travel about in this make-believe world, interact with its peoples, and seek the fabulous treasures of magic and precious items guarded by dragons, giants, werewolves, and hundreds of other fearsome things. The game organizer, the participant who creates the whole and moderates these adventures, is known as the *Dungeon Master*, or simply the *DM*. The other players have game *personae*—fighters, magic users, thieves, clerics, elves, dwarves, or what have you—who are known as *player characters*. Player characters have known attributes which are initially determined by rolling the dice. . . . These attributes [e.g., strength, charisma, intelligence] help to define the role and limits of each character. . . . [T]here is neither an end to the game nor any winner. Each session of play is merely an episode in an ongoing "world." . . . Players pit their wit and imagination against the creations of their DM, so *D & D* is basically a cooperative game where the group teams to defeat the hostile environment developed by the Dungeon Master. (TSR Hobbies 1979:1)

This role-playing is oral, and does not involve physical activity. Often players or the DM must roll dice to determine the outcome of battles or other encounters among players, or between players and hostile creatures. These dice rolls determine who is killed or the extent of injury, and provide some formal structure for an otherwise very flexible game.

CONSORTING WITH THE DEVIL

Whatever else they may be for crusading groups, fantasy role-playing games, especially *Dungeons & Dragons*, represent a decisive moral realm through which Satan gains control of individuals and unravels the social fabric of communities. Dealing with the Devil is a precarious business. One may find that a deal has been struck without one's full knowledge or consent of the transaction. Not all demons show their cloven hooves. Unlike university researchers, the Devil rarely provides "informed consent" in bargaining for a soul. Critics claim that such deals may be struck by fantasy game players whose engrossment in *Dungeons & Dragons* makes them unwitting and, hence, vulnerable customers to this salesmanship. Assessing involvement of the Prince of Darkness depends ultimately on the type of "plausibility structure" (Berger 1969) that one employs. Our belief that fantasy role-playing games are not, as a rule, havens for Satanists, is not proven, but is based on our faith in the secular character of middle-class, adolescent leisure in late twentieth-century America.

Claims of demonic involvement are often made by *D & D* opponents who frame fantasy game playing as an occult activity. On the cover of one of BADD's promotional pamphlets, for example, appears the picture and signature of Darren Molitor, an ex-player of *Dungeons & Dragons;* the caption below reads, "This young man was convicted of killing a young girl with whom he played Dungeons and Dragons." Although no further claims are made that involvement in fantasy game play was a contributing factor in this tragedy, the tract describes the game as,

> very possessive, addictive and evil. Evil may sound wrong or peculiar to explain a game, but there is no other way to describe it. It is a device of Satan to lure us away from God. It is occult. (Molitor n.d.: n.p.)

Another opponent of fantasy games suggests that we are witnessing a battle between good and evil:

> *Dungeons & Dragons* are games of fantasy that open up a whole realm of occult to players. . . . These are games that Satan has connived to bring about war on God's Kingdom. (*St. Paul Pioneer Press* 1984:C5)

The publisher of *Dungeons & Dragons,* TSR, met these charges with disclaimers that framed fantasy game playing as innocuous, but also admitted that some companies had included unsavory scenes in games. One game apparently calls for "fat of a child that has been dug up from the grave," leading Dieter Sturm, corporate public relations director for TSR Inc., to claim that "some role-playing games on the market I wouldn't even touch" (*St. Paul Pioneer Press* 1984:C5).

The claim of satanic ties also appeared in several testimonies by citizens of Putnam, Connecticut where involvement in *Dungeons & Dragons* allegedly precipitated the suicide of a local youth.

> "It is another of Satan's ploys to pollute and destroy our children's minds," said Kathy Dewey, one of nearly a dozen parents who Tuesday night urged the Board of Education to ban the playing of the game at Putnam High School. . . . "You have authorized Russian roulette," the Rev. Robert O. Bakke, pastor of the Faith Bible Evangelical Free Church, told the board. "Over the months to come there will be many thrilling and harmless clicks of the gun as Dungeons and Dragons is held to the heads of our young people. But another deadly explosion will come." *New York Times* (1985:B1)

The fact that these games are played in and sponsored by public high schools emphasizes to these critics the secular nature of schools their children attend, and lack of control parents have over education of their children. Not surprisingly, BADD proudly enumerates the schools that have removed *Dungeons & Dragons*—schools in all parts of the country: Vermont, New York, Virginia, Colorado, Wisconsin, and California. The movement to ban fantasy games in public schools resembles other attempts by parents to gain more control over their children's educations, as in battles about textbooks and school libraries.

To counter charges that their games promote occultism, TSR Hobbies offers an 18-point code of ethics that states:

> The use of religion in TSR products is to assist in clarifying the struggle between good and evil. Actual current religions are not to be depicted, ridiculed or attacked in any way that promotes disrespect. Ancient or mythological religions, such as those prevalent in ancient Grecian, Roman, American Indian and Norse societies, may be portrayed in their historic roles (in compliance with this code of ethics). (*St. Paul Pioneer Press* 1984:C5)

Dieter Sturm contends that when TSR sought to mass market *Dungeons & Dragons*, they deliberately attempted "to make the game wholesome for the family situation" (*St. Paul Pioneer Press* 1984:C5). The game provides a fantasy structure, like an empty glass into which all kinds of libations might be poured. The company's claimed intent does not, of course, limit uses to which its games might be put.

MIND CONTROL

The claim that *D & D* is a form of mind control that draws individuals away from a moral community is a recurrent theme in critics' warnings. The inimical effects that derive from fantasy play are defined as a result of both its imaginative dimension and the illusory and mystical quality of compulsion to play the game:

> It is very possible for the subconscious mind to overpower the conscious mind. Suddenly you are no longer in total control of your mind. The "fantasy game" becomes a "reality game." You begin to live it for real. Everything you do, or say involves or associates to the game itself. You no longer play the game for enjoyment, you must have it (play it) just like a person on drugs, alcohol or tobacco must have them. It is an addiction and your mind is under the control of the game. It is possessed by the game. . . . It has happened to many college students that have committed suicide or done some serious bodily harm to themselves and/or others. The destruction it can cause to the mind and soul is incredible. (Molitor n.d.: n.p.)

The mind is, from this perspective, fragilely tied to the core self, capable of being untethered. The fact that the game is played "entirely in the mind" gives it a power that other leisure activities do not have. Fine (1983) found that gamers made similar claims, but they were conscious exaggerations, given temporal and normative boundaries of actual fantasy game play.

Several players within groups that Fine observed related stories of others who had become so thoroughly engrossed in fantasy play that they had difficulty retreating back into everyday life and conventional morality. One player commented:

> I know a few people . . . who seem to think that the fantasy world is real and that the real world is fantasy. . . . They seem to think that *D & D* is real; that's their whole life—nothing else, and that this world is just something we put up with in order to go to these games, which to me is a very scary thing. (Fine 1983:218)

Because thorough engrossment and theatricality during fantasy play makes for a good game, a strong identification with one's fantasy character is desirable. Critics argue that it is precisely this engrossment in imaginative play that leads to overattachment to the *personae ficta* of fantasy games, displacing normative behavior in everyday life.

It is, however, both the engrossing quality of the play and the folklore that surrounds this enrapturing engrossment that give the game its "mystical" and subcultural quality. Games are locations for leisure "flow" (Csikszent-mihalyi 1990), that is, it is the *experience* of the game situation as mystical that helps give the game this quality. What cautions against an over-emphasis on this dimension is the fact that some games turn out to be quite slow and boring, leading players to search for more interesting ones at other tables. Boring games lack "flow," and as Goffman (1961) claims, a lack of "fun" in games is a legitimate excuse for terminating the experience. Thus, although the "best" games, according to gamers, are engrossing, there is no guarantee that all games will have this feature.

For the vast majority of players, the "mind control" of the game has temporal limits to it, and is under the gamer's control. It is rare for a gamer to become so engrossed that reality cannot intrude.

VIOLENT FANTASY

Particularly alarming to all of the crusading groups is the use of violence during fantasy role-playing in *Dungeons & Dragons*. Although violence does not automatically equate to satanism, the belief in bloody, violent satanic rituals certainly feeds into this concern. The personal testimony cited in promotional literature by BADD also describes violence:

> Not only is the game based on magic and the supernatural, it involves violence, serious violence! The type of violence not allowed on TV. There is hack and slash murder, rape, thievery, pillaging and terrorism. And in the game it is natural and expected for a character to do those things. A character must, at least, murder and rob in order to survive. (Molitor n.d.: n.p.)

Critics are quite correct that content of some fantasy role-playing games can be extremely violent, although effects of this type of violence is a matter for debate—a similar concern is raised about pornography, or violence on television—namely, the hypothetical intrusion of fantasy violence and/or sexual activity into real life. The most violent episodes in *Dungeons & Dragons* appear to occur in all-male groups. Female fantasy gamers are rare and considered by some male gamers to be an inhibiting force to fantasy play, especially where this play includes violent episodes such as the rape of a nonplayer character. Fine recounts an episode in field notes taken while observing play in *Empire of the Petal Throne* (1983:70):

> In a game of EPT our party comes across six Avanthe worshipers [female warrior-priestesses, enemies of our party] in their refractory. The leader (a nonplayer character, played by the referee) places a spell on us, but I remove the spell before it can work. Tom says, laughing loudly: "I will dive over and grab their turdy necks. (He really looks as if he is eager to kill). Tom yells: "I'm screaming at them, 'Stop and be raped, you Goddamn women!' " After all six are killed, Tom gets excited, suggests: "Let's get gems, jewels and panties." Later in the game when we meet another group of Avanthe priestess-warriors, Tom comments: "No fucking women in a blue dress [sic] are going to scare me . . . I'll fight. They'll all be dead men."
> Jack: Men?
> Roger: Is that your definition of a woman, a dead man?
> Tom: A *dead* man.

The play frame developed during fantasy games defines what would be brutal and savage attacks in real life as part of a typical routine of fantasy role-playing. Outside the game context, gamers are not overtly aggressive (Fine 1983:44). Yet, some players obviously do act out aggressive impulses within the fantasy game framework. It is precisely because this framework legitimates such action that "killing" within a game, by even espoused pacifists, becomes intelligible. To understand the definition of these attacks within the play frame of the game, it is crucial to take the perspectives of gamers themselves, to see these events through their eyes, and then to ask who or what is being served through these events.

Gamers rely on a variety of rhetorical strategies to discount criticism, seemingly plausible, that they are overinvolved deviants looking for a bloody fix. First, although gamers may be oriented toward killing and death, fantasy play in the game embodies the struggle between "good" and "evil" where "evil" is defined and personified as a fantasy character that must be exterminated. Thus, good remains good, even when characters, like theatrical performers, portray "evil." Second, some gamers claim that games have cathartic effects. One player explained his participation as a means of releasing pent up hostilities:

Unfortunately you get a lot of people that think that we are warmongers, and are the type you know, "give us a weapon and we will kill, pillage and everything," and in actuality, myself, I don't want to enter the military. As far as I'm concerned we should ban all weapons. You know, I'd rather not have them, I'll play my games. You can simulate; try and get your hostilities out that way. (Fine 1983:43)

Third, gamers point to the games' value in teaching personal self-control: "I think a lot of people through playing war games begin to get a much better sense of sadism, militarism, and thereby can limit it in themselves" (Fine 1983:43).

To accept these claims without further analysis would be "bad faith"; we should view these denials with a critical "eye." Gamers who engage in violence during a game may have a relatively high level of aggression that they need to express, and may choose to express it in this way.

KILLING, SUICIDE, AND ENACTMENTS OF SELF

A key claim made by moral entrepreneurs who oppose fantasy games is that involvement in *D & D* has led numerous adolescent players to violent and self-destructive action, a theme easily connected to the machinations of Mephistopheles. A BADD promotional booklet, *Dungeons & Dragons: Witchcraft, Suicide and Violence*, for example, asserts,

With 6,500 teens committing suicide and over 50,000 attempts every year, we cannot afford to overlook a "game" that teaches the philosophies of witch-craft, Satan worship and a cult-like institution, not to mention specific suicide phrases. What we found in this book can hardly be considered a "healthy release for suppressed hostilities" or "of educational value" in a positive sense.

Subsequent pages of the pamphlet list the names of suicide victims: "The below listed adolescents had one common denominator: ALL WERE HEAVI-LY INVOLVED IN DUNGEONS & DRAGONS." Many of these "cases" are hotly debated, as those who defend the game are eager to blame poor parenting, drug abuse, depression, or other more "serious" external forces, and to deny any moral (and legal) responsibility to the game. Presumably each youngster played *D & D,* and did many other things as well. Specifying a single cause for a death should be approached with some care, although it is often treated as a matter of moral football, as critics attempt to "run up the score," while defenders attempt to block these attempts. Also, it is impossi-ble to know how many suicides were *prevented* through lonely teens finding a social community in the world of fantasy gaming.

Gaming proponents tend to argue that claims about the extent of game-caused suicides are typically bereft of "facts." The Game Manufacturer's

Association (1988) responded with counterclaims to accusations that its games perpetuate violence and aberrant behavior. These counterclaims included a "case-by-case analysis" of suicides alleged by moral entrepreneurs to be connected to *D & D* playing. For instance, the fact that BADD was founded by Pat Pulling, mother of a suicide victim who was a *Dungeons & Dragons* player, is often emphasized, and is used by gaming supporters to launch attacks on BADD volunteers as bad parents and their children as mentally disturbed. This could be considered "blaming the victim" (see Pulling 1989:86):

> Her [the mother] story is that Bink [the son] had been playing *D & D* at school under a "gifted" program and that the teacher who ran the game as the Dungeon Master had put a "curse" on Bink (his character) to make him (his character) a homicidal killer. Bink took his life to keep from killing his family. . . , and (they say) left SIX suicide notes explaining this . . . She goes on to claim that Bink was a well-liked boy with no emotional problems. Now there is where there are difficulties. She would *have* to claim this to save face (hers is a fundamentalist household) rather than to get at what the real problem was. (Savoie, n.d.—emphasis in original)

Other observers claim that BADD's founder selectively "edits out" evidence disconfirming the organization's claims when reporting newspaper accounts of suicides:

> In the section of the article Pulling did not print the following appeared: " 'He had a lot of problems anyway that weren't associated with the game,' said Victoria Rockecharlie, another classmate of Pulling's in the Talented and Gifted program." Though she presents herself as taken utterly unawares by her son's death, at least in BADD publications, Mrs. Pulling was aware of her son's problems. During a seminar at the North Colorado/South Wyoming Detective Association 9–12 Sept 86 (and as reported in file 18) she said her son had been displaying "lycanthropic" tendencies like running around the backyard barking. Within the month before his death, 19 rabbits Bink had raised were inexplicably torn apart, and a cat was found disembowled with a knife. It seems clear that Bink Pulling was a disturbed youth. (Stackpole 1989.272)

Thus, game supporters marshal their own set of "facts" and interpretations. They suggest that Mrs. Pulling is a "fundamentalist" with a seriously disturbed child. She describers herself and her son as Jewish (see Pulling 1989:5), and claims that Bink was a "really neat son," with "excellent grades" (Pulling 1989:2). She further contends that her opponents have made threatening phone calls, even including death threats (Pulling 1989:11).

It should be no surprise that characters that *D & D* players have lovingly developed in previous games would be ones with which they might strongly identify and conjure up in subsequent games. It makes sense that players care about their characters. Yet key questions remain: to what degree do gamers see their characters as extensions of themselves, and, conversely, are there likely to be personal changes, perhaps destructive changes, resulting from the role-playing of their own fantasy characters?

In interviews with several gamers, Fine found that D & D players differed in the degree to which they identified with their fantasy roles during the course of play:

> GAF: How much do you identify with your character?
> Barry: I don't even think of my character at all, all I think about is myself in the situation, but the question really isn't how much you identify with the character, but how much you identify with yourself. . . . I still play my same character regardless of who I roll up. (Fine 1983:207)

and another player,

> I have seen few people who role-play. . . . When we play you can see no difference between that person—who he really is—and the [character] that he has taken on. (Fine 1983:208)

Few if any players are able to render performances bereft of vestiges of their nonfantasy selves. Although players who play themselves may be invested in the game, one could not claim that the character has taken over their lives. In that sense they are immune from Satan's beckoning. On the other hand, because they are playing *themselves,* any harm to their character may be painful to bear, and could in rare cases lead to clinical depression or suicide. Most *Dungeons & Dragons* characters are role-played as, and infused with, the character of one's nonfantasy self. Even the person who is an imaginative genius at role-playing still draws upon a corpus of biographical or experiential insights. As one player explains:

> I never forget my character. You always kind of play your character in the way you think he might . . . and they're usually traits that you have . . . but you're playing them in a more exaggerated form. (Fine 1983:208)

Or in another interview:

> GAF: When you say players are being themselves, do you mean their personal selves or their character selves?
> Andy: Well, with the people I play with, it's mainly a mixture. They're trying to be the character they rolled up, but it's hard to totally lock out your own feelings. (Fine 1983:208)

Just as some players seek to vest their fantasy character with attributes they themselves prize, some gamers enjoy attempting to role-play characters whose traits are totally dissimilar from their own nonfantasy selves. Most players, however, choose not to play villainous or "evil" fantasy characters.

Among the fantasy gamers observed by Fine, approximately 80 percent opted to role-play "good" or "lawful" characters (1983:210). Still, that leaves 20 percent for parents to worry about. Moreover, even when a person's fantasy role is vested with negative traits, these characteristics are commonly ignored during play. Two gamers explain:

> Alfred played his character like a geek. Most people play their characters like geniuses, even if they're geeks. (Fine 1983:211)

> If you have a character that's chaotic, if I had one, I wouldn't play it as a chaotic person, I'd probably try to play his alignment more neutral or good rather than chaotic. (Fine 1983:210)

Among more experienced players, those for whom the realism of one's character presentation is as important as having one's character succeed in the game, role-playing is true theatricality. This means creatively developing a character quite distinct from oneself and playing that character according to the logic of its nature. Older, hard-core players talk of the "schizoid" nature of their role-playing wherein the immersion of self in a character yields a persona exuding a distinctive "otherness" in relation to their non-game selves. In this sense, gamers and opponents agree. This testimony, however, is given a qualitatively different moral valuation than that given by fantasy role-playing opponents:

> Many people literally become different people when playing an FRP game. (Jacquays 1979:26)

> I like to say that I'm one of those people who will play a character like a character in a play or in a story where he is a separate entity from himself . . . I think when you're playing role-playing games you're not trying to be yourself, you're trying to experiment. You're trying to see what you can do. Why be yourself, when you can have the fun and the risk, of being someone else. (Fine 1983:212)

> The best play results when a player fully understands his character, and tries to act as he thinks his character might in a given situation. While this is not the best course of action, it makes for a much better game overall. (Kanterman 1979:10)

Successful role-playing, as opposed to successful playing of a role-playing game, necessitates that gamers identify with their fantasy characters. Such identification is not always easy. Since identification is usually critical for a successful game, players often negotiate with the referee for traits that enhance their fantasy character, their identification with that character, and, hence, the game. When *Dungeons & Dragons* players find their fantasy characters to be uninteresting, having little potential for character development, and a referee who is unwilling to negotiate, they may opt to have their characters commit suicide:

> Much of the game consists of preliminaries such as rolling up characters, a
> time-consuming process. Frank said that he had to "kill off" several characters
> whose prime requisites [traits] he didn't like. (Fine 1983:215)

Character development is a time-consuming process that readily facilitates identification with one's character. One has time to fantasize about
who one might be. Such identification, of course, can lead to an "overin-
volvement" which can itself become problematic during play (Fine
1983:217–222). Ego involvement of players in their fantasy characters,
which are products of substantial creative energy and hours of playing time,
breeds not only identification with the character but frustration and even
resentment on death or disfiguring injury of that character.

There are, of course, normative boundaries on use and type of killing
within *D & D* play, especially where such violence militates against collective success of the group's adventure and, hence, the fun of the game. Some
players may be so concerned with their own character that their play fails to
support group success and, as a result, collective enjoyment of the game is
affected. Of course, death of one's own fantasy character, especially a
character that has required substantial imaginative labor, is a catastrophe.
Players who identify too closely with a character may cause the characters
of others unnecessary risk, or even become depressed if their own character
receives a fatal injury. As one gamer explained:

> Many players get very caught up in the game, they identify so much with the
> character that they don't want to put them in any danger . . . they may be the
> strongest character there, and they want to be in the middle of the group, so
> that everybody's around them, protecting them, so that monsters are going to
> have to kill everybody else to get to them. (Fine 1983:223)

When gamers are role-playing a character whose traits they disassociate
from their own, violent episodes may be found within the behavioral repertoire of their character. Since they are actors simply enacting a part, such
situations come to be defined as action that flows from a "scripted logic,"
and not themselves. They are insulated from psychic stress, but in doing so,
they may accept the deviant "otherness" of the character. For gamers whose
characters include personifications of themselves, killing or other dastardly
deeds reflect on their own character—they are their own Satans; the moral
order of their character is their own. Some players feel guilty when, due to a
dice throw, their fantasy character is required to seriously harm or even kill
another player's character:

Tim: Before the convention ends you have to meet my friend, Ralph,
          because to him this is a real life-or-death reality.
Geoff: [One] time he was fighting someone and he scored a critical hit in the
          groin. [The location was determined by the dice.] He stabbed this guy

in the groin with a dagger, and he was upset that he stabbed someone in the groin for at least a week or so.

Tim: He'd call me up and tell me how bad he felt.

Geoff: He felt it was a low blow. He couldn't see himself doing that and he was upset that he did that. (Fine 1983:218)

Whether one plays one's fantasy role as an extension of oneself or as disassociated from oneself, these lines of action embroider both the role-playing and the social fabric of the world of gaming with meaning. Fantasy games exist as living cultures where fantasy characters evolve out of the imagination of players who bring with them varying experiences and performance skills upon which they rely.

RATIONALIZING THE DEVIL

Several systematic research studies of effects of fantasy play on cognitive and emotional development of children demonstrate the value of some forms of fantasy play. In a longitudinal study, Saltz and Johnson (1974), examining fantasy play among "socially and economically disadvantaged pre-schoolers," found that, compared to the control group, children participating in role-playing of imaginary stories tested significantly higher on a number of items measuring social and cognitive development, as well as on a standard IQ test.

Kindergartners assigned to experimental groups in a tripartite research design by Robert Fink (1976) displayed significant increases on pretest–posttest measures of understanding kinship relations and free-play imaginativeness. The substantive significance of Fink's findings is that "imaginative play can be generative of new cognitive structures, under certain conditions, by the enhancement and accommodative use of psychological processes such as reflection, role-integration, language, role conflict and representational activity" (1976:895).

Deborah Rosenberg examined elements of preschool fantasy play as "Correlates in Concurrent Social-Personality Function and Early Mother-Child Attachment Relationships." Her findings suggest that the inability of preschool children to participate in fantasy play could be considered "a form of 'social handicap'" (1984:90). Notably, "those children who showed weaker skills in fantasy, who did not come to some satisfactory resolution of conflict, or who did not practice skills and interactional repertoires in fantasy play, did not function well in nursery school settings" (1984:89).

Few studies have specifically assessed the impact of *Dungeons & Dragons* playing upon youth development and psychological well-being. Zayas and Lewis (1986) observed interaction among latency-aged boys whose behavior included episodes of "acting-out" and hyperactivity prior to their selection to play *Dungeons & Dragons*. According to their research findings, the game fostered "adaptive social interaction" among this group because it "provided for mutual aid situations" (1986:61–62).

One rigorous attempt to assess the relationship between *Dungeons & Dragons* playing and the emotional stability of the participants (Sim'on 1987) correlated the number of years a gamer had played *D & D* and Cattell's 16 PF Test (Form C: Factor C), which measures emotional instability. Unsurprisingly Sim'on found very low levels of association that were not statistically significant. He concluded:

> Notwithstanding, newspaper reports of fundamental religious parents denouncing on the one hand that D & D is Satanic and on the other hand policemen and district attorneys blaming D & D for individual cases of runaways, suicides, and various crimes, our findings show a more mundane picture. Increased exposure to D & D is not positively correlated with emotional instability. Indeed, as a whole group, D & D players obtain a healthy psychological profile, as measured by the 16PF. It appears, then, that in those cases wherein the individuals had previously played D & D, the game may have simply been an incidental, irrelevant aspect, rather than an etiological factor. (1987:332)

What all of these studies indicate, then, is that involvement in fantasy role-playing games seems unrelated to allegedly more maleficent outcomes of gaming claimed by crusading groups. Some research findings, in fact, indicate the opposite, that fantasy play in general, and possibly even *D & D*, is developmentally beneficial for children who participate.

THE DEVIL'S BREEDING GROUND?

Are games, with their constructed, artificial realms of meaning, magical worlds? Do we need such realms beyond the ordinary? An oft quoted verse lies at the end of Max Weber's *The Protestant Ethic and the Spirit of Capitalism:*

> "No one knows who will live in this cage in the future, or whether at the end of this tremendous development entirely new prophets will arise or there will be a great rebirth of old ideas, or, if neither, mechanized petrification, embellished with a sort of compulsive self-importance. For of this last stage it may truly be said, 'Specialists without spirit, Sensualists without heart; this nullity imagines that it has attained a level of civilization never before achieved.' "
> (1958:182)

Again in "Science as a Vocation" Weber tells us that "one can, in principle, master all things by calculation. This means the world is disenchanted. One no longer has recourse to magical means in order to master or implore spirits" (1946:139). "The Fate of our times is characterized by rationalization and intellectualization and, above all, by the disenchantment of the world" (1946:155).

It is, perhaps, significant that Weber, who had conscripted himself into the revelry of his father's dueling fraternity, as well as the liveliness and frolics of drinking bouts at the local *bier gartens* (Gerth and Mills 1946:6–8), should be the same Weber who later bemoaned the "mechanized petrification" of rationality in the modern age. But, if modernity was marked by disenchantment for Weber, it was also marked by the curious possibility of charisma "breaking through" those rationalized structures of modernity that he so lamented. However seemingly prophetic these pronouncements, Weber overstated his case—perhaps the older Weber should have engaged himself ethnographically in the frivolity, merry making and enchantment of those places frequented by the younger, and which surrounded him still as he wrote.

We contend that such enchantment exists side by side with processes of rationalization, in whatever small or privatized proportions. To *see* fantasy as the breeding ground of the Devil is in part to give testimony to this enchantment. To engage actively in fantasy role-playing and creative imagination *is* to enchant. In framing fantasy role-playing games as occultist activities, crusading groups share with *Dungeons & Dragons* players a sense of "the world reenchanted." What is different is that fantasy role-players, in contrast to members of the crusading groups, define these activities as inherently social, imaginative, and limited rather than cosmological and self-defining.

The social world of gaming has a "vacation appeal" (Caughey 1988:133) for many gamers; it is a world in which persons can take temporary leave of everyday concerns and embark on an adventure in an alternative symbolic universe. In so doing, everyday life seems less a monolithic, rationalized monstrosity and appears, on closer examination, to be potentially full of wonderful and mysterious "third places," places that "play host to the regular, voluntary, informal, and happily anticipated gatherings of individuals beyond the realms of home and work" (Oldenburg 1989:16).

If modernity has played host to *wertrationalitaet*, then it has acutely and terminably excised both creativity and emotion in public life (Hochschild 1979, 1983), a process of which Weber was acutely aware. Bureaucracy, after all, relinquishes the need for imaginative creativity by virtue of adherence to formalized rules while it reduces the range of emotional experience, insuring that "all feelings are institutionally channelled and individual variation controlled" (Douglas 1983).

The problem posed by modern life is not only to recapture meaning, but to reclaim expressivity, creativity, and imagination—those elements of existence that claim us as uniquely, wonderfully, and dangerously human. If modernity has tossed them on the scrap heap in the public domain, and privatization of meaning has delimited their social availability, where then shall they reside? In principle this is a concern both of gamers and their opponents. The controversy in depicting controversial leisure is to decide which moral universe we shall use to reclaim the magical world, and hence, who operates the unseen machinery that surrounds us.

We are confident that such enchanting enclaves are carved out else-where, in "third places": bars, leisure clubs, coffeehouses, and even in community centers where fantasy gamers "hang out." Perhaps these en-chanting places are, as Alfred Schutz would tender, so taken for granted within the natural attitude of everyday life that we have lost the ability to see them as such. Whether it is Satan or God who claims us, the possibility for dealing with the unknown and unknowable coexists with modern life.

REFERENCES

Berger, Peter L. 1969. *The Sacred Canopy*. Garden City, NY: Anchor Books.
Caughey, John L. 1988. "Fantasy Worlds and Self-Maintenance in Contemporary American Life." *Zygon* 23:129–138.
Csikszentmihalyi, Mihaly. 1990. *Flow: The Psychology of Optimal Experience*. New York: Harper & Row.
Douglas, Mary. 1983. "The Effects of Modernization on Religious Change." Pp. 25–43 in *Religion and America: Spiritual Life in a Secular Age*, edited by Mary Douglas and Steven Tipton. Boston: Beacon Press.
Fine, Gary Alan. 1983. *Shared Fantasy: Role Playing Games as Social Worlds*. Chicago: University of Chicago Press.
Fink, Robert S. 1976. "Role of Imaginative Play in Cognitive Development." *Psychological Reports* 39:895–906.
Game Manufacturer's Association. 1988. "The Assault on Role-Playing Games." Carrollton, TX: GAMA.
Gerth, H. H., and Mills, C. Wright. 1946. *From Max Weber: Essays in Sociology*. New York: Oxford University Press.
Goffman, Erving. 1961. *Encounters*. Indianapolis: Bobbs-Merrill.
Hochschild, Arlie Russell. 1979. "Emotion work, Feeling Rules, and Social Structure." *American Journal of Sociology* 85:551–575.
———. 1983. *The Managed Heart: Commercialization of Human Feeling*. Berkeley: University of California Press.
Jacquays, Paul. 1979. "Fun . . . Heck No/ I Do This for Money!" *Different Worlds* 1:24–26.
Kanterman, Leonard H. 1979. "Where No Man Has Gone Before." *Different Worlds* 1:9–11.
Lortz, Stephen L. 1979. "Role-Playing." *Different Worlds* 1:36–41.
Molitor, Darren. n.d. "Dungeons & Dragons." Richmond, Virginia: B.A.D.D. (Bothered About Dungeons & Dragons).

New York Times. 1985. "A Suicide Spurs Town to Debate Nature of a Game." August 22, Section B.

Oldenburg, Ray. 1989. *The Great Good Place: Cafes, Coffee Shops, Community Centers, Beauty Parlors, General Stores, Bars, Hangouts, and How They Get You Through the Day.* New York: Paragon House.

Olmsted, A. D. 1988. "Morally Controversial Leisure." *Symbolic Interaction* 11:277–287.

Pulling, Patricia. 1989. *The Devil's Web: Who Is Stalking Your Children for Satan?* Lafayette, LA: Huntington House.

Pulling, Patricia, Loyacono, Rosemary, and Dempsey, Patrick. n.d. *Dungeons and Dragons: Witchcraft, Suicide and Violence.* Richmond, Virginia: B.A.D.D. (Bothered About Dungeons & Dragons).

Rosenberg, Deborah Meg. 1984. *The Quality and Content of Preschool Fantasy Play: Correlates in Concurrent Social-Personality Function and Early Mother-Child Attachment Relationships.* University of Minnesota: Unpublished Doctoral Dissertation.

Saltz, Eli, and Johnson, James. 1974. "Training for the Thematic Fantasy Play in Culturally Disadvantaged Children: Preliminary Results." *Journal of Educational Psychology* 66:623–630.

Savoie, Pierre. n.d. "The Whole Loon Catalogue: A Look at the Anti-RPG Movement." Chapel Hill, NC: CAR-PGa (The Committee for the Advancement of Role-Playing Games).

St. Paul Pioneer Press. 1984. "Game's Maker Says Foes are Chasing Dragons." May 14, Section C.

Sim'on, Armando. 1987. "Emotional Stability Pertaining to the Game of Dungeons & Dragons." *Psychology in the Schools* 24:329–332.

Stackpole, Michael A. 1989. "The Truth About Role Playing Games: A Special Appendix." Pp. 231–283 in Shawn Carlson and Gerald Larue, *Satanism in America.* El Cerrito, CA: Gaia Press.

TSR Hobbies. 1979. "Understanding Dungeons & Dragons." Lake Geneva, WI: TSR Hobbies. Pamphlet. 4 pp.

Victor, Jeffrey S. 1989a. "A Rumor-Panic About a Dangerous Satanic Cult in Western New York." *New York Folklore* 15:23–49.

————. 1989b. "Rumors About Satanic Cults Across the Country." A paper presented at the annual meeting of the American Folklore Society. October 18–21.

Weber, Max. 1946. "Science as a Vocation." Pp. 128–156 in *From Max Weber: Essays in Sociology,* edited by Hans Gerth and C. Wright Mills. New York: Oxford University Press.

————. 1958. *The Protestant Ethic and the Spirit of Capitalism.* Trans., Talcott Parsons. New York: Scribner and Sons.

Zayas, Luis H., and Lewis, Bradford, H. 1986. "Fantasy Role-Playing for Mutual Aid in Children's Groups." *Social Work With Groups* 9:53–66.

PSYCHIATRY AND OCCULT SURVIVORS — IV

Occult Survivors: The Making of a Myth   8

Philip Jenkins and Daniel Maier-Katkin

"PROOFS OF A CONSPIRACY"

In the late 1980s, it was frequently alleged that the United States faced a serious crime-wave associated with the occult or satanism (Raschke 1990; Larson 1989; Pulling 1989; Johnston 1989; Kahaner 1988; Peterson 1988, Schwarz and Empey 1988; Frederickson 1988; Terry 1987). However, the lack of solid corroborating evidence has caused many critics to dismiss these claims (Lanning 1989; Lyons 1988; Rodgers-Melnick 1989). In response, believers in a satanic menace suggest various reasons why proof is not forthcoming. The authorities might fail to note evidence through ignorance or more sinister motives; or else the satanists demonstrate extreme cunning in concealing evidence of their crimes (Peterson 1988–1990; *America's Best Kept Secret*). Without material evidence, the focus of inquiry must shift to the first-hand testimony of witnesses and participants. These are the occult "survivors," alleged former cult members or victims, whose evidence thus attains unique significance.

There are now hundreds of individuals who claim to be "survivors," and they even maintain a self-help group, "Overcomers Victorious," led by Jacquie Balodis. Survivor accounts have become a mainstay (almost a cliché) of media investigations of satanism, providing a basis for the most lurid footage on the controversial Geraldo Rivera television documentary, *Devil Worship* (Rivera 1988). Typically, the survivor is a woman in her thirties or forties, who tells of confronting her satanic past, usually during intensive therapy. Sometimes, she will also have had a "born-again" conversion experience. Her recollections may date back to early childhood, or be limited to recent events. At a minimum, reported experiences are likely to include cult worship, blood drinking, and ritual sexual acts, often involving children and pornography. Most stories also involve ritual murder and cannibalism. One of the best-known survivors, Lauren Stratford, is the major source for the idea of "breeders," women who deliver children solely for the purpose of sacrifice. She claims to have had three of her own babies taken in this way (Stratford 1988; but see Passantino et al. 1989).

The reality of the occult threat seems to be confirmed by the similarity of accounts presented by survivors from different regions of the country. Claims-makers like Bob Larson and Ted Gunderson make extensive use of such testimony to support apparently outlandish claims about satanic crime. For example, it is the statements of "the few survivors" which prove that "a large number of missing children are victims of human sacrifice cults" (Larson 1989:125). At every point, survivors' testimony allows the claims-makers to confound their critics. For example, ritual child abuse cases had usually foundered when children's testimony proved to be inaccurate and unreliable; but now this could be explained. To quote fundamentalist writer Laura Michaelsen,

> in the past few years, adult survivors, defectors from satanist camps, and investigators have begun to shed some light on the satanists' tactics. Animals are indeed killed and buried, but are later dug up and disposed of elsewhere. The children are frequently given a stupefying drug before the rituals so that their senses and perceptions are easily manipulated in the dim candlelight of the ritual scene. (Stratford 1988: foreword; compare Michaelsen 1988)

Perhaps most valuable for the claims-makers was the lengthy history that the survivors gave to contemporary charges of "ritual abuse" (Marron 1988; Eberle and Eberle 1986). This offense is essentially undocumented before the 1980s, but now the survivors were offering accounts of such acts being performed in the 1950s or before. If accepted, this would add plausibility to the charges of cult involvement in contemporary mass abuse cases.

Assessing the objective reality of these survivor accounts is difficult. They appear wildly implausible, but that is not necessarily damning in itself. It is also likely that the individuals themselves believe firmly in the reality of their experiences, and would probably pass a test like a polygraph examination. Some appear to be reliable witnesses; but close examination of the most influential and widely publicized cases suggests numerous problems that cast doubt on the whole "survivor" genre. Most commonly, the difficulties arise from history and logic: witnesses are depicting events that almost certainly could not have happened in that particular time and place.

The fictional elements in these stories can be attributed partly to the fundamentalist religious agendas of many of those creating and publicizing the accounts. In addition, the role of the therapeutic and psychiatric procedures used to elicit much of the supposed evidence needs to be examined closely. Whatever the reasons, the whole subculture of survivor tales must be viewed as thoroughly tainted. Given the central place of the survivors in the whole structure of beliefs and myths about diabolism, the consequence must be to weaken still further the claim that society faces a real satanic danger.

A HISTORICAL CONTEXT

The stories of satanic survivors fit well into long-established traditions that have become distinctively American, above all the radical Protestant idea of conversion and the inner experience of rebirth. The saved sinner denounces and probably exaggerates former misdeeds, in order to emphasize the miraculous role of divine arbitrary Grace. This is often undertaken as an evangelistic duty, the confession being presented in a public context where others can learn from the experience. This sense of salvation from the forces of sin and the devil led many to write and publish accounts of their redemption, sometimes full autobiographies. Bunyan's title, *Grace Abounding to the Chief of Sinners,* could serve as the subtitle of any of them.

Parallel to this religious genre, we also find a secular political tradition that is particularly associated with conservative and nativist sentiment. America has experienced many previous panics directed against "dangerous outsiders," from Catholics and Freemasons in the nineteenth century to communists and the mafia in the twentieth century. In each of these cases, opposition to the supposed alien conspiracy has drawn largely on the testimony of survivors or defectors, former members of the deviant movement, who subsequently exposed the misdeeds of their colleagues (Hofstadter 1979; Lipset and Raab 1978). In the Jacksonian era, a major issue for the powerful antimasonic movement was the apparent murder of one such Masonic defector, who had been on the verge of exposing the secrets of the craft.

Anti-Catholicism, meanwhile, flourished on the testimony of the "survivor" nun Maria Monk, who portrayed convents in terms of frequent casual sexuality between priests and nuns. In a striking parallel to more recent charges, Maria claimed to know from personal experience that children born of such unions were murdered:

> [The Mother Superior] gave me another piece of information which excited other feelings in me. . . . Infants were sometimes born in the Convent, but they were always baptized, and immediately strangled. This secured their everlasting happiness; for the baptism purifies them from all sinfulness, and being sent out of the world before they had time to do any wrong, they were at once admitted into Heaven. . . . How different did a Convent now appear from what I supposed it to be! (*Maria Monk:* 39)

Throughout the nineteenth century, Protestant activism was regularly stirred by lectures and testimony from ex-priests and nuns, real or feigned; and the tradition survives today. The fundamentalist publisher "Chick" distributes not only occult survivor stories, but also harrowing memoirs and conspiracy tales by purported former Catholic priests and Jesuits (Brown 1986).

In the mid-twentieth century too, the validity of such defectors' evidence would again be a prime political issue with the numerous exposés of the American Communist movement by its former supporters. Figures such as Whittaker Chambers and "red spy queen" Elizabeth Bentley became national heroes, at least for the political Right. When attention turned to the alleged alien conspiracy known as the mafia or *La Cosa Nostra*, the most powerful evidence was again believed to come from former members of the group, such as Joseph Valachi and Jimmy Fratianno. To some extent, occult survivors are but the latest manifestation of an ancient tradition, and there are many resemblances between satanic defectors such as Mike Warnke and earlier mafia or communist witnesses. All seek to emphasize their own importance in the conspiracy and the depths of its wrongdoing, from which they were in due course converted.

The occult survivors vary enormously in their credibility, but some at least fit well into the "classical" defector genre: that is, they give a picture that attempts to be broadly plausible, if admittedly polemical. Mike Warnke's autobiography *The Satan Seller* (1972) appears largely credible, if we allow for a little artistic license, and the book provides a striking contrast to other accounts that we will consider below. He provides an internally consistent story of becoming involved with sex and drug abuse in the hippie subculture of southern California during the mid-1960s. He gradually became active in a diabolical cult, allegedly with national ramifications, and he claims to have been a satanic high priest, though occult interests never wholly displaced the life of a hustler and drug dealer. Following conversion to Christianity, Warnke led a fundamentalist ministry chiefly directed against the "occult," a term that includes "New Age" movements.

Warnke's account has a plausible locale and chronology, and the cultural environment can readily be confirmed from a range of contemporary sources. The book is written with a strong religious and political slant, but it is easy to differentiate between what Warnke reports as experience, and what he encounters as hearsay. Most of the controversial and outrageous statements are placed in the latter category, such as the opinion that American witches were millions strong, or that "drug pushers and political revolutionists are using devil worship" to subvert American society (Warnke 1972:195).

ASSESSING THE EVIDENCE

If Warnke's story follows a traditional format, most tales by occult survivors diverge from historical precedent, above all in their approach to evidence. In the earlier cases, charges could be debated and rebutted, either by members of the accused groups themselves or by critical observers.

Corroboration could be sought in the form of supporting testimony or material evidence, as both accusers and "conspirators" attempted to present a coherent and plausible case that could convince the uncommitted. None of these considerations seems to be highly valued when assessing the testimony of current occult survivors. It is difficult even to extract specific dates and places from most accounts, often because the witnesses wish to remain anonymous. Corroboration is rarely claimed or (apparently) sought.

Survivors appear to be treated according to a wholly different set of evidentiary criteria that effectively invert normally accepted principles. The guiding principle resembles the statement attributed to the early Christian, Tertullian, *Credo quia impossible est,* "I believe because it is impossible." Such a statement may be of great value in the history of religious faith, but modern accounts of occult crime offer what can only be described as a similar irrationalism in their approach to matters of evidence. Not only do they admit that the claims they report are quite outrageous, they actually cite the improbability to support the truth of the charges. Larson (1989:126) is typical in suggesting that, "satanic cults deliberately fabricate preposterous forms of child victimization, knowing that the more unbelievable their atrocity, the less likely the victim will be believed."

The concept that cults deliberately attempt to provoke incredulity can be traced to the influential television journalist, Kenneth Wooden, who originally based the idea on his observations of Jim Jones' People's Temple (Wooden 1981). Wooden has been well placed to promote this view, and to publicize material that might otherwise have been thought too shocking or *outrè.* He was an investigator or producer for many of the network documentary reports on satanism during the decade, most significantly for Geraldo Rivera's *Devil Worship* (Wooden 1988). Wooden appears in "survivor" Lauren Stratford's autobiography as a major force in persuading her to write the book (Stratford 1988:165).

Wooden and Larson may or may not be correct in their view of cult tactics, but the practical effect of their beliefs is to remove plausibility as a criterion for assessing evidence. Quite the contrary, it seems that survivors must tell fantastic tales to be credible. In the Rivera television special, perhaps the most controversial material involved interviews with women who claimed not only to have bred children for sacrifice, but to have seen them flayed. In only one recent case has a sacrifice allegation drawn forth the public outcry that it deserved, when an alleged survivor reported on national television about the prevalence of ritual infanticide among American Jewish families (Gerard 1989: compare Hsia 1988 for medieval precedents). The story, clearly absurd, drew massive criticism from a variety of groups; but most of these outrageous allegations are allowed to pass without comment.

Survivors' accounts are valued despite apparent flaws that would ipso facto discredit them in a normal criminal case. Alleged adult survivors of ritual abuse often appear badly disturbed, and it is soon admitted that they do in fact have lengthy records of serious psychiatric disorders, often combined with substance abuse. Nevertheless, believers in ritual abuse argue that the severity of the disorders is itself testimony to the extent of the traumatization. In almost every case, survivors are said to have no conscious memory of the abuse until it is released in therapy. In recent years, it has even been explained why the witnesses are so often multiple personalities: they were deliberately brainwashed into this condition by satanic psychiatrists: "Every adult (survivor) that I have dealt with is a multiple personality. That behavior, doctors believe, can be induced by mental cruelty and drugs" (Kahaner 1988:237). Jacquie Balodis makes a similar point about multiple personality, and notes a link to traditional ideas of possession.

If these views are accurate, little is gained by conventional criticism of survivor accounts. Almost any logical flaw or contradiction could be explained within this belief system, while skepticism could be rejected as demonstrating a lack of sympathy for victims, who are usually thought to be abused children. Personal conviction, rather than evidence, would determine one's attitude to this growing corpus of stories.

ANALYZING SURVIVOR STORIES

In reality, conventional methods of criticism can still be used to analyze survivor tales, even within the limits set by their advocates: in this light, the accounts demonstrate fundamental flaws and contradictions. One critical approach is through a painstaking analysis of individual cases, a necessarily laborious procedure that effectively means dissecting the whole life history of the claimant. However, the method can yield rich rewards, as suggested by the impressive demolition of Lauren Stratford's memoirs by a team of researchers reporting in the Christian magazine, Cornerstone (Passantino et al. 1989). Regrettably, the limited circulation of this journal means that the critique will become familiar to only a tiny proportion of those who heard Stratford's claims on television programs such as Geraldo or the 700 Club.

In this case, the investigators reconstructed Stratford's life history and undertook extensive interviews among her family and friends. Cornerstone noted Stratford's many contradictions and falsehoods, too numerous to report here, and generally suggested a consistent pattern of wild fantasies on her part. Her book was unreliable about matters as basic as her family structure, and her accounts of her parents and siblings have been subject to kaleidoscopic changes over the years. Her claims of abuse had similarly changed frequently, and satanism had only appeared as a claim as late as 1985, in the aftermath of the McMartin case (in which she claimed a direct role). The physical scars that she attributed to satanic abuse appear in fact to have been self-inflicted.

Of her most dramatic charge, about "breeding" and sacrificing three children, the story noted that she had variously claimed:

> she's sterile/had two children killed in snuff films/three children killed, two in snuff films, one in satanic ritual/says she had children during teenage years/her twenties/lived two years in a breeder warehouse. In reality, no evidence she was ever pregnant. (Passantino et al. 1989:27)

The most remarkable conclusion was neither that the charges were unsupported, nor that they frequently contradicted known events; it was that virtually no outlet for these claims had undertaken any serious verification. "The most stunning element . . . is that no one even checked out the main details" (Passantino et al. 1989:27). In early 1990, it was reported that *Satan's Underground* had been withdrawn by the publisher; but a number of distributors continued to circulate it.

Michelle and Jenny

Ideally, all survivor stories should be subjected to such a searching individual analysis, but more general principles of evaluation can be formulated, that cast doubt on survivor stories as a category. This can be illustrated from a critique of two similar autobiographies that are among the most important sources for contemporary ideas about satanism. Both are pseudonymous recollections of ritual abuse suffered during early childhood, and both are presented in what appears to be a critical and indeed clinical style, which apparently lends substance to their argument.

The pioneering account of "Michelle" effectively shaped the whole survivor genre (Smith and Pazder 1980). It takes the form of a recollection during months of intensive psychotherapy in 1977–1978, with the subject recalling elaborate rituals she believed to have occurred in her childhood. Over a 12-month period, she recalled what had happened to her on the corresponding dates in 1954–1955, when she was 5 years old. The traumatic memories were at their strongest on the days of great satanic rituals. Her account is so important because it incorporates virtually all the major charges that would become popular in the 1980s—satanic worship, ritual child abuse, blood sacrifices of animals and perhaps babies, mock burials, and defecation on crucifixes. Obviously, she could not have been influenced by the later storm of publicity surrounding ritual abuse, so her account, whatever its possible flaws, is at least an independent source.

Michelle's story has achieved considerable acceptance, as has the similar account of "Jenny," described by Judith Spencer (1989) in the best-selling mass-market paperback, *Suffer the Child*. This book includes a scholarly apparatus and some 40 citations, often to respectable psychiatric journals; and the author made an admirable effort to confirm the subject's sense of recall by checking biographical details. Jenny's story was hailed in reviews from therapists as well as child abuse support groups; author Larry Kahaner called the book "the best account" of its kind that he had encountered. Jenny's experiences were almost identical to Michelle's. Initiated into her mother's cult at the age of five, "the rhythms of Satan worship permeated her childhood" (Spencer 1989:14). She "stood boldly to see other dogs, and then cats, chickens, squirrels, rabbits, and goats killed. She watched the amputation of fingers and nipples, and sometimes, penises" (Spencer 1989:15). The religious life described here suggests a large and influential cult, with frequent rituals including as the centerpiece a classical Black Mass.

Both accounts include the idea that the abused child was being prepared for a special role as a "Devil's Bride," a common theme in the genre. The notion of special mission is in the context almost a logical necessity, required to resolve a paradox in the narrative. The survivors wish to describe cults as homicidal groups that regularly kill children; and yet the narrators, by definition, survived. Election as a "bride" explains this contradiction. However, the conflict is never quite resolved, and satanists are depicted both callously killing children and painstakingly brainwashing them over years. This has led writers into real confusion. Larson, for example, writes that "children are abducted and subjected to the terrible intimidation of drugs and brainwashing before being sacrificed" (Larson 1989:125). Brainwashing a person one intends to kill anyway seems a waste of time and energy; but the dilemma is explained if we understand the ambiguous nature of the "survivor" accounts.

Neither Michelle nor Jenny inspire confidence as witnesses. "Michelle's" psychiatric problems were apparent, to the point of demonstrating classic hysterical symptoms. She is reported to have developed physical stigmata that supposedly recalled her suffering. Moreover, the book demands belief in objective supernatural forces: Michelle's torment culminates with a dramatic purgation not unlike an exorcism, in which a spirit or apparition was photographed by the participants. Despite the "therapeutic" format, *Michelle Remembers* is not a standard psychiatric case study. It is also interesting to read the ambiguous commendation that a Catholic bishop provided for the book, stressing that "*for Michelle*, this experience was real" (Smith and Pazder 1980:foreword; our emphasis).

Suffer the Child lacks the spiritualist trappings, but it depicts an even more disturbed individual. Jenny had been hospitalized for mental illness at the ages of 14 and 21, with schizophrenia a possible diagnosis. She was believed by the author to have several hundred distinct personalities, 35 of whom are named in a glossary. If one accepts this as a true case of multiple personality disorder, then obvious questions arise about the causation of the illness. The author believes that Jenny evolved new personalities to help her cope with her childhood experiences. These characters included witches, sorcerers, and demons, in keeping with the ritual nature of the abuse. In contrast, we might argue that Jenny developed the personalities from reasons other than actual experience. Her mind then contained a whole cast of *dramatis personae*, such as Sandy the witch and Mindoline the demon, for whom Jenny created appropriate myths and histories.

Such criticisms would readily be countered by those who believe the survivors. In this case, though, we can seek historical confirmation for the truth of the stories, and the implied chronology of events is critical. Allegedly, both girls were introduced to satanic cults around the age of 5, and they spent several years in a continuing nightmare of ritual abuse and bloodshed. These events can be dated with fair confidence to almost exactly the same time: Michelle suffered during 1954 and 1955, while Jenny's cult experiences must have begun about 1954. The suggestion is that quite sophisticated clandestine cult satanists must have been firmly established by the early 1950s—Michelle's group in British Columbia and Jenny's group in an unspecified area of rural Dixie. The presence of many children already born into the movement means that the satanists must have long remained as a secret alternative religion in these widely separated areas. We would have to hypothesize local traditions dating back for decades. In addition, this early to mid-1950s chronology is frequently presented in the accounts of less celebrated survivors, such as Heather Cambridge (Schwarz and Empey 1988) or Casandra Hoyer (Pulling 1989:66). Lauren Stratford's cult experiences are presumably set about 1960, as are the memoirs of the pseudonymous "Elaine," recounted in yet another book (Brown 1986). Most occult survivors are baby-boomers.

There are some today who claim that North American devil worshippers run into the millions, and that cult satanists are engaged in a wholesale assault on society; but these charges are paltry besides the implications of *Michelle* and *Suffer the Child*. These survivor tales require us to believe that the sophisticated satanic rituals of 1890s Paris or 1970s California were commonplace in remote rural or suburban communities during the Eisenhower era. The regularity of blood sacrifices implies that the cults were so powerful as to have no fear of legal intervention. They could abduct and kill with impunity in a time of far lower homicide rates, when missing persons were likely to attract more law enforcement concern than today. Further, no individual from such a cult ever betrayed its secrets or ever revealed its existence to a local church or newspaper. No religious revival ever forced a defection or an investigation, and no local politician sought celebrity by exposing such heinous crimes.

This calls less for a suspension of disbelief than a complete rewriting of the history of the United States and Canada. One even older survivor reported "near total involvement of the entire village where she grew up on the affluent North Side of Chicago, Illinois, during the 1930s. Her parents "as well as Christian ministers, policemen, lawyers and socialites were involved" in a cult active in human sacrifice and Black Masses (Peterson 1988:28). The only contemporary parallel to such a picture comes from popular Gothic fiction by authors such as Robert Bloch or H. P. Lovecraft, whose protagonists so often stumbled across diabolical secrets shared by remote communities. As a portrait of the reality of rural or suburban American in mid-century, the survivors' reminiscences are monstrously improbable.

The News Media

If cults of this sort existed at all, to say nothing of the vast scale required by the accounts proliferating today, we would expect some trace in the news media—some rumor, scandal, or investigation. This should have reached a crescendo about 1954, which modern sources claim witnessed a "Feast of the Beast," with sacrifices in unprecedented numbers. We might expect increased reports, however speculative, on ritual killings, child abductions, church desecrations, or cult activity. In order to test this, we searched the index volumes of the *New York Times* between 1948 and 1960. Key words used included *crime and criminals, cult, devil, kidnapping, murder, occult, religion and churches, ritual, ritual murder, sacrifice, Satan,* and *witchcraft. Witchcraft* and *ritual murder* provided by far the richest material. Every year produced three or four stories, which did indeed depict powerful secret cults involved in black magic, ritual human sacrifice, and even the abduction and brainwashing of children. However, virtually every one of these stories occurred in Africa, as traditional cults became politically active in the last days of European colonial rule. Other Third World countries provided for most of the remaining tales, for example the 1955 lynching of an alleged witch in Guatemala.

Within North America, only three such stories were found. One concerned the efforts of the modern citizens of Salem to clear retroactively the victims of the great trials. In 1951, a semihumorous story told of a court case where a Hispanic resident of the Bronx accused a neighbor of using a "voodoo hex" (September 15). Finally, in 1959, an Alabama teacher was dismissed for a sympathetic classroom discussion of voodoo beliefs (January 6). This last story illustrates that an occult case was seen as sufficiently weird and novel to attract national attention, even without criminal or sensational elements. The implication is that a real "Feast of the Beast" would have caused a flood of media attention, if it had ever occurred, but the over-whelming evidence is that it did not.

It is useful here to compare media attitudes toward the real occult prac-tices found in many remote communities about this time, the magical healing practices and witch beliefs associated with the Pennsylvania Dutch country or parts of the Appalachians. Though these customs were almost always benevolent in intent, the communities usually attempted to keep them secret, largely through fear of ridicule. However, they were bound to fail on occasion, and the slightest rumor of occult-related crime drew widespread attention. The most celebrated instance occurred in York Coun-ty, Pennsylvania, in 1928–1929, when three boys were implicated in mur-dering a reputed local wizard for his magical "Pow-wow Book" (Lewis 1969). The case earned national and international coverage as "the witch-murder," attracting comment from celebrities such as Clarence Darrow. The media sensation was such that throughout the 1930s, journalists regularly read "hex" and ritual elements into ordinary murder cases in the area, even when the motive was clearly personal or financial. There is no reason to believe that the media of the 1950s were any more reluctant to seek a sensational story than their predecessors.

Real Satanic Groups

The question might be posed in another way. Devil-worshipping groups have unquestionably existed in twentieth-century America, but how does our knowledge of them fit the cults described by the survivors? Michelle's biographer attempts to link her mid-1950s persecutors to known move-ments, specifically the "Church of Satan," an organization "actually older than the Christian Church. . . . There's a lot in the psychiatric literature about them" (Smith and Pazder 1980:117). Despite this claim, no satanist group has even a tenuous organizational continuity dating before the pres-ent century; and the Church of Satan to which this appears to refer is the American movement of that name founded by Anton LaVey in 1966. Mi-chelle's biographer, Lawrence Pazder, also attempted to corroborate the presence of occultists in the Vancouver area, and includes as an appendix a news story about modern-day witch activity in the area. However, this only supports the possible existence of witchcraft in 1977, which is irrelevant to the situation in the 1950s (Smith and Pazder 1980:299–300).

We know of no evidence from any source of cult activity of this sort in North America before 1960. Most American satanism can be traced to the late 1960s. LaVey's group was the most celebrated, but the following years saw the creation and growth of several movements—the Process, the Solar Lodge, the Temple of Set (Lyons 1988; Adler 1979; Bainbridge 1978;

Moody 1977). There was also some development of local groups out of the whole subculture described by Mike Warnke; and a proliferation of individual satanic believers, partly inspired by media depictions in films such as *Rosemary's Baby* and *The Exorcist*.

Before 1965, however, the religious fringe was more sparsely populated. The closest approximations to "devil-worship" were strictly confined to geographic areas far removed from the locales of Michelle and Jenny—above all, to California.[1] The Agape Lodge in 1930s Hollywood had been associated with wealthy decadence; by the 1940s, Jack Parsons transformed it into the Crowleyite Church of Thelema, based in Pasadena. At least in rumor, this group was active in orgies and sacrifice, but the tiny cult was moribund by the mid-1950s (Lyons 1988). In addition, Aleister Crowley had a handful of American followers of his OTO lodge, *Ordo Templi Orientis*, some dating back to the Magus' sojourn in New York during the First World War (Symonds 1973; Crowley 1970). However, no informed Crowleyan would have been associated with the inverted fundamentalism of "Michelle's" group; and the chants recalled by Jenny fit no known magical tradition. Finally, none of the new satanic movements of the 1960s demonstrated any influence from or contact with any older American devil cults of the sort recorded by the survivors.

We cannot prove a negative. We are unable to show that organized cult satanism was wholly unknown in America before about 1966, or that there might not have been one or two isolated cults on the lines described by Michelle and Jenny. On the other hand, the evidence they present contradicts what we know from many other sources, it is wholly unconfirmed, and inherently improbable, and it fits poorly with the historical context. Similar objections would apply to any other conceivable account of ritual abuse or satanic crime in America before the mid-1960s—and that includes a large majority of all survivor stories.

THE THERAPEUTIC PROCESS

Most accounts of survivors essentially consider the role of one protagonist, the woman herself. However, even those who accept these stories as true admit that the accounts are not presented spontaneously. They are drawn out gradually in a lengthy therapeutic process in which there are at least two actors. Understanding the stories therefore requires knowledge of the process and its underlying assumptions.

One central idea is that early childhood trauma can cause the mind to bury painful memories that lie dormant until revived by therapy such as hypnotic age regression. This may not be controversial as such, but it is questionable whether the memories will come back in an accurate and unadulterated form, untainted by images or fantasies acquired at a later date. Again, early trauma might lead to later psychiatric disorders; but these same complaints could also have other origins, including biological and biochemical dysfunctions. European psychiatrists in particular would be skeptical of the unreconstructed Freudianism of some of their American counterparts. There might be cases where childhood sufferings could be reconstructed during therapy; but it would seem rash to insist on their objective reality, without extensive corroboration.

It would not be hard to suggest why survivors might formulate stories of satanic rituals, especially when their accounts were collected during the last decade. Patients under therapy in the 1980s might have heard and internalized the kind of charges initially made in *Michelle Remembers,* and subsequently repeated in child molestation cases such as McMartin, Jordan, or Bakersfield. Jenny herself appears to have begun therapy in 1984, just as these allegations were reaching their height; Lauren Stratford's tales of cults and sacrifices began about 1985. Ritual abuse became a major topic in the mass media, with new survivors regularly appearing on television talk shows and in the pages of the *National Enquirer.* Their stories involved powerful images of the sort often found in mythology and dream imagery, stories and symbols with a universal Jungian relevance. In addition, there might have been specific issues such as guilt or internal conflict about the issue of abortion that might go far towards explaining the "breeder" tales. As Gordon Melton suggests, "satanism has emerged as a reflecting board on which people have projected a wide variety of fantasies" (quoted in Rodgers-Melnick 1989).

Images and speculations then reappear as fantasies, which the patient increasingly holds to as literally true—especially if the therapist is supportive and encouraging. In this context, it is intriguing that Michelle's analyst, Dr. Lawrence Pazder, came from a rather unusual background. He practiced medicine in West Africa in the early 1960s, at the height of widespread public concern there over the activities of cults and secret societies active in blood sacrifice, cannibalism, and child maltreatment (Parrinder 1963; Scobie 1965; compare Beatty 1978). Dr. Pazder makes no secret of this background, to which he frequently makes reference; and we must obviously accept his assurance that he "never told Michelle about the correspondences he sometimes saw between her experiences and the things he had studied" (Smith and Pazder 1980:140n; compare 169, 173–174). On the other hand, the "cult" described in *Michelle* is in fact very close to the notorious African "leopard societies" to which Pazder specifically refers. African memories might have made him more prepared to accept the literal truth of Michelle's account, far more so than the majority of his North American colleagues.

We must therefore know what a therapist will be prepared to believe or accept and how directive the therapist is in the therapy setting. Observations of the profession in general suggest that these expectations have changed substantially in recent years. The alleged consistency of accounts across the nation might therefore reflect no more than the dissemination of ideas across the therapeutic disciplines. Dr. Frank Putnam of the NIMH has pointed to the influence of seminars on ritual abuse, and to published memoirs such as those of Lauren Stratford and Michelle. He remarks, "There is an enormous rumor mill out there. Patients pick up stories, and therapists trade stories" (quoted in Rodgers-Melnick 1989). We may therefore see survivor stories as the product of the dynamic process between patient and therapist.

Crucially, large sections of the therapeutic profession are now prepared to credit charges that would once have been dismissed as fantasy, and "ritual crimes" have become an issue in several ongoing debates. For example, extreme abuse during childhood was believed to contribute to multiple personality disorder, a condition hitherto viewed as a peripheral and rather faddish notion. In the last decade, however, it has become more widely accepted as a respectable issue for therapists, with occult survivors providing important case studies. One serious scholarly text on multiple personality notes cases of "forced participation since childhood in satanistic cult worship entailing ritual sex, human sacrifice and cannibalism" (Braun 1986). The author claims to know of some 60 such cases, and has also stated that his attempts to help these patients have led to threats from satanic groups (Rivera 1988).

Another debate concerns the frequency of early childhood abuse, and the veracity of accounts purporting to describe it. A bitter controversy of the 1980s involved the charge that Sigmund Freud had suppressed his seduction theory, bowing to the outcry that arose when he had originally suggested the prevalence of child molestation and incest. His revised form of the theory had portrayed memories of abuse or incest as mere fantasies or wish-fulfillment. In the political and social context of the 1980s, this approach seemed a callous betrayal of the powerless, of women and children, of victims. In the new view, it was almost an article of faith that such accounts were rarely invented, even when they involved grotesque "ritual" elements, and even when the memories appeared to come from the deepest levels of the subconscious. To reject Jenny might be to question the bona fides of any abuse victim.

But this reaction in favor of the victim may well mean a refusal to doubt even the most absurd allegation about early experiences. It is controversial whether therapists might encourage the actual creation of an idea of early abuse; but even well-founded memories might be distorted and elaborated into grand ritualistic fantasies. A medical practice specializing in ritual abuse—and these are proliferating—is likely to be receptive to these purported memories, and the therapist might shape, even if unintentionally, the patient's narrative by asking questions that support an occult context. One Texas clinic that advertises its treatment of satanic survivors from all parts of the country now reports dealing with "many women," whose early ritual abuse led to pregnancy, with the children subsequently sacrificed (Rodgers-Melnick 1989).

CONCLUSION: A NEW MYTHOLOGY

One of the recent studies of the occult threat bears the title *Satanism: Is Your Family Safe?* and the authors would certainly answer in the negative (Schwarz and Empey 1988). Their conclusion is based partly on a case study of a bloodthirsty California cult allegedly operating from the early 1950s, whose members would indirectly be connected with major criminal acts. These included the 1970 Fort Bragg murders allegedly blamed on Jeffrey MacDonald. It is possible to proceed far in this narrative before noticing that virtually every detail and accusation is taken from the purported memories of survivor (multiple personality and "Devil's Bride") Heather Cambridge. Her memoirs are subject to all the criticisms made above against works such as *Michelle Remembers,* and we would suggest that her account is not likely to be reliable as literal truth.

But what is most interesting here is the use of evidence. The survivor accounts are seen as credible first-hand testimony, and they are beginning to be drawn together to create a new synthetic history of cults and satanic activity in this country. The MacDonald case is only one example of a controversial or mysterious case where survivors have offered testimony in support of an occult interpretation; and other instances might well occur in the near future. If it is objected that Michelle portrays diabolical cults of the sort that never existed in the 1950s, it will soon be answered that in fact they did, and that there are dozens of survivor accounts to confirm it. Far from being an innovation of the 1960s, American satanism is likely to be portrayed by the claims-makers as having real historical roots. Overall, a golden age of myth making seems imminent.

We can already discern the early stages of a troubling process that permits the almost unlimited "manufacture" of survivors and their grisly tales. Ideological and theoretical changes within the therapeutic community have contributed to a dramatic increase in the numbers of self-described occult survivors. These individuals may find themselves interviewed and promoted by exponents of the "satanic threat," including occult experts from religious groups and law enforcement. In turn, these accounts gain widespread publicity in the mass media, especially on sensationalistic talk shows. Accounts appear in book form, which owe their commercial success in large part to a prurient interest in the detailed descriptions of sadism and

perversion—an appeal far removed from the intentions of the original authors. As these stories appear ever more frequently in television and published accounts, so survivors and "ritual crimes" increasingly permeate the
public consciousness, providing a vocabulary for disturbed individuals to
recount in therapy. The process thus becomes self-sustaining, and it is
difficult to see how the cycle could be broken in the foreseeable future.

As survivor tales proliferate, the sheer volume of apparent evidence may
convince some of the truth of the charges. We would suggest, however, that
many of these stories should be seen as little more than derivatives of the first
few accounts, and that those first accounts are themselves highly questionable. The study of survivors can tell us a great deal about mental disorders,
about the state of American religious belief, or the therapeutic process.
What "occult survivors" cannot tell us about is the occult.

NOTE

[1] In order to be comprehensive, we should mention the black southern cults
occasionally reported to be involved in rituals similar to voodoo. In 1912, the
"Church of Sacrifice" in Lake Charles, Louisiana, was said to be involved in 30 or
more deaths (*New York Times*, March 3, 1912; compare Tallant 1946). Southwestern Indian communities also had witchcraft traditions (Simmons 1974). However, none of the current survivors appears to be referring to these alleged ethnic
traditions.

REFERENCES

Adler, Margot. 1979. *Drawing Down the Moon*. Boston: Beacon.
America's Best Kept Secret. 1988. Video produced by *Passport Magazine*.
Bainbridge, William Sims. 1978. *Satan's Power: A Deviant Psychotherapy Cult*.
    Berkeley, CA: University of California Press.
Beatty, Sir Kenneth James. 1978. *Human Leopards*. New York: AMS Press.
Braun, Bennett G. 1986. *The Treatment of Multiple Personality Disorder*. American
    Psychiatric Press.
Brown, Rebecca. 1986. *He Came to Set the Captives Free*. Chino, CA: Chick.
Crowley, Aleister. 1970. *The Confessions of Aleister Crowley*, edited by John Sym-
    onds and Kenneth Grant. New York: Hill and Wang.
Eberle, Paul, and Eberle, Shirley. 1986. *The Politics of Child Abuse*. Secaucus, NJ:
    Lyle Stuart.
Frederickson, Bruce G. 1988. *How to Respond to Satanism*. St. Louis, MO: Concor-
    dia.
Gerard, Jeremy. 1989. "Winfrey Show Evokes Protests." *New York Times*, May
    6:50.
Hofstadter, Richard. 1979. *The Paranoid Style in American Politics*. Chicago: Uni-
    versity of Chicago Press.

Hsia, R. Po-chia. 1988. *The Myth of Ritual Murder.* New Haven: Yale University Press.

Johnston, Jerry. 1989. *The Edge of Evil: The Rise of Satanism in North America.* Dallas, TX: Word Publishing.

Kahaner, Larry. 1988. *Cults That Kill.* New York: Warner.

Lanning, Kenneth V. 1989. "Satanic, Occult and Ritualistic Crime: A Law Enforcement Perspective." *Police Chief* 56(October):62–85.

Larson, Bob. 1989. *Satanism: The Seduction of America's Youth.* Nashville: Thomas Nelson Press.

Lewis, Arthur H. 1969. *Hex.* New York: Trident.

Lipset, Seymour, M., and Raab, Earl. 1978. *The Politics of Unreason,* 2nd ed. Chicago: University of Chicago Press.

Lyons, Arthur. 1988. *Satan Wants You.* New York: Mysterious Press.

Maria Monk. 1835. *Maria Monk: The Awful Disclosures of Maria Monk; and the Mysteries of a Convent Exposed.* Philadelphia: T. B. Peterson.

Marron, Kevin. 1988. *Ritual Abuse.* Toronto: Seal Books.

Michaelsen, Johanna. 1988. *Like Lambs to the Slaughter.* Eugene, OR: Harvest House.

Moody, Edward J. 1977. "Urban Witches." Pp. 427–37, *Conformity and Conflict: Readings in Cultural Anthropology,* 3rd ed., edited by James P. Spradley and David W. McCurdy. New York: Little Brown.

Parrinder, Edward G. 1963. *Witchcraft: European and African.* London: Faber.

Passantino, Gretchen and Bob, with Trott, Jon. 1989. "Satan's Sideshow." *Cornerstone* 18(90):23–28.

Peterson, Alan H. 1988–1990. *The American Focus on Satanic Crime,* 2 vols. South Orange, NJ: American Focus Publishing Co.

Pulling, Pat. 1989. *The Devil's Web: Who Is Stalking Your Children for Satan?* Lafayette, LA: Huntington House.

Raschke, Carl A. 1990. *Painted Black: From Drug Killings to Heavy Metal—How Satanism is Besieging our Culture and Our Communities.* San Francisco: Harper & Row.

Rivera, Geraldo. 1988. *Devil Worship: Exposing Satan's Underground.* NBC television documentary, October 25.

Rodgers-Melnick, Ann. 1989. "Rumors from Hell." *Pittsburgh Press,* three parts: September 3, 5, 6.

Schwarz, Ted, and Empey, Duane. 1988. *Satanism: Is Your Family Safe?* Grand Rapids, MI: Zondervan.

Scobie, Alastair. 1965. *Murder for Magic: Witchcraft in Africa.* London: Cassell.

Simmons, Marc. 1974. *Witchcraft in the Southwest: Spanish and Indian Supernaturalism on the Rio Grande.* Flagstaff, AZ: Northland Press.

Smith, Michelle, and Pazder, Lawrence. 1980. *Michelle Remembers.* New York: Congdon and Lattes.

Spencer, Judith. 1989. *Suffer the Child.* New York: Pocket.

Stratford, Lauren. 1988. *Satan's Underground: The Extraordinary Story of One Woman's Escape.* Eugene, OR: Harvest House.

Symonds, John. 1973. *The Great Beast.* London: Mayflower.

Tallant, Robert. 1946. *Voodoo in New Orleans.* New York: Macmillan.

Terry, Maury. 1987. *The Ultimate Evil.* New York: Doubleday.
Warnke, Mike. 1972. *The Satan Seller.* South Plainfield, NJ: Bridge Books.
Wedge, Thomas W. 1988. *The Satan Hunter.* Canton, OH: Daring Books.
Wooden, Kenneth, 1981. *The Children of Jonestown.* New York: McGraw-Hill.
———. 1988. "Light Must Be Shed on Devil Worship." Letter to the editor, *New York Times,* November 23.

Satanism and Psychotherapy: A Rumor in Search of an Inquisition

9

Sherrill Mulhern

INTRODUCTION

The current revival of popular belief in the existence of an international conspiratorial satanic blood cult has been promoted primarily by public declarations of alleged cult survivors, whose testimonies have been accredited by authoritative mental health professionals. These eye-witnesses can be divided into two groups: (1) adult mental patients, who claim to have been raised in transgenerational cults that "brainwashed" them through ritual torture, and (2) very young children, who allegedly have been subjected to ritual torture by cult recruiters while in daycare.[1] Both groups are said to have dissociated their memories of these horrifying experiences, recovering them only recently in psychotherapy.

In the early 1980s, the allegations of ritual torture and animal and human sacrifices made by these professed victims were taken seriously by law enforcement agencies, which spent several years "aggressively trying to uncover the evil conspiracy" (Lansing 1989). In spite of intensive investigations, no material substantiating evidence was recovered, making it unlikely that the allegations were true.

However, the question remained, if the horrifying rituals of a network of devil-worshipping cultists had not happened, what had occurred? Mental health professionals flatly rejected suggestions that the therapeutic disclosure process, which had led to the extraordinary revelations of heretofore amnesic adult survivors and recalcitrant child victims, had decisively shaped the patients' allegations. Therapy was portrayed as disinterested, the therapist as an individual with the courage to see through society's age old conspiracy to doubt the stories of innocent young martyrs.

At the 1989 National Conference on Child Abuse and Neglect, Dan Sexton, Director of the National Child Abuse Hot Line, responded to FBI Special Agent Ken Lanning's request for a sober review of the entire investigative and disclosure process:

I'm not a law enforcement person, thank God! I'm a psychology person, so I don't need the evidence, I come from a very different place, I don't need to see evidence to believe . . . I don't care what law enforcement's perspective is, that's not my perspective. I'm a mental health professional. I need to find a way to help survivors heal to the trauma that they had as children and to help support other clinicians who are trying to help survivors and victims of *this kind of crime.* (Sexton 1989).

This polarization of the debate has had far-reaching consequences. Shielded by the mental health perspective of belief, therapists and their patients continue to spread the satanic cult rumor. Together they speak out authoritatively in public forums, describing the behaviors and practices of a network of cults that no one but the alleged victims has ever seen. Medical professionals are part of a cultural elite, presumed to speak with scientific authority that is rarely questioned. However, in this case they are using that authority to accredit the belief that thousands of apparently normal people switch into satanic alter personalities and meet on a regular basis to commit wholesale slaughter right under our noses.

This chapter describes changes in the theory and practice of psychotherapy that have shaped mental health professionals' belief in the satanic cult conspiracy rumor, as well as methods used to propagate this belief in the mental health profession. I will focus on alleged adult survivors and their therapists because they have provided most ostensibly authoritative descriptions of the organization, motivation, and finality of the elusive conspiratorial satanic blood-cult network. It is essential to remember that propagation of the satanic cult conspiracy rumor in certain sectors of the mental health profession in the United States has been sanctioned, accelerated, and amplified by the sociocultural context described in this book's other chapters.

REALITY, TRUTH, AND CLINICAL VALIDITY

During the last two decades, the fundamental Freudian theorem that most psychopathology results from intrapsychic conflict between unacknowledged instinctual drives and demands of external reality has been increasingly challenged by revived interest in the traumatic theory of psychopathology. This theory, described by Janet at the turn of the century, holds that individuals exposed to extraordinary trauma experience overwhelming emotions that paralyze their ability to take appropriate action. To survive, the individual "splits off" the memory of the traumatic experience from consciousness, through the psychic mechanism of dissociation (van der Kolk et al. 1989).

Dissociated memories do not evaporate, but are hidden by an amnestic barrier. As time passes, these hidden memories may reappear as a fragmentary reliving of the trauma, emotional conditions, somatic states, visual images, or behavioral reenactment (van der Kolk et al. 1989). Historically, the treatment of choice for patients "haunted" by dissociated traumatic memories was (1) recovery of the offending memory, frequently through hypnosis, and (2) abreaction (reexperiencing, in an altered state of consciousness) of traumatic material in a secure therapeutic environment, where the memory's disturbing content could be processed and ultimately reintegrated into unified conscious memory.

At the turn of the century, Breuer and Freud used this technique particularly in treating hysteria. However, shortly after the 1895 publication of *Studies on Hysteria*, Freud became deeply dissatisfied with hypnosis when he realized that the memories recovered by patients in hypnoid states were not necessarily accurate accounts of experienced trauma. He subsequently replaced hypnosis with his technique of psychoanalysis. Following Freud's initiative, most clinicians rejected hypnosis. It was not until the First World War that the technique had a significant revival.

Faced with the problems of treating large numbers of combat veterans, clinicians again turned to hypnotic and/or drug-induced abreaction as effective techniques for eliminating the crippling psychological sequela of battlefield trauma. Over the next 30 years the successes of military psychiatry, especially during wartime, bolstered clinicians' confidence in the legitimacy of hypnosis for uncovering the causes of psychological trauma (Laurence and Perry 1988). Since accredited medical schools did not offer training in hypnosis, practitioners were forced to organize independent seminars to meet rising demand from clinicians drawn from a broad spectrum of the medical profession. The organization of the American Society of Clinical Hypnosis during this period helped stimulate interest in hypnotic techniques.

In the United States, the dramatic effects of intensive propaganda techniques on military prisoners made understanding hypnosis a major government priority. Beginning in the 1950s, more than five million dollars in federal research funding was made available, encouraging experimental researchers to take a serious look at hypnotic phenomena. One of their initial objectives was to develop scientific scales that could reliably measure individuals' ability to enter hypnotic states. Results of this research indicate that hypnosis is not a unitary phenomena; there appears to be a spectrum of hypnotizability running from low hypnotizables, who persistently resist suggestion, to high hypnotizables, who are so suggestible that the shift from normal consciousness into the state of deep hypnotic trance is practically instantaneous (Spiegel 1973; Morgan and Hilgard 1975; Weitzenhoffer and

Hilgard 1962; Frankel 1990). This latter group is estimated at between 5 and 10 percent of the general population.

Herbert Spiegel studied the behavioral characteristics of a large cohort of· highly hypnotizable subjects who presented no significant clinical symptoms. When not hypnotized, these subjects exhibited "a clinically identifiable configuration of personality traits" (Spiegel 1974:303), which he called the Grade Five Syndrome. When tested with the Hypnotic Induction Profile, Grade 5s demonstrate the high eye-roll with a high intact profile that tends to confirm the hypothesis that "trance capacity is essentially a biological phenomenon with a psychological overlay" (p. 304). Moreover, these subjects exhibit a posture of trust, "an intense, beguiling innocent expectation of support from others" (p. 304). In the therapeutic context, this behavior is translated into a persistent demand that "all attention and concern be focused on them" (p. 304). Grade 5s have unfailing confidence in the good will of their therapists, readily assimilating whatever is suggested by the therapist as being pertinent for them.

Grade 5s' highly empathetic abilities make them particularly vulnerable to introspective therapeutic techniques. For example, when they are asked to probe their memories for additional details concerning a particular remembered image or event, Grade 5s compulsively respond to their therapists' requests by adding information from various sources into their memories to "fill in the blanks." Researchers found that although these subjects ignore the sources of confabulated details, when questioned about the fallacious information, they make enormous efforts to fit the imagined material logically into the ongoing narrative of their recovered and reexperienced memories (Spiegel 1974).

Grade 5s have a "relatively telescoped time sense focused almost exclusively in the present" (p. 306). For example, when the hypnotic technique of age regression is used and they are asked to go back in time mentally to a prior moment in their lives, Grade 5s experience the unfolding past memory as if it were happening in the present. When they narrate the internal events to their therapists, they consistently use the present tense, i.e., "I am looking out the window" rather than "I was looking out the window."

When age-regressed Grade 5s recover apparently incongruent or impossible information, even the most extraordinary details—such as bodies materializing in thin air—are readily accepted and experienced as real. This complete immersion in what Orne (1959) has described as trance logic allows Grade 5s to accept and experience logically contradictory and mutually exclusive statements as being equally true (Spiegel 1974; Orne 1959; Pettinati 1988; Laurence and Perry, 1988).

The profile of individuals exhibiting the Grade 5 Syndrome is particularly relevant when attempting to evaluate testimonies of alleged adult survivors of satanic ritual abuse, the majority of whom have been diagnosed with multiple personality disorder. In 1989, George Ganaway, reviewing a co-hort of 82 patients meeting the DSM-III R criteria for dissociative disorders whom he had treated over a 2½-year period, stated that 66 percent met the diagnostic criteria for adult multiple personality disorder (MPD). In addition, he stated: "virtually all of the patients in the MPD group also met Spiegel's criteria for the Grade Five Syndrome" (Ganaway 1989:208).

Another aspect of hypnosis that experimental researchers have studied extensively is "hypnotic hypermnesia," the apparent enhancement of a subject's memory when in hypnoid states. Research confirms that hypnosis is anything but a truth serum; recovering memories through hypnosis does *not* ensure the material's historical accuracy. Controlled laboratory studies of age regression have demonstrated a tendency of hypnotized subjects to confabulate information spontaneously. For example,

> In one instance, it was suggested during hypnosis that one subject was attending school the day after a childhood birthday. The subject replied that he was not, and explained that the day after that particular birthday was a Saturday. His birthday, March 8, when checked out for that particular year, was found to have fallen on a Sunday. Orne points out that *this same fallacious statement came out in a later session and probably would have been believed had it not been checked.* (Perry and Laurence 1983:158; emphasis added)

This persistent fallacious information in a subsequent session with its potential for becoming permanently incorporated into a believed memory if indiscriminately validated by the therapist is particularly relevant. Experimental researchers have observed that even when memories are found to be fantasy or confabulation when checked against verifiable outside sources, hypnotized subjects experience all recalled memories *as if they were equally real*. This subjective experience of authenticity significantly increases the assurance and persuasiveness with which subjects relate their recovered memories when they return to the normal conscious state (Bowers and Hilgard 1988).

Therapists often overlook these risks when they attempt to uncover hidden memories of satanic ritual abuse and when they believe and validate unfolding memories of patients exhibiting the Grade 5 Syndrome, simply on the basis of the memories' compelling emotional quality and internal coherence. For example, contrast these experimental findings with Dr. Laurence Padzer's justification for his belief in the reality of the cult experiences remembered by his patient Michelle (Padzer and Smith 1980).

> It was a gradual turning point. Every time she entered into a new area of working, everything that she had said before was totally consistent. And then, when she had completed what she had done, she was totally free of it. It had a ring of truth to it, that I said, this is not accountable from anything in the literature, except by the fact that she had been through that experience. There's no other way that I can explain it. (Padzer 1990)

Dr. Padzer's comments suggest that the concerns and conclusions of experimental researchers have had relatively little impact on therapists. In clinical practice, attitudes toward hypnosis remain enthusiastic. Therapists emphasize the

> tremendous therapeutic benefit that can be gained from using hypnosis and narcosynthesis to allow the patient to reconnect with lost memories and emotions. Because it is both relaxing and likely to help dissociate emotion from cognition, hypnosis may minimize the psychic pain that normally accompanies the remembering of traumatic, forgotten events. (Pettinati 1988:286)

Clinicians working with patients, particularly those believed to be trauma victims, acknowledge that "all the factors which contribute unintentionally to memory distortion in hypnosis . . . may be centrally important in the clinical setting and contribute in a major way to the healing process" (Pettinati 1988:287).

During the first half of the twentieth century, most patients treated by psychological trauma specialists using hypnosis had either documented histories of life-threatening trauma (such as wartime service) or overwhelming recently experienced personal losses (such as death of a loved one). In therapy they presented recognizable dissociative symptoms such as amnesia, extreme detachment, and depersonalization. When a clinician discovered that a specific traumatic memory of combat was a fantasy, produced by an overwhelming fear that the "remembered" event might occur, he or she was likely to minimize the fact that the memory was fallacious, particularly when the retrieval and reliving of the inaccurate event invariably led to relief of symptoms.

Throughout the 1950s and 1960s, growing public concern with physical child abuse, incest, and child sexual abuse encouraged therapists to take an interest in victims of family trauma. An increasing number of adult patients entered therapy seeking to resolve symptoms that were perceived as sequela of life-threatening trauma experienced in childhood. Since these patients displayed symptoms remarkably similar to veterans' post-traumatic stress symptoms, many therapists used hypnosis to assist patients in recovering their dissociated memories of child abuse. Abuse histories disclosed by these patients forced clinicians to reevaluate the traditional Freudian attitude toward women's memories of incest. Many argued that Freud's initial "seduction theory" of hysteria may have been correct (Masson 1984). Although high mobility of adults in contemporary society makes it difficult for clinicians to corroborate individual childhood histories, when patients recover memories of violent sexual trauma, therapists no longer dismiss them as phantasms.

It is easy to understand why therapists turn to hypnosis and abreaction in treating these patients, but the usefulness of these techniques may be seriously compromised when clinicians believe that hypnosis is an impartial, efficient tool for recovering lost memories. A 1980 survey of 169 individuals, 46 percent of whom had formal graduate training in psychology, found that 84 percent agreed that hypnosis was effective for memory enhancement (Loftus and Loftus 1980). Laurence and Perry hypothesize that "the assumption underlying this belief in hypnotic memory enhancement is that memory is reproductive, that is, that it functions like an accurate recording device" (Laurence and Perry 1988:319). But experimental research into hypnotic phenomena has clearly shown that this metaphor flounders because, unlike a recording device, human memory is constantly reconstructing encoded perceptions in light of new input.

Although experimental researchers have been relatively successful in bringing their findings to bear on use of hypnosis in courts and other forensic settings, clinical practice has yet to implement formal guidelines on use of hypnosis to gather information. For example, in 1974 Spiegel explicitly recommended that patients be tested in order to identify those who exhibit the Grade 5 Syndrome. However, his recommendation has never been incorporated in a standardized clinical protocol. Moreover, textbooks and programs used to train therapists in hypnosis, including those texts that discuss the diagnosis and treatment of patients with multiple personality disorder, offer no cautions against systematic therapeutic probing of patients' memories for traumatic details. There are no obligations to record therapeutic sessions. Consequently, it is usually impossible for impartial observers to evaluate therapeutic techniques employed with patients diagnosed with multiple personality, who recall large-scale criminal activities such as cult murders.

MULTIPLE PERSONALITY: FROM EVE
TO THE MANCHURIAN CANDIDATE

Most human societies explicitly recognize that the subjective experience of being taken over by an alternative identity is a very real phenomena that is radically different from behavior that could be described as simulation. The seriousness of "embodying an alternative identity" is emphasized by the fact that all societies establish rules by which they can identify and socialize the phenomena (Zempleni 1986; Stoller 1989; Devereux 1977; Lowell 1894). Traditionally, embodied "alters" are considered entities with an independent subjective history and existence in the supernatural world. Consequently, they are typically described and understood in religious terms.

However, contemporary pluricultural, secularized society lacks a religious consensus.

This does not eliminate the subjective experience. On the contrary, responses to victims of embodiment are provided by a variety of belief systems including past life regression, channelling, spirit possession, witch-craft, satanism (*not to be understood as conspiratorial blood cults*), and pathological multiple personality disorder (MPD). Stern (1984) reported that many individuals with multiple personality believe in spirits, and many understand their alternative personalities as arising from past lives or spirit possessions. This variety is consistent with anthropological data indicating that these types of subjects are highly suggestible. Once they have found a socially authorized explanation for their experiences, they invest themselves totally, until a new authorized explanation comes along. In other words, they learn to understand their preexisting, subjective experiences during the identification/diagnostic process, and they conform themselves to behavioral models that society offers them.

The first secular description of pathological MPD is generally attributed to Pareclesus (1646), who reported the case of "a woman who was amnesic for an alter personality who stole her money" (Bliss 1980 in Putnam 1989:28). Rare reports of the condition that appeared over the next two centuries remained fairly superficial; however, the behavior was generally ascribed to something wrong with the patient, rather than to a supernatural power. It was not until publication of the cases of Estelle (1849, see Putnam 1989:29) and Leonine (Janet 1889) that significant indications emerged of the importance trauma might play in the etiology of MPD (Greaves 1980; Putnam 1989). At the turn of the century, the concept of dissociation was proposed to describe the hypothesized psychic defense mechanism that broke off the organized memory isolates, or personalities that in turn acted on or intruded into normal consciousness. Although MPD was accepted as a real clinical entity, it was considered extremely rare, a phenomena that should be diagnosed with great caution.

The case of Eve (Chris Sizemore), popularized in the film, "The Three Faces of Eve," brought attention to the diagnosis again (Thigpen and Cleckley, 1954). Although Putnam (1989) notes that the film presents a misleading image of the current clinical picture of MPD, he acknowledges that the case furnished further evidence of a relationship between early childhood trauma and dissociation, as well as some indication that dissociated alter personalities presented by an adult patient were created during childhood.

Throughout the 1970s Drs. Arnold Ludwig, Cornelia Wilbur, and their colleagues in the Department of Psychiatry of the University of Kentucky published an important series of MPD case reports and papers on dissociation (Larmore et al. 1977; Ludwig et al. 1972; Ludwig 1966). According to

Ludwig the dissociative mechanism can be triggered by a variety of social and environmental circumstances, including intentional brainwashing reported by war veterans and religious rites of ecstatic cults, described as mind altering, by Sargent (Ludwig 1966; Sargent 1957). This alleged link between controversial religious practices of contemporary religious cults and pathological dissociation that had attracted the attention of certain sectors of psychology during the 1960s ultimately facilitated the spread of satanic cult rumors in the 1980s (Bromley and Richardson, 1983).

This is not to suggest that psychiatrists treating MPD were treating a population of cult victims. On the contrary, during the 1970s, most multiples reported coming from strict, often puritanical, fanatically religious fundamentalist family backgrounds (Higdon 1986). Many reported enduring severe corporal punishment for even minor, ostensibly moral transgressions. Most patients treated by the Kentucky group, many of whom recovered memories of being subjected to sadomasochistic sexual abuse, came from this type of background. Some individuals in this patient cohort had already begun "recovering" memories of gang rape, entombment, mutilation and even infant murder in the 1970s.

The importance accorded memories of such sadistic torture was notably absent in other early clinical reports. For example, in 1977 Dr. Ralph Allison proposed a description of the clinical presentation of the disorder that was much more mitigated than current descriptions, particularly those that focus on satanic programming. Although he never denied the potential importance of child sexual abuse, he hypothesized that MPD is "due to a combination of factors, including inborn inability to learn from errors, unwillingness to make moral choices, being highly sensitive to others' emotions and living in a polarized family" (Allison 1977:1). Alter personalities were described as having been created as a result of unconscious forces at a specific date, for a specific emotional purpose, in response to a life trauma of psychological need.[2]

In the 1970s the clinical picture of MPD developed bit by bit as clinicians exchanged information, particularly data obtained from increasing patient cohorts. The 1973 case of Sybil, a patient treated by Dr. Cornelia Wilbur, dramatically underscored the relationship between repeated sadistic physical and sexual torture directed at a small child and the clinical syndrome of multiple personality. Although medical journals rejected Dr. Wilbur's case report, "the popular book *Sybil* (Schreiber 1973), with its graphic treatment of the amnesias, fugue episodes, child abuse, and conflicts among alters, served as a template against which other patients could be compared and understood" (Putnam 1989:35).

In 1980, the DSM-III diagnostic manual of the American Psychiatric Association adopted the diagnosis of multiple personality. This formal recognition of validity for MPD served to legitimate serious research into the phenomenon's cause and treatment. In 1984, the First International Conference on Multiple Personality/Dissociative States was organized in Chicago. During that same year, the unfolding cases of alleged satanic ritual abuse in daycare centers became a focus of media attention.

Over the next 6 years, the annual conferences became a privileged context wherein clinicians and their patients met to discuss the etiology, diagnosis, and treatment of MPD. Researchers reported their findings and therapists came to learn the latest techniques, while patients listened to presentations and exchanged ideas and experiences in support groups. In addition to providing a useful historical framework for understanding emergence of a consensual, "state of the art" definition of MPD, tape recordings of sessions and collections of abstracts and papers presented during those meetings clearly document propagation of the satanic cult rumor.

Satanism and satanic cults were already a subject of informal conversation among clinicians and patients by 1985. A year later, the first purported description of the practices of satanic cults, a potpourri of alleged victims' stories of orgies, bloody rituals, and human sacrifice mixed with the popular brainwashing model of mental coercion and mind control, was included in the scientific program. A survey of the conference participants indicated that 25 percent of the patients in treatment were alleging satanic cult abuse. In 1986 nine papers addressed the question of satanic ritual abuse. All of these presentations treated satanic cult memories as if they were literally true. No alternative explanatory models, concomitant alternative treatment strategies, or therapeutic guidelines were proposed.

Multiple personality was no longer simply the consequence of child abuse. It was the explicit goal of intentional, diabolical cult brainwashing, mind control, and programming. Believing clinicians who accepted the satanic etiology of MPD concluded that many of their adult patients were in fact satanic Manchurian Candidates (or brainwashed satanic robots) waiting to be triggered by cult leaders lurking just beyond the therapist's door (Hammond, 1989). In 1989, 20 percent of the scientific program was allotted to the diagnosis and treatment of ritual abuse allegedly perpetrated by actual satanic cults. In addition, a full-day post conference satanic ritual abuse workshop was organized.

The glaring absence of presentations offering a critical analysis of the growing moral panic among clinicians does not indicate a general agreement among therapists and researchers on the accuracy of satanic ritual abuse allegations. In 1986, the problem of "the cult" was raised during a meeting of the research committee of the International Society for the Study of Multiple Personality & Dissociation. Researchers were confronted with an exasperating dilemma. The dramatic increase in reports of child sexual abuse since the 1960s had persuaded many clinicians that patients' recovered memories of repeated childhood physical and sexual abuse were highly probable (Kluft 1985; Wilbur 1985; Putnam 1985; Braun and Sachs 1985; Goodwin 1985). They were convinced that, for generations, society had refused to listen to victimized children, forcing them to accommodate themselves in silence to their tormenters (Summit 1983). As result many therapists were hesitant to doubt even the most extreme stories of sadistic, ritualized torture.

Unfortunately, by 1986, a substantial number of patients had already "recovered" their memories of satanic abuse and had moved on from the initial validation of their therapists to public validation offered by religious propagandists. Many of these former patients and their therapists had joined a growing network of cult "experts" offering authoritative advice at police conferences, schools, and accredited training seminars for interested mental health professionals. Given the deeply held beliefs and sense of mission that bound this network together, organizing an impartial study was nearly impossible.

Nevertheless, many serious researchers were aware that none of the hundreds of satanic ritual abuse allegations that had surfaced across the United States had ever been substantiated, even after intensive criminal investigation. They were particularly sensitive to the fact that the sheer numbers of uncorroborated allegations had moved some serious critics to suggest that patients' satanic memories must reflect something other than factual accounts of experienced trauma. They were also aware that the possibility of a contagious rumor could not simply be discarded, given the clinical profile of the highly hypnotizable multiple and the enthusiastic networking of therapists.

BELIEF AND THE THERAPY OF VICTIMIZATION

My preliminary study of spread of belief in a satanic blood cult among mental health professionals treating *adult* patients revealed that clinicians listed four types of evidence for the reality of patients' satanic ritual victimization: (1) violence of the abreaction of recovered memories, (2) abundance of vivid detail and what therapists referred to as logical consistency of descriptions of abuse, (3) manifestation of body memories, such as spontaneous bleeding, muscle contractions, appearance of marks on the skin, etc. prior to or during the remembering process, and (4) their conviction that patients who had never met were saying the same things (Mulhern 1988).

Given the highly hypnotizable profile of MPD patients, even though the first three factors may seem convincing, they emphatically do not constitute evidence. When these patients are age regressed to prior moments in their lives, they relive mental events as if they were there. Although some Grade 5s are capable of producing extraordinary body manifestations that illustrate their memories (the bleeding hands and feet of stigmatics), these types of exhibitions do not constitute evidence of a memory's historical accuracy (Wilson 1982; Didi-Huberman 1982).

In 1974, Spiegel warned therapists against using introspective methods of therapy with Grade 5s, stating that they will systematically transpose a therapist's request to search inwardly for answers into an active search of the therapist for cues to the correct answer. Moreover, he noted that Grade 5s' demand for the undivided attention and concern of their therapists "is often so tenacious as to feed the grandiosity strivings a therapist may have. The therapist must therefore know where he ends and the subject begins in order to avoid entrapment" (Spiegel 1974:304).

Unfortunately, few clinicians treating MPD have understood the importance of these warnings. Dr. George Ganaway, who has been giving consultation clinics for therapist training to treat MPD for many years, has stated that he

> continues to be surprised at the number of experienced therapists who have yet to grasp that they are treating patients who in effect are continually moving in and out of hypnotic trance states, no matter what the therapists' intent may be regarding the use of hypnotic techniques. On one occasion when [he] was cautioning that memories recovered in a hypnoid state should be understood as an admixture of fact and confabulatory material, one consultee argued that this could not possibly be the case with her MPD client, as she never used hypnosis in therapy sessions; child alters simply would emerge spontaneously in vivid reenactments of their trauma. (Ganaway 1989:208)

Patients' alleged memories of satanic torture are not simply a product of a tragic therapeutic error. A Grade 5 MPD patient's vulnerability to suggestion extends far beyond the confines of therapy. They are like sponges, soaking in whatever they focus on in their environment. They become sick with the illnesses of others and convert easily to their beliefs. The implication of this characteristic was not lost on Spiegel, who speculated that a Grade 5 who has accepted a belief that is diametrically opposed to his or her customary beliefs will probably reject the new belief once returned to the usual environment. Friends and relatives will point out the aberration and exert pressure to switch back. However, should the Grade 5 move to a new environment where the new belief is shared by many people and where espousing this belief facilitates insertion, the person may hold the belief forever (Spiegel 1968). MPD patients and their therapists are equally vulnerable to suggestion and reinforcement from both the therapeutic milieu and the general social environment where satanic panics have been common for at least two decades (Lyons 1970; Victor 1989; Balch 1989; Carlson and Larue 1989; Hicks 1990).

This brings us to the fourth factor (which is apparently not a byproduct of the therapeutic setting): patients who have never met say the same things.

MPD patients have been meeting together for years in group therapy, in hospital settings, and at conferences that focus on MPD and more recently on ritual abuse. Since the beginning of the satanic panic this networking has intensified. There are many instances where cult therapists, often former patients with recovered cult memories, are treating groups of patients still in therapy attempting to uncover similar memories. Newly "cultified" (Schafer 1990) patients attend these sessions absolutely convinced that the survivor-therapist really knows what *They* do and "whatever *They* did to her, *They* did to me." Patients and therapists have been talking together about what *They* do for at least 6 years. Although obviously some patients may not have met, the similar stories are being mystified by an uncalled for sense of awe in a world defined by mass media, where stories and images of torture abound.

Although it may be true that alleged adult survivors who have *gone public* on the satanic lecture circuit are saying the same things now, given the confidentiality rules that govern therapy, society has only clinicians' assurances that these patients said the same things when they originally disclosed. Human beings are easily hypnotized by the magic of words, easily falling under their spell, believing that when there is a word there must be a thing corresponding to it, and that the wording of a given text necessarily means the same thing that it usually means in subjective, personal experience (White 1926). This observation is relevant for understanding just what authorities on sexual abuse mean when they claim that patients are saying the same things, or when they accuse those who doubt these horrendous disclosures of revictimizing their patients. Many researchers are astounded when they discover from the clinical data that the overwhelming majority of these patients, adults and children, do not say anything about satanic cult ritual abuse when they enter therapy.[3]

The majority of alleged adult survivors have been in psychiatric treatment for years, many diagnosed as MPDs. Some are chronic self-mutilators, or have histories of drug abuse. Therapists diagnosing satanic ritual abuse report that these patients are actively recovering and abreacting memories of childhood sexual victimization before any satanic material emerges. When allegations of satanism emerge, the disclosure usually begins when a patient reports experiencing an intrusive image (such as people wearing robes, a knife slashing, or a bonfire), which is subsequently fleshed out over several therapy sessions into a description of a ritual, or when a patient recognizes a ritual scene described by the therapist during a *hypnotic interview* (Young et al. 1991). In the latter case a patient's *report* of specific satanic abuses may consist of a nod of the head or a prearranged ideomotor finger signal.[4]

Adult patients report satanic cult abuse memories while in altered states of consciousness: their personality states are altered by hypnotic intervention or autohypnotic personality switching, after which the therapeutic interview takes place. Most alleged adult survivors are described as being polyfragmented multiples (Braun and Sachs 1988; Ray 1990). Therapists postulate that the impact of traumatic events has been so intense that images and emotions attached to a single episode are scattered across layers of personality fragments. Therapists must search for pieces of a particular narrative across a complex system of personalities. The techniques used to get a given personality to disclose traumatic details vary according to the declared age or temperament of that personality. For example, therapists may use play therapy, developed for use with small children, to gain information from child alters of an adult patient (Graham-Costain 1990).

When therapists work with malevolent alters considered to be potentially violent, they may "contract with the host to enter physical restraints prior to calling the alter out. This may involve a straitjacket, wrist and ankle straps, or sheeting in various combinations" (Ross 1989:287). Authorities on MPD have suggested that this procedure will become even more prevalent as "satanically abused patients enter the mental health system" (p. 288). In hospital units already specializing in alleged satanic ritual abuse, the use of restraints is relatively common. Thus, when a satanic alter personality "comes out" in the multiple's body, it discovers that it has arrived in a physically immobilized body. At this point, therapeutic probing begins: details of ritual abuse are being *reported* to therapists by satanic alters while patients writhe and struggle against restraints.

Often it takes months before a narrative of an alleged event emerges. Some patients report having expressed doubts to their therapist concerning the accuracy of an emerging narrative, only to find that their therapist refused to validate these doubts. Some therapists apparently suggest that these kinds of doubts are part of the patients' satanic cult's programming (Ganaway 1990).

Given the context of "cultified" therapy, to equate a patient who nods when asked if she was ever taken to a place where there were people in robes chanting while they threw human body parts into a bonfire, a patient who tells of being troubled by a fragmented memory of blood, and a patient who is abreacting a violent rape while in restraints, is a paranoid interpretation of the data. In paranoid interpretation, the context of disclosure vanishes. Fortuitous illusory similarities are made to appear relevant because they are viewed through a preexisting belief filter that overestimates coincidences that can be explained in other ways. Normally, discrepancies, incongruities, and contradictory details would be interpreted as evidence that individual satanic narratives differ. However, when viewed through a belief filter, these idiosyncracies are simply added into an unfolding composite description of the invisible cult. In other words, *the alleged victims of satanic cults are not so much saying the same things as they are being heard the same way.*

When complete descriptions of the contents and contexts of adult allegations are compared with those of daycare cases, the only real links that
appear between the two are (1) the crucial importance of therapy in the
disclosure process, and (2) the fact that therapists persistently cross-
reference bits of information from one group to the other *as if* they were
interchangeable.[5]

Since clinicians learn to perfect their listening skills through training and
since these listening skills seem to be indispensable to uncovering identical
dissociated memories of satanic ritual abuse (SRA), the accredited SRA
training seminars offered for mental health professionals merit examination.

Invariably, seminars training clinicians in the diagnosis and treatment of
victims of SRA begin by creating an emotional and conceptual context for
belief. From the outset, listeners are admonished, threatened, and exhorted
to believe. Belief is vital to the definition of SRA, as the following indicates:

> The phenomena that is going around on this issue is not unlike the phenomena
> around the issue of child abuse that we saw in the last decade. That somehow
> in the early 80s and late 70s no one believed that child sexual abuse was going
> on either. It wasn't until a program like "Something About Amelia" aired on
> TV that suddenly people started to reach out and say that "this happened to me
> also when I was a child." No one believed those of us who are survivors in the
> audience and throughout the conference, who are now mental health profes-
> sionals. We are perpetuating the same process of not believing again because
> it is too impossible to believe, there is no evidence that tells me that this is
> physically in front of my face. (Sexton, 1989)

The semantic slight of hand that characterizes SRA conferences is evidence in this call to belief. By evoking an image of children crying to be
heard while adult society turns a deaf ear, presenters gloss over the fact that
these patients are being heard; they are in therapy with people who are quite
prepared to listen. The problem is that the vast majority of patients are not
coming into therapy saying anything about SRA. In reality, SRA conferences
are not asking clinicians to believe what patients are saying, but to believe
that these patients' silence results from their having been brainwashed by an
elusive conspiratorial blood cult. In other words, clinicians must come to
believe in the cult *before* they begin listening to their patients. They must be
convinced that this cult is incredibly sophisticated, that it has been practicing mind control and criminal indoctrination for generations with impunity,
and that therapists are just beginning to understand the complexity of the
cult's advanced techniques (Braun 1988; Young 1989; Greaves 1989; Hammond 1989; Beere 1989; Vickery et al. 1989).

The internal coherence of training conferences depends on the creation of
an aura of *plausibility* around the conspiratorial blood cult, which has to
appear real. Many professed cult authorities begin their lectures by ac-

knowledging that no material evidence has ever been found to corroborate the cult's existence. Once this is said, however, they invariably provide trainees with a detailed description of the organization, motivation, brainwashing techniques, and finality of the worldwide satanic blood-cult network: *Them*. This portrait is illustrated by slides showing paraphernalia from ostentatious religious rituals performed by adolescents and self-proclaimed orthodox satanists, satanic graffiti, patients' satanic art work, record covers, and scenes of alleged satanically inspired murder–suicides (Burgess and Kelly 1990; Cozolino and Laboriel 1989).

Visual aids do much to make the invisible satanic cult seem very real, but none substantiates the descriptions recovered from the dissociated memories of patients. Ironically, most of the bloody images actually contradict the authoritative description of *Them*. After all, the elusive masterminds of this murder and mayhem are alleged to be so sophisticated that they leave absolutely no evidence of ritual torture chambers, brainwashing and baby killing which are described as their stock and trade.

Only patients' art work produced and interpreted during therapy remains. It is impossible to confirm that a drawing of a fire, a spiral, or a bleeding chopped up body is not symbolic, but is instead a literal reproduction of satanic insignia or a real torture scene. Accreditation of a specific satanic meaning for a given image depends on the authority accorded to the therapist certifying such an interpretation.

In the same way, it is the therapist's authority that guarantees the accuracy of description given of *Them* and what *They* do. Most experts readily admit that they have pieced together this description by combining bits of information recovered from allegedly dissociated memories drawn from two distinct populations—adults reporting on intrafamilial sexual abuse and children reporting abuse in an out-of-home setting. Given that intensive criminal investigations have failed to substantiate allegations of either population, what justification do experts offer for consolidating this material into one narrative?

Essentially, the existence of recovered memories in one population is used to corroborate memories of the other population, in lieu of material evidence and in spite of the fact that memories of the two groups are at best only superficially similar (Mulhern 1989). In 1987, Dr. Roland Summit introduced a session on the recognition of cult phenomena by reminding the audience that the type of experiences children have gone through

run a common basis for the development of MPD and other dissociative disorders . . . The worst thing that can happen to children will turn up in MPD . . . Sure enough, a striking finding has been the number of *children speaking as alters through multiple personality*, individuals who describe blood curdling kinds of experiences that have left us reeling in our incredulity. (Summit 1987)

Dr. Summit's formulation is very revealing. Instead of referring to memories produced by an adult patient speaking in the voice of a child alter personality, he speaks of *children speaking as alters*. The two populations are blended into one silenced body. They have endured torture, they have murdered babies, and they have cannibalized their victims. The child victim of long ago was allegedly forced to accommodate herself to her satanic family by a society that refused to believe. She is now heard crying out with the same voice as the child abused in daycare, whose terror at the threats and rituals of her tormentors engenders dissociation of traumatic satanic memories in a world that still refuses to believe the children.

A close examination of the two populations reveals that this blending poses problems. Victims of intrafamilial child abuse are said to *accommodate* to abuse essentially because the family unit and proximate society refuse to take children's complaints into account (Summit 1983). This does not mean that none of these victims ever exhibited symptoms of trauma. On the contrary, much of the training in child abuse prevention given to the educators of small children emphasizes visible symptoms manifested by victims of family violence in order to facilitate early identification of those in need of help.

Nevertheless, SRA trainees are told that even the most solicitous parents of alleged daycare victims may never know their child is being subjected to horrifying torture on a daily basis. They learn of the abuse when a case breaks, and children attending a daycare are brought in for evaluation. Even getting children to indicate that something has happened is a task that only skilled professionals can undertake, and even they may not succeed.

> This is the one crime that you can perpetrate against 100 children and 100 children will not tell! And it's very important that we realize that we have to be very aggressive in an invitational way. We have to be very aggressive about finding out what happened to these children. (Graham-Costain 1990)

Professionals in child ritualistic abuse explain this extraordinary silence by evoking the concept of dissociation. One of the most circulated documents at SRA conferences states that

> the horror and fear experienced by a child who is ritually abused is processed by the child with varying degrees of *dissociation* as a defense mechanism against the overwhelming pain. Most children who were ritually abused during their preschool years will have completely *dissociated* the events within two years of the cessation of the abuse and will be unable to consciously recall and report what occurred. A skilled child therapist can help the *dissociated* ritual abuse victim to recall his/her abuse and to work through the severe trauma, which if left untreated, is likely to cause serious emotional problems for the child throughout his/her life. (Report of the Ritual Abuse Task Force, Los Angeles County Commission for Women 1988:17)

The etiology of multiple personality disorder never suggests that all victims of repeated sadistic intrafamilial abuse use dissociation as a privileged psychic defense mechanism. Those who *have the ability to dissociate* may use this capacity to tolerate unbearable trauma. This extraordinary capacity has been demonstrated by only a fraction of the general population. Nevertheless, the abundant use of the term dissociation guarantees trainees that this explication is firmly grounded in the authority of science. As a result, the shift in meaning is rarely noted. Dissociation occurs in some people when terror strikes. For those few, it is the immediate, life-preserving blacking out of the ongoing event. *How can most children dissociate satanic torture within 2 years of the cessation of the abuse?* Can this possibly be the same mechanism?

In SRA training seminars, no time is set aside to examine this enormous semantic transformation. Stripped of its meaning, dissociation becomes the passkey of belief. It allows trained professionals to *know* that persistent silence of an alleged victim is not an indication that this kind of crime has not happened, but that the child has simply dissociated it. Therapy must continue until the amnestic barriers are broken down because multiple personality and other dissociative disorders await any child whose parents refuse to recognize explicit satanic ritual abuse and present the child for therapy.

> Unfortunately, the parents of many young victims are unable to believe that their children have been ritually abused, and refuse to acknowledge that they have a problem or to seek help. Their children often have been made to believe that their parents were willing co-conspirators with the abusers, leaving the children very confused, with feelings of dread and distrust toward their own parents. The extreme severity of the abuse and the systematic attempts to indoctrinate the child into the cult's belief system, make the recovery quite difficult and protracted even with the help of skilled therapists. Children who are not treated are likely to face very poor outcomes. (Report of the Ritual Abuse Task Force, Los Angeles County Commission for Women 1988:17)

This declaration is outrageous because no studies have ever documented long-term effects of therapy with child victims of sexual abuse, let alone of ritual abuse. None of the eminent faculty expounding at training seminars ever point out this detail. Dr. Summit and his fellow experts believe:

> Because we see it clinically, we see something we believe is real, clinically and whether or not our colleagues or the press, or scientists at large or politicians or local law enforcement agencies agree that this is real, most of us have some sort of personal sense that it is; at least speaking as a bias of one, and for the members of the platform. (Summit 1987)

This is a powerful argument coming from the author of *The Child Abuse Accommodation Syndrome* (Summit 1983). Dr. Summit and his colleagues are among the most respected authorities in the fields of child sexual abuse prevention and the treatment of patients suffering from major dissociative symptoms. Their opinions are more than just idle conversation; they present them in seminars that have been accredited in Category I of the Physician's Recognition Award of the American Medical Association, by the American Psychological Association, and by the American Society of Clinical Hypnosis. The trainee has paid to learn what is expected of a clinician who would treat traumatized victims of *this kind of crime*. He or she learns that the truth lies hidden behind amnestic barriers programmed by the cult. Once clinicians treating either small children or adults break through these barriers and disclosure begins, belief is primordial. Cult victims supposedly have been warned that should they try to disclose they will not be believed, therefore, to doubt the unfolding tales of horror is to further victimize the patient.

> I don't want more survivors going into clinicians' offices feeling again that they are being re-abused by the mental health profession. If you do not believe that this could possibly happen, do not work with this issue, we don't want you a part of this because it is simply going to make the issue be more confounded and more difficult. (Sexton, 1989)

Once the belief filter is firmly in place, experts elaborate on questions of diagnosis and treatment. *The sole and unique explanation offered for evolving observable behavior of these adults and children in therapy is that they were or continue to be programmed victims of real brainwashing satanic cults.* Trainees receive lists of satanic holidays, an authoritative checklist of the signs and symptoms of satanic ritual abuse (Gould 1988), and pages of satanic symbols, and are warned that "unless prepared to identify the signs of cult involvement, even highly skilled clinicians might miss the salient cues" (Kaye and Klein 1987). Therapists treating adult MPD patients are assured that once they recognize the often subtle satanic signs, which include (1) symbols, (2) ceremonial objects, (3) practices and rituals, (4) destructive acts, and (5) victims' effects, they should feel free to probe the patient's memory actively for more hidden satanic material, which, if recovered, would facilitate the abreactive work (Kaye and Klein 1987). It is apparent that for these experts, discovery of *satanic indicators* justifies use of intensive introspective psychotherapy with highly hypnotizable patients.

Treatment techniques suggested for cultified patients vary according to the expert. Some discuss deprogramming triggers and contacting layer upon layer of cult-programmed alters, while others take a spiritual approach. In 1989, Dr. Walter Young reminded mental health professionals that cult survivors are often devastated by survivor guilt once the cult memories start to surface. "People who had thought of themselves as normal, loving parents suddenly are flooded with images of themselves torturing and murdering infants" (Young 1988). Therapists are counseled to guide patients through their emerging memories, pointing out the innate goodness of child alters as they tell of struggling with the choice between death and murdering their friends (Young 1988).

During training seminars that focus on alleged cult brainwashing techniques, adult patients who recover SRA memories are described as potentially active cult members. SRA seminars provide clinicians with lists of current triggers and cues that have been *observed* on in-patient units where many satanic cult victims are treated together. Therapists are warned to watch for such seemingly innocuous gifts as sea shells, color-coded flowers, or numerologically significant greeting cards. Birthdays and an endless list of satanic holidays are potentially preprogrammed triggers for suicide or self-mutilation. Out-patients pose a special risk because the cult may leave recorded verbal cues on telephone answering machines (Braun 1988, 1989; Young 1989; Greaves 1989; Hammond 1989; Beere 1989; Vickery et al. 1989).

Today, the cult is a terrifying reality for many patients and their therapists. Clinicians claim telephone threats to themselves, cult tinkering with their cars, and being attacked by patients when they inadvertently set off a trigger recently implanted by the cult to obstruct therapy. Therapists working with children are advised to change the words they use because "these folks get in there and find out what you're doin' and they will take these kids, reinvolve them and use the words that you're using to become triggers for pain" (Graham-Costain 1990). Clinicians working on "cultified" hospital units warn of having to censor mail and telephone calls, of cult members planted on the unit in order to contact patients, of mysterious break-ins, and of the importance of hospital security police. Units that take the satanic threat seriously report that, in spite of extraordinary efforts, patients are continually being recontacted by the cult, which triggers them to self-mutilate or attempt suicide. Significantly, at least one important psychiatric center that treats MPD patients, including those who allege cult involvement, takes absolutely no extraordinary precautions to isolate patients, but has yet to experience such "satanic heckling."

During question and answer sessions experts address individual therapists' preoccupations such as how to maintain a therapeutic alliance with patients who allege that they continue to participate in cult human sacrifices. Unfortunately, clinicians who accept the validity of these types of allegations may go to extraordinary lengths, even with patients who seriously object to the reality of the satanic memories which they have recovered. In 1990, Dr. George Ganaway treated a young woman who had been hospitalized by her therapist, who had overruled her objections that her cult memories did not seem to be real. The patient was placed under security guard while she had a baby because her therapist had discovered that intrusive memories of childhood sexual abuse, which had troubled the patient during her pregnancy, were really memories of satanic ritual abuse.

The therapist had used hypnosis to contact alleged satanic alters programmed in the patient's mind and discovered that the cult intended to sacrifice the baby. Around the clock surveillance was organized to prevent the cult from kidnapping the newborn. In addition, the mother was allowed to see the baby for only brief visits with someone else present because the therapist feared that a programmed satanic alter in the mother might come out and perform the ordained sacrifice (Ganaway 1990).[6]

PRIMUM NON NOCERE

Today, cloaked in a mental health perspective, knowledgeable experts publicly chide the legal system for applying the standard of proof in criminal prosecutions, i.e., proof beyond a reasonable doubt, as the criterion for accepting whether these kinds of acts have occurred (Rivera 1988; Braun et al. 1989). They assert in scientific journals that the traumatic sequela that *they see* in their patients and the identical stories that *they hear* constitute real evidence for the existence of the satanic cult. They fail to mention the education of the therapeutic ear, censored mail and phone calls, frantic searching for triggers and cues, use of restraints, the finger signals, and risks of engaging in therapeutic probing with highly hypnotizable patients. Consequently, no one dares to doubt when the progressive collapse of the *disclosing* adult patient into "unusual fears, survivor guilt, indoctrinated beliefs, substance abuse, sexualization of sadistic impulses and dissociative states with satanic overtones" is held up as a new clinical syndrome (Young et al. 1991).

Since 1987, Dr. Bennett Braun has begun workshops and conferences on the diagnosis and treatment of satanic ritual abuse victims by announcing "I do everything by the rule of 5 . . . Anything that I report will be well above the rule of 5, and that means from five separate people, often from different states" (Braun 1989). He admits to his listeners that although he cannot *prove* the claims he is making, he is drawing his material from the reports of over *80 victims of satanic ritual abuse* that he has either treated personally, or whose cases he has personally supervised. He further asserts that in addition to his own material, he has received material from hundreds of therapists from all over the United States. He has "gotten data from England, Holland, Germany, France, Canada and Mexico, which is (not absolutely identical) but real, real, real similar. Some of the symbolism is identical across these countries. The structure and the things people talk about, the types of abuse are very, very similar, so it's the same church, different pew phenomena" (Braun 1988).

Dr. Braun invites his listeners to forward their material to him with the assurance that it will be locked away for safe keeping, far from the intruding eyes of the threatening satanists, noting that when he receives information, all details that could indicate the real source of the data are stripped away. He suggests that he and his associates will be proceeding cautiously with the complex investigation. As a result, social researchers are left with only Dr. Braun's word when they seek to examine his data base and the analytical methods that he and his informants used to conclude that "we are working with a national–international type organization that's got a structure somewhat similar to the communist cell structure, where it goes from local, from small groups to local consuls, regional consuls, district consuls, national consuls and they have meetings at different times" (Braun 1988).

During hours of training that follow, through the magic of words, the conspiratorial blood cult with its sadomasochistic brainwashing tortures will exist. Mental health professionals will learn from recognized authorities how to ferret out proof of its insidious activities from the brainwashed memories of children and chronically ill adults. Those who hesitate in this endeavor are reassured by Dr. Braun that "if even 10% of *this stuff*, is true, then we're in big trouble" (Braun 1988). It is up to the listener to understand what *stuff* is being referred to. Is it kids dabbling in the devil, or Anton Levy and his card-carrying members of the Church of Satan, or serial killers, or the drug runners of Matamoros, or the great conspirational blood cult?

This chapter does not purport to suggest that no child or adult has ever been sadistically abused by an individual or a group of people justifying their actions by saying that "the devil made them do it." I fully recognize the sufferings of children who have been battered and raped by the very persons they rely on for survival. Moreover, I have seen the bloody mess that is left behind when charismatic leaders demand ultimate sacrifice or the final solution. However, when people come to believe that anyone could be one of *Them*, someone will usually be found. I dread the moment when self-righteous vested interest groups, which today stand side by side with the champions of the mental health perspective, place one hand on the Bible and point *Them* out. What if Dr. Braun is right? What if 90% of *this stuff* is not true?

ACKNOWLEDGMENTS

I wish to thank Dr. Louise Arnold and all of the participants at the Eighth International Contemporary Legends Seminar for their invaluable suggestions, and Debbie Nathan, Robert Hicks, and Jeffrey Victor for keeping me up to date with field materials and for sharing their ideas. I would also like to thank members of the International Society for the Study of Multiple Personality and Dissociation. Although some of them may find my judgment harsh, I wish them well as they search for answers to complex issues of alleged satanic ritual abuse. Above all I wish to thank FBI Special Agent Ken Lanning, who, by his example, has taught me a great deal about life in the middle of the road.

NOTES

1.   Recently, a third group made up of child victims whose parents are involved in custody disputes has been reported to investigators of ritual abuse allegations. This group is not included because the dynamics involved in custody disputes would require a discussion of issues beyond the scope of this study.

2.   Alters are described as having gender identities, and a potential range for good or bad emotions and motivations. Actions of the alter personalities are not limited only to times when they are *out* in *the body*. Even when they are *in* (inside the mind), they are understood to be entities that can initiate actions having a real impact on the subject (the body plus all other personalities). For example, from within they can trick a personality who is *out* by hiding memories of past experiences. Inversely, when they are *out*, they can punish a weak personality that is *in*, by getting *the body* into a difficult situation and then simply switching *in*, leaving the weak personality *out* "holding the bag," so to speak.

3.   Although the number of patients who actively seek out therapists specializing in satanic cult ritual abuse has increased recently, this may be due in part to the extraordinary publicity surrounding the issue. Some experts, speaking at MPD conferences attended by patients as well as therapists, have taken to dividing multiples into categories such as "garden variety multiples" and "ritually abused multiples" (Ray 1990). This classification has probably exacerbated the situation, as Grade 5s may react rather strongly to being alluded to as "garden variety" anything, particularly by an expert who proclaims that "many of the healed multiples out there were healed from family incest . . . by having integration . . . of only the superficial layers of the multiplicity, . . . the ritual abuse was never touched" (Ray 1990).

4.   For those unfamiliar with therapists' jargon, the term *hypnotic interview* demands some clarification. Clinicians trained to diagnose ritual abuse sometimes describe either a ceremony or a symbol that they have been taught is a satanic indicator and ask if the patient recognizes it. The patient's yes or no answer can be indicated either by a nod of the head or by prearranged ideomotor finger signals. In the latter case, the therapist asks the patient to place her hands comfortably in front of her and then invites all the hidden parts/personalities to choose a yes finger, a no finger, and a stop finger on each hand. These fingers can then be used by the hidden/unconscious parts of the patient's mind to either agree or disagree with answers given by the presenting personality, or to stop a therapist's line of questioning. (Braun's [1980] suggestion, that therapists designate signaling fingers on only one hand because of the risk for confusion, often goes unheeded.) The vast majority of therapists employing this technique with patients whom they believe to be victims of ritual abuse are convinced that answers given through finger signals always reflect unconscious true responses.

5.   Specific diagnostic and therapeutic techniques that have led to disclosures in daycare ritual abuse cases will not be discussed at length, first because the context of child therapy is totally different, and second because the content of these children's disclosures bears only superficial resemblance to the adult material. Children have no choice when they are brought to a given therapist for evaluation, and they are obliged to stay in therapy as long as their legal guardians and the therapist deem it necessary. The vast majority of children in daycare cases are brought to therapists for evaluation simply because they have attended centers where allegations surfaced, not because they complained of abuse. Most such children present no overt symptoms of extraordinary trauma. Symptoms and recognizable traumatic sequela described as being consistent with ritual abuse are invariably exhibited by the children

after the actual disclosure process begins, often several months into therapy. Only then are serious behavioral problems said to appear.

Experts explain this phenomena by theorizing that once disclosure begins the hidden memories are suddenly made available to normal consciousness (Snowden 1989; Snow and Sorensen 1989). Alleged child victims of ritual abuse in daycare cases are described as children who resist therapists' invitations to engage in therapeutic activities designed to facilitate disclosure. Alleged child victims of ritual abuse are described as *never spontaneously disclosing their abuse* (Summit 1987; Sexton 1989; Snow and Sorensen 1989; Kelly 1989; Laboriel 1989; Graham-Costain 1990).

6.   Later, this patient was successfully treated as an inpatient in a clinical setting that places no special emphasis on satanic cult allegations.

REFERENCES

Allison, R. 1977. "Psychotherapy of Multiple Personality." Unpublished manuscript.

Balch, R. 1989. "The Social Construction of Satanism: A Case Study of the Rumor Process." Paper presented at the annual meeting of the Society for the Scientific Study of Religion.

Beere, D. B. 1989. "Satanic Programming Designed to Undercut Therapy." *Sixth International Conference on Multiple Personality/Dissociative States.* Alexandria, VA: Audio Transcripts: VIIIa-512.

Bliss, E. 1980. "Multiple Personalities: A Report of 14 Cases with Implications for Schizophrenia and Hysteria." *Archives of General Psychiatry* 37:1388–1397.

Bowers, K. S., and Hilgard, E. 1988. "Some Complexities in Understanding Memory." Pp. 3–18 in *Hypnosis and Memory*, edited by Helen Pettinati. New York: The Guilford Press.

Braun, B. G. 1980. "Hypnosis for Multiple Personalities." Pp. 209–17 in *Clinical Hypnosis in Medicine*, edited by Harold J. Wain. Chicago: Year Book Medical Publishers.

———. 1988. Untitled presentation. Workshop on Identification and Treatment of Victims of Ritual Cult Abuse, Fifth International Conference on Multiple Personality/Dissociative States. Chicago.

———. 1989. "Ritualistic Abuse and Dissociation: Believing the Unbelievable." Orange County Conference on Multiple Personality and Dissociation. Garden Grove, CA: InfoMedex: B158-9a/b.

Braun, B. G., Goodwin, J., Gould, K., Hammond, D. C., Kluft, R. P., Sachs, R. G., Summit, R. C., and Young, W. C. 1989. *Ritual Child Abuse: A Professional Overview.* Ukiah, CA: Cavalcade Productions.

Braun, B. G., and Sachs, R. G. 1985. "The Development of Multiple Personality Disorder: Predisposing Precipitating, and Perpetuating Factors." Pp. 37–64 in *Childhood Antecedents of Multiple Personality*, edited by R. Kluft. Washington, D.C.: American Psychiatric Press.

———. 1988. "Recognition of Possible Cult Involvement in MPD Patients." *Fifth International Conference on Multiple Personality/Dissociative States.* Alexandria, VA: Audio Transcripts: IVd-436.

Bromley, D. G., and Richardson, J. T. (Eds). 1983. *The Brainwashing/Deprogramming Controversy: Sociological, Psychological, Legal and Historical Perspectives.* New York: Edwin Mellen Press.

Burgess, A., and Kelly, S. 1990. "Investigation of Cults and Ritual Exploitation." *National Symposium on Child Victimization.*

Carlson, S., and Larue, G. 1989. *Satanism in America.* El Cerrito, CA: Gaia.

Cozolino, L., and Laboriel, L. 1989. *Satanic and Cult Worship: The Ritual Abuse of Children.* Mid-Coast Mental Health Center, Rockport, Maine.

Devereux, G. 1977. *Essais D'Ethnopsychiatrie Générale.* Paris: Gallimard.

Didi-Huberman, G. 1982. *Invention de L'Hysterie.* Paris: Macula.

Frankel, F. 1990. "Hypnotizability and Dissociation." *American Journal of Psychiatry* 147:823–829.

Freud, S., and Breuer, J. 1893. "On the Psychical Mechanism of Hysterical Phenomena." *Collected Papers, Vol. 1.* London: International Psychoanalytic Press, 1924.

_____. 1895. *Studies on Hysteria.* Middlesex: Pelican Books, 1983.

Ganaway, G. 1989. "Historical Truth Versus Narrative Truth: Clarifying the Role of Exogenous Trauma in the Etiology of Multiple Personality Disorder and Its Variants." *Dissociation* 2:205–221.

_____. 1990. Tape recorded interview with patient.

Goodwin, J. 1985. "Credibility Problems in Multiple Personality Disorder Patients and Abused Children." Pp. 2–19 in *Childhood Antecedents of Multiple Personality,* edited by R. Kluft. Washington, D.C.: American Psychiatric Press.

Gould, C. 1988. *Signs and Symptoms of Ritualistic Child Abuse.* Conference handout.

Graham-Costain, V. 1990. "The Use of Play Therapy with Child and Adult Survivors of Ritual Abuse." Orange County Conference on Multiple Personality and Dissociation. Garden Grove, CA: InfoMedex: C153-21.

Greaves, G. 1980. "Multiple Personality: 165 Years After Mary Reynolds." *Journal of Nervous and Mental Disease* 168:577–596.

_____. 1989. "A Cognitive-Behavioral Approach to the Treatment of MPD Ritually Abused Satanic Cult Survivors." *Sixth International Conference on Multiple Personality/Dissociative States.* Alexandria, VA: Audio Transcripts: IVa-512.

Hammond, D. C. 1989. "The 'Manchurian Candidate': Antisocial Uses of Hypnosis and Brainwashing in Satanic Cults." *Sixth International Conference on Multiple Personality/Dissociative States.* Alexandria, VA: Audio Transcripts.

Hicks, R. D. 1990. "Police Pursuit of Satanic Crime, Part II: The Satanic Conspiracy and Urban Legends." *Skeptical Inquirer* 14:378–390.

Higdon, J. 1986. "Association of Fundamentalism with MPD." *Third International Conference on Multiple Personality/Dissociative States.* Alexandria, VA: Audio Transcripts: 303:VIIa.

Janet, P. 1889. *L'Automatisme Psychologique.* Paris: Félix Alcan.

Kaye, M., and Kline, L. 1987. "Clinical Indicators of Satanic Cult Victimization." *Sixth International Conference on Multiple Personality/Dissociative States.* Alexandria, VA: Audio Transcripts: VIb-383.

Kelly, S. 1989. Untitled Presentation. "Investigation of Ritualistic Abuse Allegation: Think Tank." Eighth National Conference on Child Abuse and Neglect.

Kluft, R. 1985. "The Natural History of Multiple Personality Disorder." Pp. 197–238 in *Childhood Antecedents of Multiple Personality*, edited by R. Kluft. Washington, D.C.: American Psychiatric Press.

Laboriel, L. 1989. *Ritual Abuse*. Marshall Resource Center. Children's Institute International.

Lanning, K. 1989. "Gaining Insights into the Complexity of Ritualistic Abuse." Eighth National Conference on Child Abuse and Neglect. Tape #28

Larmore, K., Ludwig, A. M., and Cain, R. L. 1977. "Multiple Personality: An Objective Case Study." *British Journal of Psychiatry* 131:35–40.

Laurence, J. R., and Perry, C. 1988. *Hypnosis, Will and Memory*. New York: Guilford Press.

Loftus, E. F., and Loftus, G. R. 1980. "On the Permanence of Stored Information in the Human Brain." *American Psychologist* 35:409–420.

Lowell, P. 1894. *Occult Japan or the Way of the Gods*. Cambridge: The Riverside Press.

Ludwig, A. M. 1966. "Altered States of Consciousness." *Archives of General Psychiatry* 15:225–234.

Ludwig, A., Brandsma, J., Wilbur, E., Bendfeldt, F., and Jameson, D. 1972. "The Objective Study of Multiple Personality, or, Are Four Heads Better Than One?" *Archives of General Psychiatry* 26:298–310.

Lyons, A. 1970. *The Second Coming*. New York: Dood, Mead & Company.

Masson, J. M. 1984. *The Assault on Truth*. New York: Farrar, Straus and Giroux.

Morgan, A. H., and Hilgard, J. R. 1975. "Stanford Hypnotic Clinical Scale." Pp. 209–221 in *Hypnosis in the Relief of Pain*, edited by Ernest Hilgard and J. R. Hilgard. Los Altos, CA: William Kaufmann.

Mulhern, S. 1988. Untitled Presentation. Workshop on Identification and Treatment of Victims of Ritual Cult Abuse. Fifth International Conference on Multiple Personality/Dissociative States.

———. 1989. "Investigation of Ritualistic Abuse Allegation: Think Tank." Eighth National Conference on Child Abuse and Neglect. Discussant #4.

———. 1990. "Au Delà du Syndrome d'Accomodation." *Actes du II° Congres National de L'A.F.I.R.E.M. Paris*.

Orne, M. T. 1959. "The Nature of Hypnosis: Artifact and Essence." *Journal of Abnormal Social Psychology* 58:277–299.

———. 1979. "The Use and Misuse of Hypnosis in Court." *International Journal of Clinical and Experimental Hypnosis* 27:311–341.

Orne, M. T., Whitehouse, W. G., Dinges, D. F., and Orne, E. C. 1988. "Reconstructing Memory Through Hypnosis." Pp. 21–63 in *Hypnosis and Memory*, edited by Helen Pettinati. New York: The Guilford Press.

Padzer, L. 1990. "The Devil's Children." CBC. Televised interview.

Padzer, L., and Smith, M. 1980. *Michelle Remembers*. New York: Pocket Books.

Perry W. C., and Laurence, J. R. 1983. "The Enhancement of Memory by Hypnosis in the Legal Investigative Situation." *Canadian Psychology/Psychologie Canadienne* 24:155–167.

Pettinati, H. 1988. "Hypnosis and Memory: Integrative Summary and Future Directions." Pp. 277–91 in *Hypnosis and Memory*, edited by Helen Pettinati. New York: The Guilford Press.

Putnam, F. 1985. "Dissociation as a Response to Extreme Trauma." Pp. 65–97 in *Childhood Antecedents of Multiple Personality*, edited by R. Kluft. Washington, D.C.: American Psychiatric Press.

———— 1989. *Diagnosis and Treatment of Multiple Personality Disorder*. New York: The Guilford Press.

Ray, S. 1990. "Treatment of Adult Ritual Abuse Survivors." *Orange County Conference on Multiple Personality/Dissociation*. Garden Grove, CA: InfoMedix: C153-20.

Report of the Ritual Abuse Task Force. 1989. Los Angeles County Commission for Women.

Rivera, G. 1988. "Devil Worship: Exposing Satan's Underground." Investigative News Group. New York: Journal Graphics.

Ross, C. A. 1989. *Multiple Personality Disorder*. New York: Wiley-Interscience.

Sargent, W. 1957. *Battle for the Mind*. New York: Harper & Row.

Schafer, D. 1990. "Multi-Level Suggestibility." *Orange County Conference on Multiple Personality/Dissociation*. Garden Grove, CA: InfoMedix: C153-14.

Schreiber, F. R. 1973. *Sybil*. New York: Warner Books.

Sexton, D. 1989. "Gaining Insights into the Complexity of Ritualistic Abuse." *The Eighth National Conference on Child Abuse and Neglect*. Tape #28.

Snow, B., and Sorensen, T. 1989. "Ritualistic Child Abuse in a Neighborhood Setting." *Eighth National Conference on Child Abuse and Neglect*. Poster session.

Snowden, K. 1989. "Satanic Ritual Abuse." Unpublished manuscript.

Spiegel, H. 1968. *The Honest Liar Syndrome*. Taped conference: 1978.

————. 1973. *Manual for Hypnotic Induction Profile: Eye Roll Levitation Method*. New York: Soni Medica.

————. 1974. "The Grade 5 Syndrome: The Highly Hypnotizable Person." *International Journal of Clinical and Experimental Hypnosis* 22:303–319.

————. 1980. "Hypnosis and Evidence: Help or Hinderance?" *Annals of the New York Academy of Sciences* 347:73–85.

Stern, C. R. 1984. "The Etiology of Multiple Personalities." *Psychiatric Clinics of North America* 7:149–159.

Stoller, P. 1989. *Fusion of the Worlds: An Ethnography of Possession Among the Songhay of Niger*. Chicago: University of Chicago Press.

Summit, R. C. 1983. "The Child Sexual Abuse Accommodation Syndrome." *Child Abuse and Neglect* 7:177–193.

————. 1987. "Recognition of Cult Phenomena in MPD." *Fourth International Conference on Multiple Personality/Dissociative States*. Alexandria, VA: Audio Transcripts: VIb-383.

Thigpen, C. H., and Cleckley, H. M. 1954. "A Case of Multiple Personality." *Journal of Abnormal and Social Psychology* 49:135–151.

van der Kolk, B. A., Brown, P., and van der Hart, O. 1989. "Pierre Janet on Post-Traumatic Stress." *Journal of Traumatic Stress* 2:365–379.

Vickery, D. M., Kaye, M., and Klein, L. 1989. "Understanding Cult Triggers." *Sixth International Conference on Multiple Personality/Dissociative States*. Alexandria, VA: Audio Transcripts: VIIIa-512.

Victor, J. 1989. "A Rumor-Panic About a Dangerous Satanic Cult in Western New York." *New York Folklore* 15:23–49.

Weitzenhoffer, A. M., and Hilgard, E. R. 1962. *Stanford Hypnotic Susceptibility Scale, Form C*. Palo Alto: Consulting Psychologists Press.

West, L., and Thaler Singer, M. 1980. "Cults, Quacks, and Nonprofessional Psychotherapies." Pp. 3245–258 *Comprehensive Textbook of Psychiatry*, 3rd ed., Vol 3, edited by H. I. Kaplan, A. M. Freedman, and B. J. Sadock. Baltimore: Williams and Wilkins.

White, W. A. 1926. "The Language of Schizophrenia." *Archives of Neurology and Psychiatry* 16:395–413.

Wilbur, C. 1985. "The Effect of Child Abuse on the Psyche." Pp. 22–35 in *Childhood Antecedents of Multiple Personality*, edited by R. Kluft. Washington, D.C.: American Psychiatric Press.

Wilson, I. 1982. *All in the Mind*. New York: Doubleday.

Worrall, W. A., and Stockman, A. W. 1987. "The Role of Multiplicity in a Cult: A Case Study." *Fourth International Conference on Multiple Personality/Dissociative States*. Alexandria, VA: Audio Transcripts: IVb-383.

Young, W. C. 1986. "Restraints in the Treatment of a Patient with Multiple Personality."*American Journal of Psychotherapy* 40:601–606.

―――. 1988. "Issues in the Treatment of Cult Abuse Victims." *Fifth International Conference on Multiple Personality/Dissociative States*. Alexandria, VA: Audio Transcripts IVd-436.

――― 1989. "Triggers, Programs, and Cues in Survivors of Ritual Abuse." *Sixth International Conference on Multiple Personality/Dissociative States*. Alexandria, VA: Audio Transcripts: VIIIa-512.

Young, W. C., Sachs, R. G., Braun, B. G., and Watkins, R. T. 1991. "Patients Reporting Ritual Abuse in Childhood: A Clinical Syndrome." *International Journal of Child Abuse and Neglect* 14: in press.

Zempleni, A. "Possession et Sacrifice." *Transe, Chamanisme, Possession*. Nice: Edition Serre.

SATANISM AND THE LAW _____ V

The Police Model of Satanic Crime   10

Robert D. Hicks

INTRODUCTION

Since 1984, satanic crime seminars taught by self-professed police experts have been featured at professional conferences of educators, social workers, mental health personnel, victim advocates, probation officers, corrections officials, and clergy. The instructors present the topic in terms of crime prevention or deterrence. By serving up a pastiche of claims, suppositions, and speculation, police cult experts link symbols, images, and unconventional behavior with incipient violent criminality.

Satanic crime presentations display criminality in huckster fashion: cult cops, as they have become known, surround themselves with makeshift altars, candles, skulls, assorted literature with illustrations of alchemical symbols, and arcana of occult practitioners such as Aleister Crowley. These tableaux furnish the atmosphere, while cult cops present a model of criminality that presupposes levels of satanic involvement, ranging from teens playing "Dungeons & Dragons" to the clandestine conspiracy of murderous satanists comprising the moneyed, the powerful, and the intelligentsia. Presenting this model within the *mise en scene* of a movie set influences audiences by dissuading critical, analytical thinking, instead fostering mystery, implied causality, generalization, false analogies, and spurious history. The model's success depends on an audience's willingness to suspend critical analysis and accept the entire package without dissection or challenge. In this chapter I describe the police model of satanic crime based on lectures and handouts for approximately 50 cult crime seminars held throughout the United States from 1984 through 1990. Virtually unchanged since it was devised, this model has been promulgated nationally by police officers whose success relies less on analysis of the model's attributes than on its slick packaging. Finally, I discuss how the police organizational environment abets and encourages the satanic crime model to flourish.

THE SATANIC CRIME MODEL

The satanic crime model coalesced from several unrelated events: the publication of *Michelle Remembers* (Smith and Pazder 1980), the identification of multiple personality disorder (MPD) as a dissociative disorder in the third edition of the American Psychiatric Association's *Diagnostic and Statistical Manual of Mental Disorders* (1980), and allegations of child abuse at the McMartin Preschool and other daycare centers (beginning in 1983). Journalist Maury Terry's book on the Son of Sam murders, *The Ultimate Evil* (1987), used peripheral, circumstantial evidence to posit an organized network of satanists carrying out a program of murder. The book, coupled with confessions of murderers such as Henry Lee Lucas, who claimed to have killed 360 people as a member of the satanist cult, "The Hands of Death" contributed to a perception among police that satanism (1) motivated violent crime, (2) was a growing phenomenon, (3) and required new investigative techniques (*Crime Control Digest* 1984:4).

By 1984, professional training seminars appeared that posited a model incorporating such diverse phenomena as Lucas's prison cell confessions of satanic murders, people's claims of having experienced abuse by satanic cults, MPD as a product of intrafamilial, multigenerational involvement with satanism, and "ritual abuse" in daycare centers.

Law enforcers who helped shape the model lacked evidence suitable for criminal prosecutions, so seminar presenters suggested investigating a wider sphere of noncriminal phenomena, which they believed were related to criminal behavior. Thus, one early seminar argued that cult or occult crime investigators must examine satanic rock music lyrics, graffiti displaying occult or satanic imagery, animal mutilations, and vandalism of cemeteries (Crutchfield 1984). Even by 1984, police had constructed an image—based not on criminal evidence, but rather on secondary historical sources, Christian literature, confessions of cult survivors, and pure speculation—of clandestine, murderous satanists, a new criminal type:

> Confirmed satanists are secretive, paranoid, and sometimes deadly, fervently devoted to their religion. Although infrequently used, human sacrifice is still an actual practice. These High Black masses are conducted with utmost secrecy. (Crutchfield 1984:5)

Although the seminar presenters claimed to respect First Amendment rights of religious freedom, they asserted that satanists a priori pledge absolute obedience to the cult, and obedience means sanctioning or participating in violent crime as a religious ritual. The seminal conference on satanic crime, "The Emergence of Ritualistic Crime in Today's Society," was held in September, 1986, in Ft. Collins, Colorado, sponsored by the North-

ern Colorado–Southern Wyoming Detectives Association; it was the first
national law-enforcement conference to establish the notion of "satanic
ritualized abuse of children" (*File 18 Newsletter* 1988:4). The conference
featured speakers who remain prominent today: Officer Sandi Gallant, San
Francisco Police Department; Ken Wooden, a writer and television producer whose *20/20* report on ritual abuse still occupies a niche in satanic
crime seminars; evangelist Mike Warnke, author of *The Satan Seller* (1972);
Patricia Pulling and Rosemary Loyacano, founders of Bothered About Dungeons & Dragons (BADD); and psychiatrist Lawrence Pazder, who helped
Michelle Smith remember. Characteristically, only two of the speakers had
professional credentials bearing on criminal matters, and only one was a
police officer. Quotations from these speakers give both a sense of the
conference itself and communicate key assertions still made about the
satanic menace:

> Satanism is the worship of the Devil and of yourself. It is a self-centered, self-
> gratifying religious system. . . . Satan's goal is to defeat God's plan of Grace
> and to establish his kingdom of evil in order to ruin man. Satan needs men and
> women alive to accomplish his work for him, because he is a disembodied
> spirit. (Sandi Gallant)
>
> Jim Jones and the People's Temple phenomenon are useful when used as a
> "blueprint of cults". . . . Near the end of his life Jim Jones was having sex with
> a goat to the accompanying amplified screams of tortured children. (Ken
> Wooden)
>
> Our daycare centers are the soft underbelly of our society; they are undergoing
> a concerted attack. (Ken Wooden)
>
> Those D&D players who irretrievably cross the imaginary line between reality
> and fantasy sometimes act out torture and killing with deadly results. . . .
> Family values are attacked . . . [The game's symbols] are used in real sorcery
> and conjuration of demons. (Patricia Pulling)
>
> The pure group of "orthodox satanists" is never seen or identified in public,
> yet it is this group of invisible satanists who plant the seeds and encourage all
> the other more visible satanic groups. . . . Unhappily for Satan, Jesus has
> authority over him. Jesus is Satan's arch-enemy. . . . He uses every tool over
> which he has dominion to trick and trap men, including materialism and
> material things, forces of nature, powers of science (the disciplines such as
> earth sciences, chemistry, numerology, astrology, etc.). . . . It is the antithesis
> of Christianity. . . . Think OPPOSITES: This is bizarre. . . . For instance,
> satanists don't love sex, they hate it, yet they use it ritually all the time. What is
> good, honorable, just, worthy to us is bad, despicable, foul and unworthy to
> the satanist. . . . Your interview techniques must be reversed. . . . You should
> develop resource teams. . . . Include a knowledgeable-but-cool clergyman,
> an open-minded-but-stable psychologist, and a survivor who has lived
> through the experience and come successfully out the other side. (Lawrence
> Pazder)

178 Robert D. Hicks

A monograph published by the Baldwin Park Police Department (California), prepared by Sgt. Randall S. Emon, completed the antisatanic ideology: it furnished lists of investigative tips and samples of satanic graffiti (including some invented iconographs, such as the 1960s peace symbol being listed as the "Cross of Nero" and therefore heretical to Christianity) (Emon 1986). It also offered undocumented, third-hand accounts of satanic violence:

> A young couple was asked by an American family to come and babysit. When the parents came home, they found the young couple, who belonged to a satanic cult, had roasted the baby on a gridiron. The horrified parents had entrusted their child to devil worshippers. (Emon 1986:4)

Of course, the lack of a citation prevents the reader from verifying the story. Similarly, in recounting how satanists sell their souls to the Devil, Emon stated, "[M]any persons who have signed their name in blood to Satan have suffered horrible deaths or have been killed in automobile accidents" (1986:6). These Faustian claims are supported by a typification of satanists: an intelligent middle or upper-class, white male who experiences some stress, perhaps with feelings of inadequacy, who may be an underachiever with low self-esteem, who may be "obsessed" with fantasy role-playing games, wears symbolic jewelry, possesses books on magic, satanism, or witchcraft, and be secretive about his activities.

The basic claims of cult seminars have continued into the 1990s, acquiring new examples of human perversity—mass murders, suicides, sensational child abuse cases—which serve to cement the causal relationships advanced by cult presenters. Although satanism remains the primary threat, other activities and beliefs labeled as cultic or occultic by police ideologues have been absorbed into the cult-crime model, particularly warnings about non-Christian beliefs such as African-derived religions (Yoruba, Santeria, voodoo).

THE FOUR-TIERED MODEL

Cult seminars present a four-tiered model of satanic crime (occasionally the model has only three tiers, ignoring Level III, the organized, public Church of Satan). The model's simplicity has led many to interpret it as a continuum of behavior, with innocent kids entering the occult realm through "Dungeons & Dragons" (Level I) and emerging at the other end as well-placed, apparently responsible citizens who practice satanism clandestinely, obtaining power through human sacrifice and child abuse (Level IV). Table 1 outlines key attributes of the four-tiered model.

Table 1. The Police Model of Satanic Crime

Level	Visibility	Primary Attributes	Character Types	Criminal Associations	Primary Evidence Supporting Criminality
I	Semipublic	"Dabblers," or young adults who listen to rock music with occult themes; interest in occult or satanic imagery; interest in fantasy role-playing games, e.g., Dungeons & Dragons	Teens, young adults of diverse backgrounds	Suicide; narcotics use; violent crime; animal cruelty	Occasional narcotics use; juvenile delinquency
II	Semipublic	Self-styled killers, e.g., Charles Manson, Henry Lee Lucas	Psychopathic or sociopathic criminals	Violent crime; narcotics use	Violent crimes actually committed, prosecuted
III	Public	Organized churches or institutions, e.g., Church of Satan, Temple of Set	Unpredictable: intelligent, curious	None, except ideology might attract criminals	None
IV	Covert	Multigenerational family involvement; child abuse; human sacrifice; kidnapping; brainwashing; sexual violence; international network	High-level public officials; police; judges; lawyers	Violent crime such as homicide and kidnapping, assault, abuse; narcotics use	Cult survivors' tales; "ritual" child abuse allegations

The types of satanic crime cited at seminars—including child abuse, human sacrifice, teen suicides, cemetery and church vandalism—all find their way into the model, linking the tiers

> together through the liberal use of the word "satanism" and some common symbolism. . . . The implication often is that all are part of a continuum of behavior, a single problem or some common conspiracy. The information presented is a mixture of fact, theory, opinion, fantasy, and paranoia, and because some of it can be proven or corroborated (desecration of cemeteries, vandalism, etc.), the implication is that it is all true and documented. (Lanning, 1989:62)

Indeed, the satanic crime continuum has become the repository for the entire domain of observed and imagined satanic behavior. Unaccustomed to sociological or anthropological typologies and their uses, police find it easy to interpolate a progression of satanic involvement. Anthropologist Sherrill Mulhern adds:

> By definition, a continuum is something in which no part can be distinguished from neighboring parts except by arbitrary division. The first thing remarkable about the alleged satanic levels is that each level is a self-contained whole, defined by specific, real or imagined, exclusive parameters. The continuum is not in observable behavior, it exists only in [cult cops] minds! (personal communication 1988)

As an example of how a cult cop easily translates the model into a description of reality, Detective Gary Sworin, Luzerne County, Pennsylvania, maintains:

> Participation . . . could mean starting out with just listening to some heavy metal rock music, starting to read satanic bibles, starting to be involved in a ritual, satanic ritual, and then gradually lead to bigger and so-called, in their perspective, better things. You generally will be involved in what they call a black mass. You'll be taken and initiated as one of their members and one of the cult people. . . . They're starting out with something that's very, very small, which is dabbling, putting markings up and drawings up. And then all of a sudden it starts to progress, and all the contributing factors we listed all come together and finally something happens where we go from what we know, what we should do, to the other extreme of what they want us to know and they want us to do. And at that point we're lost. (Satanic cult seminar, Freeland, Pennsylvania, October 4, 1988)

The continuum predicts that white male teens or young adults, the "dabblers," experiment with satanic imagery, knowingly tapping into the occult netherworld. Through heavy metal rock music, satanic symbols, or reading occult texts, teens progress to murder, suicide, harming animals, abusing others, or other violent acts. While some young adults may stop dabbling and become healthy, productive members of society, others do not; some become self-styled satanists (Level II).

Next, one finds the organized, public satanists, the third tier. Although cult cops admit that public groups such as the San Francisco-based Church of Satan espouse no criminality as part of doctrine, they nevertheless argue that such organizations' materialist, "do what thou wilt" philosophies encourage libertine behavior, which inevitably attracts sociopaths, self-styled violent satanists. The *possibility* that non-Christian public organizations might attract criminals, then, justifies police intelligence gathering. Cult seminars rail at such organizations, shocked that a belief system could defer judgment about or, worse, condone bestiality, homosexuality, and a wide range of sexual behavior among consenting adults. Cult seminars presume that such religions or beliefs raise self-indulgence to the highest virtue at the expense of all else.

Finally, one reaches the fourth tier, the covert, criminal satanist conspiracy. These people occupy responsible, moneyed positions in our society, yet covertly indulge in satanic worship involving kidnapping, child abuse, rape, mutilation, and murder. Such satanists are so clever and adroit at not leaving traces of their activities that no useful evidence has yet surfaced that even demonstrates the existence of this tier. Again, cult seminars urge audiences to ignore a natural skepticism about unseen, covert conspiracies and believe in their existence: cult survivor tales are provided as documentary evidence, although no survivor's story has to date borne legal proof.

CRITIQUE OF THE SATANIC CRIME MODEL

1. Seminar presenters often claim that this field of inquiry does not yet have experts. Investigator Jerry Simandl, Chicago Police Department, has asserted that the only experts are those who work directly with victims, the so-called cult survivors who through therapy for MPD reveal a childhood of satanic abuse (Fifth International Conference on Dissociative Disorders, Chicago, Illinois, 1988). Cult experts particularly shun academic assistance or interpretations of the concern about satanism. Cult cops consider academic views as having minimal relevance to "real" police problems:

Reference works written by non-participants (often from a psychologist's or sociologist's empirical perspective) may provide a superficial treatment of the subject, neglecting ethical/moral/legal comparisons. The basis of criminal law, however, revolves on the "rightness" or "wrongness" of people's actions. The passive observer/reporter may focus on trends, histories, and population dynamics without addressing the destructive physical, psychological, or spiritual aspects of non-traditional group membership and victimization.(*File 18 Newsletter*, 1986)

2. Seminar presenters rarely define terms, instead treating "occult," "satanism," and sometimes "cult" as synonyms. Seminar presenters never anchor their definitions in sociological or legal literature, but sometimes borrow from secondary historical sources or works by nonhistorians that offer historical arguments based on little supporting data, e.g., assertions that Adolf Hitler ate human excrement as part of a satanic ritual upon which he depended for power (Sklar 1977).

3. The satanic threat, according to seminar presenters, aims to destroy Anglo-Christian family life. To intensify the drama of conflict, cult experts use adjectives such as "moral," "good," "wholesome" when discussing families, or "innocent" and "pure" regarding children. On the other hand, seminar experts' portrait of satanists is based on the principle that everything satanists believe is a direct inversion of Christian values and those of the unblemished, middle-class, WASP American family. Cult experts ignore the ethnographic impossibility of an underground of satanic families, whose values and instincts are inversions of those held by good people, lured to the Evil One solely through a pursuit of power, and who have maintained unbroken secrecy over the years.

4. The model of satanic ideology, practices, and world view derives from Christian sources. The foremost law enforcement periodical with an openly Christian bias, *File 18 Newsletter* (produced by the Cult Crime Impact Network, Inc., Boise, Idaho, whose prominent spokesman is Lt. Larry Jones, Boise Police Department) relies on extreme fundamentalist Protestant publications, such as *Prepare for War* by Rebecca Brown, M.D. (Chick Publications), a tract that promotes anti-Catholicism. The Christian bias is evident in the cult seminars' use of "nontraditional belief" to describe any but a Christian one, and a Protestant belief at that. Cult cops also borrow heavily from Christian literature for claims that "backmasked" satanic messages in rock music can damage both psyche and spirit and lead to crime. Further, cult seminars rely on Christian sources when they promote such political stances as encouraging censorship of reading materials and music, and allying with the antiabortion movement.

5. Cult crime adherents argue that lack of usable proof to obtain an arrest, much less a criminal conviction, results from the underground satanic conspiracy's success in maintaining secrecy. The *absence* of prosecutable evidence *proves* the existence of the satanic network. Further, the lack of conventional evidence leads investigators to assert that one must seek evidence for satanic influence in unlikely places, such as canvassing libraries to ascertain who borrows books on magic, the occult, and related subjects.

6. Cult presentations assume that there is power inherent in black or white magic, witchcraft, or satanism. The "real occult" retailed in "Dungeons &

Dragons" game-playing manuals, for example, supposedly uses actual spells, incantations, and demons with which unwitting youths may tamper. The attribution of spiritual power to such "forces" enables cult seminars to displace criminal responsibility for behavior from people to unseen evil influences. The satanic crime model, then, becomes more compelling when one realizes that the enemy is supernatural. *File 18 Newsletter* advises:

> However, you may be battling with forces which are impervious to your wrist-twists, your batons, or your service firearms—and they may destroy you. These things are unseen to most of us. . . . But, in our natural state we are helpless to defend against unseen enemies: spiritual training and spiritually effective tools are required. (1987:7)

7. Scientific or technical jargon helps convince audiences that the experts' strategies for reducing the satanic threat have reliable, tested bases. This includes casual use of terms with controversial meetings in social science such as "behavior modification," "brainwashing," and "mind control." Similarly, the clinical descriptions of satanic rites convince audiences with their technical detail:

> The E.E.G. or similar electro-stimuli may be attached [by satanists] to the [victim's] head or other nerve endings for the purpose of breaking the will, encouraging obedience, layering personalities, and insuring silence through threat enforcement. (*File 18 Newsletter* 1987:2)

8. Cult seminars assert that satanic crime is increasing, an assertion safe from challenge since the FBI's Uniform Crime Reporting system does not compile occult crime data. With no dependable statistics, cult seminars include estimates of up to 50,000 human sacrifices per year. These contrived statistics support the view that satanists threaten ordered society. In particular, satanists present a supreme danger to police, and officers should not investigate satanic cases alone. The cult cop, however, armed with information supplied at the seminar, can now see phenomena invisible to untrained police peers.

9. Cult seminars proselytize audiences. Cult cops assert that officers' beliefs do not count when approaching satanists: what counts is satanists' beliefs. Supposedly, satanic beliefs acknowledge and even praise human evil, seek power at the expense of all else, and invite chaos as a social virtue. Because satanic beliefs lead to monstrous crimes and pernicious thinking, we must suspend our disbelief and critical judgment and accept what we learn from self-proclaimed cult survivors' incredible tales. Suspending critical faculties means that audience will ignore inconsistencies and not question evidence. Further, cult seminars only infrequently feature debates; they place all their weight behind the proconspiracy view.

10. The four-tiered cult model implies a progression from mindless dabbling through organized, covert worship to human sacrifice, a progression
that makes no sense. To make sense, people would have to undergo radical
changes in their personalities, predilictions, and social relationships. For
example, while many dabblers are bright but socially inept, or harbor
feelings of inadequacy and unimportance, self-styled satanists, who occupy
the next tier, are social misfits and even sociopaths, using satanic imagery as
criminal trappings. But public, organized satanists, as in the Church of
Satan, fit no personality profile except nonconformism, while covert satanists are supposedly in socially powerful positions, practicing their murderous religion in highly structured rituals.

THE POLICE SUBCULTURE AND SATANIC BELIEFS

Satanism and Police Organization Environment

The most remarkable facet of the cult-cop phenomenon is its restriction
(with very few exceptions) to field officers, either patrol or investigative
personnel, at the lowest ranks up to first-level supervisors, usually sergeants.
Police leadership pays virtually no attention to satanic crime seminars
except to consider them as skill-building in a new area of criminal investigation. Police executives merely assign one or more investigators to attend a
satanic or cult crime seminar to pick up investigative tips; they assume the
legitimacy of the subject. Cult-crime seminars resemble other police training
seminars by avoiding a forum for discussion or debate about investigative
models. One attends the seminars to comingle with others who might have
imaginative ways to do the same work: "avoiding reinventing the wheel" is
a common justification for attending conferences to pick up new ways to
manage old problems. Satanic cult seminars, however, convince officers
that a new problem exists, demanding new methods. By contrast, the topic
of satanic crime does not even appear on police executive conference
agendas: rather, police executives concern themselves with strategies, bud-
gets, manpower allocation, and acquisition of materiel.

Police executives measure productivity in terms of arrests, or the value of
recovered or confiscated property. The choice of arrests as a measure of
productivity constitutes a choice of a "social reality": the police convince
the public that a rise or fall in arrests reflects a rise or fall in crime (Manning
1977). Executives, then, in assigning personnel to cult seminars, assume
that officers will learn to detect and arrest a new category of offenders, thus
reducing crime. For police officers to conduct satanic crime seminars, under
the auspices of their agencies, constitutes a dramatic way to alert the public
that the police are vigorously fighting crime, seeking arrests.

But police executives also cite public safety and order maintenance as primary enforcement goals. Over recent years, police analysts have tried to measure order maintenance to prove to the public that the police can be productive in ways beyond arrests. Order maintenance relies on the good will and cooperation of the citizenry, and importantly, requires the beat officer or investigator to become a community advocate, employing principles of community development to rally citizens around crime-prevention strategies.

Following urban riots of the 1960s, government inquiries urged police to pursue the goal of order maintenance beyond simple arrest tallies (National Advisory Commission on Criminal Justice Standards and Goals 1973; Task Force on Disorders and Terrorism 1976). Consequently, police administrators sought to enhance the beat cop's effectiveness by decentralizing the process of deciding how to patrol communities to best detect and deter crime, and by training officers to take risks, plan patrol and investigative strategies, and become responsible for the delivery of all a community's law enforcement services. A new policing philosophy has taken root: team policing, community-oriented policing, or problem-oriented policing—all essentially similar strategies—have merged the roles of investigator and patrol officer. Under community-oriented policing, officers take a less formal approach to crime detection, relying more on community means of maintaining order, e.g., Neighborhood Watch. Such practices are driven by grassroots community organizing.

The cult cop, then, has simply appropriated the community-oriented policing model—which his own agency promotes—as the justification for alerting citizens to the satanic cult menace. When the cult cop gives public talks to sensitize the public, he allies himself with other community service professionals (e.g., social workers) and child advocacy groups (e.g., Believe the Children) and steps beyond a strict concern for criminal law enforcement to address a community's willingness to manage deviance within its neighborhoods. Of course, this means the cult cop uses his position of community leadership to brand certain citizens' beliefs and practices as satanic. The cult cop has thus invoked a community's social controls (Goldstein 1990:122).

Identifying and Managing Deviance

By incorporating satanic crime detection and deterrence into community-oriented policing, law enforcers misuse their initiative: they stigmatize noncriminal behavior, such as listening to certain rock music, wearing distinctive clothing or jewelry, or practicing Afro-Carribean religious beliefs. The informality of their law-enforcement behavior makes it possible for police to keep noncriminal intelligence records about supposed cultists or satanists from public eyes, thus making the officers unassailable, the very opposite of what police executives want from community-oriented policing. Executives may want public policing, public access to police, public access to records, and public complaint-handling procedures. But field officers, through discretion allowed them to make decisions about how best to patrol a community, may retain noncriminal records of "field interview" contacts with satanists, while sharing them with other investigators at cult seminars. These informal, noncriminal, records escape police administrative review and cannot be reached through Freedom of Information Act requests.

Police who deal with suspected pagans, witches, satanists, and practitioners of Afro-Caribbean beliefs confront people whom they do not recognize as counterparts. The police, mainly white males, often come from conservative Christian families, and they take their own culture as normative (Ehrlich and Preiss 1966). Anyone not measuring up risks a police stop, questioning, even a search. "If a policeman is unfamiliar with normal life in an ethnic community"—say, one which practices Santeria or Palo Mayombe—"and cannot communicate fluently in the local verbal and behavioral idioms, he will not use the informal means at his disposal in enforcing the law" (Cohen 1969:112). Rather, he will find ways to observe and track deviants, monitor comings and goings, and perhaps even make an arrest.

In community-oriented policing, effectiveness should be the standard for judging officers, but effective at what? At identifying and warning the public about deviance? Warning the public about satanists seems to cult cops a valued crime-prevention service in accord with the community-oriented policing model. But by instructing the community in a new form of deviance, cult cops create and shape fear, assuring citizens that the police can handle the threat. And as Goldstein has observed, police frequently respond to putative deviance by exaggerating their own capabilities in combatting what may be a small threat, thus reducing community fears (1977:48).

Where the police expect deviance, they find it. Geilhufe's study of police–Chicano relations showed that the "police expectation of crime is probably self-fulfilling," even when "police expectations have no basis in fact" (1979:78). In the case of cult cops, they have garnered enough community support, even where no provable satanic deviance exists, to successfully lobby for new criminal laws to give them the tools to pursue satanists, as in Idaho and Illinois.

Intelligence Gathering

The police have never been able to dissociate themselves from demands to regulate, control, or eliminate nonconformism, deviance, and threatening ideologies, despite the best efforts of police executives to remain apolitical. Since cult cops maintain that satanists use lawful groups (e.g., the Society for Creative Anachronism) as fronts for their crimes, the police have echoed the logic used by the FBI in its recent investigation of a noncriminal organization, the Committee in Solidarity with the People of El Salvador (CISPES). The FBI investigation of CISPES began with a suspicion of a law violation but, when the suspicion proved groundless, the FBI justified further surveillance and records-keeping by maintaining that "lawful groups are used as covers or fronts for activities of enemy agents and terrorists" (Berlet 1988:114). By analogy, cult cops investigate suspected satanic wrongdoing, and in the absence of tangible criminal leads, continue to gather intelligence on nonconformists because the police assume the *possibility* of a conspiracy to subvert family integrity. This intelligence gathering against non-Christians does not often proceed from orders by police executives. Rather, field personnel have used their own initiative to gather intelligence, with a nod from mid-managers. As in the case of the CISPES, the intelligence information comes from non-police sources. Cult cops derive (usually very poor) intelligence from cult survivors and allied advocacy groups such as BADD and Believe the Children, or from religious organizations. Cult cops routinely share information with such groups, but never with identified occult or cult groups, which are always viewed with suspicion even if they wish more open police contact to eliminate misunderstandings and misconceptions.

When the FBI emerged emptyhanded in searching for evidence of a crime, they redoubled their efforts on the presumption that CISPES had merely been very adroit at covering its tracks. Similarly, when cult cops find no evidence, they intensify efforts to uncover wrongdoing. An absence of criminal behavior merely indicates success at eluding the police.

CONCLUSIONS

The police model of satanic crime derived from several sources— sensationalized trials, publications, new therapeutic paradigms (MPD) with the abrupt appearance of self-proclaimed satanic cult survivors—which stimulated public concern or even hysteria about satanic or occult phenomena, resentment or intolerance of non-Christian religious practices, and fear of non-Christian imagery. The model unifies these diverse threats into one large satanic menace. This chapter outlines the model and places it within the police organizational environment (a more detailed discussion appears in Hicks 1991).

Community-oriented policing encourages cult cops to flourish by promoting the autonomy of the beat officer or investigator in devising strategies, with community assistance and involvement, to reduce or prevent crime.

The beat officer, then, becomes a community advocate, developer, leader. Most often, the officer's message to communities involves crime prevention: cult cops use the same strategy to raise community concern about a new form of deviance with largely noncriminal attributes.

Satanic crime seminars spawn cult cops, who in turn mimic the seminar presentations for new audiences of church groups, parents, teachers, social workers, therapists, and other police officers. Normally lower echelon personnel, cult cops have galvanized communities against a supernatural enemy without police administrative supervision or control. This may be the first time line police officers have become social activists for a quasireligious purpose. No effective controls exist for inhibiting the cult cop and his extraorganizational methods: informal records-keeping, and an off-duty alliance with political or social activist groups promote a religious or quasireligious concern that satanists' philosophy of inverting Christianity furnishes an a priori threat to public safety. Cult cops deserve closer scrutiny by academics and police executives.

ACKNOWLEDGMENTS

This chapter does not necessarily reflect the views of the Virginia Department of Criminal Justice Services nor of the Commonwealth of Virginia. I would like to thank Steve Squire and David Bromley for criticizing early versions of this chapter.

REFERENCES

American Psychiatric Association. 1987. *Diagnostic and Statistical Manual of Mental Disorders*, 3rd ed. Washington, D.C.

Berlet, Chip. 1988. "Understanding Political Repression, The FBI, and the Right-Wing: An Historical Perspective." *Police Misconduct and Civil Rights Law Report* 2(10):114–120.

Cohen, Abner. 1969. *Custom and Politics in Urban Affairs*. Berkeley, CA: University of California Press.

Crime Control Digest. 1984. "Self-Professed Mass Killer Says He Belonged to Death Cult." 18(19):4.

Crutchfield, Catherine. 1984. "California Police Finding Evidence of Satanic Cults With Links to Crimes." *Crime Control Digest* 18(19):5.

Ehrlich, Howard J., and Preiss, Jack J. 1966. *An Examination of Role Theory: The Case of the State Police*. Lincoln: University of Nebraska Press.

Emon, Randall. 1986. *Occult Criminal Investigation*. Baldwin Park Police Department (California) Training Bulletin, 86(2).

File 18 Newsletter. 1986. 2nd edition.

————. 1987. II (87-5)

————. 1988. III (88-1)

Geilhufe, Nancy L. 1979. *Chicanos and the Police: A Study of the Politics of Ethnicity in San Jose, Calif.* Society for Applied Anthropology Monograph No. 13.

Goldstein, Herman. 1977. *Policing a Free Society.* Cambridge, MA: Ballinger Publishing Company.

————. 1990. *Problem-Oriented Policing.* Philadelphia: Temple University Press.

Hicks, Robert D. 1991. *In Pursuit of Satan: The Police and the Occult.* Buffalo, NY: Prometheus Books.

Lanning, Kenneth V. 1989. "Satanic, Occult, Ritualistic Crime: A Law Enforcement Perspective." *The Police Chief* 56(10):62–83.

Manning, Peter K. 1977. *Police Work: The Social Organization of Policing.* Cambridge, MA: MIT Press.

National Advisory Commission on Criminal Justice Standards and Goals. 1973. *Police.* Washington, D.C.: U.S. Department of Justice.

Sklar, Dusty. 1977. *Gods and Beasts: The Nazis and the Occult.* New York: Thomas Y. Crowell.

Smith, Michelle, and Pazder, Lawrence. 1980. *Michelle Remembers.* New York: Congdon and Lattes.

Task Force on Disorders and Terrorism. 1976. *Disorders and Terrorism.* Washington, D.C.: U.S. Department of Justice.

Terry, Maury. 1987. *The Ultimate Evil: An Investigation into America's Most Dangerous Satanic Cult.* New York: Doubleday.

Law Enforcement and the Satanism–Crime Connection: A Survey of "Cult Cops"   11

Ben M. Crouch and Kelly Damphousse

Recent media depictions of growing satanic influence have promoted considerable unease among the public. In a telephone survey of over 1000 Texas citizens, for example, nearly 80 percent of the respondents thought satanism had increased over the past 5 years and expressed concern about it (Texas Poll 1989). While some are concerned because satanism may lead souls away from the Christian path to heaven, others fear that satanic activity often involves serious criminality. Antisatanism literature fans these fears by reporting that ritualistic crimes—such as kidnapping children for abuse and even sacrifice, drug use, animal mutilations, as well as an array of sexually perverse rituals—occur by the thousands annually (Wedge 1988; Schwarz and Empey 1988; Kidwell 1989).

This link between satanism and crime has led many law enforcement officers to become interested in "ritualistic," "cult," and "satanic" crimes. In trying to investigate such crimes, these officers face a number of difficulties, including limited training in cult criminality and disagreement as to the definition of "ritualistic" crime (Lanning 1989). These difficulties in turn hinder consensus about the nature of the problem, as well as interpretations of evidence at possible satanic crime scenes.

By the late 1980s, a large, informal network of federal, state, and local officers had arisen to respond to satanic crime (see Gates 1988). These officers developed information about such crimes as well as more general perceptions on the nature of the satanic threat. Many routinely share both, not only with other officers, but with citizens, politicians, and educators. The actions and perceptions of these officers are critical to understanding satanic crime, especially its shape in society. This is the case because police officers have the legitimate authority and apparent experience to define the seriousness of threats to social order.

This chapter presents results from a survey of "cult cops"—officers who have specifically concerned themselves with the satanism–crime connection. Although some anecdotal information on these officers and their experience with satanic crime exists (see Kahaner 1988), this survey is to our

191

knowledge the first effort to examine systematically their views and experiences. As such, the present analysis is necessarily exploratory and descriptive. In the following sections we describe who cult cops are and how they perceive links between satanism and crime. Before proceeding, however, it is necessary to discuss police reactions to satanism from a sociological perspective.

A SOCIOLOGICAL PERSPECTIVE ON POLICE CONCERNS ABOUT SATANISM

All societies reflect culturally defined boundaries that demarcate good and moral from evil and immoral. So long as those boundaries are clear, deviance is limited, or at least easy to detect. Social change, however, can blur these moral boundaries. Traditional beliefs and behavioral taboos become less binding. To the extent this blurring permits or encourages deviance, it will be perceived, by at least some segments of society, as a threat to moral order.

This country has undergone fundamental social change since the late 1960s. Politically, it has become more conservative, a trend encouraged by a "moral majority" that stressed traditional values (Timmer and Eitzen 1985; Reinarman and Levine 1989). At the same time, economic, educational, and occupational systems seem to have deteriorated relative to other developed countries. These and related changes, coupled with the uncertainty they promote, led many to turn to the occult, including satanism, for personal answers (Ben-Yehuda 1986). Others, alarmed both about the impact of social trends and the growing appeal, especially among youth, of nontraditional religions and movements, have sought to reestablish traditional values and beliefs.

Those activists seeking to reestablish traditional social and religious values in the face of rising interest in the occult may be described as "moral entrepreneurs" (Becker 1963) or "moral crusaders" (Gusfield 1986). These individuals and groups seek to bring public attention to their view of a problem, and then mobilize to eradicate it. Media preachers, antisatanism writers, and citizens pressing for bans on Satan-oriented heavy metal rock music all exemplify moral entrepreneurs.

The question in this chapter, however, concerns the nature of police involvement in maintaining moral boundaries satanism appears to breech. Clearly law enforcement officers are uniquely positioned to be involved. Their official duties and street experience make them important designators of how seriously any moral boundary may be threatened. Police pronouncements on sexual deviance, drugs or delinquency, for example, carry special normative significance. Thus, when police talk to other police about the

satanism problem, their credentials are seldom questioned, and their conclusions are likely accepted. Such acceptance is all the more true with a
civilian audience.

Police perceptions of satanism are critical to understanding this contemporary fear. First, their official duties place officers quite literally on the
boundary between culturally defined good and evil; second, their role
allows them discretion to apply a wide range of moral or normative standards in interpreting behaviors, attitudes, and crime scenes; and third, their
imputed expertise on deviance maximizes the impact of their public statements about satanic activity.

Unfortunately, within the network of cult officers there is considerable
disagreement about the nature of the satanism threat and, particularly, the
satanism-crime connection. On one hand, some outspoken officers contend
there is an international satanic conspiracy that has penetrated the media,
politics, and commerce (Gates 1988; Alexander 1990). These officers, some
with an overt Christian orientation, argue for a proactive response to the
satanic threat. Other officers see the satanic threat as largely groundless,
accusing "true believers" of sometimes using their authority as police officers to enhance their careers and even their pocketbooks (Lanning 1989;
Hicks 1989; Lyons 1988).

In addition to investigating routine criminality, police may be among
those moral entrepreneurs trying to stem what they perceive as serious
societal and criminal consequences of satanism. Yet, what police really
think about these issues, how they came to hold these views, and the extent,
basis, and implications of differences in these views are all open questions.
This chapter presents an exploratory study examining the perceptions of a
national sample of "cult cops," to shed light on these and related questions.

THE SURVEY

Conducting a survey of law enforcement personnel about their perceptions of the satanism–crime link proved extremely difficult. The first problem
was identifying an appropriate sample. Since a given police agency might
have few officers with some concern about or knowledge of satanism, we
wanted to include many agencies. Yet, because virtually no systematic
research has been done on these issues, we had little basis for choosing
agencies or even regions of the country. Therefore it was decided to rely on
lists of officers who had already identified themselves as interested in satanic
activity.

We located two lists, one of recipients of a newsletter on cult activity and
the other of class rosters from several occult seminars conducted at a police
training academy. The first list came from Larry Jones, a police lieutenant in

Boise, Idaho who directs Cult Crime Impact Network, Inc (CCIN). According to Jones, nearly 2000 subscribers, mostly police officers, receive his
"*File 18*" newsletter. At our direction, Jones compiled a random sample (N
= 993) by selecting every other officer (nonpolice were deleted), the first
person being determined by a coin toss. The second list of 800 officers,
mostly from southern and southwestern states, came from the Killeen (Texas)
police academy. Again, every other name was selected after the first was
randomly determined (N = 400). To protect the confidentiality of those on
the mailing lists, the respective directors did not release the lists to us.
Questionnaires were posted from the two agencies, although enclosed reply
envelopes brought responses directly back to the researchers. The final
sample of nearly 1400 is random only within the two lists, and cannot be
taken as representative of all officers involved with cult investigations.

A second problem was the development of a survey instrument. Given
divergent opinions among police interested in the occult problem, the
appropriate scope and content of questions were difficult to assess. To
identify key issues we reviewed an extensive literature on cult crime, satanism, and sociology of police and collective behavior. In addition, we
interviewed nearly 20 police officers with national or regional reputations as
experts on the occult and satanism. We then pretested the instrument on
several state and city officers in Texas, refining it accordingly.

The last problem concerns the rather low questionnaire return rate of 11
percent (153), despite follow-up reminders. One reason for this disappoint-
ing rate may be that police simply dislike paperwork, including questionnaires. We had hoped that contacting only officers with an interest in the
occult would offset this tendency. Another possibility involves a probable
overlap between the two lists; an unknown number of officers who attended
a Killeen seminar receive the CCIN newsletter and thus may have been on
both survey lists. If this overlap was high, then our return rate may actually
be higher than indicated, since respondents who received two instruments
would return only one.

A final reason for low returns may have been suspicions about the
researchers' motives. Nearly a dozen survey recipients telephoned to learn
whether the researchers had some ideological agenda. A few were uneasy
about questions on personal views and characteristics. Most callers, however, suspected a bias because one of the two law enforcement endorse-
ments on the survey was from Lt. Larry Jones, known in the cult cop network for his strong Christian/antioccult orientation. These officers were
worried that we had this or some other strongly held view that would skew
analysis and reporting; if so, they did not wish to participate. We stressed
that ours was a scientific orientation; mollified, all agreed to return the
survey. No doubt others also assumed researcher bias and, instead of
calling, simply discarded the instrument. These reasons may explain why

return rates were so low (CCIN sample, 14 percent and Killeen sample, 4 percent).

Despite such difficulties and limitations, we believe our survey provides unique and timely insights into law enforcement officers' views of the links between satanism and crime. We first present officers' attributes, then examine their perceptions of the satanism problem.

WHO ARE THE "CULT COPS"?

Our respondents, representing 41 states,[1] are overwhelmingly male (91%) and white (96%), with a median age of 38. They are married (80%), most with children under 15 (70%). The population of their jurisdiction ranges from 300 to 230,000, with 60 percent working in cities under 65,000. About half work in agencies with 50 or more commissioned officers, and are predominantly veteran officers; 70 percent report 10 or more years in law enforcement.

Their personal characteristics suggest they are typically middle-class, conventional and conservative. Although 24 percent reported a household gross income of over $50,000, most (55%) live on less than $39,000. Many were raised in small town settings; two-thirds grew up in a town of 50,000 people or less. Most report some college work, though only 28 percent have completed a four year degree. Politically, they tend to be either independent (46%) or Republican (30%).

Of particular interest are respondents' religious beliefs and involvements. Almost all believe in God (98%), though fewer report a belief in the devil (88%). Fewer still (70%) definitely believe in life after death, although another 19 percent reported believing that an afterlife is "probable." Most claim to be Protestant (67%), most others, Catholic (21%); none was Jewish. These officers are not, however, particularly active church goers. Over half (51%) report attending church no more than several times per year. Many, however, attend at least weekly (35%), and 17 percent hold a church office.

HOW ARE POLICE INVOLVED WITH THE SATAN–CRIME PROBLEM?

Since occult and Satanic influences on criminal behavior are not covered in routine police training, police learn about them in different ways and become involved to varying degrees. Here we examine the "trigger" or impetus for respondents' interest in satanism, then explore the extent of their involvement in the network of cult cops inside and beyond their agencies.

Preliminary interviews suggested that a particular event may trigger an officer's interest in satanism. For example, one officer reported becoming interested when his daughter attempted suicide, and he found an extensive collection of heavy metal music in her room. An open-ended question asked officers to describe in their own words what specifically led them to be concerned about satanism. The data in Table 1 indicate that there are many triggers. Seldom, however, was that trigger a heinous, local crime. Instead, the largest single trigger, cited by 22 percent of the officers, was satanic graffiti and symbols, sometimes found in association with arson, burglary, or vandalism. The trigger mentioned by the second largest group of respondents was a police cult workshop or seminar (13%).

Interestingly, most officers became concerned with satanism only recently. Though one respondent reported being interested as early as 1969, only 10 percent had an interest prior to 1980. The concern of most (73%), however, dates only from 1985.

We asked about the nature and extent of respondent involvement in the network of police concerned about satanism (see Gates 1988). The issue is how respondents might be integrated into a supportive collectivity of other officers. Network integration may involve reading materials, contact with officers across the country, or interactions within their own agency.

The simplest means of connecting with other law enforcement officers on the satanism issue is via a newsletter such as *File 18*. Many (80%) of our officers subscribe to at least one; 26 percent receive two newsletters. Nearly 70 percent began subscribing during or after 1987.

Another important means of participating in the network is through police workshops or seminars on satanism. Only 15 officers reported never having attended such a session; 80 percent had attended at least two, and 23 percent had attended five or more. Again, this activity is relatively recent: less than 20 percent report attending a seminar prior to 1986.

More informal participation in the network involves contacts with distant officers. We asked the average times per month they were contacted regard-

Table 1. "Triggers" of Initial Concerns with Satanism in Percent
(Numbers in Parentheses)

Trigger	Percent	
Graffiti, symbols alone or associated with property crime (arson, burglary, vandalism)	22%	(31)
Satanism seminars/workshops	13%	(19)
Began to hear/read more about satanism and occult	11%	(16)
Local, personal crime (murder, kidnapping)	10%	(15)
Officially assigned to problem	8%	(11)
Noticed increase in teen dabbling in occult	6%	(8)
Animal mutilations	6%	(8)
Personal/family situation	4%	(6)
Other	20%	(29)

ing satanism by someone outside their agency. For most, such contacts are rare: 29 percent report no contacts, and 46 percent report an average of only one or two contacts per month. Ten percent reported five or more contacts. Nor do respondents frequently initiate contact with others. Over one-third make no contacts, nearly that many make only one contact, and less than ten percent make five or more contacts.

Interaction with others within their own agencies on occult matters is also limited, since respondents report few colleagues share their interests. Slightly more than one-third list only one, and 59 percent report only two other officers in their agencies with similar interests. Yet, according to our respondents, other officers in the agency generally respect respondents' work on satanism, even if they are not interested themselves.

Such support is less true, however, of respondents' superiors. Sixty percent complain that support and encouragement from superiors is either tepid or absent. One officer offered an explanation: "I have noticed that my superiors don't want to admit or don't believe that this sort of thing happens. This is why I don't get much support—I get more ridicule than support." Only 30 percent had been directed by agency administrators to begin looking into the satanism–crime connection; most officers took this up on their own.

When asked to indicate their primary area of occult interest and knowledge, the largest number said satanism (44%), followed by teen suicides (11%), heavy metal music (11%), and child abuse (6%). Addressing respondents' claims of expertise from a different direction, we asked respondents to rate their knowledge of selected groups and practices on a scale from "very familiar" (in-depth knowledge) to "not familiar" (never heard of or can say nothing about). Predictably, 84 percent claim familiarity with satanism, and 69 percent know much about the Ku Klux Klan. Almost half (48%) are familiar with witchcraft, and nearly as many are well acquainted with Santeria (45%). One-third reported being familiar with Palo Mayombe and approximately a fourth with voodoo and Scientology. Of the remaining four—Macumba, Kabbalah, Abaqua, and Rochaan—one (Rochaan) is a bogus occult practice included as a validity check. Only one respondent claimed familiarity with Rochaan, suggesting that respondents were honest in their assessments here.

HOW SERIOUSLY DO POLICE VIEW A SATANISM THREAT?

Given the apparent diversity of opinions among national police experts as to the link between satanism and crime, this question is critical. The most direct index of seriousness is respondent estimations of the percent of serious crimes in the country they believe attributable to satanism. Officers were asked to provide estimates for several crimes often linked to satanism. (see Table 2)

These data indicate that officers believe one in ten homicides, about one in four incidents of drug involvement, missing and abused children, about one in three teen suicides, and six in ten animal mutilations are satanism related. It should be emphasized, however, that these figures are averages. The ranges and standard deviations (also presented in Table 2) document great variation in this sample regarding the perceived involvement of satanism in these crimes.

We reasoned that these variations in crime estimates would be related to antisatanist attitudes. To test this notion we needed an index or scale of general perceptions of the satanism problem. From a series of attitude items, we constructed what we call a "Satanism Perception" (SP) scale. Individual scores on the scale derived from respondents' agreement or disagreement with such items as: "Sometimes I think there is a secret, organized effort to promote and protect satanism in America"; "Satanic beliefs lead people to commit crimes"; "We should use any means available to stop the spread of satanism in this country."[2] The scale is scored such that a high score connotes the view that satanism is a clear and present danger in need of immediate attention. Conversely, lower scores describe officers who see satanism in much less threatening terms.

To explore relationships between perceptions of satanism as a moral danger and estimates of satanic influence on crime, we correlated the SP scale scores with the crime estimates above (see Table 3).

As expected, the higher officers score on the SP scale, the more likely they are to perceive crimes to be heavily influenced by satanism. Significantly, the highest correlations are for those crimes directly involving youths:

Table 2. Respondent Estimates of Percent of Selected Crimes in America Linked to Satanism in the Past Year

Crime	Mean Percent estimated to be Satanism influenced (%)	Range (%)	Standard Deviation
Homicide	10.0	0–70	13.5
Missing children	23.0	0–80	22.8
Illegal drug sales/use	24.8	1–97	22.7
Child abuse (including sexual abuse)	26.2	0–95	24.2

Table 3. Correlation Matrix of Satanism-Perception Scale, Estimates of National Satanic Crime and Demographics

Variable	1	2	3	4	5	6	7	8	9	10	11	12	13	14
1. Satanism-Perception	1	.475a	.496a	.505a	.422a	.345b	.330b	-.238c	-.309b	-.202d	.436a	.314d	-.259c	.277c
2. Missing Kids		1	.690a	.529a	.640a	.435a	.468a	-.377a	-.173	-.223d	.119	.308	.203d	.082
3. Child Abuse			1	.666a	.574a	.292c	.664	-.257c	-.169	-.043	.278c	.360d	.132	.088
4. Teen Suicides				1	.509a	.455a	.479a	-.293c	-.279c	-.109	.288c	.267	-.042	.199
5. Homicide					1	.299c	.590a	-.267c	-.088	-.088	.221d	.274	.114	.060
6. Mutilation						1	.128	-.308b	-.181	-.239d	.194d	.227	.042	.132
7. Drug Use/Sale							1	-.179	-.119	-.044	.249c	.403d	.045	-.046
8. Jurisdiction Population								1	.363a	.350a	.101	-.228	-.063	.133
9. Education									1	.285b	.055	-.207	-.107	-.165
10. Income										1	-.021	.013	-.066	-.028
11. Religiosity											1	.302	.172d	.310c
12. Have Children <15 Years												1	.062	.036
13. Number of Years Interested													1	.132
14. Volunteered to Speak														1

[a] $p < .0001$
[b] $p < .001$
[c] $p < .01$
[d] $p < .05$

missing children ($r = .475$, $p = .0001$), child abuse ($r = .496$, $p = .0001$), and teen suicides ($r = .505$, $p = .0001$). This pattern suggests that when officers impute a strong satanism–crime connection, they tend to be concerned particularly about children. This concern is consistent with the focus in much anticult literature on special vulnerability of children to drugs, heavy metal music, and fantasy games, all of which are said to draw youths to cults and satanism.

If perceiving satanism as a major threat leads officers to think at least some crimes are significantly influenced by satanism, then what promotes strong antisatanism attitudes reflected on the SP scale? We explored several factors.

First, we examined respondent work environments, namely agency support and size of agency's jurisdiction. Support from neither superiors nor fellow officers in the respondents' agency is related to attitudes on the satanism phenomenon. Jurisdiction size, however, is significantly and inversely correlated with SP score ($r = -.238$, $p = .007$).

We then examined the relationships of SP scores to three personal characteristics of the respondents: having relatively less education, making less money, and being more religious. As expected, these variables are significantly correlated to higher SP scores. Education ($r = -.309$, $p = .0003$) and income ($r = -.202$, $p = .02$) are inversely associated with SP scores, suggesting that officers with more income and more education are less apt to feel satanism is or should be a serious police concern. Being more religious, however, appears to be the most powerful explanation. Lacking specific data on the strength of religious values, we rely on frequency of church attendance, a common proxy variable for religiosity (Grasmick et al. 1990). This association is quite strong ($r = .436$, $p = .0001$). Clearly, active involvement in a church is an important determinant of a strong anti-satanism orientation among law enforcement personnel.

Respondents with children under 15 also tend to have high SP scores; the correlation is positive and significant ($r = .314$, $p = .04$). This relationship helps explain why high SP scorers are primarily concerned about satan-influenced crimes against children, as noted above.

Finally, we examined the length of time officers report having been interested in or concerned about the satanism issue. It is reasonable that variations in length of interest would influence their perspectives. We hypothesized that officers who have accrued knowledge and experience in these matters over a longer period of time would be less inclined to see satanism as a serious national threat, while those who have been exposed to the issue relatively recently will be more concerned. As revealed in Table 3, the correlation between SP scale score and number of years interested in these issues is negative and significant ($r = -.259$, $p = .007$). There is a clear tendency for high SP scorers to have become concerned more recently.

ARE "CULT COPS" MORAL ENTREPRENEURS?

We turn now to the question raised at the outset of this chapter: to what extent are high SP scorers "moral entrepreneurs" actively crusading against a perceived threat to society? Assuming that police who crusade against a satanic incursion would seek out opportunities to communicate their views to others, we asked officers to indicate the number of formal seminars (typically for police only) they had made presentations to or led. The correlation between SP score and seminar leadership was not significant. Thus, although some high SP scorers may be high profile seminar spokespersons, many others seldom if ever lead seminars.

A different picture emerges, however, when we examine activism aimed at groups other than police. Officers indicated the number of times they have volunteered to speak to civic, church, or educational groups on the occult. We found frequent volunteering of this type to be significantly related to high scores on the SP scale ($r = .277$, $p = .009$). In other words, while they may not lead police seminars, officers particularly concerned about satanism do take their views before nonpolice groups. Such groups might be rather uncritical of the presentations on satanism by police officers.

CONCLUSIONS

The notion that satanism is spreading in this country, especially among youth, troubles many citizens. When satanism appears to be associated with criminality, this concern takes on a new dimension. In recent years there have been several high profile, violent crimes with strong satanic overtones, including Sean Sellers' killing his parents and the California murders by Richard Ramirez, the so-called "Night Stalker." This connection between satanism and crime has become an important concern for many police officers, as well. As with other legal and extralegal norms, when police define the extent and nature of satanic activity, they play an important boundary maintenance role in society. A central concern of this chapter has been to describe views of a sample of officers active on the murky boundary that lies not just between crime and noncrime, but between good and evil. Our analysis, the first of its kind, suggests several conclusions.

First, officers in this sample certainly do not reflect a social or attitudinal monolith. They are from a variety of social and economic backgrounds and work in all levels of law enforcement in jurisdictions of all sizes. More importantly, they manifest a full range of concerns about satanism. We measured these attitudes with a "Satanism Perception" (SP) scale. Significantly, we found officers in the sample to be distributed quite evenly along this scale, with no notable clustering. This pattern not only gives us confidence in the scale, but suggests that attending seminars or subscribing to a newsletter (or returning a questionnaire) implies neither excessive zeal nor skepticism regarding the issues at hand.

Differences in perceptions of the moral threat of satanism lead to quite different perceptions of the satanism–crime connection. Officers scoring high on the SP scale are much more apt to estimate that higher percentages of crimes are satanically influenced.

What accounts for variations in police perceptions of satanism and its influence on crime? Our analysis suggests they derive primarily from personal attributes of the officers. Often from smaller towns, with less education and income and more religious, officers who perceive a greater threat appear to live and work in a relatively modest and conservative setting. Our analysis suggests another determinant of attitudes toward satanism. Namely, the longer an officer has spent exploring these issues, the greater the skepticism about the imminent moral—and criminal—threat posed by satanism. There is a significant tendency for officers who have more recently become attuned to the possibility of a satanism–crime link to score higher on the SP scale. The obverse of this tendency, of course, is that those with a longer interest take a less excited view. One well known police expert on the occult, Sandi Gallant, describes this relationship between time, experience and attitudes:

> For most of us . . . what we tended to do in the beginning was we started to hear these things (about satanism–crime linkage) and first of all, we disbelieved it. Then we felt guilty about disbelieving it when it appeared that there might be something there. And then from there perhaps we got a little hysterical in the way we responded, too. And then, hopefully, we get to a point where we go "Ah ha!" I've seen both sides of the issue, and now let me sit back and be very objective and weigh each side and come to a conclusion as to what the reality is. (Klein 1989:13).

Gallant's statement suggests a process in which attitudes of officers may change over time, especially if officers are not strongly influenced by religious or other personal factors that counter the objectivity to which she refers. With time they may come to believe that there may be much more smoke than fire in the satanism scare. Moreover, experience may demonstrate that many apparent satanic crimes are in fact not what they seem (Stewart 1981). This is the conclusion of a survey respondent from Colorado:

> I mostly investigate "occult" crimes that turn out to be false reports. For example, one woman reported a satanic burglary. As it turned out the symbolism was poorly done and I got her to admit she made it up. We also had a middle-aged woman do this to front page coverage. Her motive was to get

support for a teen center in town. I think the greatest danger now is over interpreting "occult" crime. Kids have no idea of the religious significance behind their symbolism. They could not tell you when Walpurgisnacht is, but will happily wear a pentagram because Ozzy does.

This officer cautions that, although there are satanic crimes, police should take care not to let personal or religious views on the influence of Satan in the world affect their investigations of specific crimes. Evidence from this survey suggests that serious satanic crimes in local jurisdictions are relatively rare. Most involve pranks and petty crime, and some may not in fact be satanic. Apparently, seldom is a true criminal, satanic cabal found at work. Many cult cops, although quite concerned about the issues, have little first-hand experience by which to gauge reality of the satanic threat. They read lurid accounts of satanic peril, and hear the same in seminars held by police experts. The combination of these conditions—limited, direct experience with serious cult crime and frequent exposure to information about such crime elsewhere—with personal characteristics described above lead many officers to see satanism as a major national threat. To use Gallant's words, they may get "a little hysterical" about the devil's imminence. Some of these officers will continue to cling steadfastly to a reality in which Satan looms large. Others, with time and experience, may become more inclined to see, not satanic crime, but just crime with satanic trappings.

NOTES

1. The number of respondents by state follows: 20, TX; 9, CO; 8, CA; 7, IL, MO; 6, ID, MN; 5, KS, TN; 4, FL, LA, ND, OH; 3, AR, AZ, NB, NM, OK, OR, PA, SC, WY; 2, AL, GA, MS, MT, NC, NJ, WA; 1, IA, IN, MA, ME, MI, NH, NV, NY, SD, UT, VA, WI.
2. The intercorrelation between total "Satanism Perception" scale score and each of the eight component items ranges from .641 to .774. The mean is 18.3, the standard deviation is 6.5, and scores range from a low of 8 to a high of 36. Further analysis of the scale revealed that 26 respondents scored in top quartile (high SP score) and 27 scored in the lowest quartile.

REFERENCES

Alexander, D. 1990. "Giving the Devil More Than His Due." *The Humanist* 34 (March): 5–14.
Becker, Howard. 1963. *Outsiders: Studies in the Sociology of Deviance.* New York: Free Press.
Ben-Yehuda, Nachman. 1986. "The Revival of the Occult and of Science Fiction." *Journal of Popular Culture* 20:1–16.

Gates, D. 1988. "Networking to Beat the Devil." *Newsweek* December 5:29.

Grasmick, Harold, Kinsey, Karyl, and Cochran, John. 1990. "Religious Affiliation, Religiosity and Compliance with the Law: A Study of Adults." Paper presented at annual meeting of Southwestern Social Science Association, Fort Worth, Texas.

Gusfield, Joseph. 1986. *Symbolic Crusade*. Chicago: University of Illinois Press [1963].

Hicks, Robert. 1989. "Satanic Cults: A Skeptical View of the Law Enforcement Approach." Paper presented at the 11th annual crime prevention conference of the Virginia Crime Prevention Association, Chesapeake, VA.

Kahaner, Larry. 1988. *Cults That Kill*. New York: Warner Books.

Kidwell, Kirk. 1989. "The Crime of the Nineties." *The New American* 5(5):4–6.

Klein, Dianne. 1989. "Satan Sleuths." *Los Angeles Times*. May 25:V1, 12–13.

Lanning, Kenneth. 1989. "Satanic, Occult, Ritualistic Crime: A Law Enforcement Perspective." Paper prepared by the National Center for the Analysis of Violent Crime, FBI Academy, Quantico, VA.

Lyons, Arthur. 1988. *Satan Wants You: The Cult of Devil Worship in America*. New York: The Mysterious Press.

Reinerman, C., and Levine, H. G. 1989. "The Crack Attack: Politics and Media in America's Latest Drug Scare." Pp. 115–138 in *Images of Issues: Typifying Contemporary Social Problems*, edited by Joel Best. New York: Aldine de Gruyter.

Schwarz, Ted, and Empey, Duane. 1988. *Satanism*. Grand Rapids, MI: Zondervan Books.

Stewart, J.R. 1981. "Cattle Mutilation: An Episode of Collective Delusion." Pp. 288–289 in *Paranormal Borderlands of Science*, edited by K. Frazier. Buffalo: Prometheus Books.

Texas Poll. 1989. Telephone poll conducted by Public Policy Resources Laboratory, Texas A&M University, funded by Harte-Hanks Communications, Inc..

Timmer, D. A., and Eitzen, D. S. 1985. "Controlling Crime in the 1980's: A Critique of Conservative Federal Policy." *Humanity and Society* 9:67–80.

Wedge, Thomas. 1988. *The Satan Hunter*. Canton, OH: Daring Books.

Satanism in the Courts:
From Murder to Heavy Metal

12

James T. Richardson

Accusations of satanism have been made with increasing frequency in courtrooms in recent years; several types of cases link satanic involvement with illegal or antisocial acts. A WESTLAW search of state and federal court cases using the root word "satan" revealed that there had been a total of 230 state court and 107 federal court cases with written opinions in which the term (or a derivative) appeared over the past 35 years. Of these, a high proportion were heard recently: over half (139 of 230 state court opinions and 60 of the 107 federal court opinions) occurred since 1979. This remarkable growth of cases involving satanism deserves attention from legal scholars and social scientists.

This chapter discusses four prominent types of legal actions involving claims about satanism: allegations of "satanic murder," child "ritual abuse" cases, "cult brainwashing" cases, and so-called "heavy metal" cases, including the much-publicized recent "Judas Priest" case. I will focus on similarities in the characterized of satanism in the different types of cases. All four types involve an assumption that satanism is promoted by evil people or organizations that exploit innocent victims through murder, abuse, trickery, or subliminal influences. This perception that satanists are powerful, active agents, whose victims are weak, passive individuals, underpins discussions of satanism in the various types of court cases.

"SATANIC MURDER"

Of the 20,000 murders committed annually, only a miniscule proportion involve satanic beliefs or practices, but those cases usually receive wide publicity. Indeed, given the current hysteria about satanism, any puzzling or bizarre murder may be attributed to satanists (Lanning 1989; Hicks 1989; Lyons 1988). Raschke (1990) offers an example of this propensity to "overattribute"; he suggests that many murders (and other crimes) involve satanism. After discussing a Missouri murder case with satanic trappings, he says:

"Elsewhere, a national epidemic of 'satanist-related' crime was growing faster than AIDS, even though the 'religious' motivation was frequently deleted once the cases were actually brought to trial" (Raschke 1990:56).

Most notable among so-called "satanic murders" was the recent Los Angeles "Nightstalker" case, which involved satanic graffiti spray-painted on walls of victims' homes, and the defendant's overt claims that he was a satanist. Another prominent case was that of Sean Sellers, the 17-year-old Oklahoma youth who murdered his mother, stepfather, and a convenience store clerk. Sellers claimed that he was motivated by satanic beliefs picked up through reading satanic literature and playing "Dungeons & Dragons."[1] Sensational media accounts have linked other notorious cases, including the Manson murders, Henry Lee Lucas (who claimed 360 victims), and "Son of Sam," with satanism. Media reports of these crimes foster growing concern about satanism, and encourages discussions of satanism in court.

Courtroom discussions about satanism derive from at least three concerns of triers of fact—the judges and jurors. First, beliefs and practices of those accused of murder may be relevant, as judges and juries seek to understand *what happened*. If there are accusations that a murder was part of a satanic ritual, then that ritual and any relevant evidence must be described in some fashion to assist the judge and jury in understanding what caused the murder. Second, the judge and jury must assess *motives* of those being charged with a crime. This duty also may require explanations and discussions of satanic beliefs and rituals, if claims have been made that satanism motivated the crime. Third, discussions of Satanism may be required to help assess the defendant's *mental condition*, particularly if the defense offers an insanity or diminished capacity plea. When attorneys raise these issues in cases with satanic overtones, satanism may receive considerable discussion in court, generating sensational press coverage about the alleged "satanic connection."

Consider the case of a murder of a high school student in Joplin, Missouri, by three other students using baseball bats. The murder apparently was motivated largely by conflict over paying for drugs. However, rumors of satanic connections were rampant, fueled by beliefs that the students had dabbled in the occult, including sadistic torture of animals. Two of the three accused students pleaded no contest to murder charges, but a third, Pete Roland, chose to use a "diminished capacity" defense in an effort to escape the death penalty. He claimed that his involvement in satanism led to the murder, which he said was an attempted satanic sacrifice. Whether or not this was true cannot be ascertained, but, over vigorous prosecution objections, considerable discussion of Roland's alleged satanic beliefs and involvement took place in court. Jurors may have accepted the defense; they did not sentence Roland to death. Raschke (1990:57), claims that "for the first time a satanic murder has been proved in an American court of law." [Carlson et al. (1989) offers an alternative explanation of the defense strategy.]

"RITUAL ABUSE"

The recent wave of child sexual abuse cases also has brought satanism to the courts' attention. Several well-publicized child sexual abuse cases (such as McMartin) involved accusations of satanic "ritual abuse" (Charlier and Downing 1988). Indeed, assumptions of satanic involvement help "make sense" of the sometimes bizarre activities that allegedly happened. Every crime requires a motive. Accusations about animal and human sacrifices and other bizarre activities have to be explained; satanism offers a cogent, albeit mystical and far-fetched, explanation for why the adults did what they are accused of doing. The notion that the accused were somehow caught up in satanism has been particularly useful in explaining charges against females, who would usually not be considered motivated to sexually exploit children under their care. Being "trapped in satanism" makes plausible the idea that usually caring women can treat their young charges in despicable ways.

Often, these charges do not figure in courtroom presentations of child sexual abuse cases. Investigators have not found physical evidence (bodies, blood, bones, etc.) to support accusations, and some jurors and judges apparently find claims of satanic involvement incredible.[2] Therefore, a district attorney may choose to deemphasize satanic aspects of a case, using euphemisms such as "ritual abuse" to talk about what is supposed to have taken place (Lanning 1989). However, this does not preclude the media, which have a different set of concerns, from emphasizing any alleged satanic features.

Media treatments offering satanic interpretations of alleged crimes help structure public perceptions (Charlier and Downing 1988). Many people have little experience with daycare or preschools, and depend on media for their information about what goes on in such places. Perceptions of satanism that lurk in the background of many well-publicized child sexual abuse cases encourage hysteria about "ritual abuse." Since there seems to be so much satanism about, people expect to find more child sexual abuse taking place. What we expect to find we are more prone to see. Thus, beliefs in the reality of satanism have probably borne fruit, contributing to increasing claims of "ritual abuse" of children, and additional court actions concerning alleged abuse.

CULT "BRAINWASHING"

Satanism can also play a role in so-called "cult cases," involving allegations made against one of the "new religions" that have attracted attention in the past two decades. Such allegations can be included in both criminal and civil cases. By far the most prevalent type of cult case involves accusations that groups such as the Unification Church ("Moonies") or the Hare Krishna have "brainwashed" potential recruits and used "mind control" to force them into otherwise repugnant activities.

Cult cases relying on naive brainwashing theories are quite controversial (Anthony 1990, Richardson 1989a, 1991a; Malony 1988; London 1990). Nonetheless, these theories appeal to juries and even judges; there have been sizable verdicts in some civil actions based on these theories, with several initial damage awards of over $30 million. Jurors apparently accept brainwashing theories in part because they assume that no rational person would choose to join such groups; some "evil eye" must have bewitched them into participating (Hargrove 1983). Judges and jurors who accept such ideas can force evil cult gurus to pay large damages, which serve as a punishment and deterrent.

Many cult cases are promoted by the "Anticult Movement" (ACM) (Shupe and Bromley 1980). The ACM initially focused attention on specific newer religious groups such as the Children of God and the Unification Church. However, it soon began targeting a broader range of nontraditional religious groups and experiences. The ACM has used various tactics, including counseling cult members and ex-members, furnishing information to media, legislative bodies, and governmental agencies, and even forcible "deprogramming" (Richardson et al. 1986).

One major ACM tactic has been to seek redress in the courts; hence the development of "cult cases."[3] Large damage awards may deter some groups from recruiting, or even drive them out of business. This tactic is being tested now, with several major cases having made their way through the court system, two all the way to the U.S. Supreme Court (Post 1989; Richardson 1989a, 1991a; Anthony 1990). Initial indications are that the tactic is quite successful; several dozen cases across the country have been won by plaintiffs espousing the ACM-promoted brainwashing theory as scientific underpinning for tort actions claiming "false imprisonment" or "intentional infliction of emotional distress," or related torts.

Many jurors apparently do not favor new, exotic religions, and do not believe that people voluntarily join them. Even if members join voluntarily, their decision may be disregarded because many jurors apparently have strong negative feelings about cults. Thus, they are prone to approve almost any actions that get people out of cults, even if laws appear to have been broken. This was cleary illustrated in 1989, when a Denver jury rendered a not guilty verdict in a case in which a 29-year-old woman was kidnapped out of the Unification Church, with the intent to "deprogram" her. The District Attorney charged the deprogrammers with second degree kidnapping, but was forced to accept an acquittal, even though the woman had sought out the Unification Church, and stated plainly and often in testimony that she wanted to remain a member of the group. Such verdicts, coupled with civil actions in which juries accept the brainwashing/mind control model of participation, encourage the ACM tactic of filing civil actions against cults.

The ACM exploited the 1978 Jonestown tragedy, even though the Peoples' Temple was quite dissimilar to other new religions on which the ACM had focused its efforts (Richardson 1980). Today the ACM is jumping on the satanist bandwagon, and even giving the wagon a big push. An editorial in *The Religious Freedom Alert* (1989) warns that "ominously, a number of figures prominently associated with deprogramming have added their voices to the outcry over satanism."

Having joined those promoting the idea that satanism is increasing, the ACM is taking a leading role in the effort to convince America that satanists are brainwashing people everywhere. ACM groups sponsor conferences on the topic and their publications promote their view. This serves ACM interests, meshing particularly well with the ideology of one segment of the ACM—fundamentalists who believe that Satan is active in the world. Other segments of the ACM, including some mental health professionals, are not religiously motivated, but also find it worthwhile to promote the idea of satanism as a growing threat in our society (Kilbourne and Richardson 1984).

A major ACM organization is the Cult Awareness Network (CAN), which publishes anticult literature, holds conferences, and generally promotes its perspective in the media. Thus, an article in the *Family Violence Bulletin* (published by the University of Texas at Tyler) takes as verified fact a number of claims made at a Houston CAN workshop on satanism, e.g., that women serve as breeders to produce children for satanic sacrifices, and that satanists have links to child pornography, prostitution rings, and production of "snuff" films.

Another major ACM group, the American Family Foundation (AFF), has a special "Task Force on Satanism," headed by a psychologist who has been the most prominent anticult expert witness in cult brainwashing cases (Richardson 1989c, 1991a). AFF also sells a large packet of materials on satanism consisting mostly of newspaper clippings about crimes linked to satanism by the media. Regular AFF publications such as the *Cult Observer* and the *Cultic Studies Journal* also contain articles and news stories about satanism.

Thus, the ACM has broadened its concern about "religious" cults to include "satanic" cults. However, ACM groups seem bent on promoting the satanism scare simply because it fits their agenda. Thus, ACM groups freely mix their usual message about brainwashing and mind control in religious cults with a heavy dose of atrocity tales and myths about satanism, thereby tying the ACM interest in controlling new religions or "cults" with growing concern about satanism.

Linking satanism with Jonestown and "cults" is a brilliant tactic that promises to be useful in convincing judges and jurors in cases involving groups the ACM opposes. ACM participants believe something evil and deadly is luring many people into cults; what better way to support this notion than to point to Satan himself, the personification of evil in our culture?

"HEAVY METAL" CASES

"Heavy metal" cases are another legal arena involving satanism, one which has important parallels with "cult cases." Heavy metal cases are legal actions filed against musicians and record companies for damages caused when a listener was allegedly influenced to commit antisocial and/or illegal acts by lyrics, other sounds, or record jacket art of heavy metal albums. Such cases may allege that a heavy metal rock group promotes satanism, drug use, and violence through their music, record cover art, mode of dress, on-stage antics, and general demeanor (Billard 1990).

Some people think heavy metal music is a major cause of much antisocial behavior, particularly among youth (Lyons 1988). Heavy metal court cases can be viewed as an effort to control heavy metal by those who oppose such music. Accusations of satanism help justify such efforts: Raschke's (1990:171) treatment links such varied cases as the "Nightstalker," teen suicide wrongful death suits, and cemetery vandalism to heavy metal music. He says:

> Adolescent satanism is the pedagogy of contemporary rock's aesthetic terrorism. It does indeed get things done. The stupidity of the see-no-evil crowd, the self-styled civil libertarians who prate that the music has little or no impact on social developments, becomes blatant when one considers that the emblems of satan and suggestions of so-called devil worship used in heavy metal performances are indeed, as the rockers themselves contend, stage props. The props have a purpose. They are designed to "evangelize," not so much for some sort of organized and structured church of Satan, but for a summoning of the steely determination of "young America" to take charge, as the brownshirts did in the dusky streets of Weimar Germany.

Not everyone shares this paranoid view. Heavy metal's defenders acknowledge the use of "shocking symbolism" to attract teenagers, but discount the idea that heavy metal groups try to promote a coherent ideology of satanism: "the symbols seem more intended to shock than to convert, or to give the aura of the existence of some message just beyond the audience's understanding" (Carlson et al. 1989:46). In this view devotion to heavy metal music becomes a faddish act of rebellion by youth who are tired of parents and others telling them what to do and not do. Sociologist Marcello Truzzi asks, "What is there left to shock parents with? Sex isn't shocking anymore. Only the Devil is left" (Lyons 1988:163). Devilish trappings are evident in much heavy metal music. What musicians and producers may be using as a marketing tool to increase sales to rebellious teenagers, others view as thorough-going evangelism for an international satanic conspiracy. This latter view sets the stage for legal actions in which heavy metal music is blamed for antisocial acts.

Such legal actions have been filed around the country, usually seeking damages for the suicide of a teenage male devotee of heavy metal music. The theory behind such legal actions is relatively simple: the music caused the suicide, and those who produce the music and sell it to the unsuspecting public should be held liable and pay money damages (including even punitive damages) to redress wrongs done as a result of the music. Such cases might involve tort theories of liability (harm being caused by tortious conduct), or they might develop "product liability" theories similar to those used in defective product cases. Tort theories of liability are a bit harder to prove, since they usually require proof that someone deliberately intended harm, or acted with wanton disregard for the safety of others. Product liability cases can assume intentional behavior by the producer, but they also may suggest that a defective product could have been developed unbeknownst to the producer. The producer would still be liable if the product damages someone, particularly if that damage could have been foreseen by more careful study prior to sale of the product.

Heavy metal cases have been tossed out of court until recently, on the grounds that they violate constitutional protections of freedom of speech and expression. Most courts have viewed song lyrics and record jacket art as protected forms of behavior. However, a heavy metal case that attracted national attention went to trial in Reno, Nevada, in the summer of 1990. This case involved the English heavy metal band, Judas Priest, and CBS Records, the company holding the band's performing contract, as defendants. This case may have opened the door for other such cases, and thus it is worthy of attention.

The "Judas Priest case" involved the tragic deaths of two young men who allegedly made a suicide pact on December 23, 1985, after listening to a Judas Priest album for several hours, during which time they also drank a couple of six packs of beer and smoked "low grade" marijuana. One youth died instantly of a self-inflicted shotgun blast, but the other, James Vance, succeeded only in blowing his face off. He died much later, from an apparent overdose of drugs he was taking for pain. Months after the initial suicide attempts, an action was filed by the families involved (and Vance, who was alive at the time) alleging that the Judas Priest album caused the suicide pact to be formed and acted out.

Most observers anticipated that, like other such cases filed around the country, this action would be dismissed. However, the plaintiffs' attorneys presented a novel theory that allowed the case to progress past a "motion to dismiss" that had quickly terminated other such cases. The new theory claimed that subliminal messages were embedded in the music, and that those messages were a major cause of the young men's actions. Further, the argument stated that subliminal messages should not be afforded the same constitutional protection granted supraliminal speech.

This claim of immunity from First Amendment attack was based on a simplistic psychological theory about how such messages effect the human mind. Supposedly, such messages enter the mind without the subject's awareness, but can then "surface" later, as ideas that the person thinks are his or her own, and therefore may be more prone to act on. Such invasion of a person's mind is viewed as a major violation of personal privacy that should be disallowed. In short, the constitutional protection for privacy overcomes the constitutional protection afforded speech, if that speech is subliminal in character, because subliminal speech is assumed to be invasive by definition. Those who embedded the alleged subliminal messages should be liable for damages, especially if the embedding was done deliberately (tortious conduct that could even result in punitive damages). However, they might also be found liable even if unaware of the possible impact of such messages, or if they placed messages inadvertently (relying on product liability theory).

Thus, like cult cases with their brainwashing/mind control theories, heavy metal cases depend on a simplistic psychological theory—subliminal stimulation—that also has questionable scientific support (Moore 1988; Pratkanis and Greenwald 1988; Merikle 1988; Vokey and Read 1985). However, just as in cult cases, there are experts ready to testify that subliminal messages cause suicide among youth.[4]

The Judas Priest case was one of "first impression"; there were no legal precedents for constitutional protections for subliminal messages, or whether such messages could cause suicidal behavior. Presiding Nevada District Judge Jerry Carr Whitehead held a special pretrial hearing on those two issues, with extensive briefs submitted and lengthy oral arguments by both sides.[5] The Judge also allowed plaintiffs to present expert witnesses on the question of effects of subliminal stimulation, and did not allow rebuttal testimony, relying solely on cross-examination to point out flaws in the expert's testimony.

After a 3-day pretrial hearing on evidentiary and constitutional issues, the judge ruled that there were adequate issues on which to allow a trial, and the case proceeded under the glare of national and even international publicity. The 4-week bench trial focused on whether there were subliminals present on the records in question, and what effect they might have had if they were present. A bevy of experts on both sides discussed these two issues (see note 4), as well as alternative theories about why the two young men might have committed suicide.

Three weeks after the trial ended, Judge Whitehead issued a ruling in favor of CBS Records and Judas Priest. He agreed that there were some sublirninal messages on the records in question, but did not find that they were placed there deliberately. He also ruled that a case had not been made about the effects of subliminal messages on behavior, although he explicitly left the door open for further scientific research on the issue.

The Judas Priest case contained overtones of satanism but, because the two men were not known to be actively involved in satanism, satanism received little attention in the trial. One expert used by the plaintiffs was willing to testify about heavy metal music's satanic connections, but the judge ruled such testimony irrelevant. A lengthy pretrial deposition of this witness contained numerous references to satanism, but she was not allowed to express those views in open court. There were some references to satanism during trial by counsel for plaintiffs (in opening statements, for instance), but the topic never received a thorough discussion in court proceedings.

Although satanism played a minor role in this case, future heavy metal cases may include more direct references to satanism, depending on alleged satanic involvements of those being sued, and on the views of judges and attorneys in the cases. Popular beliefs and accusations that heavy metal music and its stars are deliberately exposing youth to satanic messages are widespread (U.S. Senate 1985:15–16, 20–23). Such claims fit neatly with the religious fundamentalist belief structure, which in turn complements others' more secular concerns that heavy metal music fosters anti-social behavior, including suicide, among youth. Even the *Religious Freedom Alert* (May, 1989), a periodical opposed to the Anticult Movement, in an editorial decrying the "Great Satanism Scare," states:

> the popular press is asserting that the killings (in Matamoros) have a sociological connection, if not direct organization links, to [satanism], whose gory symbols have recently become popular among teen-age fans of "heavy metal" music. . . .
>
> There is a satanism problem in America. It involves teenage drug users who are instructed in satanic symbols and practices by the music recording industry and, to a lesser extend, the motion picture industry.

To the degree that such beliefs are widespread, we can expect to see future heavy metal cases. Under a different judge, or before a jury, or with more "proof" of plaintiff allegations and theories, such actions might succeed. To the extent they are successful, we will see more discussions of satanism in courts.

CONCLUSIONS

Alleged links between satanism and murder, child sexual abuse, cult recruitment, and heavy metal music may or may not be real. If they are real, then research must determine reasons for the linkages, as well as possible effects on those involved. But, triers of fact should not simply accept the claims made by those trying to explain bizarre murders, make child abuse charges stick, stop cult recruitment, or stamp out heavy metal music. Questions should be raised about simplistic psychological theories used to assert satanism's influence. Simplistic "Manchurian Candidate" theories that posit a conspiracy of satanists entering many areas of life, taking advantage of weak, passive individuals at every turn, do not seem particularly fruitful. There is little evidence that such a conspiracy exists, or that people are subject to such manipulations. Other, more parsimonious explanations are readily available.

Those studying alleged "satanic murders" usually find other, more "normal," motives for the killings (Lanning, 1989). Critics examining the wave of ritual child abuse cases are questioning whether much actual abuse happened, treating the cases as evidence of mass hysteria that has led to some people being made into scapegoats (Nathan 1988, 1990). Research on cult recruitment generally shows that many youth want to express their independence by trying out different life-styles and belief structures, if only for a short time (Richardson 1985, 1989b; Richardson et al. 1986; Levine 1984). Testimony in the one major heavy metal case that has gone to trial clearly showed the reasonableness of alternative theories of why the tragic acts took place: a "psychological autopsy" presented in court revealed that one of the two young men had apparently been planning to commit suicide for some time. After becoming depressed at the loss of yet another job, he became more cheerful, handed out Christmas presents early, got a haircut, told some people goodbye, and generally seemed to be putting his affairs in order—a classic pattern of behavior for some people who decide to commit suicide.

Thus, we do not have to accept the reality of satanism in order to understand murder, child abuse, cult recruitment, or youth suicide and other violence. Regrettably, the reality of a "satanic connection" with other social problems is often not what is at issue. We need to remind ourselves again of W. I. Thomas' theorem: "If people define things as real, then they are real in their consequences." If people believe that many daycare workers are satanic, then they will care for their children in other ways, and view child care workers with suspicion. If people believe that satanic impulses motivate large numbers of murders, then they will live in fear of strangers. If people believe satanic forces are at work in new and exotic religions, then traditional values of freedom of religion and association may be weakened.

If society's leaders think that music can promote satanism, then limits may be placed on artistic expression.

People who believe claims about satanism have strong motivation to act. This is of particular concern when the believers are social control agents such as law enforcement personnel and the courts. If those in powerful positions accept the reality of the satanism scare, then basic legal rights and protections may break down, leaving all citizens at risk. Erikson's (1966) careful study of the Salem witch trials shows how legal institutions can be used to harm citizens, instead of protecting them. His work reminds us that the same process is possible in today's society. Well-meaning people, trying to defend what they define as sacred, may take actions that later appear bizarre and tragic. The actions of people caught up in the satanism scare, working to defend their version of the sacred order, suggest that the Salem witch trials are not as far away as we might have thought.

NOTES

1. Some experts dispute claims of satanic involvement by murderers such as Sellers and the "Nightstalker." Carlson et al. (1989:54) state that Sellers' murder of the clerk occurred during a robbery and had no trappings of a ritual killing. Apparently Sellers had a grudge against the clerk for refusing to sell him some beer (Lyons 1988: 11). Lyons (1988) also noted that Sellers was angry at his parents for forcing him to break off with a girlfriend. Similar questions have been raised about satanic motivations of Richard Ramirez, the "Nightstalker" killer, as well (Lyons 1988).

2. One of the children in the McMartin case told of being flushed down toilets and going through sewers to a place where adults involved her in satanic rituals, then cleaned her up and returned her to the preschool before closing so her parent, none the wiser, could pick her up. This person was not allowed to testify by the prosecution, but she and her parents did appear on a Geraldo Rivera show dealing with ritual abuse at McMartin (Nathan 1990). See Charlier (1988) for discussion of problems raised when satanism is openly presented in child sex abuse cases.

3. Other "cult cases" may be filed by governmental agencies. The State of Oregon pursued many types of cases in its effort to control the Rajneesh group (Richardson 1990). Such cases depend on negative feelings toward new religions, which are fostered by brainwashing/mind control allegations promoted by the ACM.

4. A noted psychologist, Professor Howard Shevrin, of the University of Michigan, offered such testimony, stating in pretrial evidentiary hearing, the trial itself, and later in a *New York Times* interview, that he thought the suicides were caused by subliminal messages embedded in the Judas Priest album to which the two young men listened the day of the suicide attempts. Many observers of the Judas Priest trial agree that Shevrin's testimony was crucial. Had he not testified at the pretrial hearing, there probably would have been no trial; the defense would have won its motion to dismiss.

Shevrin is a psychoanalytically oriented psychologist who believes that demonstrable effects of subliminal stimulation prove the existence of the subconscious mind. Other non-Freudian, cognitive-oriented psychologists disagree. Several, including Moore, Pratkanis, and Read (all cited above), testified at the Judas Priest trial, strongly disputing Shevrin's testimony on the meaning and even existence of subliminal stimulation effects, as well as the idea that such stimulation could have led to a complex act such as suicide.

One other aspect of the testimony focused on "backmasked" messages (recorded backwards) on the albums in question. Allegations that backmasked messages contributed to the suicide pact were made, with extensive testimony and demonstrations. This effort did not succeed, in part because of testimony from Read, co-author of a well-done piece of particularly relevant research (Vokey and Read 1985).

5.   In a pretrial hearing on a motion to dismiss, the court must accept as given the allegations of the side attempting to prevent dismissal. Thus, the evidentiary threshold is relatively low, particularly since Nevada law favors allowing individuals to get to trial with their complaint. Therefore, the pretrial hearing assumed the existence of subliminal messages for purposes of argument, an assumption that Judas Priest and CBS strongly disputed, and which became a major issue in the actual trial.

REFERENCES

Anthony, Dick. 1990. "Religious Movements and 'Brainwashing' Litigation: Evaluating Key Testimony." Pp. 295–344 In Gods We Trust, edited by Tom Robbins and Dick Anthony. New Brunswick, NJ: Transaction.

Billard, Mary. 1990. "Heavy Metal Goes on Trial." Rolling Stone (July 12–26):83–88, 132.

Carlson, Shawn, Luce, Gerald, O'Sullivan, Gerry, Masche, April A., and Frew, D. H. 1989. Satanism in America: How the Devil Got More Than His Due. El Cerrito, CA: Gaia Press.

Charlier, Tom. 1988. " 'Satan Factor' Complicates Trials." Memphis Commercial Appeal (January 18, 1988):A9.

Charlier, Tom, and Downing, Shirley. 1988. "Skeptics Find Legend, Not Satan, at the Core." Memphis Commercial Appeal (January, 1988):A7.

Erikson, Kai. 1966. Wayward Puritans. New York: John Wiley.

Hargrove, Barbara. 1988. "Social Sources and Consequences of the Brainwashing Controversy." Pp. 299–308 in The Brainwashing/Deprogramming Controversy, edited by David Bromley and J. T. Richardson. New York: Edwin Mellen.

Hicks, Robert. 1989. "Satanic Cults: A Skeptical View of the Law Enforcement Approach." Pp. A1–A35 in Satanism in America, edited by Shawn Carlson, O'Sullivan, G., Masche, A., and Frew, D. El Cerrito, CA: Gaia Press.

Kilbourne, Brock, and Richardson, J. T. 1984. "Psychotherapy and New Religions in a Pluralistic Society." American Psychologist 39(3):237–251.

Lanning, Kenneth. 1989. "Satanic, Occult, Ritualistic Crime: A Law Enforcement Perspective." Pp. 205–229 in Satanism in America, edited by S. Carlson, et al. El Cerrito, CA: Gaia Press.

Levine, Saul. 1984. Radical Departures: Desperate Detours to Growing Up. San Diego: Harcourt Brace Jovanovich.

London, Perry. 1990. "Religious Cult Definitions, Legal Action, Family Counseling, and Expert Testimony." Paper presented at annual meeting of the American Psychological Association, Boston, MA.

Lyons, Arthur. 1988. *Satan Wants You: The Cult of Devil Worship in America.* New York: Mysterious Press.

Malony, Newton. 1988. "The Ethics of Psychologists' Reactions to the New Religions." Paper presented at annual meeting of the American Psychological Association.

Merikle, P. M. 1988. "Subliminal Auditory Messages: An Evaluation." *Psychology and Marketing* 5(4):355–372.

Moore, Timothy. 1988. "The Case Against Subliminal Manipulation." *Psychology and Marketing* 5(4):297–316.

Nathan, Debbie. 1988. "Victimizer or Victim:" *Village Voice* 33(31):31–39.

_____. 1990. "The Ritual Sex Abuse Hoax." *Village Voice* (June 12):36–44.

New York Times. 1990. "Research Probes What the Mind Senses Unaware." (Tuesday, August 14):C1&C7.

Post, Stephen. 1989. "The Molko Case: Will Freedom Prevail?" *Journal of Church and State* 31(3):451–464.

Pratkanis, A. R., and Greenwald, A. G. 1988. "Recent Perspectives on Unconscious Processing." *Psychology and Marketing* 5(4):355–372.

Raschke, Carl. 1990. *Painted Black.* San Francisco: Harper & Row.

Religious Freedom Alert. 1989. "Matamoros, Cults, and the Great Satanist Plot." (5):14.

Richardson, J. T. 1980. "People's Temple and Jonestown: A Corrective Comparison and Critique." *Journal for the Scientific Study of Religion* 19(3):239–255.

_____. 1985. "The Active vs. Passive Convert: Paradigm Conflict in Conversion/Recruitment Research." *Journal for the Scientific Study of Religion* 24(2):119–236.

_____. 1989a. "Battling for Legitimacy: Psychotherapy and New Religions in America." Paper presented at annual meeting of the Pacific Sociological Association, Reno, NV.

_____. 1989b. "The Psychology of Induction: A Review and Interpretation." Pp. 211–238 in *Cults and New Religious Movements,* edited by Marc Galanter. Washington, D.C.: American Psychiatric Association.

_____.1991a. "Cult Brainwashing Cases and Freedom of Religion." Forthcoming, *Journal of Church and State* 33.

_____. 1991b. "New Religions on Trial: The Oregon Experience." In *Religion in the Rain,* edited by Marion Goldman. Corvallis, OR: Oregon State University Press.

Richardson, J. T., van der Lans, Jan, and Derks, Frans. 1986. "Leaving and Labelling: Voluntary and Coerced Disaffiliation from Religious Social Movements." Pp. 97–127 in *Research in Social Movements, Conflicts and Change,* vol. 9, edited by Louis Kriesberg.

Shupe, Anson, Jr., and Bromley, David. 1980. *The New Vigilantes: Deprogrammers, Anti-Cultists and the New Religions.* Beverly Hills, CA: Sage.

United States Senate Committee on Commerce Science and Transportation. 1985. Record Labeling Hearing, September 19. Washington, DC: U.S. Government Printing Office.

Vokey, J. R., and Read, J. D. 1985. "Subliminal Messages: Between the Devil and the Media." *American Psychologist* 40:1231–1239.

The Dynamics of Rumor–Panics about Satanic Cults

13

Jeffrey S. Victor

"Perhaps no other form of crime in history has been a better index to social disruption and change, for outbreaks of witchcraft mania have generally taken place in societies which are experiencing a shift of religious focus—societies, we would say, confronting a relocation of boundaries." Kai Erikson, *Wayward Puritans* (1966:153)

Satanic cult rumors are best understood as a cultural metaphor. They do indeed have truth in them, but not a literal truth. Bizarre stories of animal sacrifice, child kidnapping, ritual torture, infanticide, blood drinking, and cannibalism must be interpreted symbolically, in terms of culturally inherited symbolic meanings. The origin of these stories can be found in the collectively shared anxieties from which they arise. Although they may not be deliberately created by any group, certain groups are more likely to believe the stories and actively disseminate them.

Satanic cult stories arise as a response to widespread socioeconomic stresses, particularly those affecting parenting and family relationships. These social stresses are products of the rapid social change and social disorganization that began during the 1960s, and that caused a deep cultural crisis of values and authority.[1] The satanic cult legend says, in symbolic form, that our moral values are threatened by evil forces beyond our control, and that we have lost faith in our authorities to deal with the threat.

THEORETICAL BACKGROUND

Persistent Rumors

A rumor is a story told in conversations between people, containing assertions of truth that cannot be confirmed by incontrovertible evidence at the time and are widely regarded as being literally true, or at least plausible. Usually communicated by word-of-mouth, rumors also may be disseminated by the mass media. Rumors are usually short-lived, locally situated, and specific in content. Rumor stories. may or may not be true, in the sense that they may be verified eventually by legal or scientific methods; truth is not the central issue in defining rumors. A story is a rumor if it is a collectively created and shared perception of reality, without any manifestly obvious evidence to substantiate it (Rosnow 1980).

Rumors usually arise when something unusual or unexpected happens. According to Shibutani (1966), rumors originate as a substitute for "hard news." He suggests that rumors are a collaborative attempt to find an explanation for an ambiguous and disturbing set of events. They usually arise when people do not trust "official" sources of news. When people lose faith in their authorities, they will regard bizarre and frightening rumors as plausible, because it seems dangerous to disregard them.

A rumor persists when it offers a plausible explanation for people's shared anxieties (Rosnow 1980; Rosnow and Kimmel 1979). Several different conditions give rumors plausibility. Rumors gain credibility when they offer specific details about an anxiety-provoking situation. They grow through a "snowball" process, as more and more people contribute supportive details to the collective story. The most crucial supportive "evidence" comes from eye-witness testimonials. There will always be people who volunteer eye-witness accounts that seem to verify even the most bizarre rumor stories. They do so to satisfy a variety of personal motives: to obtain attention and prestige, express their own fantastic fears, attack some group they hate, as a prank, or give expression to some mental delusion.

Satanic Cult Rumor-Panics

On rare occasions, fear-provoking rumor stories give rise to panics in crowds or even in whole communities. The classic case is the "War of the Worlds" panic in the region around New York City in 1939. Although there have been several studies of community-wide panics, there is no standardized definition or criterion that can be used to identify a panic. This study uses the following definition: a rumor-panic is a collective reaction to rumors about immediately threatening circumstances. A rumor-panic in a community is identified by the existence of widely occurring, fear-provoked behavior, indicated by numerous incidents of extraordinary fight–flight reaction. This collective behavior may include protective behavior, such as the widespread buying of guns, or preventing children from being in public places. It may also include aggressive behavior, such as group attacks on people perceived to be sources of threat, or destruction of property. It may also include agitated information seeking for "news" about the threat, and intensified surveillance of the community by authorities.

Rumor-panics in response to satanic cult stories do not arise from purely local events (Victor 1989). The process begins when widespread economic insecurity and family problems give rise to tension and frustrations felt by a great many people in a community. Next, an ambiguous local event, such as a teenage suicide, vandalism of a cemetery, or the appearance of mysterious graffiti on walls, becomes a concrete focus of attention for community anxiety and gossip. Satanic cult stories, coming from mass media and folklore sources, provide a plausible explanation for the ambiguity of unfocused anxieties and unclear events. These stories become incorporated into local gossip as persistent rumors. Satanic cult rumors gain credibility, as rumors usually do, through the process of consensual validation of reality. People come to believe the rumors because they are repeated so often; "everyone" they talk to says that the rumors are true. The similarity of rumor stories from location to location suggests that rumors that give rise to rumor-panics are one manifestation of a contemporary legend-making process in American society.

RESEARCH METHODS

I conducted a community study of a rumor-panic in southwestern New York and northwestern Pennsylvania (Victor 1989) immediately after it occurred on May 13, 1988, using several methods to collect data. (1) I interviewed local authorities, including police detectives, newspaper reporters, school administrators, clergymen, and the directors of the youth bureau the animal protection society. (2) Students in one of my courses conducted and recorded interviews with a sample of 50 local people in three categories: teenagers, parents, and authority figures such as teachers and ministers. (3) One student, a Methodist minister, taped interviews with 10 local ministers of fundamentalist churches. (4) Another student conducted and recorded interviews with 30 local high school students from three different teenage subcultures: "punks," "preppies," and religious activists.

In addition to this case study, I have collected data from several other sources. (1) I located newspaper reports about other satanic cult rumor-panics, as well as teenage satanism, satanic ritualistic crimes, and ritual sexual abuse of children, through the *Newsbank* microfiche collection. (2) I observed a police seminar on satanic cult crime, a church revival concerning satanism in popular music, and a psychiatric seminar about the ritual sexual abuse of children by satanic cults. (3) I collected audiotapes of antisatanist speeches presented on Christian radio programs and in churches, and gathered an extensive collection of antisatanist publications, books, magazine articles, and pamphlets—most published by Christian religious presses or volunteer crime–fighting organizations. (4) I collected transcripts of national television talk-show programs about satanism, including the episodes of "Geraldo," "Oprah Winfrey," "Sally Jesse Raphael," and "Phil Donahue."

COMMUNITY PANICS IN RESPONSE TO SATANIC CULT RUMORS
IN RURAL AREAS OF THE UNITED STATES

My search of small-town newspaper articles located reports of 31 satanic cult rumor-panics in locations across the United States, between 1984 and 1989 (see Figure 1). I also found reports of similar rumor-panics in Canada. In no case was anything found that resembled a "satanic cult"; none of the panics involved an organized group committing crimes and justifying them with a "satanic" ideology. The 31 cases probably do not include all rumor-panics in the United States, because my research source, *Newsbank*, reprints articles from only about 200 American newspapers.

This series of community-wide rumor-panics is a unique social phenomenon. There have been many examples of locally situated rumor-panics and, indeed, examples of rumors that swept the nation. However, as far as I know, there has been no other series of community rumor-panics across the country, with recurrences over several years. Curiously, this phenomenon has not been reported in the national press.

Behavioral Indicators of Collective Panic

The western New York rumor-panic I investigated featured many behavioral indicators of collective panic, including protective, aggressive, and information-seeking behavior (Victor 1989). A great many parents, for example, kept their children home from school, for fear that they might be kidnapped by "the cult." Over 100 cars showed up at a rumored ritual site in a wooded area, where they were stopped by police barricades. Some of the cars contained weapons—clubs, knives, and hunting guns. At a warehouse rumored to be another ritual meeting place, about $4,000 of damage was done to musical equipment and interior walls. The police, school officials, and youth bureau were inundated with hundreds of telephone calls reporting bizarre incidents. Several teenagers of an unconventional "punk" appearance were labeled "satanist" and received threatening telephone calls. These countercultural kids were merely scapegoat targets for community tensions, due to their publicly visible, "strange" hair and clothing style.

Indicators of behavior driven by fear were reported in newspapers throughout the 250-mile-wide region. School officials from small towns and centralized rural school districts reported hundreds of school children absent, as fearful parents kept their children home. Police departments received an avalanche of telephone calls from people who reported having seen mutilated animals, satanic symbols, hit lists of planned victims, and even human corpses. Town meetings were held in many locations; enraged parents demanded "action" from police and school authorities. Prayer

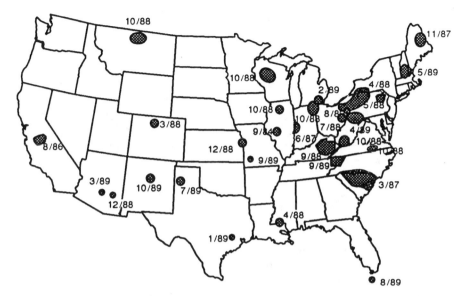

Figure 1. Locations of rumor-panics in the US and dates of newspaper reports about them.

meetings were held in some rural fundamentalist churches to pray for help in fighting Satan's influence. Sunday school instruction was given at some churches to warn children about the danger of playing with the occult. In addition, some churches invited religious satan-hunters from out of town to speak.

The newspaper articles about satanic cult rumor-panics in other locations reported similar collective behavior. I used reports of this kind of behavior as my criterion for including a location on my list of rumor-panics. I did not include locations where satanic cult rumors were merely reported to be circulating, without provoking widespread panic-driven behavior in a community or region. I did not include, for example, locations where newspaper articles reported rumors about supposed teenage satanists, or satanic ritual abuse at childcare centers.

What Are the Underlying Causes of These Rumor-Panics?

Theories of collective behavior suggest that rumors and panics arise from shared sources of social stress; underlying conditions cause widespread anxiety and frustration (Miller 1985). Clues to these sources of social stress may be found in socioeconomic conditions in locations where rumor-panics have occurred, and in the symbolic content of the rumors themselves.

Rural and Small Town Locations

In every case except one (Kansas City, Missouri), the 31 rumor-panics occurred in rural areas and small towns, rather than large cities. Rumor-panics that took place near large cities, such as Pittsburgh, Pennsylvania, or Richmond, Virginia, did not penetrate into the urban area.

My own research confirms this anomaly. The rumor-panic I studied in depth covered a huge, 250-mile-wide area of farmlands and small towns across southwestern New York and northwestern Pennsylvania. However, it did not occur in Erie, Pennsylvania, the region's largest city with about 120,000 people. People in small towns near Erie became very agitated about dangerous satanic cults, but people in Erie had not even heard the rumors (*Erie Time-News* May 12, 1988).

Interpretation.   The rural location of these rumor-panics calls for an explanation. One hypothesis is that underlying socioeconomic stresses, and the resultant cultural crisis in traditional values, are particularly acute in rural and small town areas (Victor 1989). There is good evidence for greatly increased economic stress on unskilled, poorly educated parents, due to the rapid loss of well-paid blue-collar jobs in small town America (O'Hare 1988; Porter 1989). One major study, for example, reported that "the poverty rate for the 54 million Americans who live in rural areas has climbed to 18 percent—50 percent higher than in urban areas. By 1986, one out of every five young rural families was living below the poverty line" (O'Hare 1988). There is also evidence that problems in raising children, such as alcohol and drug abuse, juvenile crime, depression, and child abuse, have increased proportionately more in rural areas than in urban and suburban areas (Helge 1990). A complementary hypothesis is that the communication networks that transmit the legend, especially among fundamentalist Protestants, are stronger in rural and small-town areas.

The Content of the Rumor Stories

The newspaper reports of the 31 rumor-panics reveal that rumor stories from across the country feature surprisingly similar content. About 75 percent of the stories mention animal mutilations; about 65 percent describe the kidnapping and ritual sacrifice of children. Many of the kidnapping stories take the form of predictions, but others claim that such crimes had already taken place and were concealed from public knowledge. Interestingly, about 40 percent of these kidnapping stories specifically mention blond, blue-eyed children or virgins—cultural symbols of innocence and purity.

Other rumor motifs are less common. About 20 percent of the rumors made claims that satanists had committed murder or mass murders (without specific mention of children). Ritual sexual abuse of children by a satanic cult appeared in only about 5 percent of the rumors. Other crimes mentioned only once each included the sacrifice of human fetuses, ritual torture, sexual orgies, and teenage suicide due to satanism.

In the western New York rumor-panic, many people claimed to have seen things that did not exist or to have knowledge of events that did not occur. The police and humane society received hundreds of reports about cats (and sometimes dogs) having been sacrificed by the satanic cult. Cats, for example, were "seen" hanging from light poles in downtown Jamestown. Many high school students "found" black roses and death threats in their lockers. Many people reported "seeing" red satanic graffiti painted on walls in the downtown warehouse area, near a site of rumored ritual meetings.

However, the most fear-provoking rumor was the "the satanic cult was planning to kidnap and sacrifice a blond, blue-eyed virgin." This rumor surfaced only about 2 weeks before the panic reached its peak intensity—on Friday the 13th, May, 1988. It served to heighten tensions that had been growing since mid-winter, as one fear-provoking rumor built upon another (Victor 1989).

Interpretation. Stories about the kidnapping and ritual sacrifice of children are at the core of these satanic cult rumors. Historical comparison shows that this motif derives from the ancient blood ritual myth, which commonly recurs during periods of cultural crisis, when people are frustrated and anxious about changing cultural values.

Many parents worry about threats to the safety and well-being of children, such as those from drug abuse, teenage pregnancy, teenage suicide, sexual molestation, and kidnapping. Many traditionalist people are morally appalled by the existence of widely available pornography, the acceptance of premarital sex, the tolerance of homosexuals, the easy availability of abortion, and other manifestations of what they consider moral decadence and threats to secure family life. (Intellectuals may regard these concerns as misplaced. Nevertheless, they are powerful themes for masses of Americans, as evidenced by popular campaign issues in national elections.) A good deal of research shows widespread feelings of powerlessness among Americans and an increasing "crisis of confidence" in institutions and authorities of American society to change things for the better (Lipset and Schneider 1983; Harris 1987).

How Do Rumor-Panics Begin?

Before a rumor-panic begins, some kind of "triggering event" acts as a catalyst to release growing social tensions. This triggering event is not the "cause" of the panic behavior, even though people may consciously point to it as the cause of their fear. However, fear is actually a response to the collective definition of social reality embedded in the rumor stories (Shibutani 1966).

Possible Triggering Events. The newspaper articles about the rumor-panics reported as important antecedent events whatever each reporter considered to be possible "causes" of the rumors. The reporters no doubt overlooked some antecedent events that may have functioned as triggering events. It was sometimes not possible for me to determine from the newspaper accounts whether the reported events had precipitated the panic or only provoked rumors long before the panic erupted.

The newspaper reports indicate that some antecedent events commonly precede community panics. These include the sighting of so-called "satanic" graffiti (mentioned in 39% of cases), cemetery vandalism (23%), or some violent, local crime, such as a murder or suicide (45%). Other antecedent events mentioned less frequently included a local church meeting or police conference concerning the dangers of satanism (16%), a mass media presentation about the dangers of satanism (13%), conflict between local youth groups involving accusations of satanism (13%), or discovery of mutilated animals (6%).

In the rumor-panic that I studied, the symbolic significance of Friday the 13th functioned as a "trigger" to release tensions that had been building for months over the region. However, other local events reported in the press triggered the preceding rumor process; different communities focused on different events—a teenage suicide, the discovery of "satanic" graffiti, or conflict between teenage cliques (Victor 1989).

In Jamestown, the rumor process started with the appearance of the new "punk" counterculture of high school students and private rock music parties attended by those youths at a warehouse rented for the purpose of band practice. Although these events were not particularly dramatic, they did give rise to anxiety-provoking gossip about supposed teenage drug use and sex orgies. Over several months, this gossip gradually transformed the countercultural teenagers into symbols of satanic cult rumor stories. One catalyst for this transformation was a "Geraldo" talk show about satanic cult influences upon teenagers (*Geraldo* November 19, 1987). Another was a national news item about a teenager who killed his mother and himself, supposedly due to the influence of satanism (*Jamestown Post-Journal* January 12, 1988). The existence of a local "satanic cult" gradually became a taken-for-granted reality in the community, through the process of consensual validation, as the rumor stories were repeated by many different people.

The acceptance of this socially constructed "reality" was by no means uniform; a great many people remained skeptical of all the rumors. (Most importantly, the local police, except for one or two officers, remained skeptical.) The key factor relevant to the acceptance of the rumor stories appeared to be participation in a communication network that constantly repeated the stories. Once the process of consensual validation gave the stories credibility, many people seemed to have a strong need to believe them.

Interpretation. It appears that antecedent to a satanic cult rumor-panic, there is usually one or more ambiguous local events that, in people's collective imagination, evoke the symbolic themes of the emerging satanic cult legend. Thus, the legend is collectively used to provide an explanation for some event of widespread local concern, for which there exists no other ready explanation (Shibutani 1966).

How Do the Rumors Spread?

Rumors spread through communication networks that are receptive to them, and not through other networks in which people remain skeptical or disinterested (Rogers and Kincaid 1981). In receptive communication networks, some people actively promote rumor stories, like propagandists. My survey of the news articles indicates that, in many cases, so-called "experts" in identifying satanic cult ritual crime contributed to the fears generated by satanic cult rumors. Newspaper articles report that experts' claims about the supposed dangers of satanic cults lent credibility to bizarre rumor stories. In about 33 percent of the rumor cases, police "experts" in satanic cult crime were active in promoting such claims, while about 25 percent of the cases featured claims about satanism by religious satan-hunters.

> In April, 1985, a local Deputy Sheriff in rural Union County, Ohio, claimed to know of five secret "cells" of satanists, with at least 1,500 members. (*Columbus Dispatch* April 14, 1985)

> In May, 1989, police satan hunters at a state-wide conference in New Hampshire said that there are over two million members of satanic cults in the United States, organized into "criminal cartels". According to these crime "experts", many unsolved kidnappings and serial murders in our country are committed by highly secret satanic cults. (*Boston Globe* May 28, 1989)

In Jamestown, fundamentalist churches functioned as an important communication network for dissemination of satanic cult rumor stories in sermons, church meetings about the rumors, prayer sessions, speeches by invited out-of-town satan-hunters, and church newsletters. Several fundamentalist ministers, responding to the growing fears of their parishioners, were particularly active in claims-making about the supposed satanic cult. These activities aggravated the rumor-panic (Victor 1989).

Interpretation.   Satanic cult rumors are spread by the mass media, but in local communities, the stories are disseminated as a "political cause." Certain groups in American society are more receptive to satanic cult rumors and more likely to disseminate them actively. These groups include small-town police and traditionally religious people.

MACROSOCIOLOGICAL INTERPRETATION: THE CONTEMPORARY LEGEND-MAKING PROCESS

My thesis is that satanic cult stories arise in Western societies during periods of cultural crisis as part of a historically recurring cultural pattern involving the spread of subversion myths and a search for scapegoats to blame for social problems. This pattern links the motifs of ancient legends to currently popular explanations for social problems.

Contemporary Legends

The scholarly study of contemporary legends by folklorists began attracting notice in the 1970s. The concept of a contemporary legend (or urban legend) provides a new intellectual tool for understanding forms of collective behavior, previously discussed in terms of persistent rumors transmitted both orally and through the mass media (Ellis 1990). Jan Harold Brunvand's first collection of "urban legends," *The Vanishing Hitchhiker* (1981), brought this concept to the attention of scholars in other disciplines, as well as the general public. Brunvand defined urban legends as a "subclass of folk narratives . . . that—unlike fairy tales—are believed, or at least believable, and that—unlike myths—are set in the recent past and involve normal human beings rather than ancient gods or demigods." In his brief survey of attempts to clarify the concept, Ellis notes that contemporary legends deal with events that are alleged to have "just happened," or with threats that have recently emerged. These stories (1) are presented as being "news" freshly arisen from the storyteller's social setting, (2) deal with some kind of perceived emergency or social problem which urgently needs attention, and (3) express attempts to gain social control over an ambiguous situation and are, therefore, "fundamentally political acts" (Ellis 1990).

It is most useful to conceptualize a contemporary legend as an interactive process of collective behavior, rather than a fixed and unchanging narrative. The collective behavior consists primarily of collaborative creation and communication of persistent rumor stories, in ever-changing variation. A contemporary legend is, therefore, always emergent out of interaction and is never finished.

The Link between Legends and Rumors

There is no clear-cut distinction between persistent rumors and contemporary legends (Mullens 1972). Both are products of people's collaborative story-telling, attempts to deal with anxiety-provoking, ambiguous situations. Mullens, for example, notes that although rumors are usually brief propositions without any long narrative about people and events, many contemporary legends are short stories about incidents alleged to have occurred recently. In discussing the connection between rumors and legends, Mullens (1972) points out that persistent rumors sometimes become incorporated into popular folklore, to be passed on from generation to generation. However, the connection most important for this study is that the themes and symbolism of legends are sometimes used by people to construct the content of rumor stories. In other words, traditional legends offer ready-made scripts, which people can use to create stories offering plausible explanations for unfamiliar, threatening circumstances.

The scripts of traditional legends learned early in life structure our preconceptions about human nature and the nature of things supernatural. Legends are not only "out there" in our shared culture. They are also "in us," psychologically. They are the exemplars and paradigms by which we live (Keen 1988). A person does not need to know all the details of a rumor built on a traditional legend to fill in the details. A good imagination will suffice. For this reason, it is usually not possible to trace the origin of a contemporary legend to any specific event; its origin may lie in ancient sources.

Origin of the Satanic Cult Legend

Satanic cult rumor stories derive from an ancient myth, usually referred to as the "blood ritual myth," which tells of children kidnapped and murdered by a secret conspiracy of evil strangers, who use the children's blood and body parts in religious rituals (Hsia 1988; Ridley 1987). This myth endures because it offers universal appeal to the latent fears of parents everywhere. Variations of the myth commonly are elaborated with symbols of mysterious evil: graveyard robberies and mutilated corpses, secret meetings of people engaged in secret rituals, strange incantations and symbols, and people clothed in black robes making ritual animal sacrifices and sometimes eating human body parts in cannibalistic rites. These are all omens that indicate that purity and innocence are endangered by powerful agents of absolute evil.

The evil internal enemy in blood ritual subversion stories is usually some widely despised group. Such groups function as scapegoats for anxieties caused by widespread social stresses. In ancient Rome, subversion stories claimed that Christians were kidnapping Roman children for secret ritual sacrifices (Ellis 1985). The murder of innocent children was a symbol of Christianity's absolute evil, for only total evil preys upon total innocence. Later, during the Middle Ages, similar stories claimed that Christian children were being kidnapped by Jews for use in secret, religious ritual sacrifices. When this myth is used in antisemitic attacks, it is known as the "blood libel" (Hsia 1988). In France, just before the French Revolution, similar stories accused aristocrats of kidnapping poor children to use their blood in medical baths.

Today, the blood ritual myth is constantly being reworked in popular culture entertainment. Many horror novels and movies use the theme of kidnapping and murder for a variety of unsavory purposes, such as ritual sacrifices (The Believers) or use of body parts (Coma). Similarly, some fairy tales depict children kidnapped, usually by witches or monsters, who may cook or eat them. Thus, popular culture keeps alive and makes familiar an ancient story's mythology. The point is that satanic cult stories are being fabricated out of these same cultural materials.

The satanic cult legend combines the blood ritual myth with another ancient subversion myth, which concerns Satan's rebellion against God and his struggle to subvert the souls of men and women, thereby destroying God's moral order. This particular combination of myths has a long history. It was frequently used in scapegoating attacks on Jews, lepers, and people accused of being heretics or witches (Cohn 1975; Tractenberg, 1983; Moore 1987). The power of this combination is that it offers both secular and sacred symbols, thus appealing to both secular professionals and religious traditionalists. The presumed satanists can be regarded as either dangerous social deviants, agents of supernatural evil, or both. The danger of such powerful subversion mythology lies in its demand to find scapegoats; inevitably, real, living scapegoats will be found.

Mythology of the Satanic Cult Legend

American society went through a very disruptive period of rapid social change during the 1960s and early 1970s. Those changes challenged traditional American cultural assumptions and values about such central issues as family roles and the meaning of work. Many people still find it difficult to adjust to those massive changes. In this context, we can recognize the satanic cult legend as an attempt to restore an idealized society to past greatness and moral purity, an attempt to locate and blame an evil enemy, a scapegoat, for the subversion of dominant cultural values.

The blood ritual myth and similar subversion myths usually arise at times when a society is undergoing a deep cultural crisis of values, following rapid social changes that cause disorganization and widespread social stress (Levack 1987; Schoeneman 1975). Indeed, subversion myths and their resulting witch-hunts can be taken as indicators of cultural crisis (Erikson 1966). These stories function as a collective metaphor to express a group or society's anxieties about its future. They say, in symbolic form, that our future (our children) is threatened by mysterious forces that we cannot fully comprehend or control.

The satanic cult legend's meaning can be found in the cultural symbolism of its metaphor (Victor 1989). Particular satanic cult claims, rumors, and stories contribute to the process of collaborative story telling. However, the overall metaphor says that very powerful, secretive, evil forces threaten the legitimate moral order. The threat derives from "heresy" against sacred, traditional values, which were once the solid foundation of our stable way of life. The evil enemy's values are opposite everything we cherish. Their power may derive from mysterious occult sources or "hidden" connections within the power elite in our society. The enemy's evil image functions, just as in times of war, to confirm our society's essential goodness.

This metaphor may be a projection of people's loss of faith in the ability of our society's institutions and authorities to solve threatening social problems. Satan symbolizes a loss of faith in legitimate moral authority. People who are most likely to take this symbol seriously are those who feel that loss of faith most intensely. The satanic cult legend is an expression of people's shared feelings of powerlessness to change our society for the better.

The Function of the Satanic Legend

Satanic cult rumors function as "improvised news" to provide an explanation for ambiguous sources of shared social stress. These stories provide fantasy scapegoats to blame for widespread feelings of frustration, anger, and powerlessness. The selective location of satanic cult rumor-panics in rural areas and small towns may be due to the greater socioeconomic stress and cultural crisis in values experienced there. Economic stress upon unskilled, poorly educated, working-class parents and the problems of parenting children may have increased proportionately more in rural areas than in urban and suburban areas.

The Dissemination of Satanic Cult Stories

Finally, we must ask: whose purposes are being served by the spread of satanic cult stories? Subversion myths commonly serve vested interests of particular social groups.

Communication networks that actively disseminate satanic cult rumors are likely to be stronger in rural and small town areas. Satanic cult stories are disseminated by local police "experts" in ritualistic crime, and by religious traditionalists (sociopolitically conservative Protestants and Catholics), whose ideological preconceptions make them receptive to satanic cult stories.[2]

Satanic cult stories serve to justify and support the power and prestige of radical-right Christians. Their ideology professes that American social problems are largely due to a loss of faith in God and a loss of patriotism in America, which is God's chosen land. Conservative Christian publications about satanism target "New Age" enthusiasts and neopagans as satanists, accusing such people of either committing or encouraging ritualistic crime (Carlson et al. 1989).

However, I suggest that these groups are only proxy targets, much like Communists were proxy targets used to attack American liberals during the 1950s "Red Scare." The real targets are liberal, modernist Protestants and Catholics. Satanic cult stories are ideological weapons in a conflict among Christians, traditionalists versus modernists. This internal conflict in American society fosters the propagation of satanic cult stories. Historical research provides evidence that "witch-hunts" for scapegoats are most common in regions and societies where internal conflict is greatest (Levack 1987; Moore 1987). Therefore, we can predict that satanic cult rumors and claims will arise in regions experiencing the greatest conflict between traditionalist and modernist Christians. As Coser notes, "the inner enemy . . . may be simply invented, in order to bring about through a common hostility toward him the social solidarity which the group so badly needs" (Coser 1956: 107).

ACKNOWLEDGMENTS

I would like to express my appreciation to several people who helped me to put together information and interpretations presented in this chapter. Bill Ellis and Phillips Stevens offered me many insights about contemporary legends, provided me with many sources of information, and gave a critical reading to an initial draft of this material. Robert Hicks, Debbie Nathan, and Sherrill Mulhern kindly shared their own research with me and sent me an abundance of research sources.

Some material appeared in my article in *Western Folklore* (1990). I want to thank the editor of that journal, Pack Carnes, for permission to include that material in this chapter.

NOTES

1.   Research evidence of this value crisis in Western societies comes from Inglehart (1990), who finds cross-cultural evidence of a value shift toward greater individual autonomy, innovation, and self-expression, and a tendency to challenge rather than accept authority. These values challenge traditionalist value priorities of

obedience to authority and unquestioning acceptance of the wisdom of the past; they particularly threaten traditionalist (but not modernist) Christian preconceptions.

2. This does not mean that all traditionalist Christians automatically accept satanic cult stories as "fact." Also, other groups with quite different ideologies may be receptive to satanic cult conspiracy stories. For example, in recent years feminists have become dedicated to uncovering the "hidden victims" of child sexual abuse and incest.

REFERENCES

Boston Globe. 1989. "Cult Scare Seen as Overrated." (May 28).

Brunvand, Jan Harold. 1981. *The Vanishing Hitchhiker: American Urban Legends and Their Meanings.* New York: W.W. Norton.

Carlson, Shawn, and Larue, Gerald, with O'Sullivan, G., Masche, A., and Frew, D. 1989. *Satanism in America.* El Cerrito, CA: Gaia Press.

Cohn, Norman. 1975. *Europe's Inner Demons: An Enquiry Inspired by the Great Witch-Hunt.* New York: New American Library.

Columbus Dispatch (Ohio). 1985. "No Bodies Found Yet in Cult Probe." (June 21), "Satanic Murders: A Great Story That Wasn't There." (June 23).

Coser, Lewis. 1956. *The Functions of Social Conflict.* New York: Free Press.

Ellis, Bill. 1985. "De Legendis Urbis: Modern Legends in Ancient Rome." *Journal of American Folklore* 96:200–208.

_____. 1990. "Introduction:. "Special Issue: Contemporary Legends in Emergence" *Western Folklore* 49:1–10.

Erie Times-News (Pa.) 1988. "Reports of Satanism Prove Unfounded"; "Far-Reaching Rumors Trigger Fear, Anxiety." (May 12).

Erikson, Kai T. 1966. *Wayward Puritans: A Study in the Sociology of Deviance.* New York: John Wiley.

"Geraldo". 1987. "Satanic Cults and Children" (Nov. 19). Transcript from *Journal Graphics,* Inc. New York.

Harris, Louis. 1987. *Inside America.* New York: Random House.

Helge, Doris. 1990. "National Study Regarding Rural, Suburban and Urban At-Risk Students." Bellingham, WA: National Rural Development Institute, Western Washington University. Research report.

Hsia, R. Po-Chia. 1988. *The Myth of Ritual Murder: Jews and Magic in Reformation Germany.* New Haven: Yale University Press.

Inglehart, Ronald. 1990. *Culture Shift in Advanced Industrial Society.* Princeton, NJ: Princeton University Press.

Jackson Clarion-Ledger. 1988. "Rumor of Satanic Cult Ritual Spooks McComb, Children Kept Home." (April 1), "Police Source Says Most Satanists in Cult to Be in Its Orgies." (April 2).

Jamestown Post-Journal. 1988. "Boy Scout Kills Mom, Then Himself." (January 16).

Keen, Sam. 1988. "The Stories We Live By." *Psychology Today* (December): 43–47.

Levack, Brian P. 1987. *The Witch-Hunt in Early Modern Europe.* New York: Longman.

Lipset, Seymour M., and Schneider, William. 1983. *The Confidence Gap: Business, Labor and Government in the Public Mind.* New York: Free Press.

Miller, David. 1985. *Introduction to Collective Behavior*. Belmont, CA: Wadsworth.

Moore, R. I. 1987. *The Formation of a Persecuting Society: Power and Deviance in Western Europe, 950–1250*. New York: Basil Blackwell.

Mullen, Patrick B. 1972. "Modern Legend and Rumor Theory. *Journal of the American Folklore Institute* 9:95–109.

O'Hare, William P. 1988. *The Rise of Poverty in Rural America*. Washington, D.C.: Population Reference Bureau (July).

Porter, Kathryn H. 1989. *Poverty in Rural America: A National Overview*. Washington D.C.: Center on Budget and Policy Priorities.

Ridley, Florence H. 1987. "A Tale Told Too Often." *Journal of American Folklore* 26:153–156.

Rogers, Everett M., and Kincaid, D. Lawrence. 1981. *Communication Networks*. New York: Free Press.

Rosnow, Ralph L. 1980. "The Psychology of Rumor Reconsidered." *Psychological Bulletin* 87: 578–591.

Rosnow, Ralph L., and Kimmel, Allan J. 1979. "Lives of a Rumor." *Psychology Today* (June): 88–92.

Schoeneman, Thomas J. 1975. "The Witch Hunt as a Culture Change Phenomenon." *Ethos* 3: 529–554.

Shibutani, Tamotsu. 1966. *Improvised News: A Sociological Study of Rumors*. Indianapolis: Bobbs-Merrill.

Tractenberg, Joshua. 1983. *The Devil and the Jews*. New Haven: Yale University Press. [1943].

Victor, Jeffrey S. 1989. "A Rumor-Panic About a Dangerous Satanic Cult in Western New York." *New York Folklore* 15: 23–49.

———. 1990. "Satanic Cult Rumors as Contemporary Legend." *Western Folklore* 49: 51–81.

14

Accusations of Satanism and Racial Tensions in the Matamoros Cult Murders

Thomas A. Green

During the early morning of March 14, 1989, 21-year-old University of Texas student Mark Kilroy was abducted from the streets of Matamoros, Mexico. Kilroy's body was recovered on April 11 from a shallow grave on a ranch outside Matamoros; the body had been mutilated, as had most of the other 12 corpses recovered on the same site. Subsequent investigation determined that Kilroy and others had been sacrificed in rituals designed to obtain supernatural protection for the drug smuggling activities of the Hernandez family.

These rituals were directed by Adolfo Constanzo, a 26-year-old Cuban-American hired by the Hernandez family to provide them with magical protection and revive the flagging fortunes of their drug smuggling empire. Before joining the family, Constanzo had established a reputation, extending to the upper echelons of Mexican entertainment and government, for personal charisma, the supernatural powers of his *limpias* (ritual cleansings), and a flamboyant life-style in Zona Rosa, Mexico City's gay district. After the discoveries at Santa Elena Ranch, he and his inner circle of followers (Alvaro de Leon Valdez; his lovers, Omar Francisco Orea Ochoa and Martin Quintana Rodriguez; and his "high priestess" Sara Aldrete) were linked to a series of particularly sadistic ritual murders in Zona Rosa. The practices that led to both series of murders, though apparently idiosyncratic and influenced by sexual psychopathy, borrowed features of Afro-Caribbean religions such as santería , to which Constanzo had been introduced by his mother. Although santería constituted a baseline for this belief system, other influences proved far more important to the final form the rituals took. For example, prior to and during her involvement with Constanzo, Sara Aldrete had been a student at Texas Southmost University in Brownsville, Texas and had studied the anthropology of religion as part of her curriculum. More importantly, she had become obsessed with the 1987 film *The Believers*, directed by John Schlesinger, which focuses on a cult that practices human sacrifice to acquire supernatural power and protection (Cartwright 1989; Garcia 1989). Her obsession led to the cult using the film as an indoctrination tool;

the discovery of the ritual paraphernalia of what she characterized as "santería cristiano" in her apartment suggests that she played a crucial role in the ultimate form Constanzo's belief system took.

The precise nature of Constanzo's practices, however, is not germane to my analysis. Rather, I want to examine the response to and labeling of the "cult activities" (the most general label imposed by the press). We may identify two distinct sorts of responses to the Kilroy case: the folk and the media. Although both reacted to the same immediate stimulus (i.e., ritual mutilation and murder), they used distinct, though occasionally overlapping, vocabularies in coming to terms with the horror. Moreover, it is apparent that both responded to and articulated other social tensions in the contemporary American environment, for example, fears caused by increased immigration from Mexico and other Latin American nations and economic depression in the American Southwest.

By a folk response to Constanzo's actions, I mean those narratives, fragments of narratives, and beliefs that circulated (primarily) orally and (primarily) among local groups as a result of the Matamoros murders. By a media response, I mean the press reports that circulated in electronic or print media and among much larger, regional and national audiences.

I collected the folk responses in the Bryan-College Station area of Texas, although I introduce available comparative data from other sources in Texas where relevant. I elicited oral materials here for the following reasons. One of Mark Kilroy's companions and his boyhood friend, Bill Huddleston, was a student at Texas A&M University in College Station; his continued attendance at the university served as a catalyst for much oral material. Even disregarding Huddleston's presence, the folk responses to the case often focused on common features of college life (spring break, roadtrips, etc.), and A&M provided an appropriate crucible for the development of such narratives. Also, A&M is a conservative Texas university whose students are primarily middle-class Anglo-Americans and, as will be seen, certain themes developed in the folk responses to the case were conservative reactions to regional problems.

FOLK RESPONSES

Folk responses draw on a repertoire of traditional tales and motifs. The folk responses to the abduction and murder of Mark Kilroy used these established traditions to highlight three areas of concern: the groups that are threatened (the young), the nature of these threats (abduction, murder, mutilation), and the categories of individuals who pose serious threats (the insane, the exploiter, the cultural "other"). Many folk narratives found in adolescent and young adult folk groups such as college students combine more than one of these themes. Such narratives most often take the form of legends—stories that are regarded by the groups that create, perpetuate, and debate them as authentic reports of events. As a result, folk interest in the Matamoros case became even more intense because of its similarity to traditional narratives.

Within days of the discovery of Kilroy's body and those of the other victims at Santa Elena Ranch, but before newspaper reports, television talk shows, and other popular media had saturated the public consciousness with details regarding the murders, oral narrative and rumor began to address the matter. The following narrative was collected on April 17, 1989. It and variants of the following text represent the important features of the initial folk response to the events.[1] The narrative was first performed by a 22-year-old female college student for her female roommate, who then reported the performance to me.

> I heard that some of the people who went down there [South Padre Island for Spring Break 1989] with them [Mark Kilroy and his companions] said that some of the people who went down to Padre left the group and went down to south, South Padre. The rest of them told them they better stick together, better not split up, but they said no they'd be okay.
> Well, anyway, they just disappeared. Went down and never came back. And that was later, that was the people they found down there in those graves, Mark Kilroy and all the others. There were 13 people who went and 13 graves in all.

Despite the lack of elaborate narrative development, this account contains a variety of the familiar themes that emerge during adolescence and persist, at least in the passive repertoires, of most contemporary middle-class Anglo-Americans (Brunvard 1981). Within this repertoire of cautionary tales—and inherent in the account above—is a warning regarding the potential danger of the mobility and isolation presented by the increased independence that comes with adulthood. If such independence is managed responsibly, all well and good. If it is mismanaged, folk tradition offers a variety of gruesome fates and brushes with potential death. Narratives about couples parked on local "lovers' lanes" and their encounters with sociopaths of various sorts (escaped convicts, lunatics, inbred monsters, and half-human/half-animal phantasms) abound in the oral traditions of the contemporary United States. The fates couples suffer range from fright (at an accidental narrow escape from the murderous "Hookman" who leaves his trademark hook hand hanging from the car door of the parking couple) to being killed and mutilated (left to hang mangled from a tree limb above the car in which one's date cowers on the floor). The mutilation theme (or at least the potential for mutilation) posed by the various Hookman/ax murderer antagonists of oral tradition was shockingly realized in the Kilroy case.

In the Matamoros folk legend, the victims venture off to seek the licentious pleasures of spring break, and then compound the risk by detaching themselves from the main body of celebrants. Leaving the protection of both the more formal and stable units of the family or the college campus, and even the informal unit of the peer group, puts the victims at the mercy of unknown, malevolent forces comparable to the fiends of adolescent legend. The phrase "south, South Padre" (i.e., a portion of South Padre Island that acts as terra incognita) is significant. One of the virtues of Padre Island for students is this vacation spot's proximity to Mexico, which has the reputation of being a supermarket of vice. *South*, South Padre is that portion of South Padre Island closest to Mexico; as a result it is that portion of familiar territory closest to the forbidden. Moreover, there is really no "*south*, South Padre." There are only those areas designated officially as Padre Island and South Padre Island. Therefore, the south, South Padre of this oral narrative is a fantasy world, a label for a marginal area where systems clash and the predictable goes out the window. Thus, we have a hint of the theme that becomes important in local media treatments of the Matamoros murders— racism and xenophobia. The foreign, and the foreigner, present a menace.

Another motif of cautionary legends that the Kilroy case echoes, and that is developed in the narrative cited above, is the nature of the threats posed to victims—who are invariably young, either adolescents or children. Many similar narratives focus on abduction and/or mutilation—the realization of the threat of figures such as "Hookman." Several legends and rumors describe a child's being abducted from a public place (department store restroom, theater, shopping mall), disguised and spirited away. In many of these legends, the child is rescued at a crucial moment. In cases of adolescent protagonists, the victim is invariably a female who has been drugged and is to be sold into white slavery.

Mutilation narratives take a more tragic turn. In these cases, the victim is male and young (often a preschooler). He is mutilated (most often by castration) in a public restroom by members of a particular racial group. Brunvand mentions examples of castration being blamed on homosexuals and "hippies," but the plot has also been utilized historically as both antisemitic and antichristian propaganda (Brunvand 1984: 78–92; Ellis 1983). The similarity to the Kilroy case is obvious. The mutilation of Kilroy's body included castration, and these acts were perpetrated by Hispanics. Although neither Kilroy's castration nor the Hispanic perpetrators were mentioned in oral narratives, facts so extensively reported by the media could hardly have escaped notice by the college students among whom cautionary narratives circulated.

At least one other significant fact, known at the time of the performance of this narrative, was not mentioned. Although probably noticed at some level, the fact that the other victims were Hispanic (sacrificial victims or threats to the Hernandez' drug trade) and only one of the recovered bodies was that of a college student on spring break was "edited out" to enhance the narrative's impact.

This legend may be considered a direct reaction to the Matamoros murders in that it is a folk account of a selected episode of the crime. Other oral responses may be characterized as indirect reactions; rather than focusing on the Kilroy case, they embody sentiments and themes in common with the case. In many cases, they allude to the Matamoros murders, and they surfaced immediately after discovery of the bodies at Santa Elena Ranch. The following rumor represents these reactions; it circulated among elementary school children and their teachers in College Station for approximately 3 weeks after the discovery of Mark Kilroy's body.

On April 21, 1989, less than 2 weeks after the discovery of the Matamoros victims, students at Southwood Valley Elementary School brought home the following memo.

> Dear Parents:
> It has been reported to us that some students have been approached by an individual trying to get them into a car. This is the description we have:
>> A big black car
>> Dark windows
>> License plate covered with either masking
>>> tape or black electrical tape
>> Wears a mask
> Please caution your children to be alert.

There were no subsequent reports of this individual, and no arrests were made. Children at the school, however, began circulating rumors of abductions. In all of the reports I collected the victim was male and mutilation was involved.[2] Each version featured decapitation; in some cases, limbs were cut off. One first grader reported that the victim's head was cut off and thrown in a ditch behind the house where he was taken. I asked how he had learned that detail, since the alleged murderers had not been apprehended and there were no witnesses. No explanation was offered, but the boy and his audience of friends remained steadfast in their beliefs.

Closer to the scene of the Kilroy murder, many students in the Brownsville-Matamoros area stayed home from school on April 19, 1989, after rumors spread that the still fugitive Constanzo, Sara Aldrete, and other "cult leaders" had threatened to kidnap children for sacrifice if their fellow cult members were not released from police custody. The rumors persisted even after police announced that the threatening phone calls were a hoax.

Simultaneously, over five hundred miles away in the East Texas community of Hemphill, hundreds of students refused to attend class on April 21, after rumors of teachers involved in cult activity and the planned kidnapping of a student as a sacrifice began to circulate. Hemphill School Superintendent Douglas Ray Butler stated that "talk of cult activity in Hemphill escalated with the recent slayings of 15 men near Matamoros, Mexico" (*Bryan/College Station Eagle* 1989c). This incident was not unique.

One year later, in a curious twist on legend scholars Linda Dégh and Andrew Vázsonyi's concept of ostension, "the physical enactment of actions [described in narrative]" (Ellis 1989:202; Dégh and Vázsonyi 1983; Grider 1984), four spring-break celebrants from Oklahoma perpetrated a 4-day hoax by alleging they had been kidnapped by young Mexican nationals in Matamoros. According to one of the accusers, Marland Crabtree, "we thought they were going to kill us because last year those people got killed during spring break" (*Texas A&M University Battalion* 1990:1). Most precisely, the actions of the Oklahoma quartet constitute an instance of what Dégh and Vázsonyi (1983) labeled "pseudo-ostension," a case of "imitating the outlines of a known narrative to perpetuate a hoax" (Ellis 1989:208). It appears likely that the College Station rumor that circulated among elementary school students was a similar example of pseudo-ostension.

The oral responses to the Matamoros murders incorporate the traditional motifs of abduction by religious or cultural others, mutilation, separation, and an ambivalence about the freedom attendant on adult status. The fact that the actual events surrounding the abduction and murder of Mark Kilroy in many ways correspond to the fictive events of folk narrative intensified interest in the case. Like the antagonists of the traditional legends which the Matamoros rumors and narratives resembled, the source of threats remained ambiguous.

MEDIA RESPONSES

Regional media reports, though erratic in their terminology, pointed the finger of accusation in a specific direction. The cult activity began being labeled as a mixture of Afro-Caribbean religions, particularly santería (a New World syncretism of Yoruba religious practices and Roman Catholicism) and *palo mayombe* (a similar New World syncretism with roots in "Congo," Bantu, traditions). Criminologist Ben Crouch (1990) suggests this labeling was a result of the media's turning to experts, genuine and self-ascribed, in an effort to make sense of Constanzo's acts. While this may be the case, these labels—like the mutilations that reverberated in folk themes—were exploited for particular rhetorical purposes. Specifically, the subtext of xenophobia apparent in the folk responses became overt in the media responses.

For example, *Rolling Stone* cited New York author Philip Carlo's claim that ritual apparatus found both at Santa Elena and in Sara Aldrete's room were accountrements of "underground Caribbean religion" and indicated a particular devotion to Oggun "patron god of criminals" (Garcia, 1989:49).[3] Gary Provost, author of *Across the Border: The True Story of the Satanic Cult*, quotes Teresita Pedraza, professor of anthropology and sociology at Florida International University, as saying, "Constanzo was a sociopath and he would have murdered people even if he was a Methodist," but cannot resist adding: "it is equally true that he was a practitioner of these Afro-Caribbean religions [i.e., santería and palo mayombe], and that the power of his own personality combined with the seductive magical religion that he preached was persuasive enough to turn several young people into murderers" (Provost 1989:120–121). Clearly Provost, like the vast majority of his media colleagues, seeks to explain the Constanzo rituals, not as primarily psychological aberrations, but as traditional practices common in exotic religion. This becomes especially compelling propaganda against non-Anglo-Americans, when coupled with the persistent folk themes noted in the previous section.

In the course of the press coverage of the Matamoros murders, a pattern emerged: a move from the most general label ("cult"), through more specific but nonracially focused labels ("satanism," "devil worship"), to race- and culture-specific tags ("voodoo," "santería"). This pattern is significant, especially with regard to Texas media. In fact, a contrast between national and regional media is easily noted. The most apparent theme in the national media was to categorize Constanzo's sadism, not as psychological abberation, but as ritual practices common in exotic religion. For example, *Time* made passing reference to palo mayombe as the "African offshoot of Santería," which formed the basis of the rituals of the "voodoo-practicing cult of drug smugglers" designed to "win satanic protection" (Woodbury 1989:30). *Time's* coverage not only labeled Constanzo's cult satanic, but used associated terms such as "witch's brew" and "demonic" when referring to the group's paraphernalia and practices. Similarly, the tabloid *Globe* carried a cover story, "How I Escaped Sacrifice by Satan [sic] Drug Cult," which characterized Constanzo's practices as "bizarre satanic ritual[s]," while omitting any mention of voodoo, santeràa, or any other Afro-Caribbean religion (Harrell 1989). *Rolling Stone* did focus on the relationship of Constanzo's rituals to palo mayombe and related New World syncretisms of African religions and Roman Catholicism, but also noted that Constanzo's psychopathic personality reformulated those practices—which normally involve animal and not human sacrifices—into an idiosyncratic and deviant form (Garcia 1989). This story was unusually careful.

Regional coverage was more culture specific and even racist in tone. The first reports picked up in South Texas newspapers tended to label the Matamoros ring as "satanic." The lead story in the April 12 *Bryan/College Station Eagle* (1989a:1A) carried the headline, "UT student's body found in grave: Satanic sacrifice by drug smugglers suspected in dozen deaths." The following day, the *Eagle* claimed that the Matamoros victims were "human sacrifices of a satanic cult" (*Eagle* 1989b:7A), and on April 14, the *Houston Chronicle* labeled Sara Aldrete a "cult witch" (Bragg and Dyer 1989:15A). Within a day or two, though, satanism began to share equal space with "voodoo" and, increasingly, "santeràa." The story, "Voodoo-cult members say Cuban directed slayings," which described Constanzo's rituals as "a sort of voodoo"· that had "overtones of . . . 'Santeràa,' " exemplifies the angle ultimately emphasized in the regional press (*Battalion* 1989:1A). Simultaneously, stories either directly connected to the Matamoros murders or sparked by them began to appear. These articles discussed santeràa, curandismo (Hispanic folk healing), and related topics. For example, one story quoted Rev. Ruperto Ayala Espinoza, a priest at Our Lady of Refuge in Matamoros, "Here there's a lot of belief in witchcraft, spells, superstition" (*Eagle* 1989d:11A). As news of the Constanzo case flagged, the void was filled by stories attesting to the pervasiveness of witchcraft, folk religious practices, and superstition among Hispanic peoples on both sides of the Mexico–United States border. Throughout the country, major newspapers devoted considerable space to Afro-Caribbean religions.

Such stories seem to suggest that adherents to non-European religions and their rites pose a growing influence on, and even an imminent threat to, white middle-class America because of both the proximity of Mexico and increasing immigration from that nation and the Caribbean. For example, an AP story reports a federal suit filed by santeràa priest Ernesto Pichardo against the city of Hialeah, accusing city officials of religious discrimination. Although the story's primary thrust is Pichardo's debunking of stereotypes surrounding santeràa, it also states that the "religion was linked to a sadistic drug-smuggling cult after human remains were found in Matamoros, Mexico, in April" (Wilson 1989:9A). By including such allusions, the press keeps popular perceptions of Afro-Caribbean religions alive.

This mistrust of syncretic New World religions and their practitioners saw its most extreme development in the handful of popular books published in the 6 to 9 months following the Matamoros murders. The titles of these works—*Hell Ranch: The Nightmare Tale of Voodoo, Drugs and Death in Matamoros*; *Across the Border: The True Story of the Satanic Cult Killings in Matamoros, Mexico*; *Cauldron of Blood: The Matamoros Cult Murders*—suggest their themes. Each book, within its own particular focus, implies that Latin America poses a clear and present threat to the Anglo-American population of the United States.

Clifford L. Linedecker, in *Hell Ranch*, makes the obligatory references to New World religions and even introduces his book with sketches of other cult crimes and serial murders discovered in the 1960s in Mexico. He goes on to note that Constanzo's rituals were a "bizarre mishmash of the worst aspects of the African and Caribbean pagan religions of *Santeràa*, Voodoo and *Palo Mayombe*, along with a strong dose of black magic and Mexican folk beliefs" (Linedecker 1989:72). Ultimately, however, he indicts general corruption and the Mexican drug trade as the culprits in the murder of Mark Kilroy.

Gary Provost's *Across the Border* also links Afro-Caribbean religions with drug smuggling. He further suggests that the rise of "Palo-related crime" can be traced to the Mariel boat lift from Cuba in 1980 (Provost 1989:201). The argument, then, becomes that Caribbean immigration inevitably creates the climate for cult-related crime such as the Matamoros murders, suggesting that there may be more Constanzos lurking in the shadows.

Cauldron of Blood by Jim Schutze, an investigative reporter for the *Dallas Times Herald*, develops the motif of the threat of Latin America and its religions most thoroughly. Schutze lumps together Constanzo's rituals, Haitian voodoo, Cuban santería and palo mayombe, Mexican curandàsmo, the teaching of Don Juan—the Yaqui shaman described by Carlos Casteneda, and satanism. The author refers to the cultures of Native America and Africa as the "original cultures" (Schutze 1989:9–10), and he maintains these cultures have perpetuated an esoteric religious tradition in Mexico and other Third World nations, which was transplanted to the United States by illegal immigrants seeking employment in the Rio Grande Valley, as well as by Caribbean immigrants such as Constanzo's mother. Thus, Schutze links the stress caused by the need for cultural accommodation to the economic decline of Mexico and its effects on the Southwestern United States. Further, this stressful situation is characterized as threatening by connecting immigrants to non-Western religious alternatives.

By focusing such social anxiety on a particular set of religions practiced by the allegedly threatening group, popular authors and the regional media gave form to the fears of the area, and provided a means for rationalizing these fears. The complexities of international politics and economics are baffling. The tangible, physical threats posed by cult sacrifice and its practitioners are not. In labeling the menace, even if the label is a misnomer, we give some hope of controlling it. Forcing the unexplainable, unthinkable actions of Constanzo and his followers into a preexisting framework— voodoo, santería, or what have you—not only categorizes the immediate event, but rationalizes fears of those other cultures and cultural practices which suffer from guilt by association.

CONCLUSIONS

Behavior seen as aberrant by the dominant system is interpreted within preexisting frameworks, rather than leading to a reorganization of the dominant group's worldview. Especially in cases of criminal deviance, there is an imperative to classify the deviant behavior, whether perpetrated by a lone individual or a group, in terms of a system (e.g., satanism), which is assumed to stand in organized opposition to the system (or systems) that provides the prevailing moral codes of the dominant group. Such deviant behaviors are rarely viewed as random and idiosyncratic. Thus, Adolfo Constanzo was portrayed as being an initiate of a secret society of bloodthirsty Afro-Caribbean mayomberos. Organizations are susceptible to being ferreted out, destroyed, and society can be purged of the menace they pose. Therefore, imagining an evil conspiracy actually lets the dominant group psychologically insulate itself from the horror of the individual psychotic's actions.

Further, the labels we impose on the actions of an Adolfo Constanzo are often dictated by larger social agendas. In the case of the folk and popular treatment of the Matamoros cult murders, a number of social anxieties were articulated in terms of a "satanic scare."

The economic distress of Mexico has had an immediate and profound effect on the border regions of the United States. As the peso has been devalued, the economies of both Mexico and the Southwest have declined while unemployment has soared. The middle and upper classes of the Mexican states that border Texas once provided a steady market for American goods and services. With the current economic slump, purchases have dwindled, while the flow (both legal and illegal) of Mexican nationals seeking employment to the north has increased. Both factors are perceived as threatening the economy of the United States.

Moreover, the amnesty program designed to grant citizenship to this immigrant population solidifies the position of these job-seekers while providing no remedy for reduced cash flow. Inevitably, the situation is perceived by American citizens as threatening the economic stability of the Southwestern United States.

In addition, increased immigration brings intensified pressure to accommodate cultural difference. The classic folk response has been to define these differences, not as viable alternatives to established cultural systems, but as inferior. For example, one folk response to mass immigration has been the emergence of legends about restaurants featuring the new arrivals' cuisine, which allegedly use unacceptable substances, particularly dog food and housepets, as covert ingredients (Brunvand 1984:121–126).

The folk and media treatments of the Matamoros murders combine a focus on overt cultural difference with the current social anxieties regarding cults, satanism, and other alternatives to traditional Judaeo-Christian religions. Clearly Constanzo drew on elements of Afro-Caribbean religion for his rituals. His use of Haitian voodoo, Cuban santeràa, and palo mayombe are adequately documented. Equally well documented, however, is the fact that his rituals, particularly the insistence on human sacrifice, deviates from the traditional practices of these religions. A primary influence on his rituals, in fact, was the film *The Believers*. Moreover, Constanzo drew from a wide range of other Afro-Caribbean, Native New World, and popular sources to create what can only be regarded as an idiosyncratic belief system whose rituals were sanctioned only by himself and the credibility of his followers.

Subsequent labeling of his practices by the media, however, led to a perception that the group was an Afro-Caribbean cult that perpetuated an esoteric tradition in the New World, a tradition to which Constanzo acquired access. No genuine evidence exists for this notion; rather the accusation is best explained as a popular response to the imperative to label incomprehensible behavior and to current anxieties (particularly those of the Southwestern United States), especially those economic, cultural, and political anxieties arising from increased immigration from Latin America.

Many of the practices of Constanzo's cult, moreover, touch common motifs in folk narrative, and these fit easily into the mold of folk tradition. For this reason, also, the Matamoros murders captured popular attention.

ACKNOWLEDGMENT

Sylvia Grider suggested valuable references and offered helpful comments on an earlier draft of this paper.

NOTES

1.   Unfortunately, I had access to induced, rather than natural, performances of this narrative. The narrative quoted in the text resulted from my expressed interest in the Matamoros case. After being given the version included above, I read it to my undergraduate folklore class. Approximately 30 percent of the class reported having heard versions of the narrative. These versions ranged from variants of the narrative collected to brief rumors that the 13 bodies had all been college students murdered on spring break.

2.   A total of six boys reported knowledge of this rumor: one kindergarten student, two in first grade, one in second grade, one in third grade, and one in fifth grade.

3.   The hypothesis that Constanzo was initiated into an esoteric religious tradition with roots in Africa and Native America is most fully developed in Schutze (1989).

REFERENCES

Brunvand, Jan Harold. 1981. *The Vanishing Hitchhiker*. New York: Norton.
_____. 1984. *The Choking Doberman*. New York: Norton.
Bryan/College Station Eagle. 1989a. "UT Students' Body Found in Grave: Satanic Sacrifice by Drug Smugglers Suspected in Dozen Deaths." (April 12):1A.

———. 1989b. "Friends Remember Industrious Student." (April 13):7A.

———. 1989c. "Students Absent from Class After Cult-ritual Talk." (April 23):7A.

———. 1989d. "Drug-cult Killings Cast Shadow of Fear, Superstition Over Rio Grande Valley." (April 30):11A.

Cartwright, Gary. 1989. "The Work of the Devil." *Texas Monthly* 17(June):78–82, 152–156, 163.

Crouch, Ben. 1990. Personal communication.

Dégh, Linda, and Vázsonyi, Andrew. 1983. "Does the Word 'Dog' Bite? Ostensive Action: A Means of Legend-Telling." *Journal of Folklore Research* 20:5–34.

Ellis, Bill. 1983. "De Legendis Urbis: Modern Legends in Ancient Rome." *Journal of American Folklore* 96:200–208.

———. 1989. "Death by Folklore: Ostension, Contemporary Legend, and Murder." *Western Folklore* 48:200–220.

Garcia, Guy. 1989. "The Believers." *Rolling Stone* 555(June 29):46–49, 63–64.

Grider, Sylvia. 1984. "The Razor Blades in the Apples Syndrome." Pp. 128–140 in *Perspectives on Contemporary Legend*, edited by Paul Smith. Sheffield: CECTAL.

Harrell, Ken. 1989. "How I Escaped Sacrifice by Satan Drug Cult." *Globe* 36 (May 2).

Houston Chronicle. 1989. "Honors Student Doubled as a 'Witch'." (April 14):15A.

Linedecker, Clifford L. 1989. *Hell Ranch: The Nightmare Tale of Voodoo, Drugs, and Death in Matamoros.* Austin, Texas: Diamond Books.

Provost, Gary. 1989. *Across the Border: The True Story of the Satanic Cult Killings in Matamoros, Mexico.* New York: Pocket Books.

Schutze, Jim. 1989. *Cauldron of Blood: The Matamoros Cult Killings.* New York: Avon.

Texas A&M University Battalion. 1989. "Voodoo-cult Members Say Cuban Directed Slayings." (April 13):1.

———. 1990. "Vacationers Kidnapped: Mexican Police Rescue Oklahoma Students." (March 19):1.

Wilson, Catherine. 1989. "Sect Comes Out of Hiding." *Houston Chronicle* (August 6):9A.

Woodbury, Richard. 1989. "Cult of the Red-Haired Devil." *Time* 133(April 24):30.

Devil Worship in Western Montana: A Case Study in Rumor Construction   15

Robert W. Balch and Margaret Gilliam

On April 14, 1974, a 39-year-old woman named Donna Pounds was found murdered in her basement near Missoula, Montana. She had been sexually assaulted, then bound, gagged, and forced to kneel before being shot five times in the head with a .22-caliber pistol. The murder weapon had been placed on the floor between her legs and small ropes were tied to the bedposts and bathroom fixtures throughout the house. The crime made front-page headlines, and Missoulians reacted with shock, outrage, and fear.

Within a few days a rumor linking the murder to a satanic cult started to spread. Supposedly Donna Pounds had been sacrificed by a "devil worshipper" being initiated into the "high priesthood of Satan." The initiation required three female victims: a Christian woman, a virgin, and a betrayer. Donna Pounds was the Christian. She worked in a Christian bookstore and her husband was a Baptist preacher. The rumor identified the virgin as Siobhan McGinnes, a 5-year-old girl who had been kidnapped and stabbed to death 2 months earlier. The third victim had yet to materialize.

The Pounds rumor was only the first of many bizarre tales about devil worshippers in Missoula. Most stories revolved around themes of human sacrifice, the ritual mutilation of animals, and witches who met on the outskirts of town to worship Satan. For the next 2 years rumors about devil worshippers appeared all over western Montana, and today many Montanans cite these stories as evidence that the current national concern about satanism is justified. Yet all the rumors proved to be false.

In this paper we will trace the history of Missoula's devil worship scare from its beginning in 1974 until the episode subsided in 1976. We will explain how the scare originated and why so many people found the stories about satanism believable in the absence of any objective evidence. Our data show that the episode was a case of mass hysteria that can be explained entirely by well-known principles of rumor construction.

Rumors are triggered by important or unusual events where factual information is absent, incomplete, or disputed. In their quest for explanations, people speculate, exchange ideas, and evaluate competing hypotheses in light of preexisting assumptions about reality. Successful rumors tend to be consistent with prevailing cultural themes. For example, rumors about police brutality are likely in neighborhoods where police are viewed with suspicion and hostility. To some observers a rumor might seem ridiculous, but others may not have the slightest doubt about its veracity. The more a rumor supports one's beliefs, the better the chance one will believe it. But even if a rumor is implausible at first, the more it is talked about and taken seriously in one's social network, the more believable it will become. Most rumors disappear quickly without lasting consequences, but sometimes they become part of local mythology where they provide fertile ground for similar rumors in the future. In short, rumor formation is a process of reality construction that can proceed quite readily even when objective support is absent. Missoula's Satan scare is a classic example of this process (Rosnow and Fine 1976; Shibutani 1966; Turner and Killian 1987).

STUDYING THE RUMORS

We started collecting data on the rumors in the fall of 1974. Seven months had elapsed since the Pounds murder, but the incident still was fresh in people's minds, and new rumors were appearing even then. Our study took two directions. We began by interviewing people who occupied key positions in local communication networks, such as reporters, law enforcement officers, ministers, teachers, counselors, and members of Missoula's occult community. They in turn referred us to people who were especially active in the rumor process. For comparative purposes we also interviewed residents of three towns in northern Idaho where a similar outbreak of satanic rumors had occurred in 1973.

For more objective data the junior author administered a 13-page questionnaire to 219 students in Missoula's two high schools and 266 sociology students at the University of Montana. Later she mailed a revised questionnaire to 300 Missoulians selected at random from the telephone book (Lynam 1978; Ms. Lynam now goes by the name Gilliam). Response rates ranged from almost 100 percent for the students to just 37 percent in the community sample, resulting in a total of 572 respondents. The questionnaires included open- and closed-ended items concerning knowledge of the murders, reactions to the crimes, confidence in the police, awareness of the rumor, religious affiliation and belief, and participation in the rumor process. Despite the problems inherent in retrospective studies, the findings from the three questionnaire samples not only agreed with each other, but they were consistent with our qualitative data. Taken together, the results provide an unusually clear picture of how the rumors developed and why they were believed.

HOW THE RUMOR STARTED

According to Allport and Postman (1947), an event must be important and ambiguous before rumors will develop. Both conditions existed in the wake of the Pounds murder. Although Missoula was a cosmopolitan city by Montana standards, its population was barely 38,000 and it was isolated from major urban centers. The nearest cities larger than Missoula were Great Falls, 160 miles to the east, and Spokane, Washington, 200 miles to the west. It had been almost 2 years since anyone had been murdered in Missoula. Then two alarming, unsolved killings occurred in less than 3 months.

The local paper printed 10 stories about the McGinnes murder and 11 about Donna Pounds. Most appeared on the front page. Both crimes were covered extensively on radio and television news programs, and a popular talk show host tried to whip up public outrage by urging vigilante action to find and punish the killers. Eighty percent of the questionnaire respondents knew about both murders, and 30 percent claimed to have been frightened by them. Twenty-four percent said they had taken precautions such as locking doors, buying weapons, and not going out alone at night. The police were swamped with calls asking for information, but only five percent of the respondents believed law enforcement officials were telling everything they knew. Over three-fourths claimed the police were withholding information, and the level of distrust was even higher in the high school samples.

Three rumors emerged almost immediately. One blamed a group of Moonies who recently had spent a week proselytizing in downtown Missoula. The Unification Church had been receiving bad publicity because of its deceptive recruitment techniques, and the Missoula contingent was highly visible since most members were orientals who spoke little or no English. Another rumor attributed the murders to the Sheriff's son who mysteriously committed suicide right after Donna Pounds was killed. Why he would have killed anyone was unclear, but some people speculated that he took his own life because he felt guilty about the murders. Both stories had limited circulation and quickly were displaced by the third rumor that blamed devil worshippers for the killings.

The satanist rumor apparently started at Missoula's Sentinel High School. Shortly before the Pounds murder a senior named Wayne Nance supposedly boasted to classmates that he was going to kill someone. Nance was a loner whose strange behavior and violent temper frightened other students. He was preoccupied with weapons and death, and often bragged about skinning cats alive. Classmates reported that Nance was fascinated with the occult, and he was enrolled in a controversial English class on occult literature. A day or two after the murder Nance reportedly appeared at school with a pentagram cut into one forearm. For a while Nance was the prime suspect in the Sheriff's investigation, but after passing a polygraph test, he was released because of insufficient evidence. Although we cannot say for sure, the satanist rumor appears to have been triggered by Nance's odd behavior.

DIMENSIONS OF THE RUMOR

The satanist rumor quickly spread through Missoula. Sixty percent of the questionnaire respondents said they had heard that Donna Pounds had been killed by devil worshippers, although there was great variation in what they remembered hearing. The cult-initiation story was followed by secondary rumors about the way Donna Pounds was killed. "Devil signs" supposedly had been cut into her body, and the killer was said to have painted a pentagram on a basement wall with her blood. Some claimed the ropes found in her house represented the ropes used to hang witches during the Salem witch trials. Others heard that a satanic book describing the ritual in which Mrs. Pounds was killed had been discovered in a trash can near her house. Parts of her body were rumored to have been found in Pattee Canyon on the south side of town.

By the time we started our field work, over 20 versions of the multiple-victim story had appeared. Most variations involved the third victim. The principal rumor said she would be a betrayer, but other versions identified her as a prostitute, an evil person, an elderly woman, a Catholic, and so on. Sometimes more than three victims were mentioned.

The most widely believed story about the third victim appeared a few weeks after the Pounds murder. A hair stylist narrowly escaped an attack by an unidentified man who had broken into her house. Some people speculated that the woman might have been the betrayer, while others identified her as the evil woman or prostitute described in other versions of the rumor because she was said to be a divorcee with a "questionable reputation." However, her assailant was never apprehended.

HOW THE RUMOR SPREAD

The rumor circulated mainly in networks of friends and acquaintances, but many people reported hearing about it through the mass media, particularly newspapers. In fact, the local paper never reported the rumor in detail, but one article mentioned that a "cult" may have been responsible for the murders, and it alluded to other cult slayings around the country. In what may have been a significant misprint, the article left the "r" out of "country," so it appeared to refer to cult murders elsewhere in "the county."

Of those who had heard that devil worshippers had murdered Donna Pounds, 31 percent claimed they believed the story, and only 8 percent were willing to say the rumor was false. The rest said they were not sure what to believe. The questionnaire data also revealed that people who believed the rumor were more likely to pass it on to someone else. Eighty-three percent of the believers told the story to another person compared to 52 percent of those who were undecided and only 33 percent those of who thought the story was untrue. The fact that a third of the skeptics still told others about the rumor is important. Even when people did not believe the rumor, many still passed it on to others because it made interesting conversation.

The idea that Wayne Nance was responsible for the rumor is supported by differences in awareness among subsamples in the questionnaire study. If the rumor originated at Sentinel High School and then spread to the rest of the community, we would expect more people to have heard it at Sentinel than anywhere else, followed by students at Hellgate, Missoula's other high school, and then by university students who presumably would have heard the story mainly from incoming freshmen. The lowest level of awareness should have been among adults with no connection to the university. These predictions were supported by questionnaire data. Seventy-seven percent of Sentinel students knew about the rumor, compared to 63 percent of the Hellgate sample, 56 percent of the university students, and 53 percent of the noncollege adults.

BUT WHY SATANISM?

It is one thing to account for the emergence of a rumor, but quite another to explain its content. It is easy to see why there should have been a burst of rumor activity after the murders, but what made the satanist theory more appealing than other rumors?

Compared to other explanations offered for the Pounds murder, the satanist rumor had the advantages of completeness and parsimony. It not only provided a coherent explanation for the bizarre circumstances of Mrs. Pounds' death, but it explained the murder of Siobhan McGinnes and later the assault on the hair stylist. It is significant that law enforcement officials and newspaper reporters did not hear rumors about satanism until after Donna Pounds was killed, but as soon as the satanist theory appeared, it was applied retroactively to explain the McGinnes murder. For 2 months the girl's death had been seen merely as a kidnap–murder case, however shocking, but suddenly it was being portrayed as the first phase in a bloody initiation rite.

Even though the satanist theory explained the facts and hearsay about the murders, it probably would not have caught on if the local culture had been less conducive. Three aspects of Missoula's cultural environment appear to have contributed to the plausibility of the satanist rumor.

The first was interest in the occult, which had been growing rapidly since 1970. At the university bookstore, astrology, eastern religions, and paranormal phenomena had replaced ecology and Vietnam as the most popular topics in the trade book section. University courses on the occult and altered states of consciousness had been attracting hundreds of students, and less conventional subjects such as astrology and the tarot were being taught in popular, noncredit evening classes.

Interest in the occult was especially widespread among high school students. One indication was the occult literature course at Sentinel High School. Seventy-eight percent of the high school sample claimed they had used a Ouija Board, and almost 20 percent reported that they had used tarot cards at least once. Two-thirds said astrology had some truth to it, and 38 percent believed it was possible to cast magic spells. Thirty percent thought *The Exorcist* (1971) was a true story.

We found that people who were open to occult ideas were more receptive to the rumor. For example, 45 percent of those who thought *The Exorcist* was true believed the rumor compared to 28 percent of those who thought the story was fictional. Seventy-one percent of those who frequently used tarot cards believed the rumor versus 30 percent of those who never used them, and 43 percent of those who had attended a seance (probably the slumber party variety) thought the rumor was true compared to 27 percent of those who had not. We found similar differences on questions about fortune telling, Ouija Boards, and the effectiveness of magic spells.

The second factor that may have made the satanist theory believable was a similar rumor about devil worshippers that swept northern Idaho just a few months before Donna Pounds was killed. In November, 1973, a young couple from Rathdrum, Idaho, a small town northeast of Spokane, mysteriously disappeared. It was a month before any clues came to light, and in the interim a rumor spread that they had been abducted and sacrificed by a satanic cult. The *Spokane Chronicle* first reported the rumor in January, 1974 and published stories about it through February. The *Spokesman Review*, which had a small circulation in Missoula, picked up the story late in February. Spokane television also reported the rumor. At the time, over 8000 Missoula households were connected to a TV cable system that carried Spokane stations.

One questionnaire item asked if respondents had heard anything about witchcraft and satanism from people living outside Missoula. Thirty-three percent said they had, and the Idaho rumor figured prominently in their replies to an open-ended question asking for specifics. Several people claimed a devil worshipping cult was located near Rathdrum, and some reports mentioned the Tridentine Latin Rite Church, a Catholic sect in

Spokane known locally for its reclusiveness and unusual customs. Although it is hard to assess the role played by the Idaho rumors, many Missoulians reported that the local rumor made sense because similar satanic crimes had been committed just 200 miles away.

The third and perhaps most important aspect of the local environment that contributed to the rumors was the growing concern about the occult in Missoula's Christian community. Fundamentalists were most likely to be upset. For them all forms of the occult, even astrology, represented the powers of darkness, and typically they lumped them all together as satanic practices. During our field work we found that fundamentalists, especially Pentecostals, were rich sources of new rumors and variations on old ones.

Books warning about the dangers of the occult were popular items in the Christian Book Center where Donna Pounds worked. Many volumes, especially the best-selling works of Hal Lindsey (1972, 1973), linked the nation's rising interest in the occult to the end-time prophesies of Revelation. These books argued that the growing prominence of the occult indicated that Satan was marshalling his forces for the inevitable apocalyptic confrontation between the powers of good and evil.

Many of Missoula's fundamentalist churches had been actively trying to counter the growing interest in the occult. A few Pentecostal ministers gave sermons about satanism that specifically linked the Pounds murder with occult activities, and several churches had sponsored films about Satan's tightening grip on the world. In one, "Satan on the Loose," scenes of devil worshippers dancing hypnotically in a demonic frenzy were followed by the stern warning that "satanic rituals like this one are being conducted in *your* community." Fundamentalists campaigned against discussion of psychic phenomena in high school classes, and they were especially upset by Sentinel's course on occult literature.

To examine the effects of fundamentalism, we correlated belief in the rumor with religious affiliation and several measures of religious belief. The data revealed that members of fundamentalist churches were more likely to believe the rumor than respondents who belonged to other denominations. For example, 42 percent of the fundamentalists said they believed the rumor compared to 23 percent of the Protestants from more liberal churches. The same pattern emerged when we divided our respondents according to their personal religious beliefs. Using a series of questions adapted in part from Glock and Stark's (1966) orthodoxy scale, we asked respondents about their belief in God, Jesus, Satan, speaking in tongues, and the authenticity of Biblical miracles. Each question had several possible responses, only one of which reflected a fundamentalist interpretation of the Bible. In the question about Jesus, for example, the fundamentalist reply was "Jesus is the Divine Son of God and I have no doubts about it."

With one exception the results supported the hypothesis that fundamentalists would be more likely to believe the rumor. For example, 20 percent of those who believed Jesus is the son of God thought the rumor was true compared with 13 percent of those who questioned his divinity, and 22 percent of those who believed the miracles happened exactly as described in the Bible said the rumor was true compared with just 8 percent of those who accepted a less orthodox view. Only the item about belief in God failed to support our hypothesis. However, belief in God, even when held with deep conviction, may not distinguish fundamentalists from other Christians, so this lack of support is not surprising.

THE EROSION OF SKEPTICISM

During field work we discovered the power of the rumor process to strip away skepticism of even the most hardened unbelievers, namely ourselves. We started the study as complete skeptics, but the more we heard about the Pounds murder and "related" incidents, the more uncertain we became. Although we never found objective evidence to support the satanist theory, we had no obvious basis for rejecting it either. After being warned repeatedly by colleagues and informants that our investigation could be dangerous, our uncertainty turned to apprehension, and the senior author began keeping a loaded gun by his bed.

This experience, along with similar accounts from our informants, led us to hypothesize that belief in the rumor would be directly related to its currency in one's network of friends and acquaintances. As Shibutani explains:

> Mere reiteration may lead some of the doubtful to reconsider, for hearing the same report from several sources tends to weaken skepticism. Unless one has built up special resistance, knowledge that others are taking an account seriously makes it difficult to dismiss. (1966:140–141)

In the questionnaire study respondents who said they believed the rumor were asked why they thought it was true. The most commonly checked alternative (28 percent) was "Everyone was talking about it, so I thought there must have been some truth to the stories." More direct evidence for the hypothesis comes from a question asking respondents to estimate the extent to which their friends believed the rumor. We found that belief in the rumor increased from 12 percent of those who said none of their friends believed it to 53 percent of those who claimed nearly all their friends thought the story was true. A similar picture emerged when respondents estimated the number of people who told them that witchcraft or satanism was involved in the murders. Twenty-five percent of those who answered "one or two" believed the rumor compared to almost 60 percent of those who indicated twenty or more.

Although these figures may reflect a tendency to project one's beliefs and concerns onto one's friends, they are consistent with our field observations. For example, we enlisted a reporter from a small town in northwestern Montana to help us look into the Idaho rumors. When we called her a month later, she nervously refused to talk to us on the phone because she feared someone from "the cult" might be listening in. All she had discovered during her investigation was the same collection of rumors we had already heard, but she had been told so many stories about satanism by so many different people that she had become a believer.

THE TRANSFORMATION OF SOCIAL REALITY

Even as the original rumor was starting to fade, new rumors were emerging. None spread as far as the first, nor were the new stories believed by as many people, but satanism was fast becoming part of the local folklore, especially in the high schools. Most stories centered on Pattee Canyon where witches reportedly had been seen dancing naked, burning crosses, sacrificing animals, and drinking blood while chanting incantations to Satan. Some rumors described sacrificial altars in the canyon where devil worshippers met on Halloween and Walpurgis Night.

The most widespread story was an "urban legend" (Brunvand 1981) of unknown origin. It described a woman who encountered a group of robed figures while driving alone late at night. The figures formed a chain across the road by linking arms, and their faces were concealed by hoods. Terrified, the woman accelerated, hitting one of them before they could scatter into the woods. She later discovered blood on her bumper, but when sheriff's deputies investigated the scene, nothing remained to corroborate her story. The "human chain" story surfaced in many parts of western Montana and northern Idaho, and several informants gave us exact locations, all different, where the incident supposedly occurred.

Two processes contributed to formation of the new rumors. First, the original rumor provided a novel interpretive framework for making sense of anomalous events. For instance, a few months after the Pounds murder the police received an hysterical call from a woman who claimed her next door neighbor belonged to the cult that killed Donna Pounds. She knew he was a devil worshipper because he had been sacrificing dogs. However, an investigation revealed that the neighbor was a coyote hunter who had draped several skins over his back fence to dry. Except for the satanist rumor the incident might not have been cause for concern in the first place.

This incident did not precipitate a new rumor, but others did. Early in 1975 a college student mysteriously disappeared without withdrawing from classes, and a rumor spread that he had been sacrificed to Satan. A few weeks later a woman jumped to her death from a bridge, and a story emerged that she was trying to escape from the clutches of a satanic cult.

The most alarming rumor in 1975 was triggered by a front-page story in the *Missoulian* (Stromnes 1975) about two "bizarre deaths" in Pattee Canyon. Two high school students had been found dead in a parked car and their two companions were both unconscious. It had only been a month since the high school survey, so we hastily administered an open-ended follow-up questionnaire at the students' school to find out if a new rumor had appeared in the meantime. The results were predictable: students who knew about the deaths attributed them to Pattee Canyon's notorious devil worshippers.

In fact, none of the new rumors turned out to be true. The college student who disappeared had merely taken a spur-of-the-moment trip to California; the woman who committed suicide had been distraught about personal problems; and the two teenagers had died of exposure after overdosing on wood alcohol. Although there were two stone altars in Pattee Canyon, they were built by a forestry club at the university to initiate new members. Since the initiation ceremony involved robes and chanting, it easily could have been mistaken for a satanic rite.

The second process contributing to the new rumors was retrospective reinterpretation (Kitsuse 1962). The term refers to the reinterpretation of past events in light of one's current perspective. We found that Missoulians not only used the satanist theory to explain current events, but they applied it retroactively to account for puzzling events in the past. For example, a graduate student's wife told us about a group of people she saw dancing nude on a river bank east of town. At the time she thought it was a "bunch of hippies," but in retrospect she wondered if the dancers might have been devil worshippers. In fact, the place where she saw the dancers was a popular "skinny dipping" spot, and no evidence of satanic activity was ever found in the area.

An instructive parallel is the famous Seattle windshield pitting epidemic of 1954 (Medalia and Larsen 1958). In the midst of nationwide concern about nuclear testing, a rumor spread that radioactive fallout was causing pits in automobile windshields. The police received over 15,000 calls from people complaining about windshield damage, and the mayor called on the governor and president of the United States for help. In their study of the incident, Medalia and Larsen concluded that the pitting was caused by ordinary road damage. The pits had been there all along but people simply had not noticed them because they had been looking *through* their windshields instead of *at* them.

Like the Pounds rumor, which drew support from tales of satanism in Idaho, Missoula's new rumors were buttressed by stories from other parts of the country. The most prominent "evidence" came from cattle mutilations in the plains states. Beginning in the fall of 1973 law enforcement officials in

Kansas began receiving reports that cattle were being found dead with their lips, udders, and genitals cut off. Although other body parts were often mutilated as well, attention focused on the missing sex organs that usually were said to have been removed with "surgical precision." In some cases the blood appeared to have been drained from the carcasses. By 1974 similar reports were appearing in eastern Montana, and at least one incident was reported in Missoula county. Speculation about the perpetrators included UFOs, Bigfoot, and government scientists, but the most common story attributed the mutilations to Satan worshippers.

Investigators from the Animal Diagnostic Laboratory in Bozeman, Montana concluded that the mutilations were caused by predators such as coyotes (Cade 1977). Microscopic examination of the incisions debunked the hypothesis that knives or razors had been used. The researchers noted that as skin decomposes, irregular tears take on a smooth appearance. They also pointed out that blood gravitates to the lower side of a carcass and decomposes rapidly, giving the impression that the carcass has been drained.

However, the laboratory's investigation received almost no attention in the media. By 1975 stories about Montana's cattle mutilations were widespread in Missoula, and the theory that devil worshippers were responsible added credibility to the local rumors about satanism. "If it can happen there," one respondent asked, "why not here?"

It was not until 1976, 2 years after the Pounds murder, that rumors stopped appearing. We continued to hear about satanism, but except for the perennial human chain story, the reports became increasingly vague. Rather than rumors about specific incidents, we heard only nebulous claims that there were devil worshippers in the area. Pattee Canyon retained its central position in the folklore, and even today some high school students refuse to go there at night, but the epidemic of rumors had passed.

Several factors appear to have led to the decline in rumor activity. Nothing on the order of the Pounds and McGinnes murders happened again, and the media eventually stopped covering the stories. Law enforcement officers consistently refused to give the satanist rumors any credibility, and, perhaps most important, no objective evidence of a satanic cult ever surfaced anywhere in western Montana or northern Idaho.

WAS THERE ANY TRUTH TO THE RUMOR?

What makes this case especially important for the study of satanism is that the crime that precipitated the rumors eventually was solved. In 1986 Wayne Nance, the original suspect in the Pounds murder, was killed while attacking a young Missoula couple in their home. A new investigation by the Sheriff's department conclusively linked Nance to other area murders, and the evidence now indicates that Nance also killed Donna Pounds. Although many fundamentalists claim the revelations about Nance have vindicated their belief in the rumor, the investigator failed to turn up any evidence that Nance was ever involved in a satanic cult. Nor have the police found any indication that such a cult has ever existed in the area. We may never know if Nance's fascination with the occult played a role in the Pounds murder, but all evidence indicates that he acted alone.

Every aspect of the original rumor has turned out to be false or highly dubious. Deputies who searched Donna Pounds' house after the murder did not find anything to link the killing to the occult. No satanic symbols had been cut into the body, no pentagram had been painted on the wall, no satanic book was found, and parts of Donna Pounds' body were never discovered in Pattee Canyon. Although the McGinnes murder is still unsolved, Nance's modus operandi strongly suggests that he was not the killer. As for the third victim, the hair stylist assaulted shortly after the Pounds murder, police believe she was attacked by a former boyfriend.

CONCLUSION

The entire episode of satanist rumors, stretching over 2 years, appears to have been a case of mass hysteria. The term refers to widespread alarm based on an unfounded belief. The Missoula incident is a classic example of mass hysteria, and it can be explained by standard principles of rumor formation.

The satanist rumor was a collective attempt to make sense of a problematic situation. It emerged in the wake of a gruesome, unsolved murder and spread rapidly, causing almost as much alarm as the murder itself. Some people believed the rumor because it dovetailed with their preconceptions about satanism and the occult, whereas others became convinced simply because they heard the story from so many people. The Pounds rumor was followed by even more bizarre tales about devil worshippers, as Missoulians used the satanist theory to explain a growing array of puzzling events. Under normal circumstances some of the events attributed to satanism probably would not have caused any concern, but in the shadow of the Pounds rumor these occurrences became troubling anomalies, and the satanist theory provided a plausible explanation.

Although the rumors eventually died out, belief in satanism did not. Instead it became incorporated into the local folklore, especially in the high schools where today students who never heard of Donna Pounds still tell stories about devil worshippers and animal sacrifices in Pattee Canyon. While writing this paper the senior author had a conversation with a high school boy who was only 2 years old when Donna Pounds was murdered. When asked what he had heard about satanism in Missoula, the boy described how the mother of one of his friends had narrowly escaped capture by a human chain. Although his account was exactly the same as the human chain stories we heard in 1974, the boy claimed the incident happened "just last year."

Of course, rumors about satanic crimes occasionally turn out to be true (Lyons 1988), but Missoula's Satan scare demonstrates the importance of approaching such rumors with cautious skepticism. The fact that a story is widely believed or told with deep conviction may be reason to open an investigation, but it is not a good basis for drawing conclusions. As Marcello Truzzi (quoted in Melton 1989) has said, when people make extraordinary claims, the burden of proof should be on them and not the skeptics who challenge their beliefs.

REFERENCES

Allport, Gordon W., and Postman, Leo. 1947. *The Psychology of Rumor*. New York: Henry Holt.

Blatty, William Peter. 1971. *The Exorcist*. New York: Harper & Row.

Brunvand, Jan Harold. 1981. *The Vanishing Hitchhiker: American Urban Legends and Their Meanings*. New York: W. W. Norton.

Cade, Leland. 1977. "Cattle Mutilations—Are They for Real?" *Montana Farmer-Stockman*. Great Falls, MT: (March 3):6–11.

Glock, Charles Y., and Stark, Rodney. 1966. *Christian Beliefs and Anti-Semitism*. New York: Harper & Row.

Kitsuse, John I. 1962. "Societal Reaction to Deviant Behavior." *Social Problems* 9:247–256.

Lindsey, Hal. 1972. *Satan Is Alive and Well on Planet Earth*. Grand Rapids, MI: Zondervan.

———. 1973. *There's a New World Coming*. Santa Ana, CA: Vision House.

Lynam, Margaret Gilliam. 1978. *Witchcraft in Missoula: A Case Study of the Rumor Process*. University of Montana: Unpublished Masters Thesis.

Lyons, Arthur. 1988. *Satan Wants You: The Cult of Devil Worship in America*. New York: Mysterious Press.

Medalia, Nahum Z., and Larsen, Otto N. 1958. "Diffusion and Belief in a Collective Delusion: The Seattle Windshield Pitting Epidemic." *American Sociological Review* 23:221–232.

Melton, J. Gordon. 1989. "Contemporary Satanic Practice." Presented at the Annual Meeting of the Society for the Scientific Study of Religion. Salt Lake City, Utah. October 27–29.

Rosnow, Ralph L., and Fine, Gary Alan. 1976. *Rumor and Gossip: The Social Psychology of Hearsay*. New York: Elsevier.

Shibutani, Tamotsu. 1966. *Improvised News: A Sociological Study of Rumor.* Indianapolis: Bobbs-Merrill.

Stromnes, John. 1975. "'Bizarre' Deaths Still Being Probed." *Missoulian.* Missoula, MT: (May 22):1.

Turner, Ralph H., and Killian, Lewis M. 1987. *Collective Behavior*, 3rd ed. Englewood Cliffs, NJ: Prentice-Hall.

Caldrons Bubble, Satan's Trouble, but Witches Are Okay: Media Constructions of Satanism and Witchcraft 16

Laurel Rowe and Gray Cavender

The 1960s witnessed a revival of interest in the occult. The counterculture of the 1960s ushered in "The Age of Aquarius," with new styles in dress, new attitudes, a commitment to sex, drugs, and rock-n-roll, and, for some, participation in the occult, e.g., astrology and the tarot cards (Jorgensen 1982). A decade or so later, that interest in the occult persisted and became a part of the "New Age" movement. The "New Age" movement generated its own styles: it filled the air with astral music, and its adherents sought power and well-being in pyramids and crystals.

The occult revival featured an array of practices: astrology, tarot cards, pyramids, crystals, shamanistic healing, voudou, channeling, I Ching, goddess worship, wicca or witchcraft, and even satanism, Although these practices had existed for many years, they became more visible during the occult revival. New religious movements such as Scientology and the Unification Church also appeared (van Driel and Richardson 1988). In general, neopaganism flourished.

Along the way, the occult revival generated a large body of written material from its adherents, mainstream media, and academics. Scholars have characterized the occult revival as a boom or explosion (see Truzzi 1972; Eliade 1976). Their explanations for the occult revival, and for why it has occurred at this time, vary, but frequently stress a common theme: the search for identity, meaning, and transcendent values in a society wherein religion and sciences have faltered (Ben-Yehuda, 1985). Like witch-hunts in earlier eras, the occult revival is seen as a bellwether of social change amid uncertainty; some scholars suggest that occult practices may even generate social change (Tiryakian 1973; Zaretsky and Leone 1974; Cavender 1988). In any case, scholars have concluded that many people of good standing participate in occult practices, and for understandable reasons. They even have found some good in satanism (Moody 1974).

Recently, however, the public has become alarmed with some aspects of the occult. The mass suicides in Jonestown and charges against some new religious movements such as the Unification Church have challenged the occult revival (van Driel and Richardson 1988). Condemnation has intensified with allegations linking occult groups with notorious crimes and other nightmarish practices. Most often, these satanic and other occult criminals are portrayed as people "who have gone off the deep end."

News media have been active in shaping this image. In past years, the media covered satanism in light-hearted Halloween interviews with the Church of Satan's Anton LeVey. Today, however, television news and newspapers cover satanic crime, ranging from sensational national stories of ritual murders to local coverage of vandalism in cemeteries. Because they present "hard news," the mainstream media lend legitimacy to allegations that satanic activity is on the rise, posing a threat to society.

However, stories about satanism, like all news stories, represent the media's social construction of reality through news frames (Tuchman 1978). News frames are selection principles whereby newsworkers decide which occurrences to cover, whom to interview, and which details to include or emphasize in a story; they help organize reality both for newsworkers and news consumers (Molotch and Lester 1974; Gitlin 1980). The media's constructed reality tends to reinforce existing stereotypes and dominant ideologies (Hall 1977; Hufker and Cavender 1990).

Our interest is in how media have portrayed the new occult reality. This paper describes a content analysis of newspaper coverage of two forms of occultism—witchcraft and satanism. We focus on four dimensions of coverage: (1) how the media depict the participants, (2) sources for the stories, (3) images of the two phenomena (e.g., rituals and symbols), and (4) connotations of deviance. On these four dimensions media coverage of witchcraft differs from the treatment of satanism.

The differences are interesting because in the distant past, both practices were considered evil; indeed, they were allied—witches were tools of Satan (Pfohl 1985). Today, however, media depict witchcraft as a harmless, albeit kooky, religion. Feminism typically frames coverage of witchcraft. Satanism, in contrast, is portrayed as a dangerous crime problem, and as a cause for concern. "Danger to" and the "threat of" youth are standard frames of coverage, consistent with media depictions of other youth subcultures (Hebdige 1979).

METHODOLOGY

Our analysis uses newspaper articles referring to satanism and witchcraft published from January 1, 1987 to June 30, 1988, which were indexed in Newsbank, Inc., a database of articles from newspapers in over 450 U.S. cities. The full texts of articles appear, listed under subject headings. We used Newsbank, Inc. because it permitted breadth of coverage, which is important because stories about the occult frequently appear in local rather than national newspapers (Shupe and Bromley 1980).

We selected index headings relevant to satanism and witchcraft. "Satanism" was a separate topic heading, with subheadings such as "criminal activity," "animal sacrifice," and "danger to youth." We considered all 46 articles under "Satanism" and its subheadings. "Witchcraft" and several other religions were indexed as subheadings under "Psychic Phenomena and the Occult." We considered all 13 articles indexed under "Witchcraft."

After examining the articles, we developed a codebook to analyze four elements: (1) participants, (2) sources, (3) images of the phenomena, (4) connotations of deviance. We also coded basic information about each article: date, newspaper, city and state of publication, and topic—satanism or witchcraft. The first author coded the articles. As a measure of reliability (see Krippendorff 1980), the second author coded a subset of them. Agreement was 100 percent.[1]

ANALYSIS

Participants

It makes a difference who we think participates in occult activities. The witch-hunts of centuries ago usually targeted powerless older women as suspects, making it more likely that the accusations would be accepted (Ben-Yehuda 1985). Today, the relative prestige of participants continues to affect public acceptance of the occult. The media's depiction of the participants of satanism and witchcraft differs markedly, affecting news consumers' identification with them.

Satanism.   Stories about satanism typically feature youth or amoral individuals as participants. Eighty-one percent of the articles depicted youth as participants in satanic activity. There were several youth themes. Many articles focused on young victims, even babies. Some addressed sexual victimization of children by satanic groups. "Young girls, from 11 to 14, began telling police about rituals in which men gave them alcohol and drugs, read from a satanic bible and forced them to participate in dozens of bizarre sexual acts" (Dallas *Morning News*—April 20, 1988). Other articles reported rumors that satanic cults kidnapped or even reared children for purposes of human sacrifice (Myrtle Beach, S.C. *Sun-Times*—March 13, 1987). Another variation on the "youth as victim" theme involved portraying teenagers as vulnerable to satanism. Some articles offered explanations for why teenagers turn to satanism: low self-esteem; isolation and alienation from family, friends, and religion; solace; and a sense of power over aspects of their immediate environment such as parents or school (Riverside, CA *Press-Enterprise*—April 12, 1987; Boulder *Daily Camera*—March 20, 1988; Rutland, VT *Daily Herald*—June 8, 1988).

Other articles focused on the consequences of children's participation in satanism. "Kids don't realize what they are getting into. And then they really get fully into it because it absorbs them" (*San Jose Mercury News*—March 4, 1987). Some pieces linked participation in satanism to delinquent activity. One reported that a burglary investigation led to a 16-year-old high school drop-out with an inverted cross carved into his back; he admitted participation in satanic rituals (*Cincinnati Enquirer*—March 14, 1987). Other articles alluded to more serious crimes, including murder (*Kansas City Times*— March 26, 1988).

Articles about adult satanists often emphasized their prestige. One noted that doctors and lawyers sometimes were among Satan's legions (Hamilton, OH *Journal-News*—October 31, 1987); another noted that several members of Mensa, the high IQ society, had been satanists (*San Jose Mercury News*— November 8, 1987). Interestingly, intelligent, professional participants not only did not legitimate satanism, they heightened its threat (Hicks 1990).

Articles frequently linked participation in satanism for youth and adults to mental illness. One described satanism as a personality disorder (Long Island *Newsday*—January 1, 1987). Others characterized satanists as sociopaths who have little conscience, are incapable of empathy, and are disloyal and untrustworthy (*Anchorage Daily News*—March 5, 1987; *Kansas City Times*—March 26, 1988). Another described the typical satanist as "an underachiever, suffering from low self-esteem, experiencing conflict in peer relationships and alienation from his family and his family's religion" (Denver *Rocky Mountain News*—March 16, 1987). Articles frequently appeared to be directed to parents, warning them that their alienated kids might become participants, inviting readers to identify with satanists' parents.

Witchcraft. Newspapers' characterization of today's witch differed significantly from traditional stereotypes. Articles noted that witchcraft still appeals primarily to women, but acknowledged that both men and women were adherents. Several different themes appeared in the stories.

The most prevalent theme was the connection to women. This theme often had a decidedly feminist cast. According to one article "Women want to be active in their spirituality, not simply the receivers of someone else's— usually a man's—expression of spirituality" (*Detroit Free Press*—October 29, 1987). Another estimated that half of the participants came to witchcraft through the feminist movement (*Boston Herald*—January 31, 1988). Sometimes, the women's theme focused on goddess worship. Goddess worship also was linked to nurturing. "Religion is attached to a loving mother. . . .

In fact . . . her initiation as a witch included a pledge to the goddess that went: I am your child, mother. I am always your child" (*Albuquerque Journal*—July 12, 1987). Articles often conveyed a celebration of being a woman.

Some witchcraft articles addressed power, a theme that also appeared in coverage of satanism. In satanism articles, alienated teenagers sought power over others. Newspapers offered a different view of power for witchcraft. One article quoted a witch who said "It's tremendously empowering for me as a woman to have female symbols and images, to feel different aspects of my potential as a woman" (Boulder *Daily Camera*—March 20, 1988). Another discussed power as a natural force that witches felt when they touched the earth (New York *Daily News*—July 5, 1987).

Newspapers also addressed secrecy, a common theme for both groups. While they portrayed satanism as a furtive practice that could not stand the light of day (*Boston Herald*—May 15, 1988), the articles depicted witchcraft's secrecy as a defensive posture against people who thought witches were dangerous (Cleveland *Plain Dealer*—March 22, 1987). One article noted that witches were not always secretive. Some were rather public about their beliefs and engaged in normal activities, like getting involved in school board elections (*Los Angeles Times*—October 31, 1987).

In sum, newspapers depicted witches as caring women, often feminists, who sought the fulfillment of their human potential; some even were depicted as hard-working, as leaders (Boulder *Daily Camera*—March 20, 1988). In contrast, articles presented satanists as alienated, disrespectful teenagers, unwilling victims, amoral adults, or crazy, dangerous people. Such differences in coverage must have affected the degree readers would identify with satanists and witches (see Greisman 1977).

Sources

The choice of sources—who gets interviewed—determines whose perspective reaches the news consumer. Newsworkers prefer sources whose apparent credibility legitimate a story's facticity (Tuchman 1978). Accordingly, they often turn to officials and experts as sources (Altheide 1976, 1985). Of course, such sources tend to legitimate established institutions and values, and media's link to them (Tuchman 1978). Sources in the satanism articles differed from those in the witchcraft articles.

Satanism. Newspapers relied on participants as sources in only 15 percent of articles on satanism. The vast majority of articles relied on experts as sources: police (78 percent of the articles), therapists (26 percent), religious specialists (15 percent), school authorities (11 percent), and parents (9 percent).

Police were the primary source of information about satanism, although the nature of their expertise varied from story to story. Predictably, police were a source in stories linking satanic activity to crime (*Cincinnati Enquirer*—March 14, 1987; *Boston Herald*—May 15, 1988). Sometimes, they advised parents about warning signs of satanic activity among children (Rutland, VT *Daily Herald*—June 8, 1988). At other times, they spoke as experts on religion and law. Thus, one police expert noted that devil worship was a religion and therefore protected by the Constitution (*Dallas Times Herald*—May 8, 1988). However, another officer observed that if satanism was a religion, it was "a sick one" (Pontiac MI *Oakland Press*—March 22, 1987).

Many articles relied on therapists as sources. Some reported psychologists' and psychiatrists' explanations for why people get involved in satanism (Riverside, CA *Press-Enterprise*—April 12, 1987; *Anchorage Daily News*—March 5, 1987; *Kansas City Times*—March 26, 1988). For instance, one professor of clinical psychiatry observed that "devil worship reflects total narcissism, a personality disorder" (Long Island *Newsday*—January 1, 1987). A few therapists expressed less concern; one psychologist said satanism had become an "all-purpose whipping boy" (Youngstown *The Vindicator*—June 5, 1988). However, most psychologists warned about either personality disorders that motivated participation, or psychological trauma that resulted from it (*Kansas City Times*—March 26, 1988).

Some articles cited religious or school authorities. Several quoted religious leaders who blamed satanism on failure of social institutions—family, government, and especially church (Boulder *Daily Camera*—March 20, 1988). Two cited academic experts on religion who said that satanism entailed a rejection of Christianity (*Cincinnati Enquirer*—March 14, 1987; Pontiac, MI *Oakland Press*—March 22, 1987). A few quoted school authorities who said satanism was under control at their schools (Jackson, MS *Clarion-Ledger*—April 4, 1988). One parent said she would have been worried had not the school handled the problem so well (Spartanburg, SC *Herald-Journal*—March 14, 1987). However, another piece quoted a high school teacher who said that a well-organized satanic group was on the look-out for vulnerable students on campus. "I've estimated that 30 to 40 percent of my class alone has been either victimized, threatened, beaten or in some way bothered or terrorized by this group" (*Fort Collins Coloradoan*—March 20, 1988). Danger to children was an important theme in many articles.

Witchcraft.   Witchcraft coverage also relied on sources, but in 92 percent of the articles those sources were witches. Articles offered information ranging from what it was like to be a witch, to a physical description of the witch who was interviewed (New York *Daily News*—July 5, 1987; *Washington Times/Insight*—June 8, 1987). They provided a tangible, accessible image of witches.

One article covered a police lecture in a community. The source, a detective, said he was investigating a specific witch to determine if she practiced black magic, which included child abuse and animal sacrifice (*Binghamton Press and Sunday Bulletin*—July 3, 1987). However, most articles let witches respond to such allegations, denying that they worshipped Satan or killed animals (Holyoke, MA *Transcript-Telegram*—October 31, 1987). One witch said, "We don't kill cute fuzzies" (Cleveland *Plain Dealer*—March 22, 1987). In other articles, witches described their activities, such as the details of goddess worship (*Albuquerque Journal*—July 12, 1987).

In sum, newspapers turned to outside experts as sources in their coverage of satanism. In contrast, witchcraft stories relied on insiders who denied negative allegations and stereotypes, and provided information about their beliefs. The newspapers' choice of sources offered an implicit statement on legitimacy of the two phenomena.

Images of the Phenomena

Articles we reviewed presented readily identifiable images of satanism and witchcraft. Newspapers constructed these images through their depiction of the phenomena, especially in terms of their rituals and symbols.

Satanism. Newspapers depicted satanic rituals as "ritualistic horror." Several different themes conveyed the horror. Many articles (33 percent) detailed sexual rituals involving both adults and children. Gruesome practices included sexual assaults, forced necrophilia, and animal and human sacrifice (*Kansas City Times*—March 26, 1988; *Fort Collins Coloradoan*—March 28, 1988). One article described mutilation of large farm animals (*Dallas Morning Star*—April 20, 1988). Animal sacrifice was mentioned in 54 percent of the articles.

Human sacrifice appeared in 76 percent of the articles. In one, a woman reported that she saw an unknown man stabbed to death (*Kansas City Times*—March 26, 1988). The situation in another article was more vague but no less ominous: police reported discovery of two female legs; they suspected satanic worship (*Cincinnati Post*—February 21, 1987). The human sacrifice references often mentioned such dismemberments.

Moreover, articles often included "blood drinking" as a ritualistic component of animal and human sacrifice (*Kansas City Times*—March 26, 1988; *Dallas Morning News*—April 20, 1988). Some stories described a combination of sexual practices, mutilations, animal and human sacrifice, "blood drinking," and "flesh eating" in describing satanic rituals. Heavy metal rock music and drug use were linked to satanic rituals among youth (*Fort Wayne Journal-Gazette*—May 8, 1988).

Newspapers portrayed ghoulish, chanting, black-robed individuals as participants in rituals (*Kansas City Times*—March 26, 1988). Black robes exemplified a symbolic dimension of satanism. Other satanic symbols included black candles, the number "666," inverted pentagrams, upside-down crosses, and the satanic bible (*Las Vegas Review Journal*—April 25, 1988). Sixty-five percent of the articles described such symbols. The rituals and symbols demonstrated the anti-Christian, blasphemous nature of satanism.

Experts often described the symbols as warning signs that parents could use. They included an obsession with heavy metal rock music among warning signs; some listed specific rock groups as culprits (*Charleston*, WV *Daily Mail*—May 5, 1988; Rutland, VT *Daily Herald*—June 8, 1988).

Witchcraft. Articles conveyed a different image for witchcraft. They treated its rituals as central tenets of a religion. Witches acknowledged that their rituals sometimes included spells, but characterized them as caring, not evil. An article quoted the Wiccan Rede: "And it harm none, do as thou wilt" (Cleveland *Plain Dealer*—March 22, 1987). Another, which described witchcraft as an "ages-old religion," noted that witches chant, "Maiden, Mother, Crone" as a ritualistic celebration of the life stages of womanhood. It also detailed myths that explained witchcraft's cosmology, its relationship to and ritualistic celebration of nature (*Boston Herald*—January 31, 1988).

Articles characterized witchcraft as ecology based and witches as nature-worshippers (*Hartford Courant*—October 31, 1987). Some described rituals that celebrated different aspects of nature, such as changing of seasons. "On a hilltop, surrounded by trees, they danced around a maypole, weaving ribbons in and out, singing in the afternoon sunshine on the first day of May" (*Washington Times/Insight*—June 8, 1987). One described a ceremony that involved the four basic elements—water, fire, earth, and air (*Hartford Courant*—March 21, 1988). They often discussed the connection between rituals and symbols.

Articles also mentioned other symbols such as crystals, herbs, stones, ribbons, and candles. Some referred to more exotic symbols traditionally associated with witches: caldrons, wands, and pentacles. However, witches who were interviewed denied that these things were used in negative rituals. They also discounted more stereotypic symbols such as black cats, warty noses, pointed black hats, and broomsticks (*Boston Herald*—January 31, 1986; Boulder *Daily Camera*—March 20, 1988), and displayed humor in their rejection of the stereotypes. One said, "she doesn't fly, not even on airplanes" (New York *Daily News*—July 5, 1987).

In sum, articles depicted satanic rituals as hideous, loathsome practices, and satanic symbols as anti-Christian, "symptoms" for identifying suspected participants. In contrast, newspapers depicted witchcraft's rituals as elements of a nature-oriented religion. Its symbols also were "naturalistic."

Newspapers allowed witches to deny many stereotypic allegations about witchcraft's rituals and symbols.

Connotations of Deviance

Both satanism and witchcraft are deviant belief structures that differ considerably from mainstream religions. However, when newspapers depicted this deviance, they offered different constructions of satanism and witchcraft.

Satanism. Articles portrayed satanism as an unacceptable deviant phenomenon. Often, several deviant themes appeared together, portraying satanism as undifferentiated deviance (Becker 1963).

Some articles specifically characterized satanism as seriously deviant (*Dallas Morning News*—April 20, 1988). They linked it to criminal behavior, ranging from vandalism to murder (*Nashville Banner*—May 5, 1988). According to one "It's only natural that many people suspected of heinous crimes would proclaim their allegiance to the Prince of Darkness, experts say" (Fort Wayne *Journal-Gazette*—May 9, 1988). Others linked satanism to mental illness (Long Island *Newsday*—January 1, 1987; *Kansas City Times*—March 26, 1988).

Coverage also mixed satanism with all sorts of cult and occult activity. They linked satanism to blood cults, the mass suicide of Jim Jones' followers, the Charles Manson murders, the Klu Klux Klan, and neo-Nazi groups (Fort Wayne *Journal-Gazette*—May 8, 1988; *Binghamton Press and Sunday Bulletin*—July 3, 1987). Some lumped satanism and other occult phenomena such as voudou (*Nashville Banner*—May 5, 1988) and even witchcraft (*Denver Post*—June 12, 1988).

Satanism also appeared to be a catch-all category for unacceptable behavior of youth. Indicators of satanic activity included such standard concerns as teenage rebelliousness and disrespect for authority, secrecy, alienation from parents and from school, drug usage, and sexual promiscuity (Pontiac, MI *Oakland Press*—March 22, 1987; Denver *Rocky Mountain News Herald*—March 16, 1987). According to one article "The practice of satanism, with beliefs and rituals that run contrary to more conventional religions, is a natural attraction for people rebelling against society" (Fort Wayne *Journal-Gazette*—May 8, 1988).

Newspapers portrayed heavy metal music as a catalyst for satanism. According to one, heavy metal was the common bond among kids who were into satanism (*Boston Herald*—May 5, 1988). In another, police experts offered a warning: "Parents should be on the lookout for their children who are 'obsessed' with heavy metal music. . . . The lyrics of so many heavy metal songs contain a potent subliminal message" (Rutland, VT *Daily*

Herald—June 8, 1988). Heavy metal, when combined with sex and drugs, symbolized a youth subculture at once threatened and a threat.

The coverage portrayed that threat as a cause for alarm, especially for parents. Despite some disclaimers that satanism had been blown out of proportion, coverage conveyed and perhaps generated hysteria. There often was a pattern to the coverage: discovery of suspected satanic activity such as mutilated animal remains, followed by police lectures to parent groups about the warning signs, speculation from police or other experts that satanic activity was widespread or on the rise, and community reaction (*Denver Post*—March 12, 1988; *Nashville Banner*—May 5, 1988; Rutland, VT *Daily Herald*—June 6, 1988). One article quoted a parent, "I think it's probably a lot more widespread than any of us really know" (*Fort Collins Coloradoan*—March 20, 1988). Others reported that rumors of satanic activity had terrified parents who kept their kids home from school (Myrtle Beach, SC *Sun-News*—March 13, 1987; Columbia, SC *State*—March 14, 1988; Jackson, MS *Clarion-Ledger*—April 1, 1988).

Witchcraft.   Newspapers also depicted witchcraft as a deviant phenomenon, but one more acceptable than satanism. Although they occasionally reported allegations that witches practiced black magic or worshipped Satan, 92 percent of the articles specifically disclaimed these practices (*Albuquerque Journal*—July 12, 1987).

Instead, articles portrayed witchcraft's rituals as deviant, but essentially harmless, perhaps even interesting. One article discussed beliefs and creeds that prohibited black magic and encouraged helping others, and described practices such as dancing "skyclad" (nude beneath the sky) (Holyoke, MA *Transcript-Telegram*—October 31, 1987). Some were tongue-in-cheek, but in a good humored vein; witches showed a sense of humor (New York *Daily News*—July 5, 1987).

Newspapers depicted witches as active individuals who control their lives, unlike passive, alienated victims of satanism. They characterized covens as closed-group environments, and frequently a witch's full legal name was not disclosed, yet there also was an "openness" to the coverage. One article said that "witches are slowly starting to come out of the broom closet" (*Detroit Free Press*—October 29, 1987). Others noted that the number of witches was increasing, but did not portray this as cause for alarm (*Washington Times/Insight*—June 8, 1987).

In sum, articles constructed an image of satanism as a vulgar, sick, dangerous phenomenon. Beyond the bounds of acceptable deviance; it constituted a threat. Witchcraft, in contrast, fared better. Newspapers depicted it or permitted its participants to depict themselves as healthy individuals who led acceptable, if somewhat unusual, lives.

CONCLUSION

Societal reaction to the occult has varied considerably over the years, from severe repression centuries ago during the witch-hunts, to relative acceptance during the recent New Age movement. Today, the occult—or at least satanism—seems in for another period of repression.

Using content analysis of newspaper coverage of satanism and witchcraft, we compared the media's treatment of both occult phenomena on four dimensions of coverage. We found that witchcraft no longer is depicted as a form of satanism.

Articles depicted satanism as attractive to alienated teenagers and people with personality disorders. Often, participants in satanism were unwilling victims. In contrast, articles portrayed witchcraft as appealing primarily to women who were strong, caring individuals. As a result, while readers might be able to identify with witches, they probably would identify with satanism's victims, such as parents whose kids had become involved.

In covering satanism, newspapers usually relied on experts who depicted it as a problematic activity, because of what they said, and because of who they were—e.g., police and mental health professionals. Witchcraft articles usually relied on witches as sources. They denied negative allegations and, simply by being interviewed, conveyed a sense of witchcraft as more legitimate.

The articles treated witchcraft's rituals as religious ceremonies; its symbols were earthy, natural. Accordingly, although witchcraft was deviant, it was tolerably so. Witches might seem a bit offbeat, but, for the most part, they "fit in."

In contrast, articles depicted satanism as a thoroughly deviant phenomenon: its rituals were vile and criminal, its symbols blasphemy. They portrayed satanic activity as dangerous—physically, emotionally, morally, and spiritually. Indeed, articles depicted satanism as a general cause for alarm. Satanism was widespread and satanic crimes were on the rise.

Newspapers framed coverage of witchcraft around women, especially feminism. However, their coverage of satanism resembled stereotypic coverage of threatening youth subcultures. Frequently, following a period of fascination with a subculture, media "discover" in it serious deviant and antisocial tendencies such as drug usage, sexual promiscuity, crime, and disrespect for authority (Hebdige 1979). The media often claim that the music of youth encourages these unacceptable activities, and leads to rejection of traditional social values (Gray 1989). Seen from the perspective of traditional social order, youth are "folk devils" who may generate a moral panic (Cohen 1972; Hebdige 1979).

The media may contribute to such a panic. As a disseminator of traditional social values, media help define what is acceptable deviance and what constitutes a threat to society. In this case, media employed very different frames in covering these two occult phenomena: one granted tentative approval to witchcraft and the other disapproved of satanism. For media and their sources, those socially accredited experts who are guardians of traditional values, satanism symbolized decline of the family and our loss of faith in government and in God. Satanism has become a metaphor for ills and anxieties that threaten traditional values at the end of the twentieth century.

ACKNOWLEDGMENTS

We appreciate helpful comments from Nancy Jurik, John Johnson, and David Altheide.

NOTE

1.   Frequently, a single article generated several different categories in our codebook. For example, if an article quoted a psychologist and a religious authority, we counted it under each source. As a result, percentages do not always total 100 percent.

REFERENCES

Altheide, David. 1976. *Creating Reality: How TV News Distorts Events*. Beverly Hills: Sage.
_____. 1985. *Media Power*. Beverly Hills: Sage.
Becker, Howard. 1963. *Outsiders: Studies in the Sociology of Deviance*. New York: Free Press.
Ben-Yehuda, Nachman. 1985. *Deviance and Moral Boundaries*. Chicago: University of Chicago Press.
Cavender, Gray. 1988. "A Note on Voudou as an Alternative Mechanism for Addressing Legal Problems." *Journal of Legal Pluralism* 27:1–17.
Cohen, Stanley. 1972. *Folk Devils and Moral Panics*. London: MacGibbon & Kee.
Eliade, Mircea. 1976. "The Occult and the Modern World." Pp. 47–68 in *Occultism, Witchcraft, and Cultural Fashions*, edited by Mircea Eliade. Chicago: University of Chicago Press.
Gitlin, Todd. 1980. *The Whole World Is Watching: Mass Media in the Making and Unmaking of the New Left*. Berkeley: University of California Press.
Gray, Herman. 1989. "Popular Music As a Social Problem: A Social History of Claims Against Popular Music." Pp. 143–158 in *Images of Issues: Typifying Contemporary Social Problems*, edited by Joel Best. New York: Aldine De Gruyter.

Greisman, H.C. 1977. "Social Meanings of Terrorism: Reification, Violence, and Social Control." *Contemporary Crises* 1:303–318.

Hall, Stuart. 1977. "Culture, the Media and the 'Ideological Effect.' " Pp. 315–348 in *Mass Communication and Society*, edited by James Curran, Michael Gurevitch, and Janet Woollacot. London: Arnold.

Hebdige, Dick. 1979. *Subculture: The Meaning of Style*. London: Methuen.

Hicks, Robert. 1990. "Police Pursuit of Satanic Crime: The Satanic Conspiracy and Urban Legends, Part II." *Skeptical Inquirer* 14:378–388.

Hufker, Brian, and Cavender, Gray. 1990. "From Freedom Flotilla to America's Burden: The Social Construction of the Mariel Immigrants." *Sociological Quarterly* 31:319–333.

Jorgensen, Danny. 1982. "The Esoteric Community." *Urban Life* 10:383–407.

Krippendorff, Klaus. 1980. *Content Analysis*. Beverly Hills: Sage.

Molotch, Harvey, and Lester, Marilyn. 1974. "News As Purposive Behavior: On the Strategic Use of Routine Events, Accidents, and Scandals." *American Sociological Review* 39:101–112.

Moody, E. 1974. "Magical Therapy: An Anthropological Investigation of Contemporary Satanism." Pp. 355–383 in *Religious Movements in Contemporary America*, edited by I. Zaretsky and M. Leone. Princeton: Princeton University Press.

Newsbank, Inc. 1986. *Social Relations*. New Canaan, CT.

Pfohl, Stephen. 1985. *Images of Deviance and Social Control*. New York: McGraw-Hill.

Shupe, A., and Bromley, D. 1980. *The New Vigilantes*. Beverly Hills: Sage.

Tiryakian, Edward. 1973. "Toward the Sociology of Esoteric Culture." *American Journal of Sociology* 78:401–412.

Truzzi, Marcello. 1972. "The Occult Revival As Popular Culture: Some Random Observations on the Old and Nouveau Witch." *Sociological Quarterly* 13:130–140.

Tuchman, Gaye. 1978. *Making News: A Study in the Social Construction of Reality*. New York: Free Press.

van Driel, Barend, and Richardson, James. 1988. "Print Media Coverage of New Religious Movements: A Longitudinal Study." *Journal of Communication* 38:37–61.

Zaretsky, I., and Leone, M. 1974. "The Common Foundations of Religious Diversity." Pp. xvii–xxxvi in *Religious Movements in Contemporary America*, edited by I. Zaretsky and M. Leone. Princeton: Princeton University Press.

THE SATANISTS ———————————————— VII

Legend-Trips and Satanism: Adolescents' Ostensive Traditions as "Cult" Activity

Bill Ellis

One of the most intriguing folk traditions active in the United States today is the adolescent legend-trip, or ritual visit to an allegedly haunted or marginal site. It normally involves the ostension, or literal acting out, of local supernatural legends. Frequently, the trip encourages teens to enter abandoned churches and leave graffiti or to vandalize tombstones to prove their courage.

Rumor-panics about alleged satanic cults frequently stem from the traces of legend-trip activity. Such trips are intended to be illegal and to shock adults; still, they are forms of entertainment, not religious rites, and the groups who commit them cannot be termed "cults." This chapter will examine a variety of legend-trips reported from rural areas in the Midwest and in northeastern Pennsylvania, areas hard-hit by satanic rumor-panics. We will see how from the 1960s on folklorists have documented as normal adolescent activities what satan-hunters present as evidence for "cult" activity. In particular, we will see how a knowledge of such folklore would help us understand the background of dramatic events like the 1984 "Toledo Dig."

THE DYNAMICS OF LEGEND-TRIPPING

Claims about satanic cults are supported by evidence such as "satanic" graffiti, desecration of churches and cemeteries, animal mutilations, stone circles in fields, decorated rooms in abandoned houses that apparently served as "altars" for occult rites, sightings of robed figures in graveyards or remote spots, and rumors about blood drinking or cannibalism (Lanning 1989; Ellis 1989; Victor 1990). Such finds may seem to be hard evidence for devil-worship practices, but these phenomena are more likely to be reflections of adolescents' legend-tripping.

279

Folkloristic Study of Legend-Trips

Documentation of the legend-trip as a U.S. folk tradition began with an article by folklorist Linda Dégh (1969), based on an undergraduate term paper describing activities at a haunted bridge near Avon, Indiana. Dégh supplemented this account with materials documenting similar visits in Indiana, Tennessee, South Carolina, and Michigan. She stressed that although supernatural experiences simply happen unexpectedly to a witness in traditional legends, in the legend-trip "the bridge-visitors condition themselves mentally for a vision they desire to have [and] perform a series of designated acts known to be effective to prompt the ghosts to appear." She suggested that belief or disbelief in supernatural phenomena was less important than the visit's role as an "initiation ritual" through which young males prove their adulthood (1969:77–81).

Other early surveys described legend-tripping at other Indiana sites (Mitchell 1969; Baker 1969, 1970, 1972; Gutowski 1970; Clements and Lightfoot 1972), and the dynamics of the participating adolescent groups in more detail (Thigpen 1971; Hall 1973). Kenneth A. Thigpen, in particular, recognized that teens' legend complexes reflected a three-part ritual consisting of (1) initiation into the story, (2) performing the acts that "cause the fulfillment of the legend," and (3) retrospective discussion of what participants believed happened, which then fed back into the core story into which newcomers were initiated (1971:204–205). Scattered studies of legend-tripping in other areas confirm this basic description (Harling 1971; Fisher 1975; Rudinger 1976; Samuelson 1979; Moss 1979; Alphonso 1981; Baker 1982; Ellis 1982–83; Johnson 1984; Glazer 1989; Orso 1989).

Cults and Folk Groups

The total number of teens participating in this tradition is unknown, but it must be large. Thigpen, surveying all grades of a rural high school, found 14 percent familiar with legend-tripping (1971:144); Johnson (1984), surveying college students at the University of Iowa, found that 28 percent had visited the "Black Angel," a local legend-trip site. Further, some legend-trippers become "experts" in the tradition, visiting the same or similar sites dozens, perhaps hundreds of times. Thigpen identified six older teens who had formed a coherent group around the concept of "The Watcher," a malign spirit invoked by secret covens of witches in the Indiana countryside. Johnson found that "five [students] had made multiple trips, ranging from several to one hundred" (1984:6). Although such small clusters of teens may specialize in "ghost-hunting," they hardly constitute a "cult."

The popular image of a "satanic cult" assumes that the adolescent mind is somehow helpless in the face of adult "recruiters."[1] Yet teens' first-hand descriptions of legend-trips make it clear that adults are not involved or welcome. "Trippers" who are 18 or older are largely shunned as outsiders. Likewise, since the philosophy of the legend-trip involves defiance of "adult" norms, it would be highly unlikely that such a visit would be organized and enforced by an older cult "recruiter." Some popular teens strongly interested in the occult may indeed gain control of some groups that engage in legend-tripping. Still, most visits are spontaneous and frequently involve skeptics. In any case, it would be hard to see anything in the normal dynamics of the tradition that would *require* belief in the supernatural phenomena invoked; in fact, as Thigpen notes, participation in legend-trips seems *not* to have any "profound or stable influence on one's belief system" (1971:207). It seems more accurate to say that such a cluster of adolescents is a *folk group*, a collection of individuals that share informal, face-to-face contacts and so generate and share specialized information and attitudes (Ben-Amos 1972; Toelken 1979). A cluster that specializes in visits to "haunted" spots may thus be termed an "occult-oriented folk group," since members often gather and share knowledge about other aspects of the supernatural and anomalous: UFOs, Bigfoot, ouija boards, and the like. We can infer that such folk groups—not "cults"—are responsible for most of what police "experts" claim is evidence of "satanism." Further, we may infer that as adults become hypersensitive to certain activities as "satanic," many such adolescent groups will adopt (or pretend to adopt) these acts out of protest.

Legend-Trips as Ostension

Traditional folklore analysis, based on performed texts, is ill-equipped to deal with legend-tripping. However, recent research has given us fresh ways of looking at the phenomenon. Dégh and Vázsonyi (1971) have argued that legends are *not* primarily "kinds of stories" that express "belief" but rather traditional ways of *testing* the credibility of certain beliefs. Thus they have redefined legend-telling as a "repeated group rite" (1978:269). To deal with legends as behavior, Dégh and Vázsonyi borrow from semiotics the term "ostension": an action that gains its primary meaning by being part of a recognized story. A person who uses a legend as a guideline for a criminal act, for instance, is performing that legend through an act of ostension; hence, "copycat" crimes based on urban legends are themselves types of legend performance.

Two common variations, they propose, are "quasi-ostension," or mistaken judgment, and "pseudo-ostension," or hoaxing (Dégh and Vázsonyi 1983:18–20). Legend-trips, then, can best be understood as a ritual activity driven by varying forms of ostension that interpenetrate and rely on each other for meaning:

1. Ostension: as part of the legend-trip's characteristic invocation of the supernatural, teens commit ritual acts that may suggest satanism.
2. Pseudo-ostension: adolescents seeking to frighten peers or parents briefly impersonate "satanists" or fabricate evidence of "cult" rituals.
3. Quasi-ostension: normal adolescent acts having nothing to do with occult practices are nevertheless seen by authorities as being part of "satanic" rites.

Some of this complex interplay between "cults" and legend-trip activities can be documented from archival and published sources.

FORMS OF OSTENSION IN LEGEND-TRIPPING

Quasi-Ostension: Mistaken Perception

Graffiti. Although few participants' descriptions of legend-trips allude to writing graffiti, nearly all locations that I have visited have been covered with inscriptions of all kinds. In only a few cases, moreover, do these graffiti allude to the legend that motivates the trip. More often, haunted bridges are covered with names of loved ones, high school names, and mottos, and favored rock bands or albums. When graffiti are mentioned in legend-trip descriptions, they generally involve high school rivalries or courtship customs: at a haunted house near Portsmouth, Ohio, for instance, there is a room with a huge heart painted on it. If you put your initials and those of your girlfriend's inside the heart, then add a number, you will marry and have that many children (OSUFA, Jones). Even at alleged "devil-worship" sites, occult graffiti is a tiny minority of inscriptions. Typical is a derelict hunting lodge just north of Hazleton that was identified as a "cult" meeting place by a student of mine, who showed me several snapshots of graffiti incorporating pentangles and "666." In fact, when I visited the site (which obviously had been used for teenage parties), I had difficulty finding those particular items among a welter of droodles, linked initials, and other notices (Figure 1).

It is important, therefore, not to give "satanic" inscriptions and symbols a disproportionate weight. A few places may sport deliberately "satanic" inscriptions, but less to invite occult practices than to heighten a site's imaginative danger. Seen from the teens' point of view, these graffiti seem neither particularly unusual nor threatening.

"Altars." In some cases, these may be the result of ostension proper: members of occult-oriented folk groups may set aside spots for some kind of home-grown "worship." More often, rock circles are simply indications of legend-trip sites' status as party spots. Peach Ridge, near Athens, Ohio, has

been connected with evil witchcraft cults at least since the 1940s (Ellis 1989:206–208), but this has not stopped teens and college students from congregating there in great numbers. Although some circles may be deliberately set up for improvised rites, most probably have a beer keg, not an altar, as their focus.

This suggests one explanation for the many rumors about mysterious groups of devil-worshippers on whom some groups of legend-trippers try to spy. Generally, the legend has it, if you can catch the "witches" or cult members at the right time, you will find them standing around a fire, dressed in black (or white) robes, chanting and preparing to sacrifice an animal. This is dangerous, as you may be spotted and chased by the "witches" or have a mysterious car accident on the way home. Ironically, in most cases, nothing more complex than a loud party is going on. In fact, one of the reasons for circulating rumors that certain popular party spots are "devil-worship" sites might well be to keep unwelcome freshmen and interfering adults away, so that participants can drink and party in peace.

Pseudo-Ostension: Hoaxing and Role-Playing

Animal Mutilations. A common allegation is that cults kill small animals as part of their ceremonies, frequently draining the blood and hanging the corpse from a tree. Some instances can be blamed on quasi-ostension: in fact the animals have been killed by cars or mutilated by predators. In New

Hampshire, apparent animal sacrifices were road kills waiting to be picked up by highway crews (Hicks 1989:A22–23). But it is also true that many legend-trips locate dead or mutilated animals specifically at the "haunted" sites. Teens in the Hazleton area claim to know several places where satanists leave dead animals. One informant told a student of mine, "We walked for about a quarter mile beyond the cemetery and John [a "satanist" friend] showed me a huge stone altar covered with blood and huge stone candle urns. I turned my flashlight upward to the trees and I saw 13 dead puppies hanging from them" (PSUHFA, Pipech).

Some of these may be adolescent boasts or creations of imagination, but some are acts of pseudo-ostension, in which animals are killed (perhaps intentionally) by teens and left in conspicuous places, although closer study shows that no occult ceremony was ever performed. During the spring of 1987, in the midst of persistent rumors about satanic cults in the Hazleton area, a group of teens stole a lamb from the Hazle Park Packing Company, slaughtered it, and left it inside a stone ring not far from "Markle's Grave," a statue that is said to grow devil's horns under a full moon. Although State Police investigated and identified the group responsible, the sensation caused by the "mutilation" was partially responsible for a rumor-panic that broke out later that spring in area high schools (Ellis 1990:41–42).

"Caretakers." A somewhat more complex situation of pseudo-ostension takes place when humans confront humans. One of the common elements in most legend-trips is the danger presented by some adult who chases and tries to punish intruders into the legend-trip site. In some cases, the "caretaker" is a supernatural being like "The Watcher," but in many traditions, he or she is a human, though perhaps with crazed, superhuman powers. At some sites, it may be a parent who, driven mad by the death of a child, attacks any teen who resembles his/her murderer. In others, the caretaker may simply be a local eccentric or farmer who tries to scare kids away. And, indeed, some locals have accepted their legendary status and set up sound systems to broadcast bloodcurdling screams or pop out of bushes to frighten carloads of teens. More often the teens themselves play at becoming "The Caretaker" temporarily. Many legend-trip accounts include descriptions of simple or elaborate hoaxes played on peers. Some are no more than reaching a hand out the back window and then into the front to tap a girl on the shoulder; others involve hiding underneath a haunted bridge to make weird noises when the next carload drives up. And some teens succeed with even more elaborate forms of impersonation. Some students have confessed to putting on a Halloween costume and prowling around "Weatherly Cemetery," a typical neglected graveyard outside of Hazleton, jumping out of bushes and chasing carloads of their peers.

This kind of pseudo-ostension seems integral to the legend-trip tradition, since it not only gives skeptics a chance to prove their adulthood by tricking more credulous peers, but it also, ironically, provides those who are hoaxed with a more complex, entertaining experience to discuss and share with others. In many teens' accounts, the possibility that one might have been tricked does not seem to matter much, so long as the trick was carried out well. The twin benefits of pseudo-ostension, then, are that it allows the hoaxer to embody the threat invoked by the legend, while also giving the witness a chance to act as if he or she were genuinely in the presence of a witch, angel of death, or ghoul. An uneventful visit to the haunted site is, for committed legend-trippers, the worst outcome.

Ostension: Vandalism and Supernatural Rites

Smashed Gravestones and Exhumed Corpses. One complex of legend-trip beliefs, derived from older English superstitions, attributes living qualities to stones. Many such beliefs are jocular, like college stories about statues that move when virgins graduate, since they refer to events that can never happen (Williamson and Bellamy 1983:122). But more serious beliefs are fully paralleled in adolescents' legend-trips, where tombstones often move, glow, become hot, and return mysteriously if stolen. Mary Jane's gravestone, near Mansfield, Ohio, is one of many that punishes vandals. One story relates how two youths tried to steal her tombstone but were killed in a car wreck on their way home. The next day Mary Jane's marker was back in place (OSUFA, Willett).

Often these rituals are accompanied by complex graveyard "ceremonies," said to bring sinister results: those who carry them out summon devils or evil ghosts or bring untimely deaths on themselves. Yet all the sites named in these traditions have in fact been heavily patronized and vandalized over a long period of time. Mary Jane's gravestone is conspicuous for being perhaps the most completely damaged marker in the churchyard. The legend, therefore, cannot be artificially distinguished from the trip that it motivates, which tests adolescents' bravery by creating an imaginative supernatural threat, then defying it. Still, there is no evidence that such rites actually *do* raise evil spirits or lead to sudden deaths. Graphic as the "friend-of-a-friend" stories are, first-hand stories of defying the curse tend to be no more dramatic than cars that won't start, near or minor fender-benders, and sudden gusts of wind. Although such acts are ostensive, directly acting out the events that the legend says will lead to supernatural dangers, on some level they are collective fantasies that the adolescents can and do distinguish from genuine religious rites.

One of the most dramatic "signs" of cults is grave robbing: in a number of cases, mausoleums have been broken into and burial vaults dug up. "Experts" suggest that satanists are after skulls or other bones to use as amulets or ritual objects. Although first-hand accounts of grave robbing are absent

from folklore archives, cases in which teens have been apprehended with
skulls or body parts have pointed more toward a legend-tripping context
than toward cult activities. In February, 1990, for instance, two youths were
arrested for entering a Lancaster, Pennsylvania, mausoleum to smash a
skeleton with a hammer. Although the cemetery association's president
blamed satanic cults, police discounted this theory. An accompanying
photograph shows typical adolescent graffiti on the opened tomb and others
nearby (AP release, 20 February, 1990).

"Dabbling" and Ostension.   The prevalence and consistency of legend-
trip stories and associated vandalism does not provide evidence for cults
directing such actions. Children's folklore has been found to be surprisingly
consistent in even small details across state and national boundaries, and it
can spread surprisingly quickly through letters, telephone calls, friendships
made during vacations, and the electronic media. So too adolescents'
folklore tends to be "silent" yet remarkably uniform, with names and motifs
cropping up in widely divergent places. Because legend-trips appeal to
universal adolescent anxieties, it is no surprise that we find similar actions
throughout the country.

An adult uninitiated into the tradition of ostension might well accept the
presence of mutilated dogs, black-robed figures, and smashed gravestones
as evidence that adolescents are "dabbling with satanism." Such teens, they
might think, are playing a dangerous game with rituals that might seem to
give them real-life powers. Perhaps because Satan gives them extra powers,
perhaps because they become confused and want to act out their fantasies,
they may be enticed into performing more elaborate rituals that involve
killing animals or humans.

The fallacy in such an argument is that there is no direct evidence that
adolescents participating in legend-trips confuse reality and imagination.
Gary A. Hall, examining a complex of beliefs and rituals attached to "The
Big Tunnel" in southeastern Indiana, observed that adolescents consider
legend-tripping primarily as recreation. Its effect, like that of a popular
horror movie, relies on a "willing suspension of disbelief" in supernatural
phenomena. Just as the movie may be enjoyed both by those who believe in
the horrors portrayed and also by those who are skeptical, so too participants in legend-trips may or may not believe that their rituals are producing
real effects. "Questions of actual belief or non-belief are largely irrelevant
during the drama and excitement of the trip," Hall concluded; rather, the
essence of legend-trips is "collectively shared emotions of apprehension
and fear" (1973:170–171).

The dynamics resemble those observed in professional "haunted houses"
set up by charities near Halloween, during which local teens and adults
impersonate cultural scare figures like Dracula. Some psychologists have
suggested that such attractions are dysfunctional, giving visitors the message

"that it is fun to pretend to kill people and chop them up" (quoted in Ellis 1989:201). But Sabina Magliocco (1985) observed that adolescents who go through such attractions adopt well-known "roles," females reacting with exaggerated fright and males with overdone macho displays. In short, both performer and audience collaborate in a dramatic event, heightening the aesthetic effect of the "scare." Similarly, no discussion of legend-trips has ever suggested that participants "embodied" the characters of legend plots in anything more sinister than hoaxes. Real-life murders committed by teenage "satanists" likewise have shown no direct connection to legend-trips, role-playing games, or haunted houses.

Allowing oneself to become "engrossed" in the reality of self-generated plots is quite different from actively believing in them (Fine 1983; Ellis 1981). Engrossment involves creating a fantasy self that is appropriate to a given play situation. It may draw on real-life roles and generate powerful emotions, but ultimately it is set off from common-sense definitions of reality. The ability to become engrossed in such situations is mastered around the age of 12 and remains a fascinating challenge throughout adolescence. The ostensive traditions reflected in legend-trips are best understood as part of this complex *recreational* activity, not as attempts to control entities or forces that affect common-sense reality. Adults who deny teens' ability to suspend disbelief and enjoy self-generated fantasy plots, inappropriately class adolescents' activities—and their minds—with those of children. Simultaneously, they miss the real value of teen folk culture.

LEGEND-TRIPPING AND THE TOLEDO DIG

When adults fail to understand adolescents' folk traditions, or try to interpret them in a simplistic fashion, the results can be bizarre and politically dangerous. One event that illustrates this confusion is the excavation of a wooded lot in Lucas County, Ohio, by deputy sheriffs seeking the graves of 60 human sacrifices. The so-called "Toledo Dig" was to some observers a total fiasco, turning up piles of rubbish and no confirmable evidence of cult activities. To others, it was a qualified success: although no bodies were located, "experts" said they found "a headless doll with nails driven through its feet and a pentagram attached to its arm," identified as part of a "death ritual," along with "a nine-foot wooden cross with ligatures attached, sacks of folded children's clothing, sixty male children's left shoes, assorted hatchets and knives, and an anatomy dissection book" (Lyons 1989:3).

The truth is rather less sensational. Sorting out the site's history and the "clues" followed by authorities, we can see that the deputies probably excavated a legend-trip site frequented by local teens for partying and imaginative scares. Nevertheless, Lucas County police were tied up for several days during the excavation, and two innocent families were publically harassed as "child killers" after their homes were described in local papers as "cult houses" (Cleveland, OH *Plain Dealer*, 7 July 1985). And as recently as March 1989, results from the dig were used uncritically as proof for human-sacrifice cults in the Ohio/Michigan area (Victor 1990:71).

Area Adolescents' Legends

The Toledo area is an especially rich one for legend-trippers. A short drive can take a teen south along U.S. 24 to Waterville to visit "Stick Lady," then a bit farther to harass "Shotgun Lady," then farther south into a rural area known to teens as "Zombieland." Here you can watch zombies with glowing red eyes run through fields carrying parts of dead bodies, or sitting comatose in barns with folded arms (OSUFA, Carroll). Farther south, in Napoleon, an abandoned house is said to be the haunt of the first white woman in the Northwest Territory. Trippers report that, as early as 1975, the walls of the building had been covered with inscriptions relating to Satan and witchcraft (OSUFA, Evans). A short drive east brings you to the Headless Motorcycle Man's several roads. To the west of Toledo one might visit Salsbury Graveyard, near Swanton. This site features a flattened gravestone that stands up straight at midnight and a caretaker who might fire a shotgun at you, not to mention witches who hold occult rituals nearby (OSUFA, Kosonovich).

North of Toledo, along the Michigan border, the "Candlemen" hold strange rituals, standing in a circle, holding candles. Adolescents believed that these strange people held a human sacrifice once a year, and if they realized that they were being observed, they would grab you, strip you naked, stab you, and leave you hanging from a nearby tree. This particular legend-trip tradition is similar to several others found elsewhere in Ohio (Ellis 1989). Well before police found rumors of teenage cults credible, then, legend-trips were a widespread and popular activity in the Toledo area.

Police Folklore and "Experts"

The Toledo area had been affected by persistent rumors about cults since a sensational case in which Leroy Freeman had fled from the area in 1982 with his granddaughter Charity. The child was later found unharmed in California (Costa Mesa, CA *Daily Pilot*, 24 October 1988), but in the meantime, police officials repeatedly aired their fears that Charity had been the victim of a cult sacrifice. These rumors became more intense in the spring of 1985, when Lucas County sheriff James A. Telb was told by an informant that a cult was planning to meet on April 30 near Holland, just west of Toledo. The informant led deputies to within 500 feet of an abandoned farmhouse, where they watched and tape-recorded about 100 "worshippers" chanting for about 2 hours. Later, in June, a nearby Methodist church was desecrated: satanic symbols were soaped on the stained glass windows and an altar, and a Bible was burned. At this point, Sheriff Telb requested assistance from Dale Griffis, Tom Wedge,[2] and other Ohio cult "experts," who claimed that animal mutilations were "routine" and that as many as five covens of 13 people each were operating in a typical rural Ohio county (Cleveland, OH *Plain Dealer*, 21 June 1985). Griffis, a police captain in nearby Tiffin, had begun to study the dangers of cults after his teenage son committed suicide, allegedly "in the name of Satan" (Elkhart, IN *Truth*, 15 April 1988). Since the early 1980s he had been accepted as an expert on satanism by many rural police officers, who referred to him for advice on interpreting cult-like evidence in their communities (Guinee 1987:6–10). His public pronouncements make it clear that he saw cults as a deadly danger for both adolescents and law officers. Fully a third of kids in satanic cults are willing to kill, he claimed (Dorfman 1985:47), and he illustrated this point with a "story that circulated among police agencies" about two officers who were killed by devil worshippers when they "crossed the boundaries of a five-pointed star used for a ritual." Griffis admitted that he could not document this incident. But the *Necronomicon*, one of the occult books he had collected to learn about cultists, warned, "If thou happenest upon such a Cult in the midst of their Rituals, do but hide well so that they do not see thee, else they will surely kill thee and make of thee a sacrifice to their Gods . . ." [Columbus, OH *Dispatch* (*Capitol Magazine*), 15 July 1984]. The Candlemen were sober reality for Griffis.

Griffis was trained in investigative hypnosis and also had special information linking northern Ohio to human sacrifices. He had brought "Jane," an Ohio cult "survivor," considerable media attention. "Jane" claimed, through Griffis, that 11 years previously she had been taken to "a mass meeting of about 100 practitioners at a huge open field in a remote area of northern Ohio." There she had watched in horror as the ritual's leader ordered an initiate to give him her baby, then cut the child's throat. Griffis admitted that "Jane's" story was impossible to confirm, but concluded, "There are indications throughout the United States that there have been babies used for sacrifice" [Columbus, OH *Dispatch* (*Capitol Magazine*), 15 July 1984]. Her testimony appeared to be corroborated by another anonymous "survivor" from Monroe County, Michigan, who told police that she had seen satanists bury a child near the site of the Toledo Dig (Michael Pratt, personal communication).

Griffis, driven by emotions created by his personal life and professional fears, gave warrant to Sheriff Telb's fears. Ironically, he too allowed traditional narratives to shape his perception of what he was helping uncover.

His involvement was another form of ostension; the difference was that Griffis, unlike most teenagers, fully believed that he was confronting evil, diabolical forces. As he told a Toledo reporter shortly after the dig, "I like going to an area where I can do my thing and leave and ride out on a white horse and never be seen again" (Dorfman 1985:47). He lived his urban legends.

The Site of the Dig: Artifacts and History

Fitting together local folklore and information from such experts, Sheriff Telb announced that a 200-member devil-worship cult was active in the Toledo area and that since 1969 they had sacrificed five persons a year, mostly children, carving them to death "in homage to Satan" in cult rituals that included sex and drug use. Little Charity Freeman, he announced, had probably been one of the children sacrificed (Cleveland, OH *Plain Dealer*, 21 June 1985). On June 20, 1985, he raided two "cult houses," seizing such cult paraphernalia as a *Raiders of the Lost Ark* poster, and began excavating a vacant lot rumored to be the site of the sacrifices. Meantime, deputies probed through two abandoned houses and several apparent garbage dumps in the area.

Perceptions of what they found varied: a "cross" with "ligatures" looked to one reporter rather more like "half of a clothes line post" (Akron, OH *Beacon Journal*, 21 June 1985). One reporter said a headless doll was found nailed to a board and holding a "pentagram"; another said it had simply been stapled to a base to make it stand alone and had been tangled up in pink yarn with other trash: an amusement-park medallion decorated with a five-pointed star, a rag, and a telephone receiver (Cleveland *Plain Dealer*, 21 June 1985; Dr. Michael Pratt, personal communication). A more telling sign were the "cryptic symbols" found around the site, including large numbers of papers with backward writing on them and "a symbol depicting horns, eyes and a goat's head painted in red on the interior of a ramshackle cabin" (Cleveland *Plain Dealer*, 22 June 1985).

Follow-up work determined that a Afro-American drifter named Lewis Williams had settled in the building a few years previously. A local deputy sheriff recalled him as an harmless eccentric who would go "off his rocker" occasionally. The site was isolated, yet easily reached from the main road, so it was often used by adolescents as a lover's lane, and Williams apparently enjoyed scaring them away. For a while he raised hogs (hundreds of animal bones were found by police nearby) and when one would die, he would bleach out the skull and set it on a stake beside the road. He would also take road-killed dogs and hang them alongside the house. As an additional touch, he would post the property with "Keep out" signs decorated with skulls and backward writing. When couples ignored these warnings, he would wait until cars were parked, then put on a large Santa Claus beard painted black and pop out of the woods. Other times, he might wave a small "voodoo bag" or homemade cross in his hand and threaten intruders with a curse. "Kids would leave," the township sheriff recalled: "Sometimes they'd even leave their cars there" (Cleveland *Plain Dealer*, 7 July 1985; James Meredith, personal communication).

Obviously the drifter's shack was a legend-trip site, with Williams and the "lovers" engaging in a mutual pseudo-ostensive relationship. The eccentric's actions were in line with those of other legendary figures who haunted isolated shacks in the area, and the skulls, hanging dogs, and cryptic signs clearly spawned a cycle of adolescent rumors about Williams as a local "lunatic" or "witch." After Williams moved on, the drifter's shack, like others in Northern Ohio, remained the focus of visits, and more cryptic inscriptions began to accumulate. Teenagers, doubtless, were willing to let police believe that their illegal beer blasts were ceremonies of "chanting" devil-worshippers.

Meanwhile, adults were engaged in their own rituals of ostension. "Expert" satan-hunters collated "survivor" tales, urban legends, and muddled legend-trip traditions to produce the temporarily convincing claim that real "Candlemen" were responsible for an unsolved "abduction" and a troublesome vandalism case. The outcome was an act of "therapeutic magic": a public act intended to focus and bring to closure a variety of diffuse and "unnamed" anxieties (Ellis 1990:31–32). By digging up a likely area on the date of the solar equinox (supposedly the date of the next human sacrifice), Lucas County Police forestalled further "satanic" acts by a show of force. They also convinced fellow believers that they were doing something concrete to fight cults and all they represented.

As often with such public acts, witnesses interpreted the "evidence" to suit their worldviews: out of several houses and piles of junk came a few items that for the faithful confirmed their beliefs in cults. For others, the dramatic nature of the dig, contrasted with the triviality of the finds, showed that fears were unnecessary. In either case, the dig cleared the air. By acting out a scenario drawn from police folklore, officials reduced anxieties fueled by their inability to resolve the Charity Freeman "abduction" and prevent teenage acts of vandalism and partying.

In truth, Sheriff Telb probably did uncover evidence of clandestine ceremonies. But the scenario he constructed had little to do with the silent adolescent rituals being enacted around his county. And, unlike teens' acts of ostention, the Toledo dig did have daylight consequences for the people falsely accused of "cult" involvement.

CONCLUSIONS: HOW SHOULD WE STUDY LEGEND-TRIPS?

Legend ostension may include genuinely violent acts by teens that incorporate "satanic" elements. But these are rare, and the media attention they receive is misleading. To understand adolescents' use of legends, we must study the many less sensational ostensive acts that represent the *norm* of the legend-trip tradition. I have called this tradition "silent"—but not because it is secretive. Materials used in this essay were freely volunteered by adolescents whenever academics were willing to ask them about their lore. We understand little about legend-trips simply because we rarely talk with teens or pay attention to their culture.

Additional study of adolescents' supernatural legends and legend-trips is badly needed. Many misconceptions could have been clarified more quickly, had legend-trip materials been widely available to researchers. We know that the legend-trip is popular from New Jersey westward to California, but we do not know its exact national distribution. We know little about occult-oriented folk groups except that they are responsible for much of the tradition's vitality. What is the peak age for participation? Do males' patterns of participation differ from females'? What religious backgrounds stand out among trippers? Psychological questions also need to be asked about other activities that might be linked with legend-tripping. Are frequent participants also interested in other common activities based on engrossment, such as storytelling, role-playing games, or school dramas? Bourget et al. (1988) suggest that individuals identified as "satanists" by parents and authorities are likely to be prone to substance abuse and express self-destructive or violent ideas. Is the same true for frequent legend-trippers?

We can arm ourselves against official misinformation about fictitious "cults" by studying the folk groups that *do* exist and educating others about the functions that legend-trips perform. Occult-oriented folk groups are not "cults." Ostension of supernatural legends is not the same as "dabbling" in "witchcraft." Folklorists and sociologists should cooperate to collect data that would combat these dangerous misperceptions.

Local and state police have invested considerable time and money to pay for "expert" information made up of garbled adolescent legends and police folklore. Religious figures such as Cardinal John O'Connor of New York City have given warrant to such claims, assuring parents that Satan is ready and waiting to hypnotize teens into conducting gruesome black masses in graveyards. While social sciences ignore legend-trips as a "trivial" subject, other authorities cooperate to perpetuate ignorance of our own folk culture.

Through the satanic scare, Americans are paying for their lack of cultural self-knowledge. Unless we cooperate to understand the rituals quietly played out in nearly every rural or suburban community in this country, we will continue to pay the price of our ignorance, through painful and unnecessary misperceptions.

ACKNOWLEDGMENTS

Research on which this paper is based was partially funded by a Research Development Grant from the Pennsylvania State University. Thanks are especially due to Patrick Mullen for allowing me access to the Ohio State Folklore Archives, and to Jeffrey S. Victor and Rita Swan for making newspaper releases about satanism available to me.

NOTES

1. See for example *Jay's Journal*, purportedly the journal of a 16-year-old who committed suicide, preserved by the boy's mother and "edited by" Beatrice Sparks; the Library of Congress catalogues it as "juvenile fiction." Introduced to Transcendental Meditation by an adult occult "missionary," "Jay" dabbles with PK, voodoo, angel dust, sadistic sex, Presbyterianism, kitten-strangling, blood-drinking, and cattle mutilation before falling completely under the occultists' control, who force him to bathe in blood and devote his soul to Satan. Over and over, "Jay" claims to have no control over what he does, commenting, "the occult movement is kind of a Pied Piper sort of thing: we want to go but we don't want to go . . . in the end we have no choice . . . we've just got to see what's in the mountain" (Sparks 1979:112; ellipses in original). Many religious leaders assume that rock and roll music exerts a similar "hypnotic" control over teens, especially through subliminal "satanic" messages recorded backwards on some pieces (McIver 1988).

2. Wedge has since become noted for his book *The Satan Hunter* (1987) and for his seminars designed to train police officers to recognize cult activities. For skeptical critiques of his work, see Carlson et al. (1989:135–138), Stevens (1989), and Pearson (1989).

REFERENCES

Alphonso, Patricia. 1981. " 'We Don't Wanna Hear the Scientific Reason': Teenage Lore of St. Bernard Parish." *Louisiana Folklore Miscellany* 1:31–32.

Baker, Ronald L. 1969. "The Face in the Wall." *Indiana Folklore* 2:29–46.

———. 1970. "Legends about Spook Light Hill." *Indiana Folklore* 3:163–189.

———. 1972. " 'Monsterville': A Traditional Place-Name and Its Legends." *Names* 20:186–192.

———. 1982. *Hoosier Folk Legends*. Bloomington: Indiana University Press.

Ben-Amos, Dan. 1972. "Toward a Definition of Folklore in Context." Pp. 3–15. In *Toward New Perspectives in Folklore*, edited by Amrico Paredes and Richard Bauman. Austin: University of Texas Press.

Bourget, Dominque, Gagnon, Andre, and Bradford, John M. W. 1988. Satanism in a Psychiatric Adolescent Population. *Canadian Journal of Psychiatry* 33:197–201.

Carlson, Shawn, Luce, Gerald, O'Sullivan, Gerry, Masch, April, and Frew, D. H. 1989. *Satanism in America: How the Devil Got Much More Than His Due*. El Cerrito, CA: Gaia Press.

Clements, William M., and Lightfoot, William E. 1972. "The Legend of Stepp Cemetery." *Indiana Folklore* 5:92–141.

Dégh, Linda. 1969. "The Haunted Bridges Near Avon and Danville and Their Role in Legend Formation." *Indiana Folklore* 1:77–81.

———. 1980. *Indiana Folklore:* Bloomington: Indiana University Press.

Dégh, Linda, and Vázsonyi, Andrew. 1971. "Legend and Belief." *Genre* 4:281–304. Also Pp. 93–123 in *Folklore Genres*, edited by Dan Ben-Amos. Austin: University of Texas Press, 1976.

———. 1978. "The Crack on the Red Goblet or Truth and Modern Legend." Pp. 253–272. in *Folklore in the Modern World*, edited by Richard M. Dorson. The Hague: Mouton Publishers.

———. 1983. "Does the Word 'Dog' Bite? Ostensive Action: A Means of Legend-Telling." *Journal of Folklore Research* 20:5–34.

Dorfman, Celia A. 1985. "Too Close for Comfort: A Look at Witchcraft in Lucas County." *Toledo Metropolitan* October:46–49.

Ellis, Bill. 1981. The Camp Mock-Ordeal: Theatre as Life." *Journal of American Folklore* 94:486–505.

———. 1982–83. "Legend-Tripping in Ohio: A Behavioral Survey." *Papers in Comparative Studies* 2:52–69.

———. 1989. "Death by Folklore: Ostension, Contemporary Legend, and Murder." *Western Folklore* 48:201–220.

———. 1990. "The Devil-Worshippers at the Prom: Rumor-Panic as Therapeutic Magic." *Western Folklore* 49:27–49.

Fine, Gary Alan. 1983. *Shared Fantasy: Role-Playing Games as Social Worlds.* Chicago: University of Chicago Press.

Fisher, Douglas. 1975. "The Four-Mile Desert: A Horror Story." *North Carolina Folklore Journal* 23:23–25.

Glazer, Mark. 1989. "Gravity Hill: Belief and Belief Legend." Pp. 165–177 in *The Questing Beast: Perspectives on Contemporary Legend IV*, edited by Gillian Bennett and Paul Smith. Sheffield: Sheffield Academic Press.

Guinee, William. 1987. "Satanism in Yellowwood Forest: The Interdependence of Antagonistic Worldviews." *Indiana Folklore and Oral History* 16:1–30.

Gutowski, John A. 1970. "Traditions of the Devil's Hollows: Relationship Between a Place Name and Its Legends." *Indiana Folklore* 3:190–213.

Hall, Gary. 1973. "The Big Tunnel: Legends and Legend-Telling." *Indiana Folklore* 6:139–173.

Harling, Kristie. 1971. "The Grunch: An Example of New Orleans Teen-Age Folklore." *Louisiana Folklore Miscellany* 3(2):15–20.

Hicks, Robert. 1989. "Satanic Cults: A Skeptical View of the Law Enforcement Approach." Pp. A1–A35 in *Satanism in America: How the Devil Got Much More Than His Due*, by Shawn Carlson et al. El Cerrito, CA: Gaia Press.

Johnson, Donald F. 1984. *Black Angel Data Notebook.* Unpublished research project, Department of Anthropology, University of Iowa, Iowa City, Iowa.

Lanning, Kenneth V. 1989. "Satanic, Occult, Ritualistic Crime: A Law Enforcement Perspective." Pp. B1–B12 in *Satanism in America: How the Devil Got Much More Than His Due*, by Shawn Carlson et al. El Cerrito, CA: Gaia Press.

Lyons, Arthur. 1989. *Satan Wants You: The Cult of Devil Worship in America.* New York: Mysterious Press.

Magliocco, Sabina. 1985. "The Bloomington Jaycees' Haunted House." *Indiana Folklore and Oral History* 14:19–28.

McIver, Tom. 1988. "Backward Masking, and Other Backward Thoughts about Music." *The Skeptical Inquirer* 13:50–63.

Mitchell, Carol A. 1969. "The White House." *Indiana Folklore* 2:97–109.

Moss, James C. 1979. "The Barrens of Southern Chester County and Their Role in Story Formation, Transmission and Maintenance." *Keystone Folklore* 23:1–27.

Orso, Ethelyn G. 1989. "The Mona Lisa of New Orleans' City Park: The Making of a Legend." Paper presented to the Annual Meeting of the American Folklore Society, Philadelphia, PA.

OSUFA. The Ohio State University Folklore Archives, Columbus, Ohio. Patrick Mullen, Archivist.

Pearson, Patricia. 1989. "In Search of the Satanists." *The Idler* 25:19–25.

PSUHFA. The Pennsylvania State University, Hazleton Campus Folklore Archives, Hazleton, Pennsylvania. Bill Ellis, Archivist.

Rudinger, Joel D. 1976. "Folk Ogres of the Firelands: Narrative Variations of a North Central Ohio Community." *Indiana Folklore* 9:52–62.

Samuelson, Sue. 1979. "The White Witch: An Analysis of an Adolescent Legend." *Indiana Folklore* 12:18–37.

Sparks, Beatrice. 1979. *Jay's Journal.* New York: Times Books.

Stevens, Phillips, Jr. 1989. "Satanism: Where Are the Folklorists?" *New York Folklore* 15:1–22.

Thigpen, Kenneth A., Jr. 1971. "Adolescent Legends in Brown County: A Survey." *Indiana Folklore* 4:141–215.

Toelken, Barre. 1979. *The Dynamics of Folklore.* Boston: Houghton Mifflin.

Victor, Jeffrey S. 1990. "Satanic Cult Rumors as Contemporary Legend." *Western Folklore* 49:51–81.

Williamson, Tom, and Bellamy, Liz. 1983. *Ley Lines in Question.* Kingswood, Tadworth, Surrey: World's Work.

Wedge, Tim. 1987. *The Satan Hunter.* Canton, OH: Daring Books.

Social Construction from Within: Satan's Process **18**

William Sims Bainbridge

The social construction of satanism is not an activity solely engaged in by hack journalists seeking lurid topics for stories, self-aggrandizing clergy seeking helpless victims for crusades, and confused members of the general public seeking simplistic explanations for contemporary evil. Satanists actually exist, and they construct the meaning of Satan for themselves. A coalition of forces in conventional society can come to believe in imaginary folk devils and even convince individuals to accept deviant roles scripted for them. But players in this satanist drama have considerable freedom to improvise in their roles (Thompson 1967; McIntosh 1972; Bainbridge 1983). Among the most creative actors to play the role of devil-worshipper were the few hundred Processeans, members of The Process—Church of the Final Judgement (Bainbridge 1978).[1]

I first met The Process on the streets of Boston and Cambridge in the fall of 1970. Popular consensus held that they were dangerous satanists, and their black cloaks and the red man-goat heads they wore on their chests gave no lie to this image. An antisatanic book claimed to know the truth about the group: "Savage and indiscriminate sex is forced on the entrants into the cult not as a means of religious communion but as a means of purging any residue of Grey Forces that might be latent in them" (Lyons 1970:133). Another accuser added: "The Process Church of the Final Judgement is an English occult society dedicated to observing and aiding the end of the world by stirring up murder, violence and chaos, and dedicated to the proposition that they, the Process, shall survive the gore as the chosen people" (Sanders 1971:81).

In the early spring of 1971, I began a 5-year ethnographic study of this fantastic and fascinating group (Bainbridge 1978). I soon learned that the Satan of The Process bore little resemblance to Satan as constructed by conventional society. There was no violence and no indiscriminate sex, but I found a remarkably aesthetic and intelligent alternative to conventional religion. For Processeans, Satan was no crude beast but an intellectual principle by which God could be unfolded into several parts, accomplishing the repaganization of religion and the remystification of the world.

SATAN'S PROCESS

The founders of The Process, Robert and Mary Ann de Grimston, met in London in the early 1960s. At first, there was nothing obviously religious about their aims or assumptions. Each sought a way of understanding the human personality and a technique for achieving greater personal satisfaction. Each had been excited by the theory of life goals proposed by Freud's renegade disciple, Alfred Adler, and each saw promise in the therapy processes devised by L. Ron Hubbard, founder of Scientology. Adler had based his "individual psychology" on the premise that each person was guided by a single hidden desire, and if compulsive distortions could be cleared away the person would achieve his particular life's goal (Adler 1927, 1929). Hubbard had amassed a huge collection of mental techniques, inventing some, ransacking the rest from therapies, cults, and science fiction stories (Wallis 1976; Stark and Bainbridge 1985; Bainbridge 1987).

Working as therapists in the London branch of Scientology, Robert and Mary Ann became partners in a quest for improved versions of Hubbard's treatment processes, and they soon broke with the Scientology organization to go into business for themselves. Calling their practice Compulsions Analysis, they recruited clients through Robert's friendship network and set about inventing a distinctive psychotherapy designed to raise normal individuals up to superior levels of functioning. Some of the work was very much like psychoanalysis, and they frequently employed the E-Meter lie detector device used in Scientology. Whatever the techniques did for individual psyches, they produced very powerful emotional bonds linking clients with the two therapists and, through group sessions, with each other.

Soon, they had leased an elegant building in the fashionable Mayfair district of London, where they held activities and a few clients could live communally. Newspapers began calling them "mind-benders of Mayfair," and a rough description of one of their therapy processes was publicized:

> The object was to discover the clients' "goals," the hidden desires that motivate them. Among constructive goals were: "to create," "to discover," "to organize;" among destructive ones: "to annoy," "to damage," "to cheat." The theory was that people must be stripped down mentally until they reached their bottom goal of all, after which they could rise to the top. Many clients found this immensely exhilarating. (Hart-Davis 1966)

My interviews with original clients drew a picture of fantastic excitement and hope, and the intense social rewards participants received were new experiences for many of them. Every day, they discovered new facets of their personalities, and the intensely positive emotions were taken as proof that the group was on the right track. Having placed all their hopes in therapy techniques which Hubbard had often called "processes," they came to think of their group as a grand process—The Process, pronounced with a long OH in the English fashion. The dreams encouraged by therapy grew without limit, and soon they began to take on a religious quality. Late in 1965, Robert told a reporter, "The Process started off purely as psychotherapy. But the more we worked with our clients, the more we realized we were closer to a religious approach. Nearly everyone kept coming up with their religious goals—with their own concept of God."

Nearly 30 clients became so involved that they lost interest in ordinary pursuits and underwent what I call a *social implosion*. Social bonds linking participants grew rapidly stronger, while those with nonparticipants reciprocally weakened, until their social relations collapsed into an isolated group of high solidarity. Now a world unto themselves, they began creating a novel culture (Bainbridge 1985), complete with a special vocabulary and set of emblems. Their mutually supported hopes knew no limits, and they came to believe they were the vanguard of a new civilization, or of a new age that would follow the destruction of the present world. Finding London a miasma of indifference and incomprehension, they resolved to escape to a tropical island paradise.

After an unsatisfactory sojourn in Nassau, they were led by images received in group meditations to a ruined coconut plantation on the northern shore of the Yucatan. Calling the place *Xtul* (pronounced *shtool*), they continued their social implosion in almost complete isolation, and the religious aspects grew. Some members began identifying with *Old Testament* figures or with Saints, and a few took new names to express these identifications. The great power of nature, represented by a hurricane they endured outdoors as well as by the food they freely plucked from land and ocean, was identified with Jehovah, a deity for whom Mary Ann felt a special affinity.

After some months, exhaustion of the excitement at Xtul and a legal challenge that carried away three of the younger members brought The Process back to Mayfair. Emboldened by their experiences, Processeans began evangelizing their new myths and exploiting the considerable interest the public showed in their weird performances. On a trip through the United States, they met with Anton LaVey and discussed satanism. I could never quite learn how important LaVey's influence was with The Process, but soon Satan had been placed alongside Jehovah in the pantheon, and a third deity, Lucifer, emerged as Robert's foil to Mary Ann's Jehovah. In 1969, a series of London newspaper articles called Processeans "Satan worshippers" who "play Satan's game" (Maxwell 1969a,b,c).

Hovering around the Three Goat Gods of the Universe was their Emissary, Christ, not to be confused with Jesus who was but one of Christ's many manifestations. The theology was constantly changing, and Christ became a coequal fourth deity. I never saw Processeans worship their gods, because the gods were inner realities rather than external deities. But much of the Processeans' day was devoted to service of "our Lords Christ, Jehovah, Lucifer, and Satan."

At various times The Process had communes in London, San Francisco, New Orleans, Paris, Munich, and Rome, but in 1970 they settled in the United States and Canada, first in Boston and Chicago, then in New Orleans again, as well as New York and Toronto. During three years of wandering, exoticism had served them well with the general public, and they fitted in well with the explosion of radical movements that marked the late 1960s. But as rooted urban residents they needed money, and the easiest source was begging on the streets as members of a formally incorporated church. The Satan image now hurt, rather than helped, and the stigma deepened when they were falsely accused of having trained Charles Manson in the satanism that led him to order his followers on a murder spree (Lyons 1970; Sanders 1971; Bugliosi and Gentry 1974).

The Processeans responded by pulling in their horns. They changed their style of dress, adopting nondescript gray uniforms in complete contradiction to their doctrines but in pursuit of public acceptance, with tiny satan goats on the lapels replacing the huge one on their chests. A period of general depression set in, as members were forced to realize that their grand hopes had achieved nothing more than a temporary high adventure. Robert had composed most of the group's radical scripture, and he remained committed to it, spinning ever more complex intellectual structures that seemed to others ever more removed from the reality that oppressed them. A rift developed between Robert and Mary Ann, and in 1974 he and a few others left to recreate the classical Process afresh, complete with all the Gods, while Mary Ann's much larger group turned to pure Jehovianism.

To protect it from mass media accusations concerning their "satanic" past, I have called Mary Ann's group The Establishment (they did take a new name very similar to this). In each chapter house, Establishment priests went with bell, book, and candle to exorcise the negative spirits, Satan and Christ. Lucifer was dismissed as a theological mistake. Frantically, the Establishment struggled to construct a new set of symbols, vocabulary, practices, and doctrines practically overnight (Bainbridge 1985). At the end of 1974, Father Aron told a New York Times reporter that members "have almost no beliefs at all, except we believe in God and working for God and that the Messiah is coming" (Blau 1974). Rituals became more like conventional worship services, and the Establishment sought to garner laity by becoming an eclectic psychic supermarket.

For a while, Jewish members held influential positions, because it was believed they were closer to Jehovah. Later, they were demoted when the Jehovian rule proved little more successful than the era of the four gods. Some Jewish members went off to Phoenix, Arizona, to start an independent

Jews for Jesus movement. At the end of 1978, the Establishment abandoned its $900,000 headquarters in New York, losing it to debts, and moved to a canyon near Tucson to meditate and seek a new vision. Today, small Establishment groups survive in Texas and Utah.

Robert's second Process was a more chaotic experiment that produced high drama but no stable group. In New Orleans he attempted to challenge the Establishment, then in Boston and Toronto he presided over dissident members trying to create communes, and finally in London he tried to spread his message through a correspondence course culled from his voluminous scriptures. A year after my book was published in 1978, he sent me a somewhat angry letter from Egypt, where he was exploring yet another spiritual possibility. Occasionally I hear from someone who wants to begin The Process again and revive the Great Gods of the Universe. Even in failure, The Process has bequeathed lasting images of how God might be divided into gods, including among them a highly provocative Satan.

THE GREAT GODS OF THE UNIVERSE

Process theology was a logical structure explaining the nature of existence and showing how people of different natures could cooperate to bring a quartet of warring Gods together and establish a new age of harmony. Satan cannot be understood apart from the other three. In the Sabbath Assembly, Satan was described as The Great God of Ultimate Destruction, whose role was "to release the powers of Destruction in the world of men, that the debt of pain and suffering might be repaid in full." This debt was partly humanity's guilt for crucifying Jesus, but more generally our betrayal of the divine plan. Thus, Satan desires "An End and a New Beginning. The End of Hatred and the Beginning of Love."

The separate deities had different roles in a grand process, beginning with the birth of the universe and progressing through the end of the present age to a new beginning. Although bearing a familiar name, Satan was not the Devil imagined in more conventional creeds. As a 1969 internal teaching document, BI-8 (Brethren Information 8), explains, Satan was formerly the Adversary, but has been "raised up and reunited with His counterpart and one time enemy, Christ, so that They might begin to become One again." Now, humanity, in its blindness and self-deception, has taken over the role of Adversary. For Processeans, "Humanity is the Devil," Satan, thus comes to cleanse the world of the Devil. As the hymn, "Christ in the World of Men" explained in 1968: "The evils of the world of men are perishing, Satan's hordes consume them. Out of the ashes of the old shall arise the beginnings of a New Age."

No longer the Adversary, Satan was free to play his new role in unity with

Christ, "The Chant of Unity" sang: "Hallelujah, Hallelujah. The Unity of Lamb and Goat, the Power of Release; Christ and Satan are at One, the Brotherhood of Life." Christ has said we should love our enemies. Christ's enemy was Satan. As "The Unity" in the Sabbath Assembly explained, "Through Love Christ and Satan have destroyed Their enmity and come together for the End; Christ to Judge, Satan to Execute the Judgement." The Unity of Christ and Satan had three aspects. First, it encouraged acceptance of one's darker, socially suppressed impulses, private and subconscious longings that a Freudian might call primary process phenomena connected with the id. Second, it was an attempt to bridge the gaps between people of very different needs and personalities, to achieve cooperation where hostility had reigned. Third, it was a structural theory of the origins of existence, part of an intellectual world.

Processeans used the gods as a personality theory, holding that different individuals were closer to one or two of the deities than to the others. While some members personified the gods, leaders and the more intellectual members saw them as principles describing psychological orientations and feelings. Once, Sister Olivia told me her perspective on the Christ and Satan within her:

> To feel mostly Christ is a very calm and tranquil, in-tune and warm feeling. It's a very healthy thing. It's a very childlike thing, a very animal-like thing in a way. To feel mostly Satan is full of energy, is full of visions, hallucinations, and awareness of the power of destruction. And also, on the other side of that, a detachment from things that are going on in the world, and detachment from the whole conflict of the mind, from any desire to figure things out—very much of an intuitive awareness of things that are happening.

Satan had two aspects, the higher and the lower. On the abstract level Satan was the principle of separation, for example of conflict between two people. According to The Universal Law, "As you give, so shall you receive." Thus, because Satan gives separation, Satan receives separation and splits into the two aspects. In a book titled *The Gods and Their People*, Robert presents this image of a dual Satan:

> SATAN, the receiver of transcendent souls and corrupted bodies, instills in us two directly opposite qualities; at one end an urge to rise above all human and physical needs and appetites, to become all soul and no body, all spirit and no mind, and at the other end a desire to sink beneath all human values, all standards of morality, all ethics, all human codes of behavior, and to wallow in a morass of violence, lunacy and excessive physical indulgence. But it is the lower end of SATAN's nature that men fear, which is why SATAN, by whatever name, is seen as the Adversary.

Satan's lower aspect represented Sub-Humanity, gripped by lust, abandon, violence, excess, and indulgence. The higher aspect represented Super-

Humanity, evaporating into detachment, mysticism, otherworldliness, magic, and asceticism. In terms of psychopathology, Jehovah and Lucifer were neurotic, the former being obsessive-compulsive, and the latter hysterical. Theirs was the "conflict of the mind."

While Satan relates to Christ through their coming Unity, he also stands in a definite relationship to Jehovah and Lucifer, representing a pair of escapes from conflict. *The Game of the Gods* explains that each individual is torn apart by this conflict. Jehovah demands self-discipline and dedication to duty. Lucifer, in contrast, urges self-indulgence, harmony, and peace, Satan's lower aspect is an intensification of Luciferianism, while the higher aspect is an intensification of Jehovianism.

The relationships between the Gods were reflected in relationships between people. Once Christ had been elevated to the status of coequal god, each person was believed to manifest one of four "god patterns"—not one for each god but one for each pair of gods who were not locked in conflict as were Christ and Satan, Lucifer and Jehovah. Thus, the four kinds of persons were the Jehovian–Christian, the Jehovian–Satanic, the Luciferian–Christian, and the Luciferian–Satanic, often simply identified by their initials: JC, JS, LC, and LS. Robert was an LC personality, and Mary Ann was its exact opposite, JS. Through the Union of Jehovah and Lucifer, and through the Unity of Christ and Satan, they could come together in harmony, combining their psychological assets rather than falling into violent disagreement.

Ultimately, the Great Gods of the Universe are parts of God. In the beginning, there was only God, and no universe. Although standard Christianity conceives of the world as partly outside God, something created by God but not itself divine, for Processeans God created the universe by splitting himself into fragments. Time and space were created when pieces of God placed themselves at opposite ends of each dimension. In 1969, *BI-13* explained: "There is division; and from the initial division of GOD and antiGOD, there springs the fragmentation of all things, and the scattering of all parts of One throughout the Universe of Time and Space."

According to *The Gods*, the fragments of God must by reunited:

> 1.5 And whilst the Three Great Gods are divided then the concept of GOD is no more than a concept. Like a shattered mirror it lies in pieces and the pieces are scattered throughout the Universe.
> 1.6 But if Jehovah, Lucifer and Satan are brought together, united in a common understanding, a common knowledge, a common bond of awareness and unconflicted intention, then the concept of GOD becomes a reality. The parts are come together to complement each other and make a whole, and the whole is Totality.
> 1.7 So GOD is the reuniting of the Gods.

The key element in the reunion is Christ, for "Christ is the Unifier." The failure of Christianity, for Processeans, was the failure of Christ to realize that he must become unified with Satan, before he can fulfill his purposes both for humanity and for the God of which he is part. Thus, we must "resist not evil" but join with it to dissolve it in Christ's name. The unity of Christ and Satan will also bring unification to Satan's separated halves, as *BI-28* says: "When Christ and Satan come together, then the two halves of Satan must also come together." The unification of Satan will draw together Jehovah and Lucifer, of whom Satan is an exaggerated reflection, and they will achieve the Union.

This combination theology and psychology thus has little to do with the satanism constructed by non-satanists. Despite the failure of The Process, its theology was a logical approach toward solving dilemmas faced by every person and society, drawing on ideas from ancient religion and modern psychoanalysis. In my book (Bainbridge 1978) I suggested that the failure of the cult was unnecessary, coming from a few poor leadership decisions, primarily from the abandonment of the recruitment techniques that served so well in the beginning. To be sure, Processeans hoped to achieve too much with their grand new system, but in their wild dreams we may all recognize parts of ourselves.

TRANSCENDENCE AND REMYSTIFICATION

When I began my research with The Process, I had just completed half a year of research inside Scientology, which was in great measure a reflection of the personality of its founder, L. Ron Hubbard. Some cults are outgrowths of the founder's personality and thus can be described in terms of a particular psychiatric syndrome (cf. Stark and Bainbridge 1985:173–177). Scientology could usefully be diagnosed as obsessive or paranoid—or Apollonian, to use Nietzsche's (1872) terminology—and I thought it would be fascinating to study an opposite group, one exhibiting hysteria or Dionysianism.

The hallmark of a hysterical cult is histrionics—a great stress on drama and the playing of roles (Shapiro 1965). The Processeans, with their splendid costumes, alternative personal identities, and scripted group performances, looked about as histrionic as a cult could get. Considered as theater, The Process was what opera composer Richard Wagner called a *total work of art* (Newman 1924). Wagner believed that all the arts should be combined into a seamless aesthetic tapestry, and he attempted to achieve this in his music dramas, notably *Tristan und Isolde*. However, Wagner himself slighted the visual arts, and it was left to later generations to fulfill his ideal. The Process is a good example, because the true *total work of art* would be an artistically created human community with a distinctive lifestyle and culture. One would not achieve a really *total* work of art merely by combining drama with music; one must go all the way and add the domestic arts, creating living human personalities and an aesthetic community to house them.

The concept of *belief distance*, an extension of Goffman's (1961) concept of *role distance*, describing the refusal to identify oneself completely with one's creed, is useful to understand The Process. Almost every time I lecture about the group, someone in the audience asks, "But could they really *believe* all that?" My reply is that the concept of belief, as used in Western religions, is a strange one. In Christianity, for example, one must have faith. The question is less one of whether Christian beliefs are true than it is of whether one is going to be true to the beliefs. Unlike many religions, Western faiths demand loyalty, and they make exaggerated demands on the convictions of their members. The Western concept of belief, construed in terms of loyalty or conviction, had nothing to do with The Process. Theirs was not a creed of belief, but of willing suspension of disbelief, a world like that of drama and the other arts.

For Processeans, the idea that the believer had a duty to believe is pure Jehovianism, and in its great schism, one half of The Process turned toward Jehovah partly to consolidate control over its small band of followers. Lucifer is the god of hypotheses, and the Luciferian–Satanic individual is very much a persona of masks and role-playing. The test of truth in the early days of The Process was the degree of excitement and hope that an idea could generate—an epistemology of possibilities rather than of certainties. The Processeans took their great chances, literally betting their lives on the Great Gods of the Universe, but they never had faith in the traditional Western sense.

The construction of deviant reality in The Process can be understood from a traditional anthropological perspective called *cultural relativism* (Cancian and Cancian 1974; cf. Benedict 1934). This is a doctrine promulgated by a number of scholars early in this century concerning the variability of human norms. It appeared that almost any conceivable custom could be found in some society. In their politically righteous crusade to make the world respect even the most feeble and primitive society, the cultural relativists made it seem that every primitive culture was a nearly perfect human adaptation to the environment. In its extreme form, cultural relativism held that all cultures were equally good.

From the perspective of cultural relativism, the Processean gods were alternative cultures. Each had a different set of commandments. Each was at war with one of the others, but the ideology asserted that the gods were nonetheless coming together for "an End and a New Beginning." Robert de Grimston's theology was Hegelianism in the extreme. For every thesis (Christ, Jehovah) there was an antithesis (Satan, Lucifer), and the cult aimed to achieve a final synthesis of all these dichotomies in the rebirth of GOD.

Through their psychotherapy, they were trying to help individuals transcend their compulsive conflicts; on the social level they sought to bring antagonistic people together with the help of the gods, and on the supernatural plane they hoped the gods could also transcend their tremendous differences. They occasionally said that the ultimate salvation was the salvation of God—that God needed saving—and Processeans could save God, with the help of the several gods that were the conflicted aspects of their own psyches. The case of this modern, polytheistic religion provides insights about the limits of cultural relativism.

Consider the comparative intellectual merits of monotheism and polytheism. Monotheism is probably more comforting to the individual believer, because it typically suggests that a single, benevolent god is in control of the individual's ultimate fate. The polytheist must always worry about becoming a pawn in a game played between warring deities, none of whom particularly wish him or her well. Monotheism probably supports political unity and strengthens any state that compellingly claims to act on behalf of the one, true God. Indeed, one explanation offered for the rage of European witch trials is that it was a tool by which central governments strengthened themselves through establishment of orthodoxy of belief (Larner 1984), something much harder to do when the official pantheon contains gods who themselves fail to agree.

Empirical studies show a historical trend toward monotheism (Underhill 1975; Swanson 1975). There are strong reasons why religious traditions should tend to move the divine further and further away from the world of experience and to reduce the number of gods and demigods, merely given a sufficiently long-lived religious tradition for these slow changes to occur (Stark and Bainbridge 1987). For one thing, religious organizations risk disconfirmation of adherents' faith if they promise to provide worldly rewards they cannot in fact deliver. Put another way, it is dangerous to be in the business of performing magic, because clients can test one's claims all too easily. Indeed, one way of explaining the failure of The Process is to note that it promised a Heaven on earth to members, yet it delivered something less.

Religions promising many magical benefits typically postulate many lesser gods (Stark and Bainbridge 1987:111), each with its own functions. At the other extreme, a religion with one god of infinite scope can no longer make specific, convincing supernatural promises, and thus it will have little to offer most people. Those Christians for whom Satan exists as a meaningful foil for God possess a faith that has not yet rendered the divine irrelevant for human hopes. The minimum number of gods that can be the basis of a popular religion is two, one good and the other evil, although Christianity pretends to withhold full deity status from Satan. The reduction of the number of gods to one, and removal of the god from the world of human affairs if tantamount to secularization. For centuries Christianity avoided the disadvantages of monotheism, while claiming its advantages, by postulating the Devil and a collection of saints ambiguously poised between humanity and divinity. But the emergence of one lonely god, as in Unitarianism, marks the gradual collapse of a particular religious tradition.

Historians have noted that Western monotheism may have been an essential precondition for the rise of modern science. In seventeenth-century England, many scientists saw the world as a mechanical creation based on logical principles (Merton 1970; Westfall 1958). One, good, logical God created the world, then withdrew leaving man free to choose good or evil. Whereas a polytheistic religion might attribute every natural phenomenon to a different deity and assume no coordination between them, the monotheist is more likely to see the world as a unified system. As Christianity has become progressively more monotheistic in practice, the world has become demystified and disenchanted, in the sense that it no longer seemed the playground of supernatural forces (cf. Weber 1958). These developments prepared the way for science.

Monotheism is a poor explanation for the natural world. It says almost nothing about why things are as they are. Manifestly, the world is not a unity. The forces and entities postulated by physicists are many, and each person experiences many conflicting social and psychological pressures. Polytheism is a better explanation of phenomena than is monotheism, and thus it is a greater foe of modern science. By unfolding God into distinct gods, The Process sought to explain the world of experience, and through its explanations to transform the world magically. In so doing, it remystified and reenchanted human experience.

In this context, Satan had nothing whatsoever to do with the Devil. Rather, the traditional existence of some supernatural being other than Jehovah was an opportunity to reestablish polytheism. A third god, Lucifer, could also be found in the old tradition, although Processeans had to explain again and again to newcomers that Lucifer and Satan were not the same, citing separate mentions of them in the Bible and suggesting that the Bible itself was propaganda on behalf of only two of the gods: Jehovah in the *Old Testament* and Christ in the *New Testament*, Christ entered Process theology first as the Emissary of the Gods, working to bring them together, then was elevated to a fourth coequal deity on the basis of his importance in Process personality theory.

As Father Malachi told me, the fact that Processeans came from Christian and Jewish backgrounds meant that concepts of Christ and Jehovah were already familiar to them. Why were the other two gods identified as Satan and Lucifer? "I think basically because those names were there. I think we were looking for opposites."

THE DEVIL AND THE DEEP BLUE SEA

Again and again, popular writers have selectively quoted Processean scripture—for example, extracting the most horrendous passages from *Satan on War*—and presented it as proof that members of the cult were murderers, or worse. But the cult's doctrines held that destructive impulses lurked within every one of us, not within members alone, and they used the imagery of Satan's "lower aspect" to analyze this part of human nature. The scriptures employed dynamic metaphors and emotional dramatizations of abstract concepts; it is a poor writer indeed who fails to recognize poetic symbolism when he or she reads it.

One difference between satanism as constructed by Processeans and by self-conscious antisatanists is that the latter impose their twisted image on other people, while the former created a myth to inhabit themselves. Harmless to others, Processeans and their kin in similar cults place only themselves at risk when they take their great spiritual leap into darkness. On average, one of them told me, life as a satanist had been no better or worse than normal life, only the extremes were greater, ranging from deepest depression to highest ecstasy. In my years of observation, I did occasionally see harm done, but no more than I would expect to see in any group of a few hundred people, probably far less than among an equal number of journalistic or evangelical Devil-hunters.

In earlier eras, society projected its fears and private sins onto Jews and other out-groups who were falsely accused of every possible evil. Today, thankfully, norms of tolerance render antisemitism and similar prejudices unacceptable, at least when familiar groups are the potential victim. In part, satanism is a fiction, imagined out of whole cloth by unscrupulous or ignorant people, accepted as truth by credulous consumers of the latest mass media myths. But it is also true that real satanists exist, and many of them are as innocent and admirable as the Processeans. To the extent that we accept the antisatanist's construction of satanism, we do injury to the brave souls who have explored the possibilities for repaganization of religion afforded by alternatives to Christ and Jehovah, and we miss the often enlightening results of their spiritual experimentation.

NOTE

1. For popular press discussions of The Process see Beckett (1971), Lipsky (1972), Mano (1974), Melton (1978), Tenner (1979), and Weissman (1979).

REFERENCES

Adler, Alfred. 1927. *Understanding Human Nature*. Greenwich, CT: Fawcett (1954).
———. 1929. *Individual Psychology*. Totowa, NJ: Littlefield, Adams (1968).
Bainbridge, William Sims. 1978. *Satan's Power: A Deviant Psychotherapy Cult*. Berkeley: University of California Press.

_____. 1983. "Review of *Folk Devils and Moral Panics* by Stanley Cohen." *Sociology and Social Research* 67:229–230.

_____. 1985. "Cultural Genetics." Pp.157–198 in *Religious Movements: Genesis, Exodus, and Numbers,* edited by Rodney Stark. New York: Paragon.

_____. 1987. "Science and Religion: The Case of Scientology." Pp.59–79 in *The Future of New Religious Movements,* edited by David G. Bromley and Phillip E. Hammond. Macon, GA: Mercer University Press.

Beckett, Bill. 1971. "Preparing For the Fiery End: Process." *Harvard Crimson* (April 27):3–4.

Benedict, Ruth. 1934. *Patterns of Culture.* Boston: Houghton Mifflin.

Blau, Eleanor. 1974. "Young Sect No Longer Hails Devil." *New York Times* (December 1):53.

Bugliosi, Vincent, and Gentry, Curt. 1974. *Helter Skelter: The True Story of the Manson Murders.* New York: Norton.

Cancian, Francesca M., and Cancian, Frank. 1974. "Cultural Relativism." Morristown, NJ: General Learning Press.

Goffman, Erving. 1961. *Encounters.* Indianapolis: Bobbs-Merrill.

Hart-Davis, Duff. 1966. "Mind-Benders in Mayfair." *London Sunday Telegraph* (July 17).

Larner, Christina. 1984. *Witchcraft and Religion.* Oxford: Basil Blackwell.

Lipsky, Jon. 1972. "Carrying a Torch for Lucifer." *Boston Real Paper* (November 29):1–8.

Lyons, Arthur. 1970. *The Second Coming: Satanism in America.* New York: Dodd, Mead.

Mano, D. Keith. 1974. "Detente with Satan." *National Review* (May 24):595–596.

Maxwell, Ronald. 1969a. "A Strange Cult." *London Sunday Mirror* (September 7):5.

_____. 1969b. "The Satan Worshippers." *London Sunday Mirror* (September 14).

_____. 1969c. "They Play Satan's Game." *London Sunday Mirror* (September 21).

McIntosh, Christopher. 1972. *Eliphas Levi and the French Occult Revival.* New York: Weiser.

Melton, J. Gordon. 1978. *The Encyclopedia of American Religions,* Vol. 2. Wilmington, NC: McGrath/Consortium.

Merton, Robert K. 1970. *Science, Technology and Society in Seventeenth-Century England.* New York: Harper & Row.

Newman, Ernest 1924. *Wagner as Man and Artist.* New York: Knopf.

Sanders, Ed. 1971. *The Family: The Story of Charles Manson's Dune Buggy Attack Battalion.* New York: E. P. Dutton (first edition only).

Shapiro, David 1965. *Neurotic Styles.* New York: Basic Books.

Stark, Rodney, and Bainbridge, William Sims. 1985. *The Future of Religion.* Berkeley: University of California Press.

_____. 1987. *A Theory of Religion.* New York: Peter Lang.

Swanson, Guy E. 1975. "Monotheism, Materialism, and Collective Purpose: An Analysis of Underhill's Correlations." *American Journal of Sociology* 80:862–869.

Tenner, Edward. 1979. "Why Not the Beast, Indeed?" *Chronicle of Higher Education Review* (February 20):11–12.

Thompson, Hunter S. 1967. *Hell's Angels.* New York: Harper & Row.

Time Magazine. 1971. "Fellow Traveling with Jesus—The Process." (September 6):54–55.

Underhill, Ralph. 1975. "Economic and Political Antecedents of Monotheism: A Cross-Cultural Study." *American Journal of Sociology* 80:841–861.

Wallis, Roy 1976. *The Road to Total Freedom: A Sociological Analysis of Scientology.* London: Heinemann.

Weber, Max 1958. *The Protestant Ethic and the Spirit of Capitalism.* New York: Scribner's.

Weissman, Paul. 1979. "My Nightmare Year in a Bizarre Satanic Cult." *National Enquirer* (May 29):8.

Westfall, Richard S. 1958. *Science and Religion in Seventeenth-Century England.* New Haven: Yale University Press.

Biographical Sketches of the Contributors ————————————

Williams Sims Bainbridge is Chairman of Sociology and Anthropology at Towson State University. He received his Ph.D. in Sociology from Harvard University in 1975. He taught for seven years at the University of Washington, where he co-authored two books with Rodney Stark, *The Future of Religion* and *A Theory of Religion*. He is also author of *Satan's Power*.

Robert W. Balch is Professor of Sociology at the University of Montana. He received his Ph.D. in Sociology at the University of Oregon in 1972, with specialties in deviance, juvenile delinquency and collective behavior. He has published several articles on new religious movements, and currently is working on an ethnographic study of a religious commune known as The Love Family.

Joel Best is Professor and Chair of Sociology at Southern Illinois University at Carbondale. His principal research interests are deviance and social problems. He is the editor of *Images of Issues* (1989) and author of *Threatened Children* (1990).

David G. Bromley is Professor of Sociology in the Department of Sociology and Anthropology and Senior Project Director in the Survey Research Laboratory at Virginia Commonwealth University. His most recent books include *The Future of New Religious Movements*, edited with Phillip Hammond, *Falling from the Faith*, and *Krishna Consciousness in the West*.

Gray Cavender is Associate Professor at the School of Justice Studies at Arizona State University. He received his Ph.D. in Criminology at Florida State University and his J.D. at the University of Tennessee. His areas of interest in research and teaching are media, criminological theory, and corporate crime.

Ben M. Crouch is Professor of Sociology at Texas A&M University. His research interests include deviance, criminality and social control. He has written extensively on prison order and litigated reform in corrections, and is currently investigating the links among drug use, gangs and delinquency.

311

Kelly Damphousse is currently a doctoral student at Texas A&M University where he is engaged in research on patterns of occult involvement among high risk delinquents. He is also examining the role of newspapers in the development of satanism as a social problem.

Bill Ellis is Associate Professor of American Studies at The Pennsylvania State University, Hazleton Campus. He is editor of *FOAFtale News*, the newsletter of the International Society for Contemporary Legend Research, and president of the American Folklore Society's Folk Narrative Section.

Gary Alan Fine is Professor of Sociology at the University of Georgia. He is author of *Shared Fantasy: Role-Playing Games as Social Worlds* (1983). He has done research on a number of leisure activities, including little league baseball, mushroom collecting and high school debate. His Ph.D. is in Social Psychology from Harvard, 1976.

Margaret Gilliam did a masters thesis in Sociology at the University of Montana on satanism rumors, and she earned a law degree from the University of Montana Law School. She is now an attorney with Brega and Winters, in Denver, Colorado.

Thomas A. Green received his Ph.D. in Anthropology from the University of Texas at Austin in 1974, and is currently Associate Professor of Anthropology and English at Texas A&M University. His research interests include symbolic anthropology, folk narrative, linguistics, and cultural revitalization movements. Dr. Green currently serves on the Executive Board of the International Society for Contemporary Legend Research.

Robert D. Hicks is a law enforcement specialist with the Virginia Department of Criminal Justice Services in Richmond. A former law enforcement officer, he obtained his B.A. and M.A. in anthropology from the University of Arizona. He has written a critical study of law enforcement's response to Satanic crime, *In Pursuit of Satan: The Police and the Occult* (1991).

Philip Jenkins was educated at Clare College, Cambridge, and is currently Professor of Criminal Justice at the Pennsylvania State University. His publications include: *The Making of a Ruling Class: the Glamorgan Gentry 1640–1790* (1983); *Crime and Justice: Issues and Ideas* (1984) and *A History of Wales 1536–1990* (forthcoming).

Daniel Maier-Katkin is Professor of Law at the Pennsylvania State University, and Chair of the Department of Administration of Justice. His publications include *The Nature of Criminal Law: Essays, Cases and Other Materials*

(1982). His current research interests focus on legal and social reactions to infanticide and post-partum depression.

Daniel Martin is a doctoral candidate at the University of Minnesota. He is presently working on a dissertation dealing with the appropriation of body ideals in advanced capitalism, and is currently doing research on the weight loss industry.

Sherrill A. Mulhern, D.E.A. is an anthropologist specializing in the study of the socialization and socio/cultural representation of dissociative states and altered states of consciousness. Co-founder and project director of the Laboratoire des Rumeurs, des Mythes du Futur et des Sectes, U.F.R. Anthropologie, Ethnologie, Science des Religions, Université de Paris, VII, and Director of the Inter-Laboratoire de Modelisation de Processus Memoriels, Inter-Institut Robotique, Anthropologie Generative et Modelisation, Université de Paris, VIII, France.

Debbie Nathan is a freelance journalist, based in El Paso, Texas, who has been researching and writing about ritual child abuse since 1986. One of her articles on the subject won the Free Press Association's H.L. Mencken Award for investigative journalism in 1988. She holds a masters degree in Linguistics from the University of Texas at El Paso.

James T. Richardson is Professor of Sociology and Judicial Studies at the University of Nevada, Reno, where he directs the Master of Judicial Studies Degree Program. He does research in sociology of religion (on new religions or "cults") and social psychology of law. He has co-authored several books, including *Money and Power in the New Religions* (1988), *The Brainwashing/Deprogramming Controversy* (1983), and *Conversion Careers* (1978), along with many articles in professional journals. His Ph.D. is in Sociology from Washington State University (1968), and his J.D. Degree is from Old College, Nevada School of Law (1986).

Laurel Rowe is a doctoral candidate in the inter-disciplinary Ph.D. program in Justice Studies at Arizona State University. She received her B.A. at the University of California, Santa Cruz. Her primary interest of study is in religion and the law.

Jeffrey Burton Russell is the author of five books and many articles on the history of the Devil and the concept of evil. His major works on the subject are published by Cornell University Press: *The Devil* (1977), *Satan* (1981), *Lucifer* (1984), *Mephistopheles* (1986), and *The Prince of Darkness* (1988). His works have also been published in Spanish, Italian, Japanese, French, and German. He is professor of History at the University of California, Santa Barbara.

Phillips Stevens, Jr. is Associate Professor of Anthropology at the University at Buffalo, State University of New York. He received his Ph.D. from Northwestern in 1973. His areas of specialization have included religion, folklore, social organization, and cultural change, and he has conducted extensive field work in Nigeria and the southern Caribbean. He was editor of *New York Folklore*, the journal of the New York Folklore Society (1983–89), and he is the author or editor of numerous books and articles.

Jeffrey S. Victor is Professor of Sociology at Jamestown Community College in Jamestown, New York. He received his Ph.D. from the State University of New York at Buffalo. He has previously published a book and articles in the areas of human sexuality and family relationships. His current research is focused upon rumors, claims and allegations about dangerous satanic cults and resultant threats to civil liberties. He is writing a book on this issue, tentatively titled, *Witch-Hunt: The Making of a Contemporary Legend*.

INDEX